W9-COH-713

Nov 2010

GOOD THINGS OUT OF NAZARETH

GOOD THINGS OUT OF NAZARETH

The Uncollected Letters
of Flannery O'Connor and Friends

FLANNERY O'CONNOR

EDITED BY BENJAMIN B. ALEXANDER, PHD

CONVERGENT
NEW YORK

Published in the United States by Convergent Books, an imprint of Random House, a division of Penguin Random House LLC, New York.
convergentbooks.com

CONVERGENT BOOKS is a registered trademark and its C colophon is a trademark of Penguin Random House LLC.

Grateful acknowledgment is made to the following for permission to use the material below:

Caroline Fallon: Previously unpublished Caroline Gordon letters used by permission of Caroline Fallon. All rights reserved.

The Mary Flannery O'Connor Charitable Trust: Letters of Flannery O'Connor copyright © The Mary Flannery O'Connor Charitable Trust. All rights reserved. Permission granted by the Mary Flannery O'Connor Charitable Trust via Harold Matson Co., Inc.

The Paul Engle Estate: Previously unpublished Paul Engle letter used by permission of Hualing Engle, on behalf of the Paul Engle Estate. All rights reserved.

The Permissions Company, LLC, on behalf of the Katherine Anne Porter Literary Trust: Previously unpublished Katherine Anne Porter letters used by permission of The Permissions Company, LLC, on behalf of the Katherine Anne Porter Literary Trust, www.permissionscompany.com. All rights reserved.

The Robert Giroux Estate: Previously unpublished Robert Giroux letter used by permission of Hugh McKenna, on behalf of the Robert Giroux Estate. All rights reserved.

Farrar, Straus and Giroux, on behalf of the Robert Lowell Estate: Unpublished letter written by Robert Lowell to Flannery O'Connor dated January 30, 1960. Copyright © 2019 by Harriet Lowell and Sheridan Lowell. Printed by permission of Farrar, Straus and Giroux on behalf of the Robert Lowell Estate. All rights reserved.

The Walker A. Percy Estate: Previously unpublished letters of Walker A. Percy copyright © 2019 by Ann Percy Moores and Mary Prett Lobdell. Reprinted with permission of McIntosh & Otis, Inc. All rights reserved.

Library of Congress Cataloging-in-Publication Data is available upon request.

ISBN 978-0-525-57506-1
Ebook ISBN 978-0-525-57507-8

PRINTED IN CANADA

10 9 8 7 6 5 4 3 2 1

First Edition

In memory of
Louise Boatwright Alexander (1920–2010)

CONTENTS

EDITORIAL NOTE

The spelling, capitalization, phrasing, punctuation, and dialect in the letters have been retained. A few obvious typographical errors have been silently corrected. Editorial conjecture in a few cases has been exercised to clarify illegible phrases, words, or omissions in the original letters. Emendations appear in brackets. Where the meaning could not be discerned, the original text has been retained. Other brackets provide factual information or clarifications. Dots appear sparingly to avoid repetition or tangential details.

PREFACE

Flannery O'Connor is a master of the American short story, joining, since her untimely death in 1964, Hawthorne, Poe, Hemingway, and Faulkner in the literary canon. Now a fixture in textbooks and collections, she always maintained a powerful ethical vision rooted in a quiet, devout faith. It informed all that she wrote and did.

She was born in 1925 in Savannah, Georgia, but she lived most of her life on a dairy farm in Milledgeville, Georgia, raising peacocks. O'Connor practiced her craft in a modest room near an ample front porch, where she received many visitors. She composed on an old typewriter with bookshelves nearby of modern fiction, philosophy, and theology unique among American writers. The novels of William Faulkner, the American Virgil, beside the rich theological writings of the angelic doctor, Thomas Aquinas, testified to wide study. Novels by the Russians, along with volumes of the serene German theologian, Romano Guardini, occupied a shelf. The massive work of arguably the most penetrating political theorist of the twentieth century, Eric Voegelin, had another space. Such works and many others in O'Connor's library gave me a rich reading list that I have tried to pursue. When I first saw the actual setup of O'Connor's room, I was moved by the austerity. In the corner was a narrow iron bed where O'Connor spent sleepless hours courageously enduring lupus, which would take her life at the young age of thirty-nine.

O'Connor left a body of fiction featuring a combination of violence and sacramental truths that continues to stun readers. Sensational action at the point of a gun or the end of a rope reminds them of what they see on television. O'Connor was a careful observer of the medium in its early days. Slow-motion, rarefied stories might have entertained readers of earlier times, but not in the age of "moviegoers," as O'Connor's compatriot writer, Walker Percy, revealed. O'Connor recognized that her readers were becoming increasingly conditioned by television and cinema, causing her to pack dramatic action into her stories. She once noted, "To the hard of hearing you shout, and for the blind you draw large and startling pictures."

O'Connor's strategy still wakes up somnambulant English classes. O'Connor can still break through a dull lecture with a story in which a Bible salesman steals the wooden leg of an atheist philosopher ("Good Country People") or an impudent teenager hurls a book at a racist old lady in a segregated waiting room, calling her an "old wart hog from hell" ("Revelation").

I will always remember I first heard that O'Connor phrase in an undergraduate class in the late 1960s. Those days of campus radicalism and opposition to the Vietnam War imbued many students with a loathing of their country that still endures on college campuses today. The Kent State shootings were shocking and paralleled the murders of the innocent in an O'Connor story. In 1969, I enrolled in a course taught by Andrew Lytle who had taught O'Connor at the Iowa Writers' Workshop. There he had witnessed O'Connor herself reading *Wise Blood* to a class. An accomplished novelist and critic in his own right, Lytle performed O'Connor's stories dramatically in the classroom. The nasal drawl of the Misfit was unforgettable. Lytle revealed O'Connor's dialect and power to distracted students, like me. We became "woke." I soon wanted to understand O'Connor better and teach her stories from the other side of the desk.

The academic vocation has proved daunting at times, but my students, many outside the South, have responded more readily to her writing than to other masters, such as Faulkner or Hemingway. Teaching O'Connor became easier in 1979 with the publication of her letters, *The Habit of Being*. New readers, my own mother among them, read and re-read her letters, delighting in the infectious humor and pithy wisdom. A less startling voice than the one in the stories often spoke. O'Connor's letters made her fiction more understandable. They also revealed O'Connor as an apologist for the faith and spiritual director for a few searching friends. O'Connor nourished my own spiritual hunger in the 1970s left unfed by the imploding Episcopal Church that had irrationally jettisoned its historic Elizabethan prayer book. Often amused at O'Connor's unparalleled sense of humor, I also was instructed by her unflinching catechesis.

Having marked up three copies of *The Habit of Being*, I heard at academic conferences that there were more unpublished O'Connor letters. She often wrote to a Jesuit priest, the Rev. James H. McCown, who appears sparingly in *The Habit of Being*. He visited her many times at the Georgia farm. This vital, unexplored friendship contributed to O'Connor's creation of Ignatius Vogle, S. J., in her story "The Enduring Chill." Father McCown introduced O'Connor to Thomas and Louise Gossett, both credentialed academics. From 1956 through O'Connor's death in 1964 and afterward, Thomas Gossett collected her letters to Fr. McCown. (He died in 1991.) In 1972, Gossett, a pioneer in African American studies (a role O'Connor admired), shared the O'Connor letters with her editor-friend Robert Giroux, who encouraged their publication. In 1974, Gossett wrote the first article about the riches of O'Connor's letters and hoped to be the first to publish them.* *The Habit of Being* pre-empted him. Since then readers have eagerly waited for more correspondence.

Some forty years later, *Good Things Out of Nazareth* contains the letters Gossett originally collected, many not in *The Habit of Being.* I also provide annotation (suggested by a wise editor) that is part spiritual autobiography, part literary history. O'Connor's serene voice from *A Prayer Journal* (2013)—writings that she kept in graduate school—is juxtaposed with her more blunt comments in her later letters. New insights appear.

Many letters concern the friendship between Father McCown and O'Connor and the Gossetts' own lively bond with her. They reveal O'Connor's support of these close friends engaged in civil rights activism, and why she herself did not become involved. Fr. McCown was a tireless social justice warrior at a time when, as Martin Luther King Jr. also discovered, the Catholic Church was resistant to change. Thomas Gossett's academic career was nearly ruined in 1958 because of his support of integration in Georgia. O'Connor concurred with Gossett's prophetic observation that the kindred of William Faulkner's "Snopes," a network of "white trash," had penetrated academic officialdom. They were "freaks in grey-flannelled suits," as O'Connor noted. Still other letters lay to rest the unseemly speculation by scholars about why O'Connor did not marry. Finally, several letters in *Good Things* silence the cruel stereotyping of O'Connor's mother, Regina, as *merely* a woman from the backwoods. Mrs. O'Connor was a rare person—astute in business, dairy farming, protocol—but especially a charitable caregiver as her daughter's illness worsened. She did ask "Mary Flannery" once about a story in which a man turns into a roach. Regina perhaps saw the connection to the bizarre scenes in her daughter's stories.

One memorable hot June day a few years ago, I delighted in reading about these lively exchanges in the letters that Thomas Gossett

---

* Thomas Gossett, "Flannery O'Connor's Opinions of Other Writers: Some Unpublished Comments," *Southern Literary Journal,* Spring, 1974, 70–82.

had collected and donated to the Duke University archives. The afternoon of the same sweltering day, I made my way to Chapel Hill and discovered another treasure trove in the Walker Percy papers. There were the letters of Caroline Gordon, an opinionated, neglected novelist, but a gifted, precise teacher of writing. She wrote to Percy in his apprentice years before the publication of *The Moviegoer,* the National Book Award winner in 1962. Signing obscure book reviews "Walker Percy, M.D.," the aspiring novelist had little knowledge at the time about writing fiction:

> After twelve years of a scientific education I [Percy] felt somewhat like the Danish philosopher Søren Kierkegaard when he finished reading Hegel. Hegel, said Kierkegaard, explained everything under the sun, except one small detail: what it means to be a man living in the world who must die. My interest began to turn from the physical sciences and medicine to philosophy and the novel.*

Percy dispatched to Gordon the manuscript of *The Charterhouse.* She also soon received Flannery O'Connor's *Wise Blood* and would scrutinize it line by line. Caroline Gordon prophetically recognizes the gifts of the two writers in long epistles to each. She made a bold claim to Brainard Cheney (December 1951), another promising novelist, that O'Connor and Percy represent,

> what the next development in the novel will be, (according to me). And it will be something new. At least something we have not had before. Novels written by people who are consciously rooted and grounded in the faith . . . people who don't have to spend time trying to figure out what moral order prevails in the universe and therefore have more energy for spontane-

---

* Walker Percy, "Confessions of a Late Blooming Mis-educated First Novelist," Walker Percy Papers, Southern Historical Collection, Louis Round Wilson Library, University of North Carolina, Chapel Hill.

ous creation. Its no accident, I'm sure, that in the last two months the two best first novels I've ever read have been by Catholic writers [O'Connor, *Wise Blood*; Percy, *The Charterhouse*]. . . . Harcourt Brace says it [*Wise Blood*] is the most shocking book they ever read but have already agreed to publish it. . . . I have been thinking about this a lot since these two novels came my way and have finally decided they do mark a turning point in some tide.*

Gordon writes Walker Percy in 1951: "Well this is the season when the good things come out of Nazareth," an allusion to the tiny (some considered backwater) town where Jesus lived with his parents.** In other words, something important was rising from a place many ignored.

Gordon encourages Percy to visit O'Connor, knowing that faith for both writers imbued all the work they did. For Gordon, O'Connor and Percy embodied the opposite of Gertrude Stein's "lost generation." Hemingway, Fitzgerald, and their disillusioned spiritual brothers stumbled through post–World War I America and Europe spiritually shell-shocked. O'Connor and Percy "found" the faith many of the "lost generation" forgot in the horrific trenches of the Great War. O'Connor and Percy in the aftermath of yet another global conflict at later mid-century were new and original in American literature: two Catholics from the South, one a cradle believer, the other a convert, to a faith they both cherished.

---

* Caroline Gordon to Brainard ("Lon") Cheney, December 1951.

** Walker Percy Papers, Southern Historical Collection, Louis Round Wilson Library, University of North Carolina, Chapel Hill. Gordon apparently appropriates the phrase from Orestes Brownson, a popular critic in the mid-nineteenth century. He has subsequently fallen into obscurity. Ralph Waldo Emerson's writings have hypnotized professors and their students for generations, but Brownson demurred. Brownson observed that Emerson in his hazy, gnostic theological speculations had turned his back on the "good things out of Nazareth."

A few years ago, I envisioned that the unpublished letters of O'Connor and her friends might become a collection. I began to assess the interest and audience. I showed the letters to a dear writer friend in Virginia, M. L. Jackson (a native Georgian), who insisted then and years after they merited publication. Robert Giroux also telephoned me encouraging publication and that "he knew most of the people." A little later a kindly manager of a credit union in "hillbilly elegy" country responded enthusiastically to the phrase, "good things out of Nazareth." Venturing forth from Appalachia of the Ohio River Valley where I was teaching—home to Dean Martin, coach Lou Holtz, and Pulitzer Prize winner, James Wright—I went on to lecture at several "Nazareths" in rural Ireland and Denmark; I even spoke at an O'Connor conference in Rome near the Vatican where I insisted O'Connor be considered for sainthood in addition to Dorothy Day.

At an Irish literary festival near Dublin dedicated to Gerard Manley Hopkins, I imparted passages of what O'Connor called a "nasty dose of orthodoxy" to scholars from Europe and the United States. O'Connor stole Hopkins's thunder. In fact, I told them, O'Connor (and Percy) would force a re-appraisal of Hopkins's conventional niche in the canon. Things were changing, as Caroline Gordon predicted. Attendees were amazed and shocked. O'Connor was an amusing yet compelling apologist for the historic faith that the deracinated Irishman, James Joyce, loathed. O' Connor had learned from Caroline Gordon to value the exquisite craftsmanship of Joyce's *Portrait of an Artist* and *Dubliners*, the short story collection. Gordon insisted Joyce's fiction not be judged according to churchmanship or piety. The teaching took root. Gordon wrote Flannery O'Connor's friend and mentor, Robert Fitzgerald, "This girl [O'Connor] is a real novelist. . . . She is already a rare phenomenon: a Catholic novelist with a real dramatic sense, one who relies more on her technique than her piety."*

This comment is the foundation of *Good Things Out of Nazareth.*

---

* Caroline Gordon to Robert Fitzgerald, May 1951.

Gordon's emphasis on "technique" over "piety" is a vital principle. It has largely been abandoned in the pedagogy of many creative writing programs today, even those in Catholic institutions. The mastery of technique requires discipline, practice, and repetition still observed in music education and athletics. The formation deters what Thomas Aquinas calls "religiosity" that leads to literary condemnations based on piety. The master practitioner of craft over religiosity originates in medieval times, in another "Nazareth"—Florence, Italy, and its most famous citizen, Dante. An exiled patriot and believer, he is remembered for his "dramatic sense" in the sensational horrors of the *Inferno* and the beauty of *Purgatorio* and *Paradiso*. Dante's faith is implicit, yet compelling because he is a storyteller first. Dante's presentation of purgatory, for example, is conveyed not in a tract but in a narrative about climbing a mountain. The *Purgatorio* is not only ecumenical but also interfaith in its appeal—in a word, "catholic." I have witnessed students of various beliefs and no beliefs absorbed by Dante's narrative; likewise, both Islamic students and a professor-friend. Dante may be the greatest of theological writers because storytelling overrides piety.

O'Connor's rootedness in Dante runs through the letters in *Good Things Out of Nazareth*. In one letter she conceives of the stories in *A Good Man Is Hard to Find* as an exposition of the seven deadly sins modeled on Dante's *Purgatorio*. Sequencing of the stories is essential. The famous lead story, "A Good Man Is Hard to Find," has for many years, like others, been studied apart from the cycle, leading to misreadings. A priest stared at me in disbelief when I told him the story is not really about a serial killer murdering a family. The letters reveal O'Connor intended larger contextual revelation rooted in a specific order of reading. O'Connor's stories comprise cycles—they are like Dante's cantos and are to be read in order. *Good Things Out of Nazareth* reveals this vital principle that enables readers to better understand O'Connor's fiction.

Stressing both "technique" and "piety," Gordon and O'Connor also exchange letters revealing their esteem for the writing of other "bad" Catholics such as Hemingway and Graham Greene. They advocate that their works need to be rescued from uncharitable pietistic critics. Gordon teaches O'Connor (and Percy) immersion in the masters of literary realism; O'Connor, in turn, passes the instruction on to her correspondents. She and Gordon react to readers, both secular and religious, often distracted by the excesses of Hemingway's personality and poor Churchmanship.

Indeed, Percy laments ill-formed religious readers policing carefully crafted fiction:

> I would only wish to call attention to a chronic confusion [to] which many readers, especially Catholics, appear to fall victim. They are apt to succumb to a quite unCatholic Puritanism and confuse the vulgar with the bad and the nice with the good . . . In certain American Catholic circles, too, the impression seems to obtain that Catholic novels must be written either by a saint or about a saint.*

O'Connor concurs with Percy. She writes Gordon in 1952: "If Catholic novels are bad, current Catholic criticism is PURE SLOP or else it's stuck off in some convent where nobody can get his hands on it."** A faithful parishioner of the church in Milledgeville, O'Connor dutifully reviews works for the diocesan newspaper. In one letter, she defends Graham Greene's *The Quiet American,* criticized as unwholesome in a Catholic magazine. The reviewer essentially missed Greene's cautionary message about the French misguided resistance to communism in Vietnam, tragically repeated in the debacle of the United States in the same country.

In other assessments O'Connor is blunter, complaining to a learned Jesuit about a novel she calls "How to Kill a Mockingbird."

---

* Walker Percy, "Sex and Violence in the American Novel," Walker Percy Papers, Southern Historical Collection, Louis Round Wilson Library, University of North Carolina, Chapel Hill.

** Flannery O'Connor to Caroline Gordon, May 12, 1952.

More comments like these appear in the letters in chapter 3, "Her Kind of Literature: Places and Folks." Some correspondence therein reprises the close friendship of O'Connor with her dear friend identified only as "A" in *The Habit of Being*. A few years ago, I met, at a conference in Denmark, William A. Sessions, one of O'Connor's old colleagues and the literary executor of "A." He told me he would soon reveal her identity. Sessions in 2007 revealed "A" to be Elizabeth "Betty" Hester of Atlanta. He facilitated more letters of O'Connor to her becoming available. Their correspondence adds to the roster of rare personal alliances of writers: Adams and Jefferson, Melville and Hawthorne, C. S. Lewis and J. R. R. Tolkien, for example. O'Connor and Hester in their remarkable correspondence belong in such company.

Good Things Out of Nazareth also contains correspondence about another vital friendship. Caroline Gordon esteems Dorothy Day and attends a retreat at a Catholic Worker house of hospitality. Gordon believes she was a "saint." O'Connor and Percy were muted in their response. They did not agree with Day's criticism of capitalism rooted in her pre-conversion adherence to Marxism. The economic orientation of O'Connor and Percy is especially vital with the re-emergence of socialist political candidates and their frequent criticism of capitalism. By contrast, both O'Connor and Percy knew and admired entrepreneurs in their families and in larger society. O'Connor's letters present economic and historical truths that emphasize that American capitalism is not the narrative of greed and exploitation that journalists often claim. At a time when old politicians couch the statist governmental re-distribution of wealth as something new, O'Connor provides vital insights.

O'Connor remained an exemplary citizen and believer to the end, cheerfully enduring exhaustion, sickness, and recurrent hospitalization. She often beseeched intercessory prayers from her friends. In her last months, she still read Thomas Aquinas twenty minutes a night, but devoted correspondents urged her also to read C. S. Lewis. The letters in the last chapter, "Removing Choice Souls So Soon," reveal O'Connor's delight in his writings. More "good things out of Nazareth" came from a modest cottage in rural England where Lewis crafted *Miracles*, a work that inspired O'Connor. Lewis struck a chord in O'Connor about her own fiction. Its apocalyptic, dynamic orthodoxy, rooted in the angelic doctor, Thomas Aquinas, as well as the incomparable Dante, comprises what Lewis calls "mere Christianity." O'Connor's letters sparkle with wit and show a dedication to her vocation in the face of protracted suffering. What a friend wrote about the letters in *The Habit of Being* also summarizes the riveting new ones in *Good Things Out of Nazareth:* "As I read I felt myself saying over and over what a marvelous gift she has been to this country, to the Church, to the human spirit!"*

Benjamin B. Alexander
Pawleys Island, South Carolina
April 2019

---

* Robert McCown, S. J., to Sally Fitzgerald, November 20, 1981.

CHAPTER 1

GOOD THINGS OUT OF NAZARETH

Residing in a sparse room in New York City, Flannery O'Connor, a promising writer from Georgia, in 1949 gladly accepted Robert and Sally Fitzgerald's invitation to live with them in rural Connecticut to finish *Wise Blood*. She first had written the novel at the Iowa Writers' Workshop and had hoped that it would be published while she was in residence at the Yaddo artists' colony in Saratoga Springs, New York. Fitzgerald recalls O'Connor's mornings dedicated to *Wise Blood*, after which "she would reappear about noon in her sweater, blue jeans and loafers, looking slender and most tall, and would take her daily walk, a half mile or so down the hill to the mailbox and back."[1] In the evenings, we would "put a small pitcher of martinis to soak and call the border. Our talks then and at the dinner table were long and lighthearted, and they were our movies, our concerts, and our theater."[2] In 1951 Robert Fitzgerald, a professor of rhetoric and oratory at Harvard, sent Caroline Gordon the manuscript of *Wise Blood*.

Caroline Gordon at the time was married to Allen Tate, a contributor to the 1930 Southern Agrarian manifesto, *I'll Take My Stand,* and the author of "Ode to the Confederate Dead" (later often anthologized). Gordon was a meticulous novelist in her own right. She for years deferred to Tate to the neglect of her own work. Ford Madox Ford and other critics believed Gordon's Civil War novel, *None Shall Look Back,* published in 1937, was superior to other canonical war novels such as *Gone with the Wind* and *The Red Badge of Courage.*

When Gordon received O'Connor's *Wise Blood* she was already tutoring a physician and would-be novelist, Walker Percy. She soon concluded that both O'Connor and Percy had great promise—and was one of a few in the early 1950s to recognize their potential. When Gordon first came to know them, the two writers were working in remote Southern settings—Milledgeville, Georgia, and Covington, Louisiana—far removed from publishing centers and the literary establishment. During their initial efforts at fiction writing, before they achieved fame, Gordon wrote Percy in 1951, "Well this is the season when the good things come out of Nazareth."[3]

The promise of both Percy and O'Connor was fragile. O'Connor was suffering from lupus, while Percy had survived tuberculosis contracted during his medical residency in New York. While recuperating, he began to retool himself as a novelist and read himself into Catholic conversion from agnosticism. Gordon undertook, for a meager $100, a tedious, sometimes line-by-line criticism of Percy's first novel, *The Charterhouse.* In 1952 Gordon sent him O'Connor's *Wise Blood* as an example of what she considered the opposite weakness of Percy's abstract tendencies in his fiction.

Gordon was dogmatic, opinionated, and undaunted by popular reputation. She took on anybody, including such luminaries as Faulkner and Hemingway. She wrote to another aspiring novelist, Brainard Cheney. She observed that William Faulkner was not the writer that Dostoevsky was. The Russian "rests squarely on the Christian myth, the responsibility for which rests on God. He did not have to create a new heaven and earth, as some secular writers seem to feel called on to do."[4] Gordon also applied this theological insight to both O'Connor and Percy, who followed, she noted, in the tradition of Dostoevsky.[5]

The first letter introduces Flannery O'Connor when she first appeared at the Iowa Writers' Workshop in the fall of 1945. Shortly she would begin crafting *Wise Blood,* published in 1952.

PAUL ENGLE TO ROBERT GIROUX

Paul Engle writes to Robert Giroux, Flannery O'Connor's friend and editor, his recollections of her when she was a student at the University of Iowa Writers' Workshop from 1945 to 1947. Engle was the director of the Workshop and was crucial in establishing the curriculum upon which other institutions would draw for their own programs. Engle's recollections of O'Connor made their way into Giroux's Introduction to Flannery O'Connor: The Complete Stories, *which would win the National Book Award in 1971.[6]*

THE UNIVERSITY OF IOWA

IOWA CITY, IOWA 52240

INTERNATIONAL WRITING PROGRAM

SCHOOL OF LETTERS

JULY 13, 1971

ROBERT GIROUX

FARRAR, STRAUS & GIROUX

19 UNION SQUARE WEST

NEW YORK, NY 10003

Dear Mr. Giroux:

Please forgive my long delay in answering your letter of April 26. After it arrived, I have written hundreds of letters in reply to the immense correspondence which this Program demands. However, I did not want to send you merely a quick note. As so often, the really important subject, which is of course Flannery, was put off for the magical moment when an answer in any way worthy of her (and probably there is no way worthy) could be written.

Too many years ago, when I was Director of The Program in Creative Writing in the first years of its growth, Flannery came to the University of Iowa, although I did not know her. She was, I think, a graduate student in journalism. One day I was in my office when a shy knock on the door preceded a shy person, who stood at my desk in silence. By her eyes, I could not tell whether she was looking at me or out the window at the Iowa River below. I asked her to sit down. Fine dignity in the withdrawn way she shared that place with me.

Finally she spoke, uttered sounds which were surely in a secret language. I asked her to repeat. No comprehension again. A third time. No communication. Embarrassed, suspicious, I asked her to write down what she had just said on a pad. She wrote: "My name is Flannery O'Connor. I am not a journalist. Can I come to the Writer's Workshop?"

She had been speaking her native Georgia tongue (most of which disappeared later). Of the world's many difficult languages, this must be one of the most impenetrable. I told her to bring examples of her writing and we would consider her, late as it was. Next day, stories arrived. I read them with disbelief. Like Keats, who spoke Cockney, but wrote the purest sounds in English, Flannery spoke a dialect beyond instant comprehension, but on the page her prose was imaginative, tough, alive: just like Flannery herself.

For a few weeks we had this strange and yet trusting relationship. Soon I understood those Georgia pronunciations. The stories were quietly filled with insight, shrewd about human weakness, hard and compassionate. They were the original basis for her book WISE BLOOD. She was shy about having them read, and when it was her turn to have a story presented in the "Workshop," I would read it aloud anonymously. Robert Penn Warren was teaching a semester while Flannery was at the University of Iowa; there was a scene about a black and a white man, and Warren criticized it as "unreal." It was changed. Flannery always had a flexible and objective view of her own writing, constantly revising, and in every case, improving. The will to be a writer was adamant; nothing could resist it, not even her own sensibility about her own work. Cut, alter, try it again.

One day Flannery brought a story involving a scene between a young man and young woman about to make love. I began to give my opinion, especially about what seemed to me a lack of intensity, of conviction. She stopped me and said, "Not here." Looking around at the corridor she added, "People. Can we go to a safer place?" With the manuscript, we went out of the building and across the street to a parking lot and there, sitting in my car with the windows rolled up, we discussed the appropriate phrases for the love situation. She was uncomfortable, but the wish to have it right dominated. It was obvious that she was improvising from innocence.

Sitting at the back of a room, silent, Flannery was more of a presence than the exuberant talkers who serenade every writing class with their loudness. The only communicating gesture she would make was an occasional amused and shy smile at something absurd. The dreary chair she sat in glowed. I have a large photograph of a writing Workshop having a party at a house in the country where I once lived. People are drinking, laughing, making faces, holding up children. It was wholly typical of Flannery that the part of her visible is her right knee, covered by a black-and-white checked heavy skirt which she commonly wore. There is spirit about that knee . . .

I am writing this in a little cottage on the beach in California, without carbon paper. Would you be so kind as to send back to Iowa City a xerox copy? I'd be grateful.

Paul Engle
Director

FLANNERY O'CONNOR TO BETTY BOYD

A steadfast yet quiet anti–Communist, O'Connor had left abruptly in 1949 the Yaddo artists' colony in Saratoga Springs, New York. O'Connor's friend

Robert Lowell, the Pulitzer Prize–winning poet, had exposed an FBI investigation of Yaddo's director, Elizabeth Ames, for colluding with a Soviet agent, Agnes Smedley. Lowell's revelation is historically important because both he and O'Connor knew the crucial difference between "Soviet Communists" and "Russians" who appear in the fiction of the country's great writers. Nobel Prize winner Aleksandr Solzhenitsyn, for example, is a Russian writer who writes about his countrymen suffering the cruelties and predations of the Communist government. Lowell's exposure of an American colluding with a Soviet Communist is politically accurate. He was not stoking paranoia about someone colluding with generic "Russians," a politically inaccurate and dangerously glib formulation. Lowell and O'Connor objected to the Yaddo director actually colluding with a known Communist committed to Marxist ideology. O'Connor and two others supported Lowell's demand that Ames be dismissed because her association with Agnes Smedley compromised the artistic integrity of Yaddo. O'Connor and Lowell eventually left the community, O'Connor ending up in New York City.

Unlike most American writers, even the theologically astute Martin Luther King, Jr., O'Connor, as a Thomist, consistently understood the heretical nature of Marxism in theological terms. In the last paragraph of the letter O'Connor writes of the ideology's demonic origins and its familial nature. Similar to C. S. Lewis in The Screwtape Letters, *she sets forth the idea from the master of demonic, familial conspiracies, Dante, in his presentation of a vast, escalating kingdom of evil in the* Inferno, *which he describes in the present tense—hell is an eternal state of being. O'Connor also provides another Dantesque formulation that also appears in* A Prayer Journal: *"No one believes more strongly in God than the devil."*

255 W 108

NYC

6/8/49

Dear Betty,

Your letter was most interesting to me re questions the FBI asked people about your mentioning Yaddo + Mrs. Elizabeth Ames. As Dr. B. probably told you I + 3 other guests, the total there at the time, left

Yaddo after asking the Board of Directors to fire Mrs. Ames. We felt, although, we couldn't prove anything, that there had been at some-time some measure of collusion between her and Communist guests who had spent time there—notably one named Agnes Smedley who stayed there five years + whose actions there were notably suspicious and who is to common knowledge an active Communist. Our action gained a good deal of publicity—not through us—and we have been assailed as people who want to destroy civil liberties etc. etc. Mrs. Ames continues in her post.

We found that the FBI had been watching Yaddo for years. The explanation to the questions asked about your mentioning the place can be one of two: either all the mail that left Yaddo was noted (I don't mean opened, but looked at in regard to the distribution +the same recorded) and since I wrote you two or three times from Yaddo, they knew your knowledge of the place; or, Yaddo has played a prominent enough part in espionage activity for it to be more or less a routine question. After what I have experienced lately, neither seems too fantastic although I incline to the former explanation.

If you know of anything else being asked about Yaddo or Mrs. Ames, it would be interesting to know what it is. After my experience there, my admiration for the FBI has greatly increased and my opinion of sociologists, never high since I got out of the shadow of GSCW, has got lower + lower unto death.

As to the devil, I not only believe he is but believe he has a family which in the extent + scope of its activities is a power to be reckoned with as stronger than all the dead and unborn put together. Also I believe no one believes more strongly in God than the devil, he having so much cause, and that in the end, we being what we are, its his testimony we will take. Yaddo has confirmed this in me.

I would be pleased if your literate friend would call me, although I don't feel literate. Let me hear from you.

Regards,

FOC

FLANNERY O'CONNOR TO CAROLINE GORDON

O'Connor recalls difficulties writing Wise Blood *while she was a student at the Iowa Writers' Workshop, and she seeks counsel from a Jesuit priest. Her Prayer Journal reveals that she accepted the Church's authority, even though she might be disappointed with the literary knowledge of priests. O'Connor also is averse to parochial girls' schools, a perspective present in these letters. Gordon was teaching at the College of St. Catherine in Minnesota and had written favorably about her experiences.*

[NOV. 1951]

Thank you so much for your letter and for wanting to help.[7] I am afraid it will need all the help it can get. I never have, fortunately, expected to make any money out of it, but one thing that has concerned me is that it might be recognized by Catholics as an effort proper for a Catholic; not that I expect any sizable number of them who arn't kin to me to read it—reading is not necessary to salvation which may be why they don't do it—but I have enough trouble with the ones who are kin to me to know what could be expected. You can't shut them up before a thing comes out but you can look forward to a long mortified silence afterwards. I used to be concerned with writing a "Catholic" novel and all that but I think now I was only occupying myself with fancy problems. If you are a Catholic you know so well what you believe, that you can forget about it and get on with the business of making the novel work. This is harder to do, knowing what you believe, but Catholic writers ought to be freer to concentrate on good writing than anybody else. They don't, and I wouldn't know why. When I first started my book, I was right young and very ignorant and I thought what I was doing was mighty powerful (it wasn't even intelligible at that point) and liable to corrupt anybody that read it and me too so I visited a priest in Iowa City and very carefully explained the problem to him. He gave me one of those ten cent pamphlets that they are never without and said I didn't have to write for fifteen year old girls. The pamphlet was by some Jesuit who did reviewing. He seemed to think that *A Tree Grows in Brooklyn* was about as good as you could get. Somebody ought to blow the lid off.

Since your letter to Robert [Fitzgerald] this summer, I have been examining my conscience on the business of writing about freaks. I didn't start out with that intention or any other but I found that I couldn't sustain a whole character. Andrew Lytle [professor, Iowa Writers' Workshop] saw a few of the early discarded chapters and said you keep out of that boy's mind, you'll get yourself messed up if you don't. It appeared to me to be good advice, but then the only way I seemed to be able to make clear what Haze was thinking was to have him do extreme things. I suppose what I needed to do then was make it plain that he was a freak in the philosophical order and not the kind that belonged in a clinic and I don't know if I've done that or not. This occurs to me now; nothing occurred to me while I was doing it.

I went to school to the sisters of St. Joseph of Carondelet in Savannah and liked them but I wouldn't much relish having a ring of them around my seminar; however, I don't think it would hurt them any to be there. I have always had a horror of Catholic girl's colleges. There seems to be a peculiar combination of money and piety and closed forms about them—this is all pure prejudice, I never attended one, and times may have changed. We have three of those sisters here, trying to start a school for the children. Two of them are former Baptists.

All these comments on writing and my writing have helped along my education considerably and I am certainly obliged to you. There is no one around here who knows anything at all about fiction (every story is "your article," or "your cute piece"?) or much about any kind of writing for that matter. Sidney Lanier and Daniel Whitehead Hickey are the Poets and Margaret Mitchell is the Writer. Amen. So it means a great deal to me to get these comments.

I had felt that the title wasn't anchored in the story but I hadn't known how to anchor it. I am about that now. It won't be a stout stake but it'll be something.

I had also felt that there were places that went too fast. The cause of this is laziness. I don't really like to write but I don't like to do anything else better; however it's easier to rewrite than do it for the first time and I mean to enlarge those places you mentioned. I've been reading a lot of Conrad lately because he goes so slow and I had thought reading him might help that fault. There is not much danger of my imitating him.

The business about making the scenery more lyrical to contrast with their moods will be harder for me to do. I have always been afraid to try my hand at being lyrical for fear I would only be funny and not know it. I suppose this would be a healthy fear if I had any tendency to overdo in that direction. This time, working so long on the book, I may have cultivated the ugly that it's become a habit. I was much concerned this summer after your letter to Robt. [Fitzgerald] to get everything out of that book that might sound like Truman Capote. I don't admire his writing. It reminds me of Yaddo. Mrs. Ames [Elizabeth] thought he had about achieved perfection in the form of the short story. I read in the Commonweal that his last book was better than the first one. The reviewer quoted something from it with great admiration about private worlds never being vulgar. I can think up plenty of vulgar private ones myself.

O'Connor mentions a friend, Robie Macauley—novelist, teacher, editor, and critic—who taught at the Iowa Writers' Workshop and also admired Wise Blood. *She also hopes to return to Connecticut to resume living with her friends Sally and Robert Fitzgerald.*

MILLEDGEVILLE
GEORGIA
MAY 2, 1952

I'm sorry you won't be able to review the book but I am glad to have the comment on the jacket, where it will give pause. I thought you would be interested in Waugh's comment which was as follows: "You want a favorable opinion to quote. The best I can say is: 'If this is really the unaided work of a young lady, it is a remarkable product.' End quote—It isn't the kind of book I like much, but it is good of its kind. It is lively and more imaginative than most modern books. Why are so many characters in recent American fiction sub-human? Kindest regards." Well, I am determined there'll be no apes in the next one.

I have heard from Robie Macauley who liked it. He says his own novel has been accepted by Random House and will be published in November. I am very glad because I like him and what he writes. Today I had a letter from Cal [Robert Lowell]. They are in Saltzburg and he is teaching at the American school there. The letter was very nice and very much like him but it makes me sad to think of the poor old boy.

I haven't worked my way up to *The Golden Bowl* yet, but I have just finished *The Portrait of a Lady*. The convent in that is the most awful I have ever read about. It beats the place where Julien Sorel was a seminarian. When the Mother Superior said she thought the child had been there long enough I thought I would jump out the window. This winter I read that book of Max Picard's, *The Flight from God*. I was knocked out by that.

I do hope I will see you all this summer. I hope to get to Ridge-field [Connecticut] by taking it easy. I am about ninety-two years old in the matter of energy and will have to travel with the sterilizer and syringe and all such mess but I am looking forward to it.

O'Connor addresses an unusual topic for the modern short story. She also discusses the differences in prayers of believers.

5/12/52

I was very pleased to be able to read this piece on James and I have read it a couple of times by now and with wonder every time. Since my critical training, such as it was, took place in a lump at Iowa, I've always felt that it would be horribly gauche to voice any insights on a novel or poem that came via Catholic conviction. At the same time I've thought that if a thing is art, it has to take in enough to be catholic—at least with a little c—and that if it's that, it is penetrable by Catholic standards. But aesthetics is way over my head. I don't have enough of the proper kind of words. Anyway, as I read it, I felt that this was surely the normal natural way to react to Henry James; I mean the way God and Henry intended.

I get so sick of reading all this stuff about his "accident." I am sure you mean to dismiss it once and for all when you say, "If he had been congenitally incapable of the marriage relation he would have written books different from the ones he wrote," but this statement confuses me. I'm not very subtle; to me, it puts the emphasis back where you intend to take it off. I think he could have been physically incapable of marriage and still have written the books he wrote because I don't think that that would have had anything to do with his talent or the Grace that he had to write them with. I guess you mean that if he had been morally or emotionally unfit for the marriage relation, he would have written different books, which I can readily see. Maybe I am being knocked over by a gnat here but I wish you would enlighten me. I arrive at the obvious only after lengthy research.

Most of the stories you used in it, I hadn't read but I did find a copy of THE GREAT GOOD PLACE [Henry James] and read it yesterday. I thought the vision was more one of Purgatory than of Heaven. It wouldn't have been much of a Heaven to a Catholic anyway. While he didn't suffer there the young man who took his place was a suffering figure and wasn't there a kind of communion of saints atmosphere between them? Also, although the Brother called it the Great Want Met, it was only a great want for contemplation and regaining of the self—it wasn't the great want you think of as being satisfied in heaven. The presence of God is in the place but it is experienced only vaguely and never seen. Wasn't St. Catherine of Sienna rewarded with self-knowledge in her visions of Purgatory, or rather when she felt she was actually there? I don't mean that James thought of the great good place as purgatory but only that Dane was probably not as far up as he thought he was, or James maybe thought he was.

I will certainly pray for Mr. Tate in the air but my opinion is contrary to his. I always thought converts' prayers availed more else they wouldn't be where they are and that born Catholics are only born Catholics because they would be too lazy to save themselves any other way. But maybe this only applies to the Irish.

I am certainly indebted to you for letting me see this piece and I think it ought to be a book.

If Catholic novels are bad, current Catholic criticism is PURE SLOP or else it's stuck off in some convent where nobody can get his hands on it. Sr. Mariella Gable ought to disguise herself as Freudina Potts and undermine the Partisan Review from inside. She could send the whole place to the devil.

O'Connor mentions working on a story about rural arson and the terrorism of cross burnings. She may have reworked the scene to craft her later story "A Circle in the Fire" and the ending of The Violent Bear It Away.

MILLEDGEVILLE

6/2/52

All this is very helpful to me and I intend to take the slow tour through *Madame Bovary.* I read *The Craft of Fiction* [Percy Lubbock] periodically but I am still at the stage where I have to worry more about if anything is going to BE then How. I notice Mr. Lubbock says Flaubert never had to hold down his subject with one hand while he wrote it with the other. Me neither. I have to go in search of it. I don't know whether I get blood out of the turnip or turnips out of my blood. The novel I am writing now is very exciting to me but I keep writing the wrong thing, proceeding like the mole. It has three boys for heros—all very guilty and sharp. They burn a cross on one [of] them's papa's lawn and the cross is something different to each of them and something else for the papa, etc etc. It is going to be kind of impossible to do but I think it must be the impossibility that makes the tension.

My method is more liable to be affected by my mother's dairyman's wife than by Mr. Henry James. She hangs around all the time and all her sentences begin: "I know one time my husband seen . . ." It works like you say. He sees everything and she sees twice as much as he sees but she has never looked at anything but him. They both read my book and said: it just shows you how some people would do.

Don't be amused by my profession of gratitude. It's drastic and the fact I have had a few people apply to me for advice about their manuscripts but they are always hopeless, and have a mission, or are just plain crazy. One of them, a lady, said, "You use the block style, don't you?" Another is a disciple of Henry Miller. The other is a bank clerk and when he brings a paper, he sits on the arm of the chair smoking heavily while I read it and every now and then his finger descends on a word and he says "See? That's where I use much iron-ny." It scares me to death when I think how good the Lord is to give you a talent and let you be able to use it. I reresolve to become responsible, and to *Madame Bovary* I go.

I do pray for you but it strikes me I ought to be praying for the logical positivists. A distasteful business.

Affectionately,

O'Connor mentions a visit to her friends the Fitzgeralds and their loss of a child. She also disciplined their son, Benedict, who years later became a skilled screenwriter and co-wrote with Mel Gibson the screenplay for The Passion of the Christ *(2004). Fitzgerald also collaborated in writing the script for O'Connor's* Wise Blood *(1979), directed by John Huston.*

MILLEDGEVILLE

9/11/52

Last night I happened on this picture of your connection here. Since I had sent him two bucks in memory of Mark Twain (before I asked you about him), I figure I must have at least paid for the license. He [is] mighty well preserved.

I am up again now and looking forward to a recessive period of my come-and-go ailment. It's very good working again. I am just writing a story to see if I can get away from the freaks for a while.

This summer while I was at the Fitzgeralds, I read "The Strange Children" [Caroline Gordon]. I thought it was a beautiful book, part one probably in the development of Grace in these people. Of the characters I noticed that the Catholic, Mr. Reardon, was the least filled in. Was that because he would have taken the book over if he had been? It was not his story of course but it takes some doing to put a Catholic in a novel.

I have just read "Victory." Everything I read of Conrad's I like better than the last thing. I've also just read the "Turn of the Screw" [Henry James] again and to me it fairly shouts that it's about expiation.

Have you seen the Fitzgeralds? Sally seems to be having a bad time still. I had to leave in a hurry on account of my fever a few days before she lost the baby. Benedict [Fitzgerald] has had the chicken pox but they say it has only given him more zest—which he didn't particularly need. The day before I left, he climbed in the car, drove it twelve feet over a chair and into a pile of rocks, climbed out the window, looking exactly like Charles Lindburg, and received a whipping from me (Sally was in bed sick) as if it were a great honor.

I suspect you are getting ready for Minnesota.

O'Connor is pleased that Gordon approves of "The River." O'Connor is also working on a story that would become a novel a few years later, The Violent

Bear It Away. *She also praises one of Gordon's most famous stories, "Old Red," which taught O'Connor much about writing fiction* (The Collected Stories of Caroline Gordon, *Baton Rouge: LSU Press, 1981*).

[SEPTEMBER, 1953]

I am highly pleased you liked that story "The River." I had been thinking about a woman baptizing a child that didn't know what it was about for a long time and finally I thought myself up to the point of writing it. The Churches ceremony of Baptism is so elaborate! I keep trying to think of some way in fiction that I could convey the richness against the threadbareness of the other but my thought is none too productive. The Church takes care of everything and I am always struck fresh with it on St. Blases Day when you have your throat blessed. The One True Holy Catholic & Apostolic Church taking time out to bless my throat! And these people around here have to scratch their religion out of the ground.

Which brings me around to what I wish you would do in Rome— see those Texas Baptists that are there to convert the Italians. I think that is the story of the century and if I knew anything about Rome I would be at it myself but I'll probably never get there. I saw the picture of one of them in Time—he looked like a clipped lion with a raging headache, a little like a stupid Cal. You could wring that subject dry!

Guess what I did this summer. I spent a weekend in Nashville with the Cheneys [Lon and Fanny]. They had me and Ashley Brown [professor, University of South Carolina] and we had a lovely time, mostly listening to Lon whom Fanny says is a non-stop talker. They had some people in one night and let me read "The River." I like to read once I get started and quit thinking about it. They had a picture of yours of a peacock and some other birds and wild animals that I was much taken with. It was the only peacock I'd ever seen with the face of a mandril. My peafowl seem to just die for meanness. I have a cock and two hens left. She hatched one peachicken this summer and raised it big enough for a weasel to eat before he went to bed. Next year as soon as they hatch I am bringing them in the house and going to raise them in the bureau drawer. The Cheneys have been in Ripton, Ver. and were going by to see the Fitzgeralds on their way back home. I got to the Fitzgeralds too. You are the Oracle around there. Everytime those children do something awful which is none too infrequent they say Aunt Caroline let me do that etc etc. Benedict is very superior, having visited you. Things finally got evened up when they let Hugh visit the Maxwells. Now when Benedict says Aunt Caroline had a ferry boat, Hugh says the Maxwells had a bear-skin rug that was a real bear. When I left they hadn't been able to rent the house yet and their trip to Europe was hanging fire but I am hoping they have got it rented by now.

You will see quick enough that I am enclosing two things. The one called "Whom the Plague Beckons" is the first chapter of my novel and that is all. There ain't no more and I do not know where the next word is coming from. By the time I get it finished we may both be dead and gone to our reward. My intention is to take Tarwater on to his uncles, the ass in town, pursued all the time by the cross he didn't set up—which he finally sets up on his uncle's lawn with the appropriate consequences. It's full of stuff but I am no where near it yet. The other is a long story (long for me) that I don't know whether [it] comes off or not but would appreciate your word on the subject. I have sent both of these to Mr. Ransom [John Crowe, *Kenyon Review*] and have asked him to send me back the one he doesn't want. Nothing like presumption. I would like to send something to Bottegha Osura but I would also like to paint the side of the house so I will be sending it to Madam McIntosh [Mavis] instead to have it buried in some fashion magazine for a price. I had one in the Sept. *Harper's Bazaar,* wedged in between all the skeletons in pill box hats. It made me sick to look at it.

Since I aim to be so long about the novel I have inveigled Giroux [Robert] into saying they will publish a book of my short stories in the fall of 54—to be called *A Good Man Is Hard to Find*. They take a dim view of it of course and I take a dim view of it myself though it's my idea. The fact is I am uncertain about the stories. Three early ones would have to be included and I can't even bring myself to read them over. If you say so, I would like to send them to you and get you to say if you think they ought to be included. Did you see that one of mine in the Spring *Kenyon* [*Review*] called "The Life You Save May Be Your Own"?

One of these stories, the first I ever had published, was written after I had read one called "Old Red" which you are doubtless familiar with. "Old Red" was the making of me as a short story writer. I think I learned from it what you can do with a symbol once you get a hold of it. Beforehand I hadn't even known such a thing existed.

I was mighty glad to hear from you. I live in a Bird Sanctuary but the birds are not enough.

O'Connor writes to Gordon, who is living in Rome with her husband. Gordon comments on stories that would make up the collection A Good Man Is Hard to Find and Other Stories *(1955). She also has written O'Connor about her visits to different sites. Invoking the allegory of her own fiction, O'Connor applies the technique to Gordon's experiences.*

MILLEDGEVILLE

2 OCTOBER 53

You will think I never appear but what I am loaded. I don't know if I'm writing these stories to keep from writing that novel or not but I suspect myself. Tarwater is a mighty sullen companion. Anyway it cheers me that you find him worthy. I'm distressed that dogs don't root things up but we don't know anything about dogs here. My mother won't allow one on the place because she has the grande dame cows, all neurotic. There's no such thing as a contented cow. If one of hers sees a particularly fierce horse fly, the milk production falls off. Also she won't have a hog on the place. She just don't like to look at them. I guess I will change it to hogs and then I'll have to insert a couple of hogs somewhere in the scenery. I am a city girl. One time Mr. Ransom [John Crowe] had to point out to me that you don't hunt quail with a rifle.

I've been scouting around in the Book of Daniel for a better title for the story but all the stuff there is too heady. What the angel really did was to make a wind in the heart of the furnace, like the wind that brings the dew. I need something that won't wag the dog but perhaps I'll think of the right thing before the book comes out.

I'll send you the old stories by a slower freight. I have just finished this one and as is my habit I am very pleased with it. I always am for about twenty four hours. You are mighty good to look at these things and it means a great deal to me.

The Fitzgeralds [Sally and Robert] have found themselves a tenant and say they set off Oct 12 for Milan. This will be an experience for the Italian Airlines.

All I know about these people from Texas is they're Baptists. I haven't seen anything about them lately but last year they were raising cane about how they were being persecuted in Rome. Maybe by now some Swiss guard has walled them up in an unused catacomb or they have moved on to see what they can do about Spain. I think I could handle their end of it; what I have no idea about is Rome. You must feel you are living on several levels of reality, or maybe I mean see you are, right clearly—coming up from the catacombs to catch the streetcar or whatever. The Fitzgeralds sent me a clipping about The New Jerusalem—to be built by Eddie Dowling at Pinellas, Florida. A 4.5 million dollar project, an exact replica, the smell of camels, real olives from Gethsemane, etc etc. Dowling said, "Once the site is determined, you can have the custodian come over from the Garden of Gethsemane. Right from that day, you're in business with an attraction." All this is in the vicinity of Palm Beach. Non-sectarian. Big name stars for the major roles (Jesus—Gregory Peck; Mary Magdalen—Rita Hayworth). Tourists from all over the world. I see Haze and Enoch [characters, *Wise Blood*] prowling around here, sniffing the camels.

The enclosed from Peacock. His regards, my love.

FLANNERY O'CONNOR TO BEVERLY BRUNSON

O'Connor responds to one of the few local readers who has carefully read Wise Blood.

MILLEDGEVILLE

GEORGIA

9 DECEMBER 53

Dear Miss Brunson:

I am pleased that you can suffer to read my novel twice. Some months ago I met a lady who said, "Oh I haven't read your novel. I can't read much on account of my eyes so I only read books that improve my mind!" room for improvement I thought. Having a novel behind you is like having an idiot child at your elbow: people feel they must make some discreet remark.

A shrike looks something like a masked mocking bird. I don't think it shrieks at night. What it does do is impale large bugs and mice on thorn bushes so it can eat them at its leisure. Altogether a good bird for a writer to have around but I forget where I have used it. Bird watching is actually too strenuous for me but I have a backyard full of various ridiculous looking chickens: Polish crested, Japanese silkies, pheasants, peafowl (these are beautiful), mallards, geese.

As for the abbot, he was not looking in the grave gratuitously; he was burying the dead, one of the corporal works of mercy which we are more or less required by necessity to perform from time to time. The contemplative vocation doesn't thrive in cafes. H. Motes was actually a contemplative but the means to that life not being at hand for him, the only way he could achieve it was by violence—binding himself.

A Georgian cannot of course be against Coca Cola. We feed it to our babies, serve it to our guests, console the dying with it and expect it to make us loved throughout the world. It was invented right here, sprung full blown from the head of somebody, and we are very happy that its natural merit raised it in the public appreciation above some horrid New England drink called Moxie. I daresay the claptrap we have to make our way amid is no more ridiculous than it ever was or is. The point is to see it and beyond it to what it hides.

Regards,

CAROLINE GORDON TO ROBERT FITZGERALD

Gordon writes that Flannery O'Connor "is already a rare phenomenon: a Catholic novelist with a real dramatic sense, one who relies more on her technique than her piety." This comment is the foundation of the correspondence between O'Connor and Gordon and the letters O'Connor wrote to her Jesuit friends. The emphasis on "technique" over "piety" extends back to medieval times, to another "Nazareth"—Florence, Italy—and its most famous writer, Dante. He is remembered for his "dramatic sense" in the sensational horrors of the Inferno *and the beauty of* Purgatorio *and* Paradiso. *Relying on technique, Dante presents his faith in an implicit yet compelling way. His argument for the necessity of purgatory is conveyed not in a tract but in a story about climbing a mountain in the* Purgatorio. *Dante may be the greatest of ecumenical Catholic writers because storytelling overrides piety. This is the foundation of Gordon's instruction of O'Connor and Walker Percy.*

[MAY 1951][8]

I'm glad you gave me Flannery O'Connor's novel to read. I'm quite excited about it. This girl is a real novelist. (I wish that I had had as firm a grasp on my subject matter when I was her age!) At any rate, she is already a rare phenomenon: a Catholic novelist with a real dramatic sense, one who relies more on her technique than her piety.

I hope that old GS 40 hasn't gone to my head, but I find myself wanting to make a few suggestions about this book. I think that it has real objectivity, but I think, too, that certain technical imperfections deprive it of its proper frame of reference and actually limit its scope. I believe that a touch here and there and a re-writing of two key scenes which she has muffed would do wonders for the form. I feel so strongly about this that I am going to go ahead and make the suggestions I have in mind and you can pass them on to her or not, as you see fit. After all, I know her very slightly. She may find me presumptuous.

But I am much interested in the book itself. Her general procedure seems to me sound. She is, of course, writing the kind of stuff people like to read nowadays: about freaks. Her book, like those of most of the younger writers, is full of freaks, but she does something with them that Buechner [Frederick] and Capote and those boys seem to be incapable of doing. Truman's people, all seem to me, to belong in some good clinic. Her characters started out real folks but turned into freaks as the result of original sin.

She has one line of dialogue that I contemplate with envy: on page 142: " 'Blind myself' he said and went on into the house." You remember two lines of Ernest's in *To Have and Have Not*: "Are those girls any good? . . . No, hon . . ." I always thought that those were the two fastest lines of dialogue that any of my contemporaries had written, but this "Blind myself" strikes me as being just as good. If this girl is capable of writing a line like that she is certainly capable of making the revisions this manuscript needs. I hope she won't think I'm being presumptuous in pointing them out.

We—all of us, including the prospective godfather—await news from you all. Do let us hear as soon as you can,

CAROLINE GORDON TO FLANNERY O'CONNOR

A convert, Gordon is enthusiastic about teaching at a Catholic college. Reference is also made to the political extermination of an order of nuns during the French Revolution. This vital detail illustrates Gordon's precise perspective on history. She distinguishes between the American War for Independence and the French Revolution. Conventional civic education in the United States rarely observes the crucial distinction and often conflates the War for American Independence with the French Revolution.

1801 UNIVERSITY AVENUE SOUTHEAST
MINNEAPOLIS 14, MINNESOTA
[MAY 1951]

I am delighted to hear now that you are feeling better that you have finished your novel. As you know, I was much impressed by the novel in its original form. There are so few Catholic novelists who seem possessed of a literary conscience—not to mention skill—that I feel that your novel is very important. I shall be glad to read it whenever Robert [Fitzgerald] sends it. I am going to write to Robert Giroux, too, and tell him that I want to review the novel when it comes out and that I would like to do anything I can to help—though, of course, there is little that one can do, or needs to do to help a good novel.

I had a letter yesterday from Will Percy's nephew, Walker Percy, who lives at Covington, Louisiana. He says he has written a novel which he guesses is "a Catholic novel, though it has no conversion or priests in it." I don't know that your paths are likely to cross, but if they ever should I imagine that you'd find it interesting to know each other. He has been in the Church about five years.

Allen and I are crazy about Minnesota. Everything is on such a grand scale, and the city itself is very handsome, with the Mississippi river, to my continual surprise, running right through it. Frank Lloyd Wright was here, all right. There are a lot of modern churches, Mother Cabrini's, shaped like a Viking ship, St. Ignatius, shaped like a fish, and then there is one church that has a dialogue Mass. St. John's Abbey, sixty miles away, is the largest Benedictine community in the world. Three hundred monks and three thousand acres of this fat black earth.

I am teaching a seminar in fiction at the College of St. Catherine. I have about twelve girls and, each week, an outer circle of auditors, alumnae and nuns. The presence of the nuns made me rather nervous at first, but I am getting used to them. They are sisters of St. Joseph of Carondelet, an order that was almost exterminated during the French Revolution—I believe they had to give up the habit and lived about in caves or sheltered by peasants—till the order was finally re-planted and six nuns were sent to St. Louis, Missouri, from which community nuns were sent here.

I shall await the manuscript with eagerness. Many thanks for sending it.

CAROLINE GORDON TO WALKER PERCY

In 1951, Walker Percy sent Caroline Gordon his novel The Charterhouse *for copyediting. Gordon foresees the ecumenical scope of Percy's fiction that enabled him, like O'Connor, to reach a wide, diverse audience.*

1801 UNIVERSITY AVENUE SOUTHEAST

MINNEAPOLIS, 14 MINNESOTA

Dear Walker:

First, let me tell you how very glad I am that you have entered the Church and then let me add that I'll be glad to read your novel. I remember having a conversation about writing with you years ago at some party and in that conversation you revealed the fact that you already realized that techniques were involved in the writing of novels. A Catholic novelist who relies more on his technique than his piety is what is badly needed right now. I wouldn't want to pass up a chance of discovering one.

Ordinarily I shouldn't accept a fee for reading your novel, but since you are a Catholic I will ask you a fee of one hundred dollars. I need an extra hundred dollars for a sort of Catholic project with which I imagine you'd be in sympathy. Allen and I have two godsons, a young man and a young poet, both very gifted, whose lives have been re-made since they entered the Church a little over a year ago. They are truly Benedictine in spirit and were long before they knew anything about the order and they are anxious to attach themselves to some monastery where they can put their considerable talents to the service of the Church. We both feel that St. John's Abbey, near St. Cloud, is the place for them, but they are in Massachusetts, where they run the Cummington Press, and before they could do anything at all is quite expensive. If I read your novel I'll apply the fee to their railroad fare. I think it may mean a turning point in their lives.

St. John's Abbey, incidentally, is the largest Benedictine community in the world. It is great fun living so near it. In fact, Minnesota is a wonderfully exciting place for a convert. The Church here is more like the mediaeval Church. I suppose the French influence hasn't quite died out.

My own order—I feel quite proprietary about it since I am teaching a seminar in fiction at the College of St. Catherine—the sisters there are an order that was almost exterminated during the French revolution and then re-planted at Carondelet in Missouri and sent from St. Louis to which at that time was known as "Pig's Eye." The sisters hastily christened it St. Paul.

I am delighted to be teaching in a Catholic college. I was getting tired of teaching—or trying to teach Protestants. One wastes so much time defining terms.

Allen and I both send you our best wishes and congratulations, or perhaps you ought to be sending them to us. I'm not sure which of us got to the fold first. Percy and Nancy [Mr. and Mrs. Percy Wood, daughter and son-in-law] and their two children were all baptized last spring. Our neighbor, Jacques Maritain, said that it was like the conversion of Clovis and the Franks.

Yours sincerely in Christ,
Caroline

CAROLINE GORDON TO FLANNERY O'CONNOR

Gordon mentions that her husband, "Allen" [Tate], is reading Wise Blood. *As the letters reveal, however, Gordon does the hard work of copyediting O'Connor's stories but often defers to Tate for commentary.*

[MAY, 1951]

The book arrived just after I wrote you. I think the end comes off marvelously. And that was a ticklish job, too. I have been holding my breath for fear I had been giving you a bum steer, but I really don't think so, now I see what you've made of my suggestion. It was all there implicit in the action, anyway, of course, just needed a little more bringing out.

Waugh's [Evelyn] comment on your book is interesting. I don't really think that he is a novelist. His *Edmund Campion* is a beautiful thing, but *Helena* is amateurish, at times embarrassingly so.

I am enclosing the piece of James I have been labouring on all winter. I'd like to know how it strikes you. I don't feel that James has been read yet. Certainly, when read from the Christian view-point he yields some results he hasn't yielded to any of the critics. I have a lot of other notions about his work that I couldn't get into the essay. It is strange, for instance, that so many of his big scenes take place in churches. Strange, on the other hand, that he will present a convent, say, in the most stereotyped way: the one Claire de Cintre retires to, in *The American,* for instance. Graham Greene, in a piece called "Henry James; An Aspect," says that the fact is that James was abysmally ignorant both of the dogma and the rites of the Catholic Church, though he was strongly attracted to it.

This house is in turmoil. Allen leaves Friday morning to fly first to Princeton where he will inspect Little Caroline Wood and other members of the family, then he'll take off for a cultural congress in Paris, to be gone about three weeks in all. He's scared to death of flying, but not as scared as he used to be before he joined the Church. I told him I would pray all the time he was on the ocean. He said that was all right, but he'd like to have a few nuns' prayers, as well. He'd appreciate yours, too, no doubt, even if you aren't a professional. He doesn't seem to think that a convert's prayers avail much.

We look forward to seeing you this summer. I do hope your health continues to improve, affectionately,

Allen read the first paragraph of your book and said "You can tell from that first paragraph that she is a real writer." It is such an original, strong book! I am delighted by it all over again. You've got something that none of the rest of them seem to have.

CAROLINE GORDON TO FLANNERY O'CONNOR

The original eighteen-page letter is excerpted.[9] *It illustrates Gordon's copyediting detail. O'Connor, of course, benefited from such scrutiny, which is rare in American literary history. Gordon perhaps engaged in such precision because she understood that O'Connor's* Wise Blood *was a witty and dramatic satire of a fashionable theme in modern Catholic writers, such as James Joyce in* Portrait of the Artist as a Young Man. *Joyce's autobiographical novel presents a favorable "portrait" of the sterile strictures of many facets of Irish Catholicism— drunken Churchman, mean Jesuits, and bullying in religious schools that the novel's protagonist experiences. Recanting his faith, Stephen Daedalus becomes a cult figure of theological rebellion that O'Connor ruthlessly mocks in Hazel Motes in* Wise Blood. *He seeks to found an atheistic Church complete with his evangelical proclamations about the "Church without Christ Crucified." Emulating other famous epiphanies such as St. Paul himself and St. Francis, Motes ends up blinding himself as a penance. He also has a version of a medieval hair shirt in the form of barbed wire he wraps around his chest.*

1801 UNIVERSITY AVENUE SOUTHEAST

MINNEAPOLIS 14, MINNESOTA

ST. DIDACUS' DAY

[NOVEMBER 13, 1951]

Your manuscript has come. I spent yesterday reading it. I think it is terrific! I know a good many young writers who think they are like Kafka. You are the only one I know who succeeds in doing a certain thing that he does. When I say that I am merely reaching out for some phrase that will partly convey my notion of your work. I do not mean that it is in any way derivative of Kafka. In fact, this book seems to me the most original book I have read in a long time. But you are like Kafka in providing a firm Naturalistic ground-work for your symbolism. In consequence, symbolic passages—and one of the things I admire about the book is the fact that all the passages are symbolic—passages echo in the memory long after one has put the book down, go on exploding, as it were, depth on depth. As that old fool, E. M. Forster, would say: "You have more than one plane of action." (And what a contrast they are to the maunderings which he presents as his planes of action!)

Robert Fitzgerald reported to me something that you said that interested me very much, that your first novel [*Wise Blood*] was about freaks, but that your next book would be about folks. It is fashionable to write about freaks—Truman Capote and his followers write about little else. It astonishes—and amuses me—to find a writer like you using what is roughly the same kind of subject matter. But what a different use you put it to! Whenever I read any of the homosexual novels that are so popular nowadays I am reminded of something Chekhov said, that "he and she are the engine that makes fiction move." That strikes me as profoundly true. One can write about homosexuals if one shows them as differing from normal people, as Proust does, but when a writer gives us a world in which everybody is a freak it seems to me that he is doing little more than recording the progress of his disease.

But homosexuality, childishness, freakishness—in the end, I think it comes to fatherlessness—is rampant in the world today. And you are giving us a terrifying picture of the modern world, so your book is full of freaks. They seem to me, however, normal people who have been maimed or crippled and your main characters, Sabbath, Enoch and Haze, are all going about their Father's business, as best they can. It is a terrifying picture. I don't know any other contemporary who gets just such effects. Genet achieves remarkable effects but for me they are all marred, finally, [by] his sentimentality. You are never sentimental.

I think that you have done a good job on the revision. I don't really see how you managed it. The Fitzgeralds told us that you have had a severe illness and are only recently out of the hospital. There comes a time for any manuscript when one must let it go with no more revisions. I think that having done the job you've done you could let this manuscript go with a good conscience. But I am going to make a few suggestions and comments. They are really suggestions for your future work, but I have to have something to pin them to, so I am going to take passages from *Wise Blood* as illustrations of the points I am trying to make. If I seem overly pedantic it is doubtless the result of teaching. When you are reading a manuscript for a fellow writer you can say "I like this" or "I don't like that" and he figures it out for himself, but if you are dealing with students you have to try to relate your reactions to some fundamental principle of the craft.

I admire tremendously the hard core of dramatic action in this book. I certainly wouldn't want it softened up in any way. I am convinced that one reason the book is so powerful is that it is so unflaggingly dramatic. But I think that there are two principles involved which you might consider.

It is the fact that in this world nothing exists except in relation to something else. (I take it that being a Catholic you are not a Cartesian!) In geometry a straight line is the shortest distance between two points. Theology takes cognizance of a soul only in its relation to God; its relation to its fellow-men, in the end, help to constitute its relations with God. It seems that it is the same way in fiction. You can't create in a vacuum. You have to imitate the Almighty and create a whole world—or an illusion of a whole world, if the simplest tale is to have any verisimilitude.

As I say, I admire the core of dramatic action in this book very much, but I think that the whole book would gain by not being so stripped, so bare, by surrounding the core of action with some contrasting material. Suppose we think of a scene in your novel as a scene in a play. Any scene in any play takes place on some sort of set. I feel that the sets in your play are quite wonderful but you never let us see them. A spotlight follows every move the characters make and throws an almost blinding radiance on them, but it is a little like the spotlight a burglar uses when he is cracking a safe; it illuminates a small circle and the rest of the stage is in darkness most of the time. Focusing the reader's attention completely on the action is one way to make things seem very dramatic, but I do not think that you can keep that up all of the time. It demands too much of the reader. He is just not capable of such rigorous attention. It would be better, I think, if you occasionally used a spotlight large enough to illuminate the corners of the room, for those corners have gone on existing all through the most dramatic moments.

What I am trying to say is that there are one or two devices used by many novelists which I think you would find helpful.

Often one can make an immediate scene more vivid by deliberately going outside it. A classical example is the scene in *Madame Bovary* in which Charles and Emma are alone together for the first time. Charles' senses are stirred by Emma, he is looking at her very intently. At the same time he hears a hen that has just laid an egg cackling in a hay mow in the court-yard. Going outside that scene somehow makes it leap to life. The very fact that the sound is distant makes the people in the room seem more real. Hart Crane uses the same device in a poem called "Paraphrase." A man is standing beside a bed looking down at the body of a dead woman and grieving for her death. His grief is made more real by "the crow's cavil" that he hears outside the window.

I think that this very device could be used very effectively in *Wise Blood*. Occasionally you get a powerful effect by having the landscape reflect the mood of the character, as in the scene where the sky is like a thin piece of polished silver and the sun is sour-looking. But it seems to be monotonous to have the landscape continually reflecting their moods. In one place I think you could get a much more dramatic effect by having it contrast with them. For instance, in the scene where Haze, Sabbath and Enoch meet, I think that the landscape ought to actually play a part in the action, as it does sometimes in Chekhov's stories. If the night sky were beautiful, if the night were lyrical the sordid roles the characters have to play would seem even more sordid. After all, here are three young people trying to do as best they can what they feel that they ought to do. Sabbath wants to get married. Enoch wants to live a normal human life. Haze, who is a poet and a prophet, wants to live his life out on a higher level. You convey that admirably, I think, by emphasizing his fierce dedication to his ideals. But the scene itself is too meager for my taste. Your spotlight is focused too relentlessly on three characters.

There is another thing involved: the danger of making excessive demands on the reader. He is not very bright, you know, and the most intelligent person, when he is reading fiction, switches his intellect off and—if the author does what he is trying to do—listens like a three or thirteen year old child. The old Negro preacher's formula for a perfect sermon applies here: "First I tells 'em I'm going to tell 'em, then I tells 'em, then I tell 'em I done told them." It takes much longer to take things in than we realize. In our effort to keep the action from lagging we hurry the reader over crucial moments. But anything that is very exciting can't be taken in hurriedly. If somebody is killed in an automobile accident people who were involved in the accident or who merely witnessed it will be busy for days afterwards piecing together a picture of what happened. They simply couldn't take it all in at that time. When we are writing fiction we have to give the reader ample time to take in what is happening, particularly if it is very important. The best practice, I gather, is to do the thing twice. That is, the effect is repeated, but is so varied that the reader thinks he is seeing something else. Actually the second passage, while it interests the reader, exists chiefly to keep him there in that spot until he has taken in what the author wants him to take in. Stephen Crane uses this device often and to perfection in *The Red Badge of Courage.*

Yeats puts it another way. He says that in poetry every tense line ought to be set off, that is, ought to be preceded and followed by what he calls "a numb line." He is constantly doing this in Major Robert Gregory ["In Memory of Major Robert Gregory"]. His numb lines do not slow up the action. They make it more powerful . . .

There is another thing that I think the book needs: a preparation for the title. Henry James says that at the beginning of every book "a stout stake" must be driven in for the current of the action to swirl against. This stout stake is a preparation for what is to come. Sometimes the writer prepares the reader by giving him a part of what is to happen. Sometimes he conveys the knowledge symbolically, sometimes he does it by certain cadences, as in "A Farewell to Arms," when at the beginning the narrator says "The leaves fell early that year"—another way of saying "My love died young." At any rate, however it is done, the reader must be given enough to go on, so that, in the end, he will have that comfortable feeling that accompanies "I told you so!" . . .

To sum up, there are three places in the book where I think a few strokes might make a lot of difference, this scene and the scene where the patrolman pushes the car over and the scene where Haze and Sabbath and Enoch first meet.

And one more thing: I think you are just a little too grim with Sabbath when she is nursing the mummy. I don't like the use of the word "smirk" there. It is almost as if the author were taking sides against her. I think it would be more dramatic if you were a little more compassionate towards her. After all, she is a young girl trying to lead a normal life and this is the nearest she'll ever come to having a baby—since she'll probably end in the Detention Home. At any rate, the situation is grim enough without the author's taking sides.

I will now—God help us both!—make a few, more detailed comments . . .

Well, that's enough of that! I would like to see you make some preparation for the title, *Wise Blood,* and I'd like to see a little landscape, a little enlarging of the scene that night they all meet, and I'd also like to see a little slowing up at certain crucial places I've indicated, but aside from those few changes I don't think that it matters much whether you make any of the revisions I've suggested. I am really thinking more of the work you'll do in the future than of this present novel which seems to me a lot better than any of the novels we've been getting. But of course in writing fiction one can never stand still. Once you learn how to do one thing you have to start learning how to do something else and the devil of it is that you always have to be doing three or four things at a time.

But my heartiest congratulations to you, at any rate. It's a wonderful book. I've written to Robert Giroux, expressing my admiration. My best wishes to you. I do hope that you continue to feel better.

Yours,
Caroline

NEXT MORNING:

I realize that in all this long letter I've said little about what I admire in the book. It is, first of all, I think, your ability to present action continually on more than one plane. Only writers of the first order can do that. Everything in your book exists as we all exist in life, mysteriously, in more than one dimension. When Haze runs the car over Solace Layfield he is murdering his own alter ego as well as Layfield. His Essex is not only a means of locomotion. It is pulpit. When he finds out that Sabbath's father is blind he finds out much more than that. This goes on all through the book and yet you never succumb to the temptation to allegorize. I admire, too, very much, the selection of detail. You unerringly pick the one that will do the trick. And the dialogue is superb. But you will have gathered, by this time, that I am tremendously enthusiastic about the book. My heartiest congratulations on the achievement. It is considerable.

my little sister's Godmother

CAROLINE GORDON TO FRANCES NEAL CHENEY [MRS. BRAINARD CHENEY]

Godfather

Mrs. Cheney was a professional librarian. Her husband, Brainard (known as "Lon" because of his resemblance to the actor Lon Chaney), was a novelist, political speechwriter, and essayist from Georgia. The Cheney home, Cold Chimneys, near Nashville, was a place of festivity and conversation for Gordon, Tate, and O'Connor, who enjoyed stimulating fellowship when they visited.

Gordon praises O'Connor and Percy.[10] She also mentions friends, Andrew Lytle and Donald Davidson, a poet, essayist, critic, and faculty member at Vanderbilt University. Davidson, Allen Tate, and other Vanderbilt faculty formed the Fugitives, a network of writers who wrote modernist, intellectual poetry influenced by T. S. Eliot.[11] Many of the Fugitives were members of a related sociopolitical group, the Southern Agrarians—Andrew Lytle was one of the most ardent and colorful. Some of the writers converted to Catholicism, including Gordon, Tate, and the Cheneys, while Lytle, calling himself an "old Christian," did not.

Gordon also refers to another vital literary community, "the most unlikely Nazareth I know of: Sewanee," currently known as Sewanee, the University of the South, an Episcopal college and seminary founded in 1856 in Tennessee. Walker Percy's uncle, William Alexander Percy, had a home at Sewanee, Brinkwood, and taught at the university. He devoted a chapter in Lanterns on the Levee *to fond memories of teaching there. The Sewanee Review is published by the university and frequently featured the writings of Gordon, O'Connor, and Percy while Andrew Lytle, mentioned several times in this collection, was the editor.[12]*

465 NASSAU STREET.
PRINCETON, NEW JERSEY
DECEMBER 29, 1951

Darling Fannie:

How sweet of you to think of me! This flowery square is going right downstairs on one of Joseph Warren Beach's little tables to remind us of you every day. We think of you practically every day. We think of you particularly at holidays for I believe we have had more fun at youall's house, whether on West Side Row or Cold Chimney's, than any other house we know of. I would write you oftener, in spite of having absolutely no time to spare, if it weren't for your hellish address. The first time I saw all those bristling numbers I knew I could never master them, and wrote them down carefully and parked them in a special place—not alas, in my ordinary address book—so I could have them handy. But the place was so safe I have never been able to find it again. I have repeated this maneuver several times. The last time was when your letter came a few weeks ago. Thank God, I have got it again, thinks I, at which moment the door bell rang. When I got back upstairs Allen, who, as you know, has few housewifely instincts, had come along and burned the envelope with the address on it up. Just trying to get the place straight, he said. Evidently I am not fated to possess your devilish address. Never mind, Lon will have it to forward this . . .

Walter Sullivan [professor of English, Vanderbilt] dropped by here a few weeks ago. He is on a Ford foundation grant observing creative writing classes. He was going to observe one or two other people and then hole up in Florida to write his own novel, and observe Andrew [Lytle, novelist and professor, University of Florida] for the rest of the winter.

Speaking of novels, strange things are happening. Twice in the last month I have seen the novel of the future—the novel they will all be trying to write—right here in this study. The two best first novels I have ever read have come to me last month. One is by Flannery O'Connor of Milledgeville, Georgia. Harcourt, Brace who have finally been persuaded to publish it, say that it is the most shocking book they ever read. It is a picture of a world, the world turned over to Protestantism. A sort of Kafkan effect that goes on exploding in your mind long after you have put the book down. There is no Catholic apology in it and Catholicism is mentioned in only one scene. A Catholic boy named Murphy invites the hero, a hill-billy who has lost his Holler Roller faith in the army and is now dedicated to spreading his faith in unfaith: "The Church without Jesus Christ"— well, better start again. This Murphy invites Haze Motes, the hero, to visit a whore house with him. When they come out he informs Haze that what they have done is mortal sin and that they will go to hell if they die without confessing it—and proposes that they go back the next night. But Haze is a real Protestant martyr and prefers to spend his time preaching the gospel of unfaith. The action is stripped to the bone. The light that plays on the action is like the flashlight a burglar turns on the safe he is going to rob—which is one reason HB were unwilling to publish it. Robert Giroux couldn't make out what it was about, though he knew that it was something damned unpleasant.

The other novel came out this season of the year when good things come out of Nazareth, out of what I would have said was the most unlikely Nazareth I know of: Sewanee. Walker Percy, Will[iam Alexander] Percy's nephew, after cutting a good many Didoes among the young ladies of the mountain—one was on the point of leaving her Episcopal minister husband for his sake—after all this Walker suddenly leaves the mountain, gets married to a little Mississippi girl whom Sewaneeans had never heard of, and lies doggo for four or five years. We had heard that he had joined the Catholic church, but had had no other news of him till he wrote and asked me if I'd read his novel, and sent it on in a suit case. I saw the size and groaned, then read a few pages and threw away the bottle of Wolfe-bane I kept on my desk for young writers who are taken with running fits, or as Uncle H. James puts it, "the terrible fluidity of self-revelation."

None of that here. There are a few things he needs to learn, it seems to me, but he is learning them fast—all by himself, too. When he really gets to going good I don't see what there is to stop him. He knows what its all about and knows what he wants to do. Allen and I both feel that he is just about the most intelligent young person that has ever come our way. Of course he is not so awfully young. Nearing forty.

not so unlikely! [handwritten marginal note]

Speaking of novelists, Lon doesn't write as often as we wish he would. Still he's pretty good about it. In every letter we've had he bewails the complications of his life which are certainly pretty considerable right now. (I also get a good many letters from Tommy Mabry [Thomas, *The White Hound: Stories by Dorrance and Mabry*] not so much bewailing the complications of his life as asking wistfully for a sort of certification to the effect that he is a writer. If he only had some of Lon's courage!) I will be glad when he either gets that novel published or lays it aside and gets down to a new one . . .

The Catholic note creeps in sooner or later, doesn't it, my fine feathered Buddhist Fellow Traveler? By the way, Eric Bell, Don Davidson's son in law, is taking instruction from a priest. I expect to see Don himself in the Church within the next few years. Wont that be fun? We'll just baptize Alfred while we're at it. Poor fellow. He certainly needs it.

Allen is sending Lon today a book that he has been reading, with exclamations for the last week. Thomas Merton's new book, *The Ascent to Truth*. That boy has finally learned how to write. But he had the sense to get him one of these greatest masters: St. John of the Cross. It is amazing to compare this book with *The Seven Storey Mountain,* which I still consider one of the most important documents of our time, but certainly no literary masterpiece.

This is a poor letter. I came home to find my desk piled even higher than usual with letters that had to be answered. One result of moving out here has been a perfect avalanche of semi-business letters. I am glad teaching a seminar in fiction at the College of St. Catherine here, and am going to teach at the Methodist university, Hamline, next term. After four years at Columbia, where you had to set the universe up fresh for each seminar, as there were no moral values which could be easily referred to, it is a relief to be teaching Catholics, even Catholic jeunes filles. I have twelve of them around a big table, with an outer circle of nuns. I was positively thrilled the other day when Mother Antonine wrote me that I was doing all right.

This recent re-reading of James has given me the illusion that I have discovered something about his work that has never been treated in print, though I certainly cant be the only person who has been struck by it. There is no use in inflicting an outline of the essay I propose to write. It will be in *The Sewanee Review* or something like it soon enough. I am going to call it "The Figure at the Window on the Carpet." Now isn't that a nice title?

We have no pets here, so I have become an indoor bird-watcher. I feed the birds three times a day. Mostly I just get sparrows, but there are two jay birds who come every day. I have got real attached to them.

June seems a long way off. But you certainly will be coming home then, won't you? We hope to spend the summer at Nag's Head [North Carolina] and are already trying to rent a cottage there throughout Huntington airn's [sic] real estate agent. We decided it was best to leave the Woods in possession of Benbrackets [Gordon home], and there isn't room there for both families. And we are both just dying to have some months by the sea. Maybe you and Lon can join us there during July or August!

We both send our fondest love. We can't tell you how much we miss you.

CAROLINE GORDON TO WALKER PERCY

In January 1952, Caroline Gordon writes Walker Percy that Allen Tate concurs with Gordon's criticism of Percy's novel:

> One trouble with the book is that the first sixty pages don't engage. A man is shown in flight but since we see only what is going on in his head it is hard to realize that he is in flight and we have no idea what he is fleeing from. I believe it is almost axiomatic to say that you cannot begin a novel with a long soliloquy. The character must be shown in relation to other objects and other characters before we believe in his existence.

Gordon never fully grasped that Percy was writing fiction more concerned with "being" than "doing." This view may be rooted in her teaching college students not attuned to existential fiction of "being." Gordon's reactions are not unusual—college students then and now are more drawn to O'Connor stories in which violent action predominates, such as a family murdered on the roadside or a Southern matron gored in a pasture by a bull. Gordon advises Percy to revise The Charterhouse *to make it more like an O'Connor story: "The last chapter must be presented more dramatically."*

WALKER PERCY TO CAROLINE GORDON

Writing fifteen years later, when his second novel, The Last Gentleman, *was published, Percy politely explains the existentialist fiction he has been writing. He notes, ironically enough, that Allen Tate's famous "Ode to the Confederate Dead" inspired his novels. Despite the poem's title, it is not about war dead nor is it a formal ode; rather, the so-called "ode" is about the paralysis of what Percy identifies as "solipsism." The condition afflicts the protagonists of his novels.*

TUESDAY [MARCH 1966]

Dear Miss Caroline:

Well, I do give myself credit for knowing the people to impose on. Plenty of people will tell me they like the book even though they may have reservations. A few will tell me that they like it except for such and such. But you're the only one who can say what is wrong and why it is wrong.

You must know that I attend very carefully to what you say. And I even know you are right. The only trouble is that my faults are incorrigible. At least the fault which really raised your hackles: beginning a book with a solitary young man thinking. It reminds me of the time you were teaching at Columbia and some girl gave you a manuscript which dealt for the first two hundred pages with a girl lying in a bed in Paris and gazing at the wall—you saying you were so pleased when, on p. 201, somebody finally got in bed with her. Yes, right. I even knew what light I was sinning against and hoped to redeem myself by saying in the 4th sentence that in the course of the next five minutes something was going to happen which would change his life.

It is a deliberate sin and therefore all the more mortal, I reckon. I mean to say that, what with the times being what they are, one almost has to begin a book with a solitary young man. All my writings, for better or worse, take off from the solipsism which Allen described in his essay about "Ode to the Confederate Dead." The best I can do is break him out of the solipsism.[13]

You are right about the tone.

My Uncle Hughes sent me a story-and-picture about you in his son's newspaper.

It was very good seeing you and Fr. Charles—though I think Fr. Charles is nutty as a fruitcake. As good as he can be and delightful, and knowledgeable, and maybe even a good writer—but all I could think was, I would hate to be Father Abbot and try to figure out what was best for Fr. Charles. Father Abbot! I am haunted by the recollection of his goodness and sweetness of nature. My Uncle, an old-style Georgia Catholic and nephew of Archbishop Spalding, didn't say so but I had the hunch he thinks the Trappists are a bunch of kooks, new-fangled Protestant Catholics etc.

Love and thanks again
Walker

CAROLINE GORDON TO WALKER PERCY

Replying to a letter from Percy on January 7, 1952, Gordon sends him O'Connor's Wise Blood *as an example of a novel with a plot and vivid action. She also warns Percy about the flaws of Brainard Cheney's protagonist in his novel. Percy predictably is respectful but does not heed her advice in his published fiction.*

Dear Walker:

The Express Company swears it will come and pick your ms. up today. I put Flannery O'Connor's novel in, partly for ballast, and partly because I thought you might like to read her book. It is an old copy. She has revised it twice since then and may not want it. So don't do anything about it unless she calls for it. I should say that she and you have the opposite weaknesses. It's hardly possible, I suppose, to "render" too much, but her story is too bare, too stripped, I think of all but the essential core of action. She presents none of the peripheral action which helps make the main action seem real. As I wrote her, her focus seems to me like the spotlight a burglar plays on the safe he is cracking. You don't see anything else in the room. But she is sure good. This novel is more like Kafka than anybody else I know of. Every damn thing in it—and practically everything in it is damned. That's one trouble with it: a world consisting entirely of freaks—everything in it stands for something and you only find out what it stands for after you've left the book and the events sort of explode in your mind. She has some dire illness and may die. You might pray for her.

Yes, I think a novel about New York City, with scenes laid in Bellevue, might be terrific.

But to our moutons.

You said one thing in your letter of January seventh that made me shudder, that you were reluctant to give up your angelic escape from the mountain-top. One reason I shudder is that I think you are in danger of falling, as a writer, for what Jacques Maritain calls the sin of the age; angelism. The shudders in me come from the teacher. I have just had the grisliest experience of my career as a teacher. Our old and cherished friend, Brainard Cheney, has been working for six years on a novel which he calls THE IMAGE AND THE CRY. He turned down good jobs, quit everything and plowed doggedly through it. There are five hundred pages. Red [Robert Penn] Warren read it, Allen read it, I read it, his agent read it and half a dozen publishers read it and all of us told him exactly the same thing. It is a prime example of angelism. He gives his hero a chair to sit on in his office but does little else to locate him in time and space. The poor fool sits there and <u>thinks</u>, thinks, thinks sometime for eighty pages at a time. It was done deliberately. He believed that he could focus the reader's interest on thought, rather than action. This stubborn belief leads him into all sorts of absurdities. The hero and his mistress get in bed and have a good, long talk about freight rates and the C. I. O. Once when he pinched her leg I found myself writing "Thank God!" in the margin.

His story is, in a way, the same as your story: The modern man who wanders bewildered with no help from above. Lon's hero is essentially a religious man. He finds what he is seeking in the primitive faith of the Holy Rollers and dies as the result of a snack-bite. A lot of these "Illuminists," as Fr. Knox would call them, turn wistful eyes on the Holy Rollers. They see real faith there but don't realize that the poor dopes are heretics.

But to go back to Lon. He is not a skillful writer, to begin with, and doesn't understand the limitations of his medium, limitations which in masterly hands are often turned to great advantage. He doesn't really know what a novel is and persists in doing something that can't be done in a novel. He is, in other words, trying to use his feeble intellect as if it were an angel's—what we are almost all trying to do, in one way or another, according to Jacques.

Let me sum up in my own Credo, in the hope that I can make what I am trying to say clear. A novel, any novel, in the first place, must be about love. There is no other subject. It is a <u>romance</u>. That is, it deals with something that is part of a whole. Human love—between man and woman, is the proper and only subject, as an analogue for Divine Love. St. Catherine of Siena says that we cannot love God directly. We must love him through our neighbour in order to be more like God, who loves us even if we don't deserve his love.

The proper subject of a novel, then, is love, and it must be incarnated, as Christ was. Christ could not have accomplished the redemption of mankind if he had stayed in Heaven with His Father. He had to come to earth and take human shape. So does every idea in your head that goes into your novel. It cannot float in the aether—that is, you cannot have a scene that is not located in time and space. Your business as a novelist is to imitate Christ. He was about His Father's business every moment of His life. As a good novelist you must be about yours: Incarnation. Making your world flesh and making it dwell among men . . .

fascinating

CAROLINE GORDON TO BRAINARD CHENEY

Unlike in the previous letter, Gordon praises Cheney's novel This Is Adam, *published in 1958, which featured a prominent racial theme. She also comments on Cheney's possible conversion to Catholicism. Sponsored by the Tates, the Cheneys became Roman Catholics in 1953. Gordon concludes by praising O'Connor and Percy.*

2-16-52

. . . I have put my money on a good many horses, in my time, as you know. Scatter-brained though I be, I occasionally get a glimpse of the wheels going around. I saw them revolving here in this study several months before Christmas. When I was working on Flannery O'Conner's novel and then Walker Percy sent me his novel. He's got a lot to learn, that boy, almost everything, but reading that novel was like suddenly getting down on your knees on a long, dusty walk to drink from a fresh, cold spring. His novel and Flannery's suddenly convinced me of something that I had been feeling vaguely for a long time. The Protestant mystique (which is what everybody who isn't a Catholic, even Communists, are writing out of, whether they know it or not) is out-worn, sucked-dry, beginning to rot, to stink. That accounts for the curious dryness which almost everybody remarks in homosexual novels. There's no juice left in that orange. Everybody has suspected it for some time, but the fact is now being brought into the open.

Flannery's novel—as grim a picture of the Protestant world as you can find—and Walker's novel, which is the story of a man's desperate effort to stay alive spiritually, will be sensations when they come out. They will show so clearly that the tide has turned. One gets hints of it in almost any novel one picks up, but they come right out with it. Here's another sign. Dwight McDonald is writing a profile of Dorothy Day for *The New Yorker* and has asked me to help him. Two years ago, even, they wouldn't have touched Dorothy with a ten-foot pole. But the world is changing—fast—these days. Here's another item that will interest you. Father Henry came to give Nancy his blessing after her accouchement and told her that a Jewish gentleman, who was so famous that his conversion would make international news, had just been baptized in his church by Fr. John LaFarge. Old Wise Woman Tate knows who it is, though Fr. Henry wouldn't tell Nancy. Bernard Baruch, don't you think? The Good News has got to the man on the park bench. Novels will take a different form from now on.

But you are stuck, half in, half out of the shell. The way you've been using your mind all your life is not going to help you. I don't mean that you'll have to give up using your mind that way, but you're going to have to learn to use other faculties. Reason, the way you've used it, just won't do the work. While I'm at it, I may as well compare you to another great man. Has it occurred to you that your situation much resembles the situation Allen [Tate] was in a few years ago? Except that you aren't making a fool of yourself [as] openly as he did. His situation is very different now. I believe that he is happier than he's ever been in his life. For the past two weeks he's been getting up at six or seven and almost has his long poem in the bag. I don't think that there's any question that it's the finest thing he's ever done. It lacks that unmotivated violence that his work has so often had heretofore. And the writing is certainly the most beautiful that he's done. Realizing what its all about has released energies that for years were chiefly bent to the service of his neuroses. If you didn't know him so well I wouldn't be saying all this, but I'm probably not telling you anything you don't already know. You yourself must have marked the change in him. It is the result of the exercise of faith.

Please forgive me for lecturing you at this great rate. Somehow couldn't stop once I got started. I'll promise not to do it every time I write, though. And please write again. We can't help but worry about you when we don't hear from you. There's just not anybody we're fonder of than you and Fannie. Anything that concerns you two concerns us deeply. Allen sends his love and so do I.

CAROLINE GORDON TO WALKER PERCY

Aware of the precarious health of both Percy and O'Connor, Gordon (winter 1952) addresses Percy's monitoring the recurrence of tuberculosis. She notes, "Many good writers have had their way smoothed by some such affliction." Gordon enumerates (mistakenly) the American writers kept out of the Civil War by maladies:

> Of the James boys, only Wilkie and Bob, the two dopes of the family, fought. Both William and Henry were hors de combat. Henry Adams was safe in England with his father and Mark Twain was 'roughing it' in the Rockies. Only poor Ambrose Bierce got into the front line, and he was not much of a writer. If we keep up our present draft system, which is so efficient that it's hard for anybody to slip through its meshes, we'll probably kill off all our geniuses.[14]

In an undated letter written a short time later, Gordon is delighted "to hear that you [Percy] are reading Henry James." Gordon recommends two other books: "One is Advent *by Fr. Jean Danielou, the foremost Patrologist in France. It is terrific. He tells you things about both the Old and New Testament that pretty near take the top off your head." Gordon also praises (as she does to O'Connor) the "Life of St. Thomas More, by R. W. Chambers," noting "this is above all, the book for Southerners, for Confederates, for any English-speaking person."*

CAROLINE GORDON TO ANDREW LYTLE

Gordon and her friends were developing a vision of history rooted in the patriotism of Thomas More. More's defense of liberty was applicable to their struggle to come to grips with Southern defeat in the Civil War. In an earlier letter to Percy, Gordon had recommended a biography of More, noting that he "seems to me the greatest Englishman that ever lived. And the man above all whom we should follow today." Percy responded by setting forth his view of More, which Gordon enthusiastically shared with Lytle. He was an ardent admirer of More, repeatedly quoting his dying words in his teaching and writings. Percy's analysis may have influenced Lytle's observation that More was one of the last defenders of Christendom against Machiavelli's Prince, *which "showed the princes of Europe they might rule free of spiritual counsel, looking only to their wills for guidance."[15] To Lytle, Gordon, Percy, and O'Connor (implicitly), the kind of liberty for which More was martyred was a resistance to the modern conglomerate nationalist "state" of Henry VIII.*

APRIL 4, 1952

I had a letter from Walker Percy (Will Percy's nephew) the other day in answer to some things said about St. Thomas More. That boy is sure smart: His letter is so good that I have copied the excerpt from it and sending it to you and Edna [Mrs. Lytle], for I think it will interest you.

> Hastily,
> Caroline

WALKER PERCY TO CAROLINE GORDON

I agree with you about St. Thomas More. He is, for us, the Road Back. For our countrymen, I mean, for southerners. For More is the spiritual ancestor of Lee. He is the man to pray to for the conversion of the south. One of the stumbling blocks to the Southerner (or the

American) who is drawn to the Church is that he sees, not the Church of More, not the English Church which is his spiritual home, but the Church of St. Alphonsus Liguori by way of the Irish Jesuits. If he does go in, he must go in with his face averted and his nose held against this odor of Italian-Irish pietism and all the bad statues and architecture. Of course this is somewhat exaggerated and prideful, because it is a salutary lesson in obedience and humility to take St. Alphonsus. (Hell, he was a great saint!) But if Allen is forming a St. Thomas More Society I want in.[16]

I got the New York edition of James. (I would never tell you what it cost me.) But it is worth it . . . What gets me (in connection with your paper) is the way James' heroes go diving in and out of Catholic Churches to collect their wits, or to hold interminable conversations. I have a theory about James' indifference to the Church, or rather for the strange dissociations of his attitude: splitting off his great aesthetic reverence for St. Peter's, for instance, from any necessity for taking seriously the claims of the Church upon him. It was the Age of Unbelief, if ever there was one. It would have been absolutely unthinkable for any man, however knowing and intelligent, to see his way clear to conversion. It would have taken an heroic amount of grace. Of course there are obvious reasons for this; it was the Age of the Success of Science; the great Victorian edifice was still mighty and secure. But I believe that there is a dialectic of Faith. Of course this is nothing new. But the dialectic is in our favour now; we are certainly coming into the Age of Faith. It is not so much Faith as the polarity of Faith-Unfaith. This alternative simply did not exist for our grandfathers or for James. There must surely be a providential allowance for the fix that they were in. I thank God that I didn't live then. When I look at my father's library, comprising as it does, many religious works, but all of the liberal-scholarly-protestant variety which stemmed from 19th century German rationalism by way of English divines, it gives me the creeps. It is much more lethal to the Faith than, say, the violent atheism of a Spanish Mason. They had a big middle ground in those days. Now it is being cut away.

James never had a chance. I am sure that the Road to Rome never even occurred to him, except as something "European" and therefore traditional and pleasant. The trouble was that all the other buildings were still standing and the Dome of St. Peter's wasn't especially conspicuous. Now the others have all fallen down and even I can see it.

CAROLINE GORDON TO FLANNERY O'CONNOR

Gordon mentions teaching a new interpretation of James Joyce's Portrait of the Artist as a Young Man *to nuns. The interpretation may have been inspired by her copyediting* Wise Blood, *a dramatic satire of* Portrait. *She also praises the Chambers biography of Thomas More. The biography clarified for her that Henry VIII's government was essentially a modern state with an intelligence apparatus. Informants of the Crown were bent on crushing dissent and consolidating power of the Machiavellian king who often instilled fear in his subjects.*

1801 UNIVERSITY AVENUE S. E.

MINNEAPOLIS 14, MINNESOTA

I am not going to be able to review your book, after all. I stupidly forgot to caution HB [Harcourt, Brace] about using my name as a blurb and am therefore ineligible to review the book, Francis Brown tells me. I'm sorry. I am vain enough to think that I understand better what you're getting at than the next reviewer.

The sisters who sit in on my lectures will read it with great interest, I'm sure. They continue to astonish me. The other day, after I had finished giving my interpretation of Joyce's *Portrait,* which, to say the least, is not the interpretation that I was, so to speak, brought up on, one of them sighed softly and murmured: "That's what Sister Mariella Gable has always said!"

I am so glad to hear that you have been feeling well again. If you visit the Fitzgeralds in June maybe we'll see you. We hope to land in Princeton around the first of July.

Spring has come at last! All the ice is gone from the river. The sidewalks are at last clear of snow and ice and the grass is turning green. It seems to happen overnight here and a damned good idea it is. I don't think we could have stood much more of that other stuff.

I have been having a great time all winter reading and re-reading *The Golden Bowl*. If you take into consideration three facts: a, that it is the only one of James' novels that has a happy ending, b, that it is the only one in which a child is born to the hero and heroine, c, that it is the only one in which the hero and heroine are both Catholics, you don't see James turning into a Catholic but you see the book turning into something quite different from what F. O. Matthiessen [*American Renaissance*] et al. would have you believe it is.

Allen appalled me when I had finished an essay on this subject by saying that I ought to expand the essay into a small book. The idea does fill me with horror—I can't write expository prose. However, the fact that nobody will be anxious to publish such a book will probably save me from having to write it.

Another book we have read this winter is R.W. Chambers' *Life of St. Thomas More*. It is simply terrific. Not having read it is for me a little like studying the Civil War from the Yankee point of view— you don't get much idea of what it was all about.

I hope the stories go well and we look forward to seeing you soon.

CAROLINE GORDON TO FLANNERY O'CONNOR

Gordon writes about a retreat to a Catholic Worker House of Hospitality, which had a significant spiritual impact on her. Gordon praises Dorothy Day frequently to both O'Connor and Percy. Over a half century before Pope Francis in a papal visit to the United States cited Day as one of "four great Americans," Gordon offered her own praise many years earlier.

SEPTEMBER 20, 1952

1908 SELBY STREET,

ST. PAUL 4, 1952

I was indeed glad to hear from you and so awfully glad to know that you are up and at work again. We were disappointed not to have a visit from you at Princeton. I found myself wishing that I had kidnapped you and taken you on there that day we had lunch together . . .

Allen is still reeling all over Europe—Rome one week, Venice the next, but he will have to come home by September twenty ninth as the U. of Minnesota, an institution that is doubtless far from his thoughts these days, opens on that date. He has had such a good time that he is positively dazed. At some time or other he was due to have a talk with the Holy Father. He had things he much wanted to discuss with His Holiness. I am curious to see whether awe in the pontiff's presence will keep him from saying all he thinks about his fellow Scribner-author, Francis Cardinal Spellman.

I got to St. Paul about a week ago and have been busy settling into our new (rented) house. It is just heavenly to be able to unpack and hang your clothes up in your own (rented) closet. This has been a hellish summer. I have not got a chance to put in as much as one hour's work on my novel and in the last few weeks I have been getting pretty peevish about it.

About *The Strange Children,* I think you are right about Reardon. He isn't quite right. I think now that he is mis-cast. He had to be a "little" man, one whom they could all rather look down on, but he could have had another variety of littleness. I see a different character in his role now—a man who has little intellect and who would reveal himself more than Reardon does, trying ponderously to account for his conversion and never being able to, yet holding on to whatever it was stubbornly, nonetheless. Ah well—one reason for writing another novel is the chance to avoid the mistakes you made in the first! While we're on the subject, I'll point out another flaw in that novel . . .

I took advantage of Allen's absence to go up to Dorothy Day's "Maryfarm" at Newburgh to what she calls "the basic retreat." It lasted five days. I had to come back in the middle to see Allen off, so got in only three days in all—rushed right back the minute he took off. It was an extraordinary experience. Dorothy says that for several years after she entered the Church she got little help, little more than platitudes from parish priests.

Then she went to a retreat given by Fr. La Couture in Canada. He is dead now but she keeps the retreat alive, training first one and then another priest to give it. It is tough sledding—this particular retreat is frowned on in many quarters.

They call their joint a "Hospitality House"—any bum is free to wander in off the road, and many do. The audience was therefore pretty motley. But you ought to have heard those bums sing the Latin Prime before Mass and two conferences in the morning, then dinner and a short rest and an afternoon conference and supper and another conference. I don't think I could have stood up under five days of it, but when I got back from Princeton towards the end of the retreat they were all as fresh as daisies.

The approach was frankly mystical and I was reminded often of what Jacques Maritain says, that every real novelist is a mystic, "for nobody else knows what is in the human heart." Jacques was invoked often. So were Aristotle and other worthies. And the whole series of talks was based on a figure of St. Augustine's "pondus animae"— spiritual gravity, as it were. The father also threw in the mediaeval schoolmen's demonstration of the existence of God and a good many other things that have hardly been heard of in the academic circles in which I move. It really was something! I had such a good time that I didn't even envy Allen his trip to Italy. I guess we are going there in 1954, though. Allen has got himself a Fulbright professorship at the University of Rome for that year—I reckon Minnesota will let him off.

I do hope you get good news from Sally [Fitzgerald]. I haven't heard from her since her illness. I do so hope things are going better there. I was dreadfully disappointed not to get over to Ridgefield but Sue Jenkins whom I was visiting at Sherman was ill and I couldn't get transportation over at the time I'd planned.

Let me hear from you when you feel like writing. If I don't answer you'll know it's because I'm wrestling with my novel. Getting back to work after a four or five months interruption is a grim business, isn't it? Luck to you, always,

FLANNERY O'CONNOR TO CAROLINE GORDON

O'Connor mentions suffering from the deadly sin of sloth. She was a student of Dante and Aquinas; the seven deadly sins suffuse her writing. Robert Fitzgerald, who taught The Divine Comedy *at Harvard, recalled, "I am almost sure I lent Flannery the Binyon version."*[17] *Her handwritten notes to* The Divine Comedy of Dante Alighieri *(Modern Library, 1933), show a close familiarity with the poem. O'Connor enumerates Dante's seven deadly sins in a list beside a diagram of* Purgatorio's *mountain. Learning from Dante, she identifies pride, envy, and anger as "sins of perversion," anger and sloth as "defective love," and avarice, gluttony, and carnality as "excessive love."*[18] Good Country Pictures *is preparing a television series,* 7 Deadly Sins, Seven Films Based on Flannery O'Connor's Stories.[19]*

O'Connor also refers to a visit from a Danish textbook salesman who cannot fathom works of charity.

MILLEDGEVILLE

5/20/53

I thank you the Lord knows for haranguing me twice on the same counts and at the expense of boring yourself stiff. This is Charity and as the good sisters say Gawd will reward you for your generosity. I hope quick. But you are wrong [in] one place—I do not suffer from the modern complaint of Abstraction; I suffer from the 7th Deadly Sin: Sloth. The slothful are always in a big hurry. I know all about it. And how it catches up with you before the end. My contrary disease is called lupus but it's only the Aggressive Sloth made Manifest. I'd like to persuade myself that I hear time's winged chariot and so on and so on but then I think you take such good care of yourself you'll have the embarrassment of being around like your cousin when you're 85, in spite of the ailment and the agony and the outrage. The effort to achieve some intensity is terrible but it isn't as terrible as it must have to be or there'd be more intensity coming out somewhere.

Anyway I will work on this story longer. I keep asking myself: how would the dam [*sic*] woods look after two pistol shots? The Omniscient Narrator is running me nuts. I thought he could ease into a brain and rifle it and ease out again and look like he had never been there in the first place. Mine is just a bungler. Also I think I will start talking like Dr. Johnson as a matter of course—if this is possible. My mother says I talk like a n——— and I am going to be out sometime and say something and everybody is going to wonder what kind of people I come from etc etc. Her predictions turn out on the double and worse than true and here it is has affected the Om. Nar.

There was a man at Yaddo [Saratoga Springs, New York] who used to say Gide was the "great Protestant spirit." I was glad they put him on the Index as it meant I wouldn't have to read him. Otherwise I would have thought I had to. If I had charge of the Index, I'd really load it up and ease my burden.

Somebody brought a man out here, a textbook salesman for Harcourt, Brace [Erik Langkjaer]. He was a Dane and had studied at Fordham with Fr. Lynch and was interested in Dorothy Day. He wasn't a Catholic and said what he couldn't understand was why she fed endless lines of endless bums who crawled back to the gutter after every dish of soup. No results. No hope. No nothing, he said. The few Scandanavians that I have seen have impressed me as being very antiseptic about everything. I said it was Charity and there was nothing you could do about it. He seemed to be fascinated and disgusted both. What I can't understand about them is the pacifism. If Charity were in the form of a stick I can imagine beating a lot of people over the head with it.

[illegible]. I will pray for you. St. Simons and I hope very much they'll do this.

FLANNERY O'CONNOR TO ETHEL DANIELL

A few years after Gordon asked Walker Percy to teach in a "School of the Holy Ghost" at a Catholic Worker House of Hospitality, O'Connor reveals her skepticism. She may have thought such a "school" could lead to misleading literary categorization. O'Connor distances herself from literary movements, a consistent theme in the letters.

MILLEDGEVILLE

6 FEBRUARY 56

I so very much appreciate your letter and your interest in my books. Fr. McCown told me something about you and I had asked my editor at Harcourt, Brace to send you a copy of a novel called *The Malefactors*, which they are going to publish in March. It is by Caroline Gordon (Mrs. Allen Tate) who came into the Church six or seven years ago. She's a fine novelist—has been a fine one for a long time—and should be known by more Catholics. Her husband, a poet and critic, became a Catholic a few years after she did. They were both part (in the 20s) of that Nashville group that called itself The Fugitives—they were "agrarians"—such people as John Crowe Ransom and Robt. Penn Warren. The Tates were the only ones that ended up in the Church, although the Church seems a logical end for the principles they began with. That was all part of what is now pompously called the Southern literary renascence.

As for myself and wanting to be a "Catholic writer"—well, what I want, of course, is to be a better Catholic and a better writer. Sorry professional writers, no matter of what degree of piety, don't do much good for the Church—I suppose I have to exempt sorry <u>un</u>professional writers like St. Theresa of Lisieux. Your Catholicism affects your art, no doubt about it, but an intense application to the discipline of an art or even some craft should intensify your Catholicism. I have about decided that form is one's moral backbone transposed to the subject at hand.

I have written one novel, *Wise Blood* and a collection of short stories. The stories are the better of the two but both were the best I could do at the time and could not have been written, by me, a line different. I am afraid some of my characters are even more unpleasant that M. Mauriac's and that you wouldn't want to know them either. However, they're all, even the worst of them, me, so my tolerance of them is supreme. I have pious and even intelligent friends who write me that the Catholic writer must write about love and redemption and not so much the lack of it. It's quite possible to agree with this and to add, "Yes, and we're all supposed to be saints." I find the advice I get from the inexperienced is always correct but seldom possible. One writes what one can and prays to do better.

I heard little about Grailville [Ohio], not much. Is that writing center a press or a school for writers or what? I would be suspicious of a school for Catholic writers, as there's no way special for Catholics to write.

I live in the country on a dairy farm with my mother. Milledgeville is 40 miles from Dublin and if you visit your connections there again, you must come to see us too. I don't get about much as I walk on crutches—this, thank the Lord, makes me no good around the house so most of my time is spent writing and reading and watching some peachickens I have. My avocation is raising peachickens. I hope that when you read my stories you will let me know what you think of them. I don't require my friends to like them and am inured to the fact that most of them don't. All I hope is that all aunts who burn my books have to buy them first.

Sincerely and with many thanks,

CAROLINE GORDON TO WALKER PERCY

On November 25, 1952, Caroline Gordon writes Walker Percy, praising his revisions of The Charterhouse *as well as the novel's treatment of the "Negro problem." Gordon probably had heard the phrase from Allen Tate, who had professional connections with Langston Hughes and wrote, "I know I am / The Negro Problem / . . . Wondering how things got this way / In current democratic night" ("Dinner Guest: Me").*[20]

Gordon, as she often does, addresses syntax and grammar. "There are not many different kinds of sentences that can be written. But you ought to have in your repertory at least three kinds." She provides a recipe for a good paragraph:

> Short declarative sentence. Declarative sentence a little longer than the first. Short declarative sentence. Sentence beginning with a subordinate clause or sentence formed by putting two clauses together. Declarative sentence. Declarative sentence. Long declarative sentence.

As in previous letters, Gordon also corrects Percy's misuse of pronouns. She adds apologetically,

> I am going on at such length, partly out of my natural irritability, and partly because I am so tremendously interested in your work. I think you ought to try to form the habits that make good writing. Maritain says that art is habit, anyhow. If you try to observe just these few things I have been talking about in no time at all they will become habitual.

Gordon concludes, "Well, you will have gathered that I am all for this book. In all the years I have been trying to help writers I have never had one who so richly repaid my efforts." Citing an elderly nun, she notes, "You [Percy] are in a position to receive help from the Holy Ghost, which none of my other students have been in."

Having finished the novel, Gordon writes the next morning that she plans to submit the novel to Charles Scribner's Sons and "minor corrections" can be incorporated later. She recommends Percy read Mauriac and Bernanos, but observes,

> They are criminally bad craftsmen, and hence, I think, theologically unsound, both of them—less Christian, according to Maritain's definitions, than a man like

James Joyce—There is Manichaean contempt for their craft, for, in fact, the whole natural order, that is fatal to a novelist. Damn it, they are not good novelists, either of them. Any first year student in a "Creative Writing Workshop" could point out the technical flaws in any book either of them ever wrote, but they have a range, they reveal a whole register—a plan of action—that is practically unknown to the contemporary "Protestant" novelist. I mean a man who writes out of the "Protestant" myth. They make a man like Hemingway seem flat, one-dimensional. I would not have you write like them. All my lecturing has been to keep you from writing like them, but I do wish you'd investigate them, nevertheless. I think that you might find them helpful in showing the way to some things that might be done but haven't been done yet in the novel.

WALKER PERCY TO CAROLINE GORDON

Writing some years after having won the National Book Award in 1962, Percy praises the teaching of grammar and mythology in a creative writing class. He also recollects his friend's wrestling with a frozen turkey at a Thanksgiving gathering at the Trappist monastery in Conyers, Georgia.[21]

FEBRUARY 14, 1974

Dear Miss Caroline,

A letter from Bob Giroux today reporting among other things, you'd sent him a mythology quiz you gave your students. He took it and flunked it.

Your life in Dallas sounds lovely.[22] Since with God all things are possible, it even appears that the country and the church might be saved in <u>Dallas</u>! (Certainly not in Princeton or New Orleans.)

Either we must see you there, or you must drop by here on one of your visits East. You could fly into New Orleans, we'd pick you up at the airport and whisk you across the Lake.

I keep getting inquiries about your creative writing program out there. A smart alec Ph.D. at Tulane asked me if it was true you were teaching <u>grammar</u>. I said I hoped so.

Caroline II sounds lovely. Allen Tate II stopped by my brother, Phin's on his way to Mexico last Fall. They liked him very much. Said he planned to be a farmer. A sensible choice.

If you come by to see us, you can wear your red flannel night-gown like in Conyers but you'll not be required to deal with a frozen turkey.

Good luck on your antepenultimate novel—I'm hopelessly stuck with mine, hopeless because I can't get it right and I can't let it go. A rotten life—I should have stuck to pathology. At least after polishing off a body a night, one had a feeling of accomplishment. For the present, all I have is a title, *The Knight, Death and the Devil* [Percy's novel *Lancelot*]. (Remember the Durer engraving?) (Don't tell any thieving Texas novelists.)

Love,
Walker

CAROLINE GORDON TO WALKER PERCY

In the late fall of 1952 Gordon writes Charles Scribner's Sons that Walker Percy is "the most important talent to come out of the South since Faulkner."[23] *On December 8, 1952, Gordon writes Percy that Scribner's is considering his novel and that she is "simply crazy about your book." She notes, "I prophesy that it will sweep the country."*

Capturing the essence of Percy's later published novels, Gordon specifically praises "Catholicism being implicit in the action (without even being mentioned)—*maybe so. In this novel you are really treating of conversion—or lack of conversion, though, aren't you?" She also mentions again her love-hate opinion of the "Catholic revivalists" (Bernanos, Mauriac, and Bloy). She criticizes "their poor craftsmanship," which "would disgrace a first year student in a 'Creative Writing' course most of the time." She does praise, however, the "higher plane" of their characters, which surpasses the "spiritual adventures" of* Hemingway's Lieutenant Henry in A Farewell to Arms *and* Jake Barnes *in* The Sun Also Rises.

FLANNERY O'CONNOR TO CAROLINE GORDON

O'Connor discusses the perpetual tension between her writing and pietistic, didactic fiction, in particular a novel, The Foundling, *by Francis Cardinal Spellman. She also is gratified by Brainard Cheney's penetrating review of* Wise Blood, *which proved vital in advancing her career. She also cites William Faulkner's appreciation of a new theistic element in Ernest Hemingway's* The Old Man and the Sea.

MILLEDGEVILLE

JAN. 29, 53

Thanks so much for looking for the missing page. It was the one before the one you sent but I will look for it in *The Sewanee Review* and send that to such of my kin as will be impressed with the sight of this much stately printed matter mentioning a niece. The size of it will fairly stun my 83 yr old cousin. Nothing stuns her but sheer bulk. Mr. Monroe Spears wrote me and asked if I had a story. My stories are adequate, there's nothing in particular wrong with them but they sicken me when I read them in print; however, there's that money.

I liked the piece in *The New Republic* very much but where it ought to be expanded is Thought. Though who reads Thought that don't go to Fordham? Maybe it ought to be in *Our Sunday Visitor*. Could His Eminence keep it out of *Our Sunday Visitor*? My attitude toward him and his works (literary) is more lenient than yours and more crafty. It is—if we must have trash, this is the kind of trash we ought to have. This states your case and at the same time flatters the Cardinal. Somebody has to write for my cousin and she might as well have a prince of the church and with him so well-suited to the task etc etc. I suppose its a problem that there's nothing for but the Holy Ghost. I dreamed one night about a Pope named April the 15th, and woke up thinking this must be Francis. Then I realized Francis would be the 1st and this would be one of his descendants. It was a mighty comforting dream.

I read *Middlemarch* a few years ago and thought it was wonderful all but the end. I suppose that was a concession to the century or something.

I got me the Modern Library edition called the *Best Known Novels of Geo. E[liot]* then and thought I would have a great time with them but I didn't. I started on *The Mill on the Floss* but that thing must be a child's book or I don't have any perseverance or those big books are just too heavy to hold up. I started on one about some Methodists and didn't finish that either. I remember something from *Middlemarch* about "the roar on the other side of silence." That's what you have to pick up in a novel—I mean put down in one, I suppose. I want to read *Middlemarch* again and see if she wrote about freaks.

Do you know a man named Brainard Cheney? I found a review of my book by him in a quarterly called the *Shenandoah* that I hadn't known but that comes from Washington and Lee [University, Lexington, Virginia]. It was a very good review, one of the only ones. This quarterly had a review of *The Old Man and the Sea* by Faulkner. He said Hemmingway had discovered the Creator in this. It was just a paragraph. I think where he discovered the Creator in it was that sentence about the fish's eye—where it looks like a saint in a procession. I thought when I read it that he's seeing something he hasn't seen before; but I haven't really read many of his books.

I guess you are right about Cal [Robert Lowell] I remember about the preacher who bought the sailor's parrot but finally had to give him up because whenever he cried "How shall we get god into our hearts?" the parrot hollered, "Pull Him in with the rope! Pull him in with the rope."

CAROLINE GORDON TO WALKER PERCY

Caroline Gordon informs Percy (January 31, 1953) that John Hall Wheelock, editor in chief of Scribner's, had written her that Percy's novel showed "flashes of great talent" as well as "serious weaknesses." She also warns that Percy is almost "falling into one of the first snares that the Devil lays for young writers." She warns about "stylistic laziness." She cites Hemingway's criticism of Gertrude Stein:

> Ernest used to say that she was lazy by nature, though gifted and that when she found out how tough the going was she set about devising a way to spare herself and so created the style which is so admired by fairies.
> I never saw one who didn't dote on her.

Gordon believes Percy is not "fitted by Nature, evidently, to take Gertrude's way, so you gaze wistfully after Maugham [Somerset] and Marquand [John P.]." She encourages him to reread the Odyssey and to study the precision of James Joyce and Henry James. She also beseeches him to study her own technical virtuosity in the crafting of scenes in her books and to compare them to scenes in the novels by George Eliot. She concludes, "It is not necessary or even desirable that you try to write like me, but if you take to trying to write like Maugham please don't ever tell anybody that I ever gave you any advice about your work."

CAROLINE GORDON TO BRAINARD CHENEY

Gordon congratulates Cheney for his "political job" as a speechwriter for Governor Frank G. Clement of Tennessee. Even though Cheney published four novels, he is better known for journalistic commentary, speechwriting, and the vital article he wrote about O'Connor's Wise Blood.

2-4-53

1908 SELBY AVENUE

ST. PAUL 4

You sure are smart! To work out a political job that will make you a living and give you time to write, too. Well, you deserve it. I am glad the new governor realizes how much he is indebted to you. And I'm awfully glad that you've got things worked out to suit you.

In the mail with your letter came a letter from Flannery O'Connor asking me if I knew a man named Brainard Cheney. I started to say "Like a book" when I reflected that our oldest and dearest friends are all sealed books to us, so I just said that I aimed to become your god-mother. How about that? Any hope for me?

What you say about your not being worthy to partake of the Eucharist reminds me that several weeks after I had been baptized my eighty three year old Jesuit instructor asked me if I was taking Communion regularly, whereupon I astonished the good soul by saying that as yet I didn't feel worthy. "You never will be!" he snorted. "That's the reason you take it." I am also reminded of another pearl that dropped from the lips of Monsignor Cummings after some weeks of instructing the Cummington boys, "I never feel easy about a convert till I've buried him."

I hope you and Fannie will run into Flannery O'Connor some time. I think you'd both like her. Cal [Robert] Lowell says she is a saint, but then he is given to extravagance. She may be, though, at that. She is a cradle Catholic, raised in Milledgeville where there are so few other Catholics that the priests would come to the house and make the piano into an altar, but she sure is a powerful Catholic. No nonsense about her! She has some dire disease—some form of arthritis—and is kept going only by a huge dose of something called ACTH. We are expected to adore all the Lord's doings, but it does give you pause when you reflect that this gifted girl will probably not be with us long, whereas Truman Capote will live to a ripe old age, laden down with honours . . .

But I am leaving here March fifteenth to go to Seattle to teach a ten week course at the university there. Everybody tells me it will be pretty nice in Seattle then. I can hardly wait, though the winter here has been extraordinarily mild.

Allen is rushing all over the country this spring, making as much money as he can by lecturing and I am picking up every fee I can, too, so we can leave some dollars here for them if we go to Italy next year. All the scholastic committees have passed on Allen's Fulbright application and it's up to the FBI now, and as he hasn't done a single subversive thing since he went over last August, they ought to pass him. But you never know . . .

Do let us hear from you again. We miss you both so much and long to see you. We think now that we'll go abroad around the last of July. Any chance of your getting up our way before then? We also think of renting us a cottage or at least some lodgings at Seaside Heights, fifty five miles from Princeton. Why not join us there?

Sleep deprived, Gordon praises Cheney's article on Wise Blood. *She also resents the comments of famous writers, a practice that made her at times appear small.*

2-10-53

I am so tired I can't see straight but I can't wait to tell you how good I think your review of Flannery's novel is. Allen thinks it's fine, too. It's a long time since I've seen so much acute perception united with common sense in a review. Your remarks on Caldwell [Erskine] are marvellous: the best thing anybody has said about him. Your points are all telling, we both thought, and were made tellingly. I don't blame Flannery for being pleased. I don't know of any other reviewer who did half as well.

Faulkner's remarks on Hemingway seem to strike a new low. Flannery remarked that "he seems to think Hemingway found God in a fish's eye." I wonder if he wrote those paragraphs when drunk.

They read like it. I fear the Nobel prize has done him little good. Too bad . . .

I am making plans to leave this frigid zone on March 15. I am going to Seattle for ten weeks at the U. of Washington as visiting professor.

Do let us hear from you all again soon.

FLANNERY O'CONNOR TO CAROLINE GORDON

O'Connor distances herself from Brainard Cheney's article in which he refers to the Christ "myth." O'Connor also refers to an image of the Church in a book by a Dominican that may have inspired her story "The River." She also disagrees with a critic who suggests there is a lack of charity among writers.

MILLEDGEVILLE

2/22/53

I am much obliged for Mr. Cheney's address. I wrote him that I liked the review though I had to admit that I hadn't thought of the patrolman as the tempter on the mt. top or H. Motes as embodying the Christ "myth." I leave the word myth to Mrs. Roosevelt anyway. The Fitzgeralds have a friend in the UN who took his eleven year old daughter to one of the sessions one day. He told her to act intelligent and to show that she knew who the people were he introduced her to and to say something to show that she knew. She did very well, he said. He introduced her finally to Mrs. R. and she said, "Oh hello, Mrs. Roosevelt, I always listen to your radio program while I'm waiting for the Lone Ranger." Which is how I know myth! Maybe its the myth business that [is] keeping him out of the Church.

I do think with you all that the Cardinal is last person who ought to be giving the world fiction and verse and what I mean by its being the kind of trash we ought to have is that it's several cuts above Mickey Spillane. I suppose Prudence is all you have to worry about in the order of trash and the Cardinal is very prudent though I think he sins against it in ways he don't know exists. Anyway, you tell Allen its just as well he doesn't acquaint himself with the great masters of the novel in the 19th century. That would be exactly your point of too much reading. He would go on fattening the foundlings with even more horrible prose. Somebody was so good as to give me *The Foundling* when I was sick in the hospital. I was taking big doses of ACTH which prevents concentration, but this wasn't necessary for that. It was the purest pablum and if I had been fifteen years old, I would have liked it fine.

My trouble I suppose is the usual Catholic sin of not paying much attention to the Church's temporal hard times, knowing the gates of hell won't prevail. I certainly enjoy watching them prevail here and now, or anyway, when they're prevailing in the Protestant body. Chief Thurn and the Sunshine Evangelistic Party are nothing to laugh at but I would mighty well like to hear the musical paint buckets and see the fourth singing heart in the world. When it gets around to Catholic vulgarity, that is too Business-Pious and being too close to home; hurts too much; hurts too much to write about. I've often wondered how JF Powers stands to write about it. It certainly must be a torture and be a strong man. The whole subject sharpens my sympathy for him. The other day I got a "check" for One Hundred Hail Marys on "The Bank of Heaven," from a nun in a convent in Canada where I had sent a dollar for some mission or other. All made out with a picture of the Christ Child on it in the corner—"President," and signed by the sister who said the prayers. Now this is worse than the Cardinal's works. This is bringing it too close to the altar; his is a good distance away. I know the Hail Marys were said in all charity and may save my soul.

Have you read that history of the Church by a Dominican, Phillip Hughes? He says something to the effect that the Church is like a river and the times like a river bed and when the bed is low, the river is low but still pure.

I have just finished reading a piece in the *Commonweal* by a man named Lukac who says there's no more literary correspondence and that good writers don't pay any attention to young ones because there's no more charity among them. This has not been my experience. I think of your detailed letters to me about my book and wonder what makes him so sure of what he says.

CAROLINE GORDON TO WALKER PERCY

On Easter Tuesday 1953, Caroline Gordon writes from the University of Washington in Seattle, where she is the Walker Ames lecturer. Viking Press has recognized her brilliance as a teacher of creative writing and has asked her to write a handbook, later published as How to Read a Novel *(Viking, 1957). She writes, "One chapter, (thanks partly to you,) will be a comparison of Proust and Gide."*

In a letter of April 27, 1953, Gordon writes Percy a rambling, judgmental letter. She commends the submission of The Charterhouse *to Viking Press. On May 6, 1953, however, the editor, Malcolm Cowley, writes Susan Jenkins, Percy's agent, that Viking will not publish the novel. Subsequently, in another letter Gordon asks if Percy has cut the length of* The Charterhouse *for a submission to Regnery Publishing. Regnery, however, would not publish the novel.*

FLANNERY O'CONNOR TO CAROLINE GORDON

According to Caroline Gordon, modern fiction's canonical goalposts shifted with the publication in 1952 of Flannery O'Connor's Wise Blood. *The process continued in 1953 when Gordon, living in Rome, scrutinized, often line by line, the stories that would make up O'Connor's* A Good Man Is Hard to Find and Other Stories, *published in 1955. The exchange of letters with Gordon shows that O'Connor conceived of* A Good Man Is Hard to Find and Other Stories *as a cycle with a coherent unity that set forth a dramatic exposition of the seven deadly sins modeled on Dante's* Purgatorio.

I enclose my new ending which you can plainly see is a heap better than the other one. That last one was just one more thing attributable to the 7th Deadly Sin, too lazy to do what ought to be done. The view point at the end may not be that of an eagle exactly but it's at least a buzzard on a very high limb. I have also done away with the word—the not-word—"squinch." This is very difficult as I have a natural fondness for it.

Will you please tell Allen [Tate, her husband] that Mr. Ransom [John Crowe, *Kenyon Review*] decided he wanted to use "A Circle in the Fire," so it can't be sent to *Encounter*. I was quite surprised as I thought he would want the chapter. Anyhow, he thought I ought to work on the story more, said it wasn't as economical as it ought to be—Mrs. Pritchard talked too much and some other things, so I have written it over and sent it back to him. The speed with which I did this is probably unequaled but I told him he could send it back as many times as he could suffer to. I can't stand to have them hanging around, over. He thought the chapter was a little complicated, that the reader had to work too hard, but he said he would print it too if I liked. I am afraid to fool with that right now. I rather think it's all right as it is, and I have to get on with Tarwater even though it kills me.

My mother has a D.P. [Displaced Person] family along with her regular dairyman and his family. They are becoming Americanized fast. The little boy asked my mother the other day if gold came from Mexico, where did silver come from? My mother didn't know. He said from under the Lone Ranger.

It's getting cold here and my peafowl have ruffled necks all the time and step very high. I heard a great commotion out there the other day and went to find that the cock had taken on the entire flock of turkeys—about ninety five. When they would charge him, he would fly straight up and land on the shed roof and look at them a while, then he would descend straight down and scatter them. This would have gone on all afternoon if I hadn't put a stop to it.

I'm much obliged for the Fitzgerald's address. I reckon they decided Siena [Italy] was too cold.

CAROLINE GORDON TO FLANNERY O'CONNOR

Writing from the American Academy in Rome, Gordon notes the seminal importance of one of O'Connor's stories. Gordon was one of the first to recognize the unusual ecumenical appeal of O'Connor's stories.

SEPTEMBER FIRST, 1953

Yesterday I read your story, "The River," sitting in the little inside court of our hotel on the rue Saints Peres. I am convinced that Lambert Strether once sat on the very chair I was sitting on to read that communication from his formidable fiancee, while Waymwars watched him through the glass. Jack Matthews thinks it was another court, but let us leave that aside for a moment. The point is what a beautiful story you have writte[n]. I had a feeling that it was going to be good from the moment Mrs. Connin took that little boy by the hand, and you sure didn't let me down. Just as I finished the story, John Prince, a young friend of ours who practically knows every word of Eudora Welty's "Petrified Man" by heart, came along. "There you are," says I and he, too, was charmed. As was Ward Dorrance, another friend of ours and a very gifted fiction writer, who is staying at this same hotel. There are so many of these people about that I call them the "saints peres." I seem to be the only mere. But to get back to your story, or rather, to your work in general. I see even more clearly with this story what you are about. It is original. Nobody else has done anything just like it. And it is something that much needs to be done. I'd sort of like to write something about your work—I'm beginning to feel that I might be able to point out some things about it that other people may not have noticed—and I'd like to review your novel when it comes out. Will you let me know as far ahead of time as you can so I can ask either the *Times* or the *Herald-Tribune* to let me have it. I suppose Francis Brown would let me have it. But I gather that he got a lot of indignant letters about my Willa Cather review . . .

Allen [Tate, her husband] flew over to England July sixth for some sort of conference at Oxford. I followed by boat, with our impedimenta. We had a fine time at Oxford—I spent most of my time on the river, with the swans. There are five cygnets this year, all still the colour of lead . . .

To go back a moment to your own work. I know that it's nearly always dangerous to say anything about anybody else's work, and, in a way, dangerous to become too conscious yourself of what you are doing. But I do feel that one reason your work is so original and powerful is that—for the first time that I know of—the Catholic viewpoint is brought to bear (however unobtrusively!) [for] all sectarian country people in America. It is a rich field and you are certainly the one to work it. I do congratulate you most heartily.

Write and let us know how things go with you. I am wondering whether you made the visit to the Fitzgeralds [Robert and Sally]. We are looking forward to seeing them in October,

With love,

CAROLINE GORDON TO WALKER PERCY

Writing Percy in the fall of 1953 from the American Academy in Rome, Gordon encourages him to keep writing and urges him to come "to Rome, not only for the sake for your enjoyment but also in the course of your apostolate." The idiom is new in American literary history. Gordon informs Percy that she will send via Percy's brother, Phinizy, who is visiting Rome, a "fine relic" from "St. Pudenzianas, which to me [Gordon] is the most exciting church in Rome." Gordon's sending Percy a sacramental reveals her faith is not abstract but incarnational.

FLANNERY O'CONNOR TO CAROLINE GORDON

Reference is made to a lecture at Georgia State College for Women that O'Connor herself attended. She also mentions prayerful intercession for a philanthropist who made possible a writing fellowship. O'Connor consistently did not judge wealthy persons, realizing that perhaps wealth made possible charity. She also admired the business acumen of her own parents.

MILLEDGEVILLE

10 JANUARY 54

You are certainly right about that story but at least I console myself with the fact that it was written five years ago and I've improved some. Right now I am back on the subject of Displaced Persons. Anything to get away from Tarwater; also I decided that I had not exhausted the possibilities in that particular situation so now I am busy displacing Mrs. McIntyre. I am going after it very slowly and hope to send it to you in a few weeks. I have a peacock in this one. I aim to render the highest possible justice to the peacock. Have you ever read anything about the peacock as a symbol for the transfiguration? I don't know if it appeared as that in medieval paintings or tapestries or what. If you know of anywhere I could read about it or see it I would be obliged to hear.

Mr. Ransom [John Crowe] has renewed my Kenyon Fellowship which is a great help. How many minutes a day do you suppose I ought to pray for the repose of Mr. Rockerfeller's soul? I suppose I ought at least to learn how to spell his name—that don't look right. I sold that story called "A Temple of the Holy Ghost" to *Harper's Bazaar.* I object to having them in there because nobody sees them.

I had a note from Cal [Robert Lowell] who said he was fed up with teaching and wished he lived in a world of illiterates. I thought Brother you may and don't know it.

I'm afraid my mother doesn't think highly of my fiction. Anyway she likes the fact that I do it and her tone is greatly softened by the situation of my being her child. If I was anybody elses I would hate to hear what she'd say about it. Robie [Macauley] says that after his mother read his book, she said, "Is it funny? Chuck said it was funny." When my mother read mine she took it to bed with her every afternoon for about a week. She would start reading and in about ten minutes, she would be snoring. She always says, "That was very interesting," when she hands anything back to me.

Two weeks off I have to give a talk on the novel to the local college—600 girls who don't know a novel from a hole in the head. I asked the head of the English Department how she wanted me to approach the subject, what they knew and what they were interested in. She says, "I don't care how you approach it. They don't know anything and they aren't interested in anything but personality." I am going to tell them that Henry James said that the young woman of the future wouldn't know anything about mystery or manners. Then I am going to tell them that the novel is a celebration of mystery. It's going to take me a half hour. Afterwards I am promised a Coca Cola in the Student Union. Pray for everybody.

FLANNERY O'CONNOR TO CAROLINE GORDON

O'Connor continues to work on individual stories for the collection that would be published in 1955, A Good Man Is Hard to Find and Other Stories. *She recounts tensions between "displaced persons" and an African American on the dairy farm, a conflict that would reappear in "The Displaced Person." Regina O'Connor, however, unlike the matriarch in the story, exercises charitable authority to resolve issues.*

MILLEDGEVILLE

8 FEBRUARY 54

I am fixing up the front of that story. It does read very flat. Miss Caetani wrote me a note asking for the one Mr. Ransom [John Crowe] had and I wrote her a politeness to the effect that he had it and told her I had sent you another but I didn't think I was finished with it; as I am not. If she likes it, I suppose she can have it when I am through with it but my concern right now is to get them published before Fall so I can have out this collection. I think she only has two issues a year or something; maybe she won't want it which will suit me just as well. Incidentally, I called her Miss. What am I supposed to call her? The Mozely T. Sheppard in me objects to calling her anything else. I refuse to be any urbaner than I have to be. Anyway, if she likes it well enough to want the corrected version, would you ask her to let me know and I'll send it to her.

It has been on my conscience to send Poor Ritt something. Do you know Poor Ritt? I don't know why I should call him Poor but he has written me about how much money he has lost on A. D., and of other of his trials. A. D. was something they started at Fordham, or something somebody started at Fordham, anyway it was no good, just terrible in fact, and he has taken it over and is trying to make something of it. Poor Ritt and I remember each other in our prayers but I have never met him. He has a nine year old child that he hasn't seen in nine years—wife departed and "remarried." M. Maritain is now a contributing editor, I think, and other people.

I was thinking about going to see the Fitzgeralds in the spring but my doctor squashed that one. Too much risk, said he. He says I have enough blood to be a Southern girl, I better not be anything else.

The D.P. and Shot nearly choked each other in the wagon the other day and now my mother is almost afraid to send them to the field together for fear one won't come back. She gave him a long lecture that night through Alfred, the 12 yr old boy. She kept saying, "You tell your father that he's a gentleman, that I KNOW he's a gentleman, and that gentlemen don't fight with poor negroes like Shot that don't have any sense." I think he then told his father in Polish that she said Shot didn't have any sense. Father agreed. Too much agreement. She knew it hadn't gone through and started again. "You tell your father that he is, etc." Finally Alfred admitted he didn't know what a gentleman was, even in English. She was very successful in communicating with Shot, however. "Now Shot," she said, "you are very intelligent. You are much too intelligent to fight with a man that we can't understand very well, now you know you are above this, etc. etc." He agreed with every word, but said Mr. Matysiak had hit him first.

I had a note from Paul Engle [Iowa Writers' Workshop] today after I had written to congratulate him on his O. Henry collection. He said the *Saturday Review* had just attacked it and the Workshop. He seemed sad about it but I think it's obviously an honor.

Love and thank you for seeing that story. I am going after it.

FLANNERY O'CONNOR TO PETER TAYLOR

A publisher had apparently sent O'Connor a collection of Taylor's stories. The publisher perhaps hoped to obtain a blurb for the dust jacket from O'Connor.

MILLEDGEVILLE, GA.

15 APRIL 54

Harcourt, Brace sent me a copy of your new collection [*A Long Fourth and Other Stories*] and I reckon I ought to thank them instead of you but I would rather thank you so that I can say that I admire your stories so very much and have for a long time. I always read them several times, hoping I will learn something painlessly. This may be an extravagant hope. My favorite story is still the one called "Skyline" in the other collection and I would like to write one that good some day.

It occurs to me to say also that I have just seen *Kenyon Review* and observe with horror that my story has got a new last line. I suppose this is my fault as I added it to the proofs—but not at that point. I attribute its removal to the end to some learned printer. In any case, it doesn't do much for the story.

FLANNERY O'CONNOR TO CAROLINE GORDON

Reference is made to a publisher, including in O'Connor's collection The Artificial Nigger. *The title story became one of her favorites. At the end of the story she created a powerful crucifixion image of African American suffering that functioned like a Station of the Cross in the liturgical penitential rite of Lent. Penitents meditate on images of suffering from the Passion of Christ. In "The Artificial Nigger," a dedicated racist is convicted of his own bigotry when he gazes at a cruciform statue. O'Connor's intentions are laudable, as revealed in* A Prayer Journal, *where she beseeches God, "Please let Christian principles permeate my writing."[24] In the reception of the story, however, over the years, O'Connor's intentions, like those of Twain and Faulkner, have been eclipsed by the emotional impact of the racial slur she used, even leading to the banning of O'Connor's stories in some Catholic schools.[25]*

MILLEDGEVILLE

27 OCTOBER 54

I met Bob Giroux in Atlanta yesterday and he told me your daughter had been ill and that you had been back some time. I will pray for her—he said she was better. I have not heard from anybody in great lengths of time but I suppose all my acquaintances are as glad to get shut of the summer as I am. Grace after the season. He told me about Cal [Robert Lowell].

We've been besieged lately by rabid foxes—to the extent that we've lost three cows, one a good one, of hydrophobia—so the government has come in and set traps. Every morning the traps have to be investigated. I never knew so many skunks, possums & coons had been created. Every night the negroes take home a possum or so and yesterday they went with two possums, a coon, & a fox-squirril. I asked the colored woman how she cooked the coon and she said, "First I boils him and then I bakes him." I was going to ask her to send me a piece but now I'm not sure I want him.

Where are the Fitzgeralds? I last heard they were in some kind of moated castle belonging to one of Mr. Pound's connections and this was teeming with theirs and other people's children.

I have a new story called "The Artificial Nigger," that I want to send you if you are not too busy & if you are really in Minnesota. Apparently Harcourt is going to put out my collection of stories in August. I have ten & have gone over them and removed all such words as "squinch," "skrunch," "scrawnch," etc.

I managed to raise two peachickens this summer. They are fearfully tame and both are vicious. I can't tell what sex they are yet though a man we had working out here told me that the way to tell is you hold the chicken upsidedown by its two front toes and if it tries to turn rightsideup again, it's a hen and if it just hangs down, it's a rooster. He swore this was a sure way and that he had used it many times to separate three-day-old chickens. One of mine turned up and the other hung down but they still look exactly alike.

Remember me to Allen.

FLANNERY O'CONNOR TO CAROLINE GORDON

O'Connor mentions Lon Cheney's working for the Tennessee governor, Frank G. Clement. O'Connor also mentions a televangelist and connects the scene of his preaching to a character in Wise Blood.

MILLEDGEVILLE

10/23/53

This is absolutely the last one of these things I am going to let myself write until I have my foot well on Tarwater's [early version, Francis Marion Tarwater, *The Violent Bear It Away*] neck again. I would like to know if it works or not. I'm afraid the end is too abrupt. After about 18 pages I always get the to-hell-with-it feeling and sign off. I think the reason I don't help the reader over the stile is because I am too busy getting myself over it. I don't always know what's happened even after it has.

Let me know where the Fitzgeralds [Sally and Robert] are when you find out and give them my blessings. My mother wants to know where to send their fruit cake. She has her fruit cake seizure about this time of year and there's nothing to be done about it but get out of the way.

Robie [Macauley] writes me that the Lowells [Robert and Elizabeth] have bought a big old house in Duxbury, Mass. Mansion about 300 years old, from which they aim to commute to Iowa. Cal also has a big old Packard named "The Green Hornet." I hope Elizabeth does the driving. The Fitzgeralds thought Cal was going to be at Cincinnati this year but apparently he is still at Iowa [Writers' Workshop].

Lon [Cheney] wrote that he was back at fiction after doing the Governor's paper work for his conference with the President [Eisenhower] about TVA [Tennessee Valley Authority]. It was very successful he says. His Governor Clement is a big friend of Billy Ghrame [Graham, the evangelist]. I saw old Billy on the tellyvision this summer at my aunt's in Boston. They had a real repulsive announcer—the good-looking cream variety—and then a real repulsive singer—same kind—and then Billy. Billy was very vigorous and less repulsive than the other two but I suspect they were chosen so that this would be the case. He looks like Onnie Jay Holy only he's better dressed.

I think Mr. Ransom [John Crowe] has forgotten I sent him the story and the chapter. Incidentally Cal [Robert Lowell] has a long review of Warren's poem [Robert Penn, *Brother to Dragons*] in the last *Kenyon* [*Review*]; he read it three times, he says. I read the part that came out last year but haven't read the whole thing; I have no perception about poetry though. I can tell Edgar Guest from Shakespear—that is about all.

LON CHENEY TO FLANNERY O'CONNOR

Three years have passed since Cheney wrote a seminal article on Wise Blood. *A speechwriter for Governor Clement of Tennessee, Cheney writes (July 19, 1956) to enlist O'Connor in support of his efforts to influence the 1956 Democratic convention.*

. . . The chief reason for my using a dummy committee—which I will call the Committee for Renewing the Democratic Party, or something of the sort—is that I must publish under a soubriquet or anonymously in order not to embarrass Governor Clement before the Convention. The article is, of course, freely critical of the Democratic Party as well as the Republican Party and could prove embarrassing for him if my name was connected with it. I intend to by-line it A Life Long Democrat . . .

As you can imagine, I am in a terrible swivet in preparation for the Convention which Our Boy [Governor Clement] will keynote . . ."[26]

FLANNERY O'CONNOR TO BRAINARD CHENEY

O'Connor agrees to serve on a political committee, noting she will listen to Governor Clement, whose speech, written by Cheney, electrified a sleepy Democratic convention.[27] Bill Clinton, elected President of the United States in 1992, also listened to Clement's speech in which the governor famously accused President Eisenhower of staring down the "green fairways of indifference." Criticism of presidential golf has remained a bipartisan topic from President Eisenhower to Donald Trump. President Bush gave up golf during the Iraq war, while Donald Trump criticized President Obama for too much golfing. Once elected, President Trump has happily enjoyed the fairways with famous champions such as Tiger Woods and Jack Nicklaus, and awarded the Medal of Freedom to Woods on May 6, 2019.

I'll be real pleased to have my name on the dummy committee . . .
it sounds mighty congenial.

I've been sitting with my ear glued to the radio when Brother
Clement makes his oration. May St. Thomas balance Billy Ghrame.[28]

CAROLINE GORDON TO FLANNERY O'CONNOR

Gordon is working on a novel, The Malefactors, *while reading O'Connor's
story about Tarwater, who would eventually become the rebellious prophet in*
The Violent Bear It Away. The Malefactors *features a moody, conde-
scending, unfaithful husband given to financial mismanagement and advancing
his literary career. Gordon mentions the sullenness of the characters in the two
works, perhaps reflecting her own troubled marriage.*

VIA ANGELO MASINA 5

(PORTA SAN PANCRAZIO)

ROMA

[OCT. 31, 1953]

I finished the first section of my novel the other day [*The
Malefactors*]—it took only seven chapters to carry the hero from
breakfast to the time when he sank around four o'clock in the morning into a troubled sleep. I hardly know which is the more sullen
companion—he or Tarwater. You wouldn't think it to look at—or
listen to him—but he's busy with his Fiery Crosses, too. Seems they
all are, one way or another. Anyhow, I made the mistake of turning
my back on him long enough to do a bit of sightseeing and here it's
three weeks I been letting him lay—and without the kind of excuse
you have for turning your back on Tarwater . . .

"The Displaced Person" has some of the most brilliant passages
you've written, notably Mrs. Shortley's conversations with the two
Negroes. I like them so much I've read them aloud to various people,

all of whom have gone into the proper stitches over them. Allen [Tate] likes them, too. In fact, our reactions to the story seem to be about the same. I'm going to give them to you as best I can, but for Heaven's sake remember that I may very well not know what I'm talking about. I'm really just thinking aloud—mulling over what seems to me to be the problem. We both feel that the story doesn't quite come off at the end, though superb up till then. Neither of us is quite sure what the trouble is. I'll hazard some guesses.

Mrs. Shortley's vision, though fine in itself, doesn't seem to be integral to the story. The connection between the vision and the denouement isn't established, really, seems to me. If the vision is in there it ought to "work," ought to have some particular job to do.

I am wondering whether the trouble, after all, isn't in the handling of the viewpoint at the end? I don't like the touch of levity ("I have been made regular etc.") in this context. It cuts the ground out from under Mrs. Shortley's feet, makes her pathetic rather than tragic. But you have been building her up for a tragic role—a mountain of a woman, or at any rate, a woman of larger size than most of her companions, a woman who thinks as deeply as she can, and, certainly, ponders even if she isn't capable of ratiocination.

It seems to me that the denouement ought to take place on a larger stage. Mrs. Shortley ought to see herself in somewhat the same position as those heaps of bodies dead, naked people that she saw in the movies. Damn it! She ought to see or feel herself and Mr. Shortley being dismembered!

As I see it, the structure of the story rests on three supporting scenes, the way a roof might rest on three columns: the sight of all those naked, dead bodies in the movies, the vision and the command to prophesy and, lastly, her realization of what it is she is prophesying: hers and her husband's destruction.

Mr. and Mrs. Shortley are Displaced Persons, Dismembered Persons, more displaced, more painfully dismembered than the Gobblehooks [Guizacs], if they only knew it, and your story is Mrs. Shortley's realization of what is happening to them. It's all there—and magnificently—it seems to me. All you have to do is bring out a little more what is already implicit in your action . . .

Hastily, with love,

By the way, it's "carcase," not "carcus." Also, I don't at all like "squinch" on page 21. Here is an example of the thing I was talking about in my last letter. There is no such word as "squinch." It is not in the vocabulary of the omniscient narrator, who is above colloquialisms and that sort of thing. The word therefore can come only from Mrs. Shortley's vocabulary. The use of Mrs. Shortley s vocabulary, which is to say, her view-point here, abruptly contracts the field of vision and also lowers the tone of the action—at the moment when you need a wider vision and an exalted tone.

You have here, in a nut-shell, it seems to me, the chief weakness in your work: the tendency to use too restricted a viewpoint at crucial moments, thereby cutting down the scope of your action. You are superbly agile in slipping in and out of your characters, borrowing their eyes and ears and mouths in the interest of verisimilitude. In fact, it is through this very agility that you achieve some of your finest effects but I would like to see you learn to do something else—to soar above the conflict, to view it as if through the eyes of an eagle, at certain crucial moments. And this passage is one of those moments. After all, you have a more exalted subject matter than any of the other young writers. Your language ought to match it—but without relinquishing anything of what you have already got, not even one double negative. Of course this will be hard to do but you have got what it takes to do it. I feel very certain of that.

I think that this group of stories you've just done are among the finest that have been written by any American.

FLANNERY O'CONNOR TO CAROLINE GORDON

O'Connor mentions visiting friends at Cold Chimneys in Smyrna, Tennessee. O'Connor entertained her friends, including the editor of The Sewanee Review *and his wife, by reading a story.*

MILLEDGEVILLE

18 DECEMBER 53

I have just got back from spending a weekend with the Cheneys. I like them both very much. Lon seems to be in the middle of one novel but wanting to write a different one. I suppose you always want to be writing a different one. They had the Spears [Dr. and Mrs. Monroe] up Saturday night and I read them the Displaced Person, having doctored on the end of it according to your directions. I took off the mama and papa business and added a sentence to the effect that they (the girls) had never known that she had been displaced or that now her displacement was at an end. You were right: it gives it another dimension.

The D.P. is currently telling Shot, the colored man, that he can get him a wife from Germany but that he'll have to pay five hundred dollars for her. My mother says "Oh get out, Mr. Matisiak, you know all those folks over there are white." She has had a lot of trouble anyway with Shot's matrimonial complications. He is estranged from his first wife who used to have him put in jail every month because he wouldn't support his child. My mother finally after paying his bond several times has it arranged so that she sends the check for the child every month—twelve dollars. She was talking to mother the other day and told her that she was mighty tired of having to be Shot's bookkeeper (she also pays his policy man, his board, & his incidental debts). His mother said well she wished he'd go back to his wife and then he wouldn't have to send out that twelve dollars every month. My mother says why you know that woman doesn't want him back. "Oh yesm she do," his mother said, "she wants him worsen a hog wants slop." I happened to be present and nearly fell off my chair but my mother didn't bat an eye until the old woman had gone, then she said, "I hope you are not going to use that in one of those stories." Of course I am as soon as I can find me a place to.

You would probably be interested in Mrs. Steven's children's Sunday school organization. It is called the Meriwether Mites. Meriwether is their community. Very Very Very Methodist. The Mites are mostly interested in the social opportunities in religion; the decent ones that is. They have "no drinking, no smoking, and no setting around in cars."

The story I enclose is one of those old ones that I am undecided about including in the collection. It is very funny when read aloud but I'm afraid there's not much to be said for it otherwise. Anyway I'd like to know what you think.

I hope your mobbing experiences are over. The people I saw in Nashville were powerful interested in it. Merry Christmas.

CAROLINE GORDON TO FLANNERY O'CONNOR

Gordon engages in copyediting, even the colloquialisms in "The Artificial Nigger." Earlier she had praised Walker Percy's presentation of "the Negro problem" in The Charterhouse. *The title, however, of O'Connor's story at the time of its composition in the 1950s does not present a similar "problem," perhaps because the spiritual meaning of the story was obvious to Gordon and O'Connor, but would not be to many others in later years.*

Gordon also embraces the Swiss psychologist Carl Jung both for counseling and aesthetics. Unlike Gordon, O'Connor and Walker Percy would remain steadfast in their skepticism of Jung as a helpful influence on their writing and faith. In the late 1950s, Percy would concur with O'Connor in a long, unpublished essay, "An Apology." Percy argues that Jung was unable to embrace the central claims of Christianity. Instead, Percy notes, he essentially grouped Christianity with other world religions. They all shared similar archetypical or mythical patterns.[29] In another unpublished essay, Percy notes that Jewish ex-

iles in the Old Testament are little different from any other dispossessed people in world history. As a result, the biblical chronicle of the Jewish quest for the Promised Land is just another mythical pattern for categorization.[30]

1409 EAST RIVER ROAD

MINNEAPOLIS, MINNESOTA

[FALL 1954]

Business before pleasure—as our vagabond cook, Willie, said when Allen wanted her to sweep the front porch and she felt called to the post office, to get a real special delivery letter. You asked for it and here it is:

As usual, I think you have improved your story by revision. (one reason that makes me reluctant to advise you is the danger that in reworking a story you will lose some of the good stuff. People nearly always do. But I don't think you do). I shall now treat this revised version as if it were coming out of my own work-shop. I would read it over now, for God knows the how manyeth time,) for tone and dramatic effect.

I think you can improve your first paragraph. The tone is not yet elevated enough, authoritative enough for the story you have to tell. Its subject matter is even more important than the subject matter in Joyce's "Araby," and look at the high and mighty tone he takes throughout that story of something that has happened to every one of us in our time—to be promised a treat as a child and then disappointed. Joyce takes that universal experience and makes it an analogue of man's situation in the universe, a small, lonely figure under a vast, dark dome, a figure whose eyes "burn with anguish and anger" as the child-man realizes his plight. Your story is about an old man who realizes that all along he has been no better than a child. Your subject matter entitles you to take an even higher tone. So does your Christianity, which Joyce forsook and which you didn't.

Have you ever studied any of the paragraphs in Joyce's short stories or in "The Portrait"? It is very rewarding. Each paragraph has in it at least three kinds of sentences and each sentence does its appointed task with something that approaches perfection. You should learn to write the long, complicated—in the sense that it carries a lot of stuff—kind of sentence with which Joyce ends "The Dead." You ought to have a sentence like that to end this story with. The sentence you end isn't quite strong enough, not weighty enough . . .

Your story has the same form, the same three great supports: First, Mr. Head in the moonlight, second, Mr. Head and Nelson waiting for the train. I don't think you give this scene enough attention. III corresponds to Dante's "mid-way in the forest of our life." You ought to set this scene more carefully—that is by using more sensuous detail—ought to make it more mysterious, for it is the "forest" out of which your action will emerge. You go at it too fast and don't choose your words carefully enough; "Stuck" is not good there. Set the scene. Were there any trees there? If so, how did they look then? Did the tracks run through a flat place or did the train emerge from a small defile? Were the tracks straight or was there a bend? You do put the trees in but too late to have the right effect . . .

It's dangerous for me to say this to a young writer who is such a master of colloquial dialogues as you are, but I dare say it just because you are such a master. Your dialogue delights me. I wouldn't like to see less of it in your stories. I ask only to see it more set off, better displayed. That can be done, I think, by elevating the tone of the rest of the story—more beautiful, high-toned sentences. More paragraphs without a colloquial word or phrase in them. In that way you would get contrast that would make you[r] dialogue sparkle even more than it does.

Faulkner can do it—when he's in the groove, but he, poor fellow, is bogged down, I judge from his last book, in what Allen calls "Mississippi theology." You have an advantage over him there. For God's sake make the most of it!

Allen and I have been reading a lot of Jung recently. It's amusing and exciting to watch him making his way to the Church by way of alchemical symbols in the dreams of his patients! We are also reading a book by a Fr. Victor White called "God and the Unconscious," a discussion of Jung and Freud, which Allen is going to send poor Cal [Robert Lowell] for Christmas. (How I wish I could wrap that boy up and mail him to a good Jungian practitioner). I think you'd find this book very interesting, also a book of Jung's called *Religion and Alchemy* (Pantheon Press.) It is fascinating and ought to be very helpful to any fiction writer. It is to me, at least.

By the way, you ought to be able to get any book you need through your local library. They ought to purchase any book you need for your work if they follow the almost universal custom of extending special courtesies to writers. If they don't you can get them to order books from the Library of Congress' Inter-Library loan service.

I've got to get to work on the ill-wrought paragraphs of a promising old writer named Gordon. Love and congratulations on your revision. I don't think you've lost a thing and you've gained an awful lot by the revision.

ALLEN TATE TO FLANNERY O'CONNOR

As the detailed copyediting of O'Connor's fiction proceeds, Tate's presence is primarily through absence. In this letter, however, he praises "Good Country People," and plans to read it to a class. O'Connor—not Hemingway, not Faulkner, not Joyce—could better capture the attention of distracted college students in a story about a Bible salesman stealing an atheist philosopher's wooden leg.

While Tate recognizes the dramatic power of O'Connor's story for teaching, he himself was uninspiring in the classroom. He usually entered class with a patrician air wearing a tweed jacket and sometimes puffing from a cigarette in a holder like President Roosevelt. He dispensed C papers to undergraduates struggling with poetry expositions—Eliot, Yeats, Lowell, for example. Tate once returned an essay to me with a superior admonition: "What that poem says is obvious to me but not to you."[31]

Other critical observations by Tate in this letter reveal his brilliance. The "maimed souls" reference in relation to "Good Country People" reiterates the story's rootedness in Dante's Inferno, a harrowing narrative of dismemberment and cannibalism in the darkest places of Hell. Tate recognizes that O'Connor's storytelling emanates from the Florentine master, Dante himself.

FEBRUARY 22, 1955

I have just read "Good Country People," and I admire it greatly. It is without exception the most terrible and powerful story of Maimed Souls I have ever read. This kind of soul is obviously your subject, in whatever situation you may embody it; and this new fiction is a landmark in your treatment of it.—Much of your power comes of isolating the world in which these maimed persons live; they suddenly appear with the mystery of a natural force, or perhaps of the supernatural force of evil. So this is just a note to congratulate you. Here and there, I was disturbed by details and little touches that I didn't understand. When in the expository and narrative passages Hulga is referred to as the Child, I can't tell who thinks of her so. Here the "point of view" is in question; for if it is the narrator calling her the Child, I fear it won't do; for the narrator has not established herself in the action or as an observer; and she can't really have any views. Moreover it seems to me that Hulga's Ph.D. is unreal as you present it; nothing in Hulga's conversation or behavior, before the coming of the Bible salesman, indicates that she has this side to her character. We simply must take your word for it. If you could give it fictional reality, it would do better the work that I suppose you intend it to do; that is, to stand for the spiritual maiming corresponding to her physical maiming, and thus to make quite plain her vulnerability to the advances of the Bible salesman. I am sure that Caroline has mentioned these points and commented on them more searchingly than I have. You are a wonderful writer, and you started out with the first instinct of a good writer: you write only about the life you know. I am wondering whether you know Chekhov's little story "On the Road." The scene is as limited as yours, and the characters suffer, not exactly a spiritual wound, but a failure of charity which is also an aspect of your typical theme. Nevertheless, without seeming to do so, Chekhov manages to place the crisis of the story in a larger spiritual world.

I have mentioned to my class in Southern literature the names of three Southern writers who are masters of Southern rural dialect: Elizabeth Roberts, Caroline and you. Before you can ask me not to, I am going to read "Good Country People" to my class on Thursday. The way your people talk is a marvel to read.

> Ever yours,
> Allen

Why can't the story be in your book?

ALLEN TATE TO WALKER PERCY

Three years before Tate's praise of O'Connor, he expresses reservations to Percy about The Charterhouse. *Tate, however, recognizes Percy's gifts, in particular the implicit theology of the novel that Percy would fully explore later in a penetrating essay, "Stoicism in the South."[32] Tate's theological speculation leads to a "digression" about a fellow Southern Agrarian—and novelist. In the postscript Tate recognizes the beginnings of Percy's satirical treatment of Anglican gentility and faith. Once the satirical seed was planted, Percy distanced himself from the Anglican patrimony that appears in nuanced mockery in later novels such as* The Moviegoer *and* The Second Coming. *A convert to Catholicism, and having experienced, unlike most readers, the high-toned Anglican community of Sewanee, Tate appreciates Percy's satire.*

> 1801 UNIVERSITY AVENUE SOUTHEAST
> MINNEAPOLIS 14, MINNESOTA
> JANUARY 1, 1952

Dear Walker:

I finished reading your novel yesterday. I am not sure that I can add anything to what Caroline has written you, and I may merely repeat what she said; I didn't read her commentary. It is a most impressive job, and I hope that you will be able to do the revisions necessary to round it out. I don't think there is anything fundamentally wrong with the book, but I do feel that there must be more work in detail . . .

Assuming, as I think you also would assume, that a literary technique from one point of view reflects the moral and even religious ideas implicit in the material, I am struck by the shadowy quality of the minor characters. Many of them come to life for a moment, only to sink almost immediately from sight. This literary effect would follow from Ben's moral condition, a state of sin that maybe described as using others for one's own ends, even though those ends may be compulsive and irrational, and generally destructive. It seems to me then that one of your problems in revision is to offset this moral implication of the subject-matter by giving the other characters a little more life of their own . . . What I am trying to say was first said by Aristotle about tragedy—that it is an action, not a quality; that character cannot exhibit its full meaning unless it is involved in an action; and one man isolated, as Ben is isolated, cannot make an action . . .

I am certain that you can almost at will actualize any portion of the novel, or any character: the minor characters, in so far as we know them at all, we know well. Miss MacGahee is wonderfully done—but what happens to her? She is, of course, the female version of Ben, and not too much could be done with her. I am not sure that you oughtn't to make Ben's marriage to Abbie a partial realization of the righting of a wrong: he need not know the full meaning (i.e., the full "conversion") of the righting of this wrong, but a dim perception of it would give him greater dignity than he has at the end: he would be a man of stature whose imperfect "contrition" would give him a tragic implication.

One more thing. Your Southern business men are beautifully conceived but I think they are overdone: they represent the satire of the author rather than the actuality; they are almost allegorical. They don't, of course, in life, constantly refer to their "class," etc. By highlighting all this you almost caricature them; and I take it that this quality is scarcely the right coefficient of the seriousness of the hero. Ben's father, I repeat, is excellent; he has real "specification"; but he tends to be dissolved in the exaggeration of his friends. You are absolutely right that the Roman myth still hangs on the South, and that the South is not really Christian; it is merely reactionary without being traditional.

(When Andrew Lytle [editor of *The Sewanee Review,* and novelist and professor] says he can't join the Catholic Church because it isn't in the Southern tradition, what he ought to mean is that the South has no tradition without the Church; for the thing that we all still cherish in the South was originally and fundamentally Catholic Christianity. Andrew's position is sheer idolatry—worship of a golden calf, mere secularism—and alas his views are more representative today than yours or mine—or yours and mine. Twenty years ago I knew that religion was the key to the South [as it is to everything else] but I didn't see far enough then.)

Well, that digression is not criticism of your novel. One more suggestion, I hope a practicable one: why not review the progression of incidents, and decide which ones are crucial? Then develop each one as if it were a distinct bit of action? This wouldn't necessitate as much rewriting as you might think. It seems to me that this process might correct the faulty scale of the book as it is. There is too much before Ben returns to the Retreat, if there is going to be so little after; I think there's just about enough after; so perhaps the other end should be scaled down.

The dream about the Church is not convincing, and I can't think of a way to make it convincing. I see what you are up to, and the equivalent at least is probably necessary. My hunch is that the rounding out of Ignatz from the beginning would almost do the equivalent thing.

I congratulate you. You have great intelligence and power, and you're going to be a valuable novelist.

Ever yours,

Allen

P.S. The satire of Sewanee [University of the South] as a psychiatric retreat is wonderful—effective in itself, but with an added dimension for those of us who know Sewanee.[33]

FLANNERY O'CONNOR TO CAROLINE GORDON AND ALLEN TATE

O'Connor mentions the autobiographical theme in "Good Country People," revealing that without faith she might have been like the story's atheist intellectual, Hulga. Another O'Connor story, "A Temple of the Holy Ghost," contains insights about her adolescence, while "Revelation" contains autobiographical elements of her struggles as an adult with a deadly illness.

MILLEDGEVILLE

I MARCH 55

I do appreciate both your letters and I am glad to have my opinion on that story confirmed. I really thought all the time it was the best thing I had done. Hit (it) was a seizure. Anyway, Mrs. Freeman's remarks are not much credit to me. She lives on this place and all I have to do is sit at the source and reduce it a little so it'll be believable. As for the other lady I have known several of her since birth and as for Hulga I just by the grace of God escaped being her; the Bible salesman also came without effort. I am mighty afraid he is my hidden character.

I have corrected the business about the child and now only use it from the mother's point of view. This is a great improvement. Then I have added two touches to support the intellectual life of Hulga; one, like you said about the name, and the name's working like Vulcan in the furnace, etc. Hulga thinks that one of her greatest triumphs is that her mother has not been "able to turn her dust into Joy, but the greater one was that she had been able to turn it herself into Hulga." That helps some. Then while Mrs. Hopewell is thinking about Hulga and how she is getting more bloated, rude and squint-eyed every day, I stick in this (from Mrs. Hopewell's viewpoint):

"And she said such strange things! To her own mother she had said—without warning, without excuse, standing up in the middle of a meal with her face purple and her mouth half full—"Woman! Do you ever look inside? Do you ever look inside and see what you are not? God!" she had cried sinking down again and staring at her plate, "Malbranche was right: we are not our own light! We are not our own light!" Mrs. Hopewell had no idea, to this day, what brought that on. She had only made the remark (hoping Joy would take it in) that a smile never hurt anyone."

Anyhow, with these changes, I sent it airmail to Giroux and he wired me he would try to get it in the collection if it didn't cost too much to throw away the old type and do the resetting [A Good Man Is Hard to Find and Other Stories, 1955]. Seems there can't be but so many pages or they will go broke. I was to get the proofs this week so I suppose he could wring my neck.

I know you are glad to get out from under that novel, or anyway where you can see out. If I could just get where I could see a little daylight in mine I would be happy. It hasn't moved an inch in 18 months and when I stop it and write a story I feel like I am letting myself down from the penitentiary by a rope. I mean a thread.

The story of Powers [J. F.] in the O'Henry collection is better than any of the others in the book. If you ever see him I wish you would tell him he has one solid admirer in Georgia.

CAROLINE GORDON TO MR. AND
MRS. ANDREW LYTLE

Gordon writes from Sherman, Connecticut, where she is visiting Walker Per-cy's agent, Susan Jenkins. Gordon describes the impact of a public reading by Flannery O'Connor. Serial murders interwoven with discussion of the Resur-rection were meant to both entertain and provoke genteel critics.

Lytle would have appreciated O'Connor's reading. Trained as an actor at the Yale School of Drama, Lytle was a gifted teacher who mesmerized students in his classroom performances of O'Connor's stories at the Universities of the South [Sewanee] and Florida [Gainesville]. When he was editor of The Se-wanee Review, *students from his classes and other admirers congregated at the "Log Cabin," Lytle's ancestral home in Monteagle, Tennessee. Lytle would simply resume his class on his front porch or beside the fire, where more unfor-gettable teaching occurred.*

An undergraduate might imbibe highballs served in silver cups with "Mr. Lytle," and assorted luminaries in town might appear for the evening. These might include the novelist, Eudora Welty; the Faulkner scholar, Cleanth Brooks; Lytle's fellow Agrarian, novelist Robert Penn Warren; the biblical scholar, the Reverend William H. Ralston, Jr.; Thomas ("Tam") Carlson, of the English faculty at Sewanee; the Reverend K. Logan Jackson, dynamic president of the national campaign to preserve the Elizabethan Book of Com-mon Prayer, his wife, Mary Lyman [Scott] Jackson—concert pianist, bril-liant writer, and the cofoundress of Exodus Youth Services (Washington, D.C.), and many others. Sometimes appearing in black dancing slippers, Lytle might recall his adventures as an actor or his experiences boxing.[34] *He praised O'Connor, while noting Faulkner's shortcomings. He lauded Joyce, noting that* Portrait of the Artist *was about the integrity of the artist who would not serve a corrupt Church. (The observation has renewed cogency with the unfold-ing scandal in the Catholic Church.) Lytle lamented the liturgical revisions of the Elizabethan* Book of Common Prayer *that resulted in the gutting of Anglicanism's claim of Catholic orthodoxy. Mr. Lytle proclaimed that the "Episcopal bishops no longer believed that Jesus was the son of God." He de-*

cried "the puritans" and admonished his guests to "use the gifts of God." Lytle repeatedly praised Thomas More, often quoting his famous line "I die my king's good servant but God's first."[35] *"Mr. Lytle" as a host, conversationalist, and raconteur was a legendary, magnetic personality who had an impact on many students and admirers.*[36]

SHERMAN, CONNECTICUT

JUNE 15, 1955

Dear Andrew and Edna:

Here is a letter which I thought I had mailed to you two months ago. Seems I wrote it just before I went to that symposium where I had to preside over a "Faulkner panel." There were two talks on Faulkner, by young profs from Catholic universities. They swallowed the symbolism—and the screwy theology—in "A Fable," hook line and sinker. I had only two or three minutes in which to set forth my views. I read from your piece: the part that says that this work is begotten by an act of will etc. The speakers did not like what you said at all, but the sisters loved it. It really went over big, and it was handy for me to quote from another writer instead of trying to set forth my own views. But enough of Faulkner panels . . .

I am still reading Erich Neuman's *The History and Origin of Consciousness* and think it is about the best book I ever read, next to holy Writ.[37] I am anxious to see what you all think of it and asked Sue Jenkins to send you the copy I lent her but she never got around to it and now I have to keep the copy to use in a lecture I am trying to get ready for Indiana.

I see by some advertisement I read, Andrew, that you think as much of Flannery O'Connor's work as I do. She is certainly a remarkable person and a remarkable writer. She spent a week end with us recently. We had the Van Wyck Brookses [*The Flowering of New England*] and the Cowleys [Malcolm] over for dinner. After dinner Van Wyck insisted that Flannery read one of her stories. She was quite willing and wanted to read "Good Country People," but there were several elderly ladies present and I simply could not see them taking that scene in the hay-loft, where the Bible salesman tries to seduce the one legged Ph.D. and switched her on to "A Good Man Is Hard to Find," which is shocking enough, God knows. Van Wyck said later that it was sad to see such a talented young writer have such a pessimistic view of life. He said that he found the experiences of her characters "alien to the American way of life." He said that he and Gladys had driven all over this country and found nothing but loving-kindness!

James Waller is going to visit us ad Dulce Donum this summer and we hope the Cheneys will come by on their way up here. They expect to spend September with Sue. I wish you all were coming, too. We expect—and fervently hope—that this summer will be less hectic than last summer. The Lord does sometimes temper the wind to—elderly—shorn—sheep.

Love for both of you and for the girls,

as ever,

FLANNERY O'CONNOR TO ANDREW LYTLE

The letter is representative of O'Connor's respect for a vital mentor and teacher. He had instructed O'Connor at Iowa about Wise Blood *and recognized its originality and power. He witnessed a rare occurrence in the classroom: O'Connor's classmates giving her a standing ovation after her reading the novel. Over a decade later, O'Connor remains grateful for his consistent support and understanding.*

MILLEDGEVILLE

4 FEBRUARY 60

Dear Andrew,

I feel better about the book, knowing you think it works. I expect it to get trounced but that won't make any difference if it really does work. There are not many people whose opinion on this I set store by.

I have got to the point now where I keep thinking more and more about the presentation of love and charity, or better call it grace, as love suggests tenderness, whereas grace can be violent or would have to be to compete with the kind of evil I can make concrete. At the same time, I keep seeing Elias in that cave, waiting to hear the voice of the Lord in the thunder and lightning and wind, and only hearing it finally in the gentle breeze, and I feel I'll have to be able to do that sooner or later, or anyway keep trying.

There is a moment of grace in most of the stories, or a moment where it is offered, and is usually rejected. Like when the Grandmother recognizes the Misfit as one of her own children and reaches out to touch him. It's the moment of grace for her anyway—a silly old woman—but it leads him to shoot her. This moment of grace excites the devil to frenzy.

The book [*The Violent Bear It Away*] is going to be published by Longmans, Green in England. After they read the manuscript, they wrote to inquire what the significance was of Tarwater's violation in the woods by the man in the motor car. Besides the fact that nobody knows about the devil now, I have to reckon on the fact that baptism is just another idiocy to the general reader. A lady-librarian reviewing it in the *Library Journal* said that there was not "enough convincing action to bring this macabre tale to a successful conclusion." She also noted that Tarwater added to my "band of poor God-driven Southern whites." God-driven means underprivileged.

Well any, I am most grateful to you and steadied by you. If you get up this way, please stop with us. Ashley enjoyed his visit with you all. That boy is on the road more than Kerouac, though in a more elegant manner.

Yours,

FLANNERY O'CONNOR TO FATHER SCOTT WATSON

O'Connor writes an erudite Jesuit friend who identified the dramatic sacramentalism and biblical element in The Violent Bear It Away. *She also qualifies its connection to a British novel and also quotes a revered teacher.*

8 FEBRUARY 60

You can't know how very much obliged I am to you for your letter. Reading it I felt for the first time that the book actually did work, for you got out of it what I intended to put into it. Of course I won't find many readers with your equipment to read, either in the literary or religious sense. Most people find baptism just another idiocy, prophecy an anachronism; the Eucharist nothing but a symbol, or rather just a sign. When one writes, or anyway when I do, I have constantly in mind the kind of person I am trying to get my vision across to. For me, this person is always an unbeliever and the strain of making him see is considerable. Perhaps it is too much to ask to make him see. All I really hope to do is disturb him, lose him a night's sleep maybe.

I've read *Till We Have Faces* [C.S. Lewis] and had mixed feelings about it. It was pretty much allegory. A friend of mine, Andrew Lytle, a very fine novelist [*The Velvet Horn, The Hero with the Private Parts*], wrote me about my book and said this, "I felt the end of *Wise Blood* got too allegorical, almost fantasy, in my belief that always there must be the natural action which contains and represents the supernatural or imaginative. Allegory can exist only in an age of belief. People exist today in their personalities, so desperate is our plight." He felt that this last book of mine was better than *Wise Blood* because "the symbols seem true symbols, that is containing the action, not signs in place of action." I am interested in this subject of allegory and symbol. There is a book by a man named Erich Heller called *The Disinherited Mind* which has a good chapter on the subject.

Once again, my very inadequate thanks.

CHAPTER 2

"THE FIRST PRIEST WHO SAID TURKEY-DOG"

One of O'Connor's lasting friendships was with the Reverend James Hart McCown, who called on her at Andalusia in January 1956. When she opened the door, he said, "I read your stories, and I just wanted to meet you. I liked them very much." She never forgot that he "was the first priest who said turkey-dog to me about my writing."[1] Father McCown soon introduced O'Connor's stories to other Jesuits. These included Robert McCown (his brother), Scott ("Youree") Watson of Spring Hill College in Mobile, Alabama, and Harold Gardiner, the literary editor of the Jesuit journal *America*. O'Connor writes to her friends the Fitzgeralds, "These Jesuits work fast. Ten days after I had the visit from the one in Macon, I receive a communication from Harold C. Gardiner, S.J. asking me to contribute to *America*."[2] In March 1957 O'Connor's "The Church and the Fiction Writer" appeared in the journal.

In 1956, Father McCown introduced O'Connor to Thomas and Louise Gossett. Thomas Gossett at the time was an English professor at Wesleyan College in Macon, Georgia. As the friendship between the Gossetts and O'Connor flourished, Tom Gossett pioneered in the new academic fields of African American history and literature. Gossett supported racial integration, which in 1958 led the president of Wesleyan College to suspend him from the faculty. O'Connor steadfastly supported him and admired his scholarship.

Gossett's seminal *Race: The History of an Idea in America* has become a canonical work in African American studies. Writing in a time and place of entrenched segregation, Gossett undertook to examine thoroughly the origins and development of racism in the United States from colonial times to civil rights activism. Father McCown, a civil rights activist himself, delighted in Gossett's original scholarship and writes his enthusiastic congratulations in April 1964.

Professor Gossett's scholarship also included collecting the letters O'Connor wrote Father McCown. He recognized the daily sanctity of Father McCown and the genius of O'Connor. Gossett and O'Connor admired the relentless zeal of Father McCown. Writing in his 1990 autobiography, *With Crooked Lines,* Father McCown catalogs his fifty years of ministry, including

> [teaching in] Jesuit high schools in New Orleans and Shreveport; parish and youth counseling in Macon; setting up a racially integrated country parish in Fort Valley, Georgia, in the early sixties, working in retreat houses on the Gulf Coast, Atlanta, Lake Dallas, and Grand Coteau, founding a poor kids camp near San Antonio, traveling through the southern states conducting parish retreats, working in slum parishes in El Paso and San Antonio, and posh parishes in New Orleans and Dallas.[3]

During their friendship, Gossett requested that Father McCown send the letters that O'Connor had written him. Father McCown cheerfully did so. The correspondence of these lively friends would span nearly a decade, from 1956 until O'Connor's death in 1964. The first letter recounts Father McCown sending Gossett his letters from

O'Connor. (In a few letters Tom Gossett's appended clarifying information is included.)

FLANNERY O'CONNOR TO
FATHER JAMES H. McCOWN

Mr. Ridley [Horace], a friendly whiskey salesman, drove colorful Cadillacs and was a parishioner of Father McCown's church in nearby Macon, Georgia. He ferried books and people back and forth to Andalusia, O'Connor's home. He once told Father McCown that he did not think O'Connor's stories were "trashy enough." O'Connor instructs Father McCown about Catholic fiction, including the benefit of reading "bad Catholics."

MILLEDGEVILLE

19 JANUARY 56

Thank you for the books sent in the mail and the ones Mr. Ridley brought. I'm returning the Michelfelder novel and several of the magazines that I have enjoyed very much, and I also enclose in that package a pocket book copy of *Wise Blood* which I forget whether you said you had seen or not. [If] you have time to read it sometime I'd like to know what you think of it.

The Michelfelder book [William Michelfelder, *A Seed upon the Wind*] is amazing and I am very glad to have read it. It interests me particularly because it deals with loss of faith which was the underlying subject of my novel, though I didn't use a Catholic background. A Catholic has to have strong nerves to write about Catholics.

I have read almost everything that Bloy, Bernanos, and Mauriac have written. The Catholic fiction writer has very little high-powered "Catholic" fiction to influence him except that written by these three, and Green [Julian]. But at some point reading them reaches the place of diminishing returns and you get more benefit reading someone like Hemingway where there is apparently a hunger for a Catholic completeness in life, or Joyce who can't get rid of it no matter what he does. It may be a matter of recognizing the Holy Ghost in fiction by the way He chooses to conceal Himself.

I hadn't read the Eric Gill [*Autobiography*] and am enjoying it. If Mr. Ridley doesn't stop in the next few weeks I'll mail these library books back to you unless you want them sooner.

Again I'm very grateful for the visit and the interest. I asked Harcourt, Brace to send you a copy of Mrs. Tate's [Caroline Gordon] book which I trust they will do sooner or later.

FLANNERY O'CONNOR TO LOUIS RUBIN

O'Connor declines to write an apologetic essay about her region. Writing stories, by contrast, enables her to present both regional and religious patrimony. O'Connor uses the idiom of regional autonomy and subsidiarity in speaking of the South as a "country" with its own traditions, customs, and language—the region is not a province or a section and has historically been resistant to cultural and political uniformity imposed from the outside. Reaching a diverse nonregional audience, O'Connor blends together both regional and theological elements in stories such as "The Displaced Person." O'Connor's stories reveal deeper historical complexities. Like the writings of Faulkner, Foote, and Percy, they contain an implicit counternarrative to the victory narrative of American exceptionalism rooted in colonial Puritan rhetoric of dissent.

MILLEDGEVILLE

GEORGIA

24 JANUARY 56

Thank you so very much for asking me to contribute to the book of essays that you are going to edit. Unfortunately, all my views about the South have to be expressed in the form of fiction. I simply know no other and if I set out to write an essay, it would very shortly turn into a story and wouldn't serve the purpose.

My own experience as a Southern writer is complex because I am not only a Southerner but a Catholic and thus have two regions to deal with. This is a complication that can best be shown in fiction, and by me, only in fiction.

Please let me say that I have read two of your reviews of my stories and that I find them very understanding; and that I'll be looking forward to reading the book when it comes from Regnery.

FLANNERY O'CONNOR TO FATHER JAMES H. McCOWN

On February 6, 1956, O'Connor sets forth her literary instruction that emphasizes realism. She recommends well-crafted works written by Catholic, irreligious, and dissenting writers.

However, it does seem to me that you don't have to rely on the virtue of prudence to prevent pornography in your writing, but that you must first anyway rely on the virtue of art. Pornography and sentimentality and anything else in excess are all sins against form and I think they ought to be approached as sins against art rather than as sins against morality. At least this is practical in these times when most writers are pagans and if you are going to talk to them at all, you have to talk in terms they can understand. The pious style is a great stumbling block to Catholics who want to talk to the modern world . . .

I enjoyed *Black Popes* [Thomas D'Esterre Roberts] very much and found an article by Archbishop Roberts in *The Month* which I enclose in returning the book. I haven't read *Weeping Cross* [Henry Stuart Longan] but I judge it is historicalish from some ads I saw. I have just read a very funny book by a priest named Fr. Robo [Etienne]—on St. Therese of Lisieux. It's called *Two Portraits of St. Therese.* He has managed (by some not entirely crooked means) to get hold of a photograph of her that the Carmelites have not "touched up" which shows her to be a round-faced, determined, rather comical looking girl. He does away with all the roses, little flowers, and other icing. The book has greatly increased my devotion to her.[4]

O'Connor mentions (February 20, 1956) reviewing books for diocesan publications.[5] These reviews rehearse her tutoring strategy with Father McCown to make him a discerning reader of well-crafted (but not necessarily pious) works. She also reveals the origin of a story with a racial slur in the title. Ugly lawn statues originally revealed a tragedy for her region. The story challenged such distortions with a cruciform image of suffering at the end.

I had a nice letter from Fr. Gardiner [Harold], giving me five or six names of reviewers who would be interested in Caroline Gordon's book [*The Malefactors*]. He said my ideas for a critical piece were very interesting and he hoped I would come up with one before too long. However, there is a good deal more that I must come up with right now.

My mother went cow-buying a couple of years ago and asked an old man for directions how to get to a certain man's house. He told her to go thus and so and that she couldn't miss it because it was the only house in town with an artificial nigger. I was so intrigued with that that I made up my mind to use it. It's not only a wonderful phrase but it's a terrible symbol of what the South has done to itself. I think it's one of the best stories I've written and this because there is a good deal more in it than I understand myself . . . [6]

O'Connor seeks spiritual counsel. The letter also revisits a theme of her most famous story, "A Good Man Is Hard to Find," featuring a theological debate about the identity of Jesus.

MILLEDGEVILLE

4 MARCH 56

The enclosed letter is from one of my correspondents whom I've never seen. I helped him to get into the University of Iowa and now he favors me with letters describing his friends. He has been telling me for some time about this Mrs. De Luna whose chief characteristic is that she can't stand Jesus. Thinks He was a lunatic. She is of the psychoanalytical school. In the letter before this Steele told me that Mrs. De Luna's thought for the week was that nobody would have paid the least attention to Jesus if he hadn't been a martyr but had died at the age of 80 of athlete's foot. I told Steele she was absolutely correct and that her trouble was probably that she was orthodox and didn't know it. So now I get this further information about her background. It should doubtless be posted on the bulletin board at the Sisters of Mercy's Mother House.

What I want to know is if I am right in contradicting the Sister who told Mrs. De Luna that anybody who hadn't heard of Jesus would be damned? So far as I understand it the Church does not teach any such thing, but then I know this is a matter with complications and I don't want to tell him what I am not absolutely sure about.

I have finished *Weeping Cross* [Henry Stuart Longan] and I must say it is a fine novel and your note in the front of it well justified. I hadn't expected it to be so good. I am now on *The Devil Rides Outside* [J. H. Griffin], but I haven't got far enough to have much opinion about it. If you want the *Weeping Cross* before Mr. Ridley appears, let me know and I will mail it, along with another book for your library—this time a good one—*The Presence of Grace* by J. F. Powers, which I have reviewed for *The Bulletin* [diocesan newspaper].

I never thanked you for the letter in the newspaper or the pamphlet about the brothers but I appreciated both. I haven't heard from the brother again and hope not to.

I don't know anybody in Augusta. I visited there once when I was four—at the convent where my cousin was Mother Superior and celebrating her something-or-other jubilee. They had ice cream for dessert in the shape of Calla lilies. That was the only time I was ever tempted to join an order—I thought they ate that way every day. We hope you will get over on the 19th.

Father McCown apparently is scheduled to deliver a literary talk. O'Connor politely declines an invitation to attend.

MILLEDGEVILLE, GEORGIA

2 APRIL 56

Thanks very much for the (very elegant) invitation to hear your review. I wish I could. I also wish we had some such movement afoot in Milledgeville but we prefer Bingo. I'm a Baptist about Bingo.

I had a letter from Dale Francis who said that in an editorial in *America* commenting on the National Book Award it was said that either Robert Penn Warren or I would have been better people to get it. That may mean Fr. Gardiner read my book. I had it sent to him.

The enclosed will interest you. I'd like it back as I often have to refer to it to get my own bearings.

I hope you have heard that Mrs. Daniel is better.

Father McCown initially tried to enlist O'Connor "to do some polemical writing to defend Holy Church against her enemies" and sent her pious novels.[7] *She reacts (May 9, 1956) with judicious comments.*

However, after taking as much as I could stand of *Affair of the Heart* [Margaret Long], I decided that since I might get a chance to meet her, it would be better not to have read her books—as I wouldn't possibly be able to say I like them . . .

I think a person who didn't know anything about fiction could read it and enjoy it. It's all done with dialogue and the dialogue could have been tape-recorded from Macon or Atlanta. She has an awfully good ear but absolutely no discrimination in using it. *Affair of the Heart* is just propaganda and its being propaganda for the side of the angels only makes it worse. The novel is an art form and when you use it for anything other than art you pervert it. I didn't make this up. I got it from St. Thomas (via Maritain) who allows that art is wholly concerned with the good of that which is made; it has no utilitarian end. If you do manage to use it successfully for social, religious, or other purposes, it is because you make it art first. She doesn't.

The Griffin novel [John Howard, *The Devil Rides Outside*] is not as good as I thought it was going to be but very interesting and more convincing than the last—which may be because it's about savages and you have to take his word for it . . . [8]

O'Connor recurrently suggests parallels for her Jesuit friend from fiction and in this letter (May 20, 1956) likens him to a character in a novel by a British novelist.

It was good to see you turn up with that crowd from Macon. It reminded me slightly of one of those early books of Waugh's that has Fr. Rothschild, S. J. in it [*Vile Bodies*]. He is always appearing in unlikely company, usually in disguise, and if I remember correctly, usually on a motorcycle.[9]

O'Connor complains about an editor's unauthorized changes in an article she wrote. She also plans to lecture at Notre Dame University. Her lecture established a lasting interest in her on campus. For example, in the fall 2003 Litera-

ture Series, "A Reason to Write: Two Catholic Novelists: Flannery O'Connor and Walker Percy," scholars and students discussed the works of both. Ecumenical in nature, the conference featured a non-Catholic lecturer on O'Connor who commanded the audience's attention by beginning, "I thank God for Notre Dame because it always gives me something to protest against." After the lecture, O'Connor might have enjoyed the lively discussions that extended into the night at the Morris Inn. A few libations were shared.

MILLEDGEVILLE

30 MARCH 57

I am certainly much obliged to you for sending me the copies of *America*. We enjoyed the priest who brought them but we didn't manage to catch his name. He and my mother had a lively discussion on the relative merits of retreats. He was in favor of retreats. She was not.

I was disappointed in the piece in *America* ["The Church and the Fiction Writer"]. He [the editor] changed entirely the paragraph about the responsibility of the artist, so that it sounded to me contradictory. Now I have no objection to being corrected and made orthodox on these matters, but I think I should have been allowed to correct it myself, in my words, inasmuch as my name had to be on it. If in one paragraph you say the writer is free, and in the next say the responsibility for souls will turn him to stone, and in the next say he has it anyway, and in the next say it doesn't matter, it seems to me you are only muddying an already muddy situation. If the writer has this responsibility then it ought to be defined—is it to fifteen year old-years girls? is it to the ignorant reader? is it to children? is it the same, in kind, as the responsibility of the Church? If you know anybody that answers such questions, please put me onto him.

I have had two letters from your friend Mr. Watts. The last enclosed. I don't know what idea he has got in his head about the Mercer professors but I wouldn't want him to think that I didn't appreciate their visit or admire their intelligence. Anyway I liked his letter to the paper and you were right to make him chop off that last sentence—all the Baptists in Georgia would think that the Pope was about to take over the legislature.

I am going to talk at Notre Dame on the 15th of April so I'll be able to report first hand on Cathlick eddication pretty soon.

Come to see us when you can and thanks again for the books.

O'Connor mentions "Billy," William A. Sessions (1928–2016), an enduring friend of both Father McCown and her. An entertaining scholar and story-teller, he had his own distinguished academic career as recounted by an acquaintance:

> I knew Bill only in my guise as a beginning Renaissance-lit scholar who admired his work and was, in turn, encouraged by him in my own studies . . . Alas, I only saw him at conferences and once when he invited me to his home to meet with him and the circle of Tudor-era historians and literary scholars he knew . . . I remember listening to him one evening spend a great amount of time with a historian debating some of the more arcane significations of English heraldry. The topic was essential to his account of the poet, the Earl of Surrey's death in his well-known and well-received biography of Henry Howard [*Henry Howard, the Poet Earl of Surrey: A Life*]. He had a deep knowledge of Tudor culture, so it always surprised me when I found out how much he knew about 20th-century American literature as well. I envied him his broad knowledge![10]

MILLEDGEVILLE, GEORGIA

8 MAY 57

We're sorry you can't come to dinner but if you can get over in the afternoon, I know Mary Harty would like to meet one of William's friends (That sentence don't parse.)

No, don't quote me to Fr. Gardiner [Harold, editor of *America*] because I have forgotten what I said and also because I should write him myself. The thing don't seem so bad to me now but I still feel that no self-respecting magazine should make changes without asking the writer himself to do it. They printed one letter (April 20?) which I thought entirely beside the point. Some Jesuit wanted to know what you could read to preserve your innocence. Answer: the telephone book. He also seemed to object to Original Sin.

The only one of those books that I need back is Baron [Friedrich] von Hugel's *Letters to His Niece*. You can send it by Billy [William Sessions].

I appreciated your brother's [Robert McCown, S.J.] kind comment on the article. I hope you rake up a good crowd from Mercer for Fr. Tavard.

MILLEDGEVILLE

14 MAY 57

We killed off the bottle you sent in short order and were all very much obliged to you. Fr. Tavard negotiated the opening of it and got it all over himself as my mother had shaken it vigorously before bringing it in—she handles liquor as if it were milk of magnesia, or as if it would be better if it were.

After the 20th we will be home and certainly will be glad to have you and Mrs. Daniell over for lunch. On the 20th we are going to Savannah to spend the day but after the 20th will be here. Let me know when you'll come.

That was an elaborate dirty trick played on Fr. Tavard, getting him to go to Dublin to take the place of what he thought was a dead priest. They came back by here Sunday and gave us an account of it which was very funny. We certainly liked Fr. Tavard.

We'll expect to see you and Mrs. D.

O'Connor likens her Jesuit friend to a priest in a novel by a British author. She also declines to visit Koinonia Farm, founded in 1942 in Sumter County, Georgia. Like the utopian communities of New England established in the nineteenth century, such as Brook Farm formed by Transcendentalists, Koinonia envisioned "transcending" the segregation of Georgia in the establishment of an integrated, ecumenical community. Koinonia's radical sociology during the civil rights era led to conflicts. Dorothy Day, cofoundress of the Catholic Worker Movement, visited the farm and narrowly escaped violent conflict.

MILLEDGEVILLE

GEORGIA

22 MAY 57

I think you will soon be known as The Whiskey Priest [Graham Greene, *The Power and the Glory*]; the Christian Brothers should put you on the payroll, not just send you a case of brandy. That is the funniest controversy I have seen in years. Send Brother Matthews a bottle when the case comes.

I'm mighty sorry to have missed the Daniells but I'll hope maybe they will come again.

Thanks for the invitation to Koinonia with you and the Gossetts but I won't be able to make it. I will not be found under the potecoshay [porte-cochère, a covered porch at the entrance of a building]. I wish you and the Gossetts would drive down some afternoon.

FLANNERY O'CONNOR TO THOMAS GOSSETT

O'Connor mentions (November 24, 1957) the Irish representative to the United Nations. O'Connor's skepticism of literary categories continues. She also refers to one of the "Twelve Southerners" of I'll Take My Stand *(1930).*

O'Connor maintained distance from the Vanderbilt professor perhaps because of his right-wing politics. Other Southern Agrarians—Andrew Lytle, Robert Penn Warren, Allen Tate, and John Crowe Ransom—were vital, however, in either teaching O'Connor or publishing her stories in journals they edited.

We certainly would like you to come over and bring Mrs. MacEntee [Maire]. She sounds powerful formidable with all them degrees and what not but we'll look forward to the visit. I have been meaning to write and ask you and Louise to come over some afternoon. I hear you are teaching something called southern Literature. What is that? . . .

I hope Donald Davidson [professor, Vanderbilt] didn't cure them of having Southern lecturers. At least they started at the extreme. How far to the right can you get? etc.[11]

FATHER JAMES McCOWN TO GERALD KELLY, S.J.

Hosting an ecumenical reading group, O'Connor seeks a dispensation in order to read a Nobel Prize winner listed on the "Index" in 1952. Centuries earlier, in 1542, the Catholic Church established the Index Librorum Prohibitorum *to prohibit the faithful from reading works of Protestant Reformers and others. The* Index *grew to a list of works the Church considered dangerous to faith and morals. Father McCown consults his professor from seminary. He (identified as "my old teacher") appends a possible way to accommodate O'Connor's request.*

> TO GERALD KELLY, S.J.
> [BEST AMERICAN CATH. MORALIST
> MY OLD TEACHER]
> JANUARY 13 [1958]

Greetings from the sunny south! I am writing to ask your opinion on something. First, let me quote a paragraph from a letter from Flannery O'Connor, O'Henry Award winner for the best American short story for 1956, a devout Catholic, tremendous knowledge of

Catholic thought (all gotten on her own from extensive reading), and dear friend. Quoting:

> Two or three things have come up on which I need some expert SOS spiritual advice. Not long ago the local Episcopal minister came out and wanted me to get up a group with him of people who were interested in talking about theology in modern literature. This suited me all right so about six or seven of them are coming out here every Monday night—a couple of Presbyterians, the rest Episcopalians of one stripe or another (scratch an Episcopalian and you're liable to find most anything) and me as the only representative of the Holy Roman Catholic & Apostolic Church. The strain is telling on me. Anyway this minister is equipped with a list of what he would like us to read and upon the list is naturally, Gide, also listed on the Index. I despise Gide but if they read him I want to be able to put in my two cents worth. I don't think there is any use to ask the local reverend father for permission. Some women in the parish, college graduates & pillars of the church, asked if they could read some Jehovah Witness pamphlets. They wanted to see what the Witnesses believed. He told them flatly no. He is a letter of the law man, no ifs, ands or buts, and very hard to approach anyway. You said once you would see if you had the faculties to give me permission to read such as this. Do you and will you? All these Protestants will be shocked if I say I can't get permission to read Gide . . .

Now, I have read Aregui, Jone, and Davis. All three seem to have been copied from the same original, no "ands, ifs, or buts" about it. They quote the canon and that's about all. Now the trouble is that the bishop of Atlanta (in whose diocese Miss O'Connor resides) has a well-known case of scruples, and I am as sure as I am sitting here, that he would never give such a permission, even for this kind of case. The gal in question has read more fathers of the church, and more St. Thomas than His Excellency ever saw. Now, does any moralist or recent ruling allow me, her spiritual father, to allow her to read Gide? Can I allow the Catholic students of the local state College to read assigned books that happen to be on the Index, or do I have to have toties quoties [Latin term meaning "repeatedly" or "as often as necessary"] recourse to the bishop? I might say in passing that I agonize over the whole Index anyway. I am sure it is the obstacle keeping countless intellectuals a million miles away from the Church. They laugh at us because of it. I am now where this letterhead indicates. A lovely place and a most comfortable house. Why not come down here for your annual retreat? I'll take you fishing. Sure hope your health has improved. I was much saddened to learn of your heart attack.

God bless you.

Mac

[J. H. McCown, S.J.]

Dear Mac [Father McCown]: P.C.

You're not the only one who doesn't like the Index. But you have no faculties to give permission to read forbidden books. However, there's a principle that even this law ceases to bind when the keeping of it would result in harm to the Cath. faith. If what the lady says in her last sentence is true, then it looks as if she could apply this principle to the reading of Gide.

God bless you,

CAROLINE GORDON TO FLANNERY O'CONNOR

Caroline Gordon copyedited "The Enduring Chill." She notes its originality; with revisions, it can surpass stories of canonical authors such as Hemingway. Gordon prophetically continues to locate her student in the mainstream of modernist fiction. O'Connor's A Prayer Journal *reinforces Gordon's insight. O'Connor observes that "if I ever do get to be a fine writer" it will be "because God has given me credit for a few of the things He kindly wrote for me."*[12] *Gordon also links grammar and colloquial language to theological revelation.*

COMMENT AND ANALYSIS 3RD REVISION, 1-26-58.

What facility you have! I'm amazed at the way you've taken my suggestion and built it up into a convincing scene. I think that bringing people of this kind into the action does a lot for the story structurally. Association with people who are not like the people at home helps to explain his horror of dying at home.

The priest seems fine, too—a splendid contrast for Fr. Finn, just what Fr. Finn needed to bring him out in all his full bloom!

And now I come up with another admonishment, being, as you know, never satisfied. This is, really, a comment on your prose style in general but I will try to show what I mean by using some sentences from this story as examples.

I suppose that in common with everybody of your generation, you were brought up to feel that any concern you might have with grammar took place long ago and is now no concern of yours. But I think reflection on the parts of speech and their function is helpful for any of us at any time.

Do you, for instances, ever reflect on the respective nature of the "loose" and the "periodic" sentences and the differences in their functions?

In a strong prose style the periodic sentence—the sentence which saves its punch for the end—predominates. There is a psychological basis for this. You put the thing you want the reader to remember last . . .

"While Goetz had listened enthralled . . . strictly reserved interest" is a "loose" sentence—it trails off. The important thing, the fact that Asbury's gaze had rested on a priest, is buried in the middle of the sentence. The reader's the laziest and stupidest of God's creatures, is not going to dig it out but will carry a blurred impression away from the reading. If I were writing this sentence I'd automatically end it on the word "priest."

You make this mistake several times in the story, and make another mistake which is allied to it. Anything that is important ought to have a sentence all to itself. Asbury's approaching death is the most important thing in this story: You introduce it in a subordinate clause. It ought to have a sentence all to itself . . .

Ernest Hemingway has won a good deal of fame and fortune by a complete mastery of the principle I have been setting forth. His style is founded on it. He cannot write the long complicated sentence which is the glory of Joyce's style, but he never has two ideas fighting each other in one sentence. The structure of his style is relatively simple. When he needs a complicated sentence he forms it by joining two of his short periodic sentences together. It works—for him. He doesn't tackle any very complicated or elevated theme. His style is suited to his subject matter.

I suspect that you are unconsciously following his example of late. You have got to the point where the flatfooted simple sentence won't always serve. Instead of writing another kind of sentence you take several of your flatfooted sentences and link them up. You do that quite often in this story.

But you are after bigger game than Ernest, the biggest game there is in this particular story. There ought, in this story, to be some sentences, indeed, passages, which show forth the grandeur of your theme and the height of your aspirations. The structure of your story ought to be antiphonal. We ought to have throughout a contrast between Asbury's present situation and his imminent fate—a fate which is pretty grand, for all his horror of it. To have the H[oly] G[host] descend upon you in any form makes a hero of you. Asbury is just a boy from Georgia, but he is made in the image of God and will shortly confront eternity. If the HG is to descend upon him—in whatever form—in the end that fact ought to be foreshadowed in the beginning. We will sympathize with his sufferings more keenly if his heroism is foreshadowed from the start.

In the first version, as I recall, you foreshadowed the fact that his spirit had a wider horizon than his mother's or his sister's by one grudging sentence about a red sun. One sentence! You can't turn around on a dime. One sentence like that won't create the effect that is needed here. You have improved the story enormously in your revisions. Enormously.

What I have to say further is about your style in general. This takes me back to first principles—principles which I can name outright to you but which I have to approach cautiously with my secular pupils. There is only one plot, The Scheme of Redemption. All other plots, if they are any good, are splinters off this basic plot. There is only one author: The HG. If He condescends to speak at times through a well-constructed detective story, which I think he does, he certainly will condescend to speak often through FO'C. Your chief weakness as a writer seems to be a failure to admit the august nature of your inspiration. You speak almost always like FO'C. That is fine. You have the best ear of anybody in the trade for the rhythms of colloquial speech. In this particular story what the negroes say in their last conversation with Asbury is exquisitely rendered. I don't know anybody else who could have brought that off. Red Warren [Penn Warren] couldn't. Andrew Lytle [teacher, novelist, and editor of *The Sewanee Review*] couldn't. Their ears are not delicately enough attuned and they are always forcing things, too. But you have this enormous advantage: of what Yeats called the primitive ear. He had it, too and got a lot out of it.

But you have another kind of ear, one that is attuned to—shall we say the music of the spheres? It is attuned to that music or you would not choose the subjects you choose. The nature of your subject—its immensity, its infinity ought to be reflected in your style—antiphonally. Asbury, conversing with his mother, his sister, the negro hands, ought to speak down to earth, flat sentences. But he ought to take a more elevated tone when communing with his soul—in which presumably God may dwell. If he did you would have a wonderful contrast in tones—an antiphonal effect—which would reinforce our dramatic effects.

Muir [Edwin], who is himself a considerable stylist, gives an illustration of what I am trying to say in his translation of Kafka's "Hunter Gracchus." The action of the story is recounted in flat down to earth narrative. The denouement is, however, foreshadowed in the first paragraph which is like a painting by a primitive painter . . . a window seems to open into the blue distance of infinity. The heroism of which the human soul is capable is implied by the fact that a hero is flourishing a sword on high on a monument—still flourishing it even if a man uses the monument only to rest in its shadow while he reads a newspaper. Everything is kept keyed down to the concrete till the last sentence which carries the notion of infinity in its very cadence: "My ship has no rudder, and is driven by the wind that blows in the undermost regions of death."

Every time I read your last sentence in your story I balk. I balk on the phrase "with ice, instead of fire." It is vague, inexact. This magnificent climax to which you have built up so well is not the place for careless inexact phrasing. You cannot say that the HG is coming with ice instead of fire. The phrase is colloquial. If I am having a party and don't have enough ice cubes I can say properly "The Johnsons are coming, with ice" but you are talking about the HG and your diction and the construction of your sentences ought to reflect, as far as is humanly possible, the enormity of his presence. Couldn't you say, "enveloped in ice instead of flames"? And couldn't you give Asbury and the HG each a sentence to himself? "He blanched in recognition. But HG, enveloped in ice instead of fire, continued, implacable, to descend." . . .

In my day we diagrammed sentences. This is what we call a compound sentence: a sentence made up of two or more equal and coordinate clauses. The sun rose with power and the fog dispersed is what Nesfield gives as an example of a compound sentence. I don't think that a compound sentence is what you need here. Asbury's blanching and the HG's descending are not ideas of equal importance. Asbury's blanching in recognition of the presence is our chief concern in this story but the descent of the HG is what Balzac called the "consta-tion," the summing up, the appeal from the particular to the general. Each ought to have a sentence to itself.

If you were less stout-hearted and less talented I wouldn't dare to say the things I am saying to you but I expect you to do not only bet-ter than any of your compeers but better than has been done hereto-fore. In this martial spirit I shall comment on your last paragraph even further . . .

Have you ever read a story of mine about Andre Gide called "Em-manuelle! Emmanuelle!"? In the climax of this story a young man looks into eyes that are, in turn, contemplating an eternity of tor-ment. The action of the whole story is sunk in those eyes.

Anyhow, suppose you made his eyes mirrors of infinity or about to become mirrors of infinity. He shudders, naturally, and rather than contemplate his own soul, looks out of the window. What does he see? You don't feel like putting your extraordi-nary imagination to work on this passage so you write—carelessly and inexactly— ". . . over the treeline." An awkward phrase to begin with. If you are going to use those trees give them a chance. Really put them in there. The trees that lined the whatever it was or surrounded the so and so were so and so. The sun that heralds the descent of the HG ought to have a sentence to itself. The next sentence, which ought to be one of the strongest, is weak and poorly constructed. "Like some magnificent herald" and "as if it were preparing for the descent of an unspeakable presence" are really repetitious of the same idea. Similes are dangerous, any-how. It is usually better to show how something looked and then say that it was like something else rather than try to convey the notion of what it is by telling us what it is like. You ought to make us really see this sun and in order to do that you've got to create it. I'd leave out the word "aghast." The fact that the boy fell back on his pillow and stared at the ceiling conveys the fact that he was aghast.

I think that you are going to have to elevate the tone a little here. You keep on being flatfooted till the end, but it won't do. The tone should be gradually rising all the way to the denouement.

Here I can only say what I'd do or try to do in this case. I think that after he falls back on his pillow and stares at the ceiling that I'd have a passage about his body, a passage which would do two things at once, prepare for the enduring chill and also engage the reader's sympathies by reminding him that this is the frail body of a young doomed creature. Oh, something like "His limbs, which in the past weeks had been racked alternately by fever and by chill now seemed to have no feeling in them. It was then that he felt . . ." Oh hell, it would take me days, perhaps weeks to do it. I see that going the way I'm going I'd get into "chill" too fast. What I'm saying so poorly is that this passage must be elevated in tone, but so gradually that the reader doesn't know what's happening. You can't go straight into the Presence talking Georgia. There must be a moment in which Asbury—being a hero—must stand for all mankind, as Liharev does in Chekhov's "On the Road," as Gabriel Conroy does in "The Dead." Words, indeed, phrases, consonant with the hero's high calling must be used in your denouement . . .

Your concluding passage ought to reflect Asbury's status as a hero by a gradual elevation of the style. This can be done partly by identifying Asbury with all mankind, partly by using words that may not even be in his vocabulary, words and phrases such as a really omniscient and hence all-compassionate observer might use. And I come up with another objection: the phrase "The fierce bird with the icicle in its beak" worries me the same way "with ice instead of fire" worries me. If I were doing it I'd say something like "The fierce bird that during the long nights had seemed to his feverish fancy to hold an icicle in its beak now appeared to be in motion."

That's corny. I'd have to revise it a dozen times, but still I'd start out working in that direction. The bird, with an icicle in its beak, is an awkward construction. Do get rid of it.

FLANNERY O'CONNOR TO
FATHER JAMES McCOWN

Through Father McCown's efforts, O'Connor is becoming more well known among Catholic institutions. An effort to categorize her elicits a typical demurral.

MILLEDGEVILLE

20 JANUARY 58

I don't actually know that cousin well enough to write him and tell him to go to see you but you might run into him some time by accident as he doctors at that hospital there. I think the name of it is Confederate Memorial.

They sent me one of the Anderson lecture reprints and I thought it was fine. Also, I'm pleased to announce that I got a letter from one John J. Quinn, S.J., of Scranton University, saying he admired my works and wanted me to judge a short story contest that he is in charge of at his school. The which I will do. I also had a letter from a Rev. Gerard Nolen from a St. Norbert's College in Wisconsin. This one said that the promise of my work reminded him of the prediction in Whitman's poem "Old Ireland." Never heard of the poem so I looked it up. It was a long rigamarole about how old Mother Ireland, wo' out and bedraggled, had laid down her harp. BUT it would be picked up again in America. I guess the point was I am Old Mother Irelands descendent, picking at the old girl's harp in America. I consider this a doubtful compliment but I thanked him for it.

"A View of the Woods" is not the O'Henry thing. That one was Greenleaf. I have just answered 15 questions on writing for *The Motley.*

FLANNERY O'CONNOR TO THOMAS GOSSETT

O'Connor praises and quotes from a poem by her friend. O'Connor also enumerates interesting people who had visited or were planning to call on her.

MILLEDGEVILLE

23 JANUARY 58

Louise has obviously missed her calling and is wasting her time at Mercer [University]; she had better set up as a poet at once. I won't mind the competition as long as it's poetry she writes but if she ever sets her hand to stories, I'll shake in my shoes.

We enjoyed Miss McEntee [Maire] no end and having supper with you all. We met her the next day at the bus and gave her a copy of my book and if we have a day or two in Dublin, I'll call her up.

By all means bring Miss Katherine Anne [Porter] over if Miss Katherine Anne chooses to come. I'd love to meet her.

My mother is very happy today as she has three jack-leg carpenters at hand and is supervising the construction of a carport in the back yard. I think the peachickens are going to enjoy sitting both over and under it.

Regards from another "marble in the mud."[13]

FLANNERY O'CONNOR TO
FATHER JAMES H. McCOWN

Aware of Father McCown's interest in civil rights, O'Connor shares with him discussions of a reading group. She also shares with him theological inconsistencies of a friend's letter.

[FEBRUARY 1958]

MILLEDGEVILLE

GROUND HOG DAY

Well I am certainly much obliged to you for asking that foremost theologian about my Monday night clashes with the Index. They seem to have forgotten about Gide for the present and I am keeping their attention directed to 35¢ editions. Ostensibly this group is discussing theology in modern literature but none of us knows anything about theology, not excluding the Episky minister. Last week they started talking about a Presbyterian preacher that had talked at the college for Religious Emphasis Week (big thing with them). This preacher was talking about why Catholics had made more progress with race relations etc than Protestants and he said the reason was because the Protestant emphasis in the church was on family and the Catholic on community. I thought this was pretty good as far as it went.

As for yr. spiritual advice, I will follow it to the letter. And it relieves my mind of a burden that was keeping me off and on from doing my work. When you can't resolve these things it is a great relief to be told what to do.

I have got several postcards from Billy [William Sessions] from Spain. He is supposed to be studying philosophy but that I can see he isn't doing anything but travelling, from which I guess he will get more in the long run.

I still ain't looking forward to my visits to the shrines. I will send you a post card from the Baloney Castle or whatever it is we are going to be forced to view in Ireland. My lapsed Catholic friend in Missouri wrote me about *The Stumbling Block*. I think it affected her however she said that a lie within the truth was still a lie. I mean to tell her that Mauriac sees that too, but that what he means is that the direction of the Church is not changed. She allowed that her trouble was that she couldn't believe in the divinity of Christ. In the same paragraph she announced that she believed in Lourdes. I am not going to tell her that that don't make sense. I have been invited to the University of Missouri in May so I expect to meet this girl.

FLANNERY O'CONNOR TO SALLY AND ROBERT FITZGERALD

O'Connor's friends were living in Italy, and she hoped to meet them while she was on a pilgrimage to Lourdes, France.

MILLEDGEVILLE

9 MARCH 58

These travel people say that they can arrange it for us to fly to Milan but before I turn over Cousin Katie's money to them I want to find out definitely if this is going to be allright with you—to meet us in Milan on I think the 23rd and for us to spend about six days with you. You may have sick children or you may not have the room or you may not be able to meet us. Any and all of which we can perfectly understand. I don't even know how far Milan is from you. And we can easily change the plans and meet this tour in Paris please feel free to be frank about this. If we do come to Levanto we thought you might go with us on the train to Genoa or Florence or somewhere. I would like to see St. Catherine myself. There will be an extra day at Lourdes and I thought if you went with us we might arrange to get to Vincinnes to see that Matisse chapel. I wish I had the proper pious attitude to Lourdes but it has not been cooked up yet. A letter from Billy [William Sessions] declares he wants to meet us in Lourdes too. He would be the ideal one to write up the place for the Msgr. After they leave Lourdes they seem to fly through Spain to get to Rome but it don't look like to me they are going to do more than look out the plane door there. I see what an old sister I am. I am spending most of my time thinking how glad I will be to get back home again.

I may hear from you when I put this letter in the mail so if you have already answered it you can ignore it.

Cheers,

TUESDAY

We have the tickets and other paraphernalia in hand. The hotel in London is the Park Lane in case you fetch upon calamity and have to head us off. Otherwise we will be in Milan at 12:10 PM on Thursday the 24th.

There are only going to be twelve pilgrims. We have the list—2 Clancys, 2 Brennans, 2 O'Connors, mostly they look like retired school teachers or retired lawyers, from the list that is. My uncle who is a dentist in Savannah has made the Msgr. an extra set of teeth for the trip. My mother informs me that they arrest you if you have more money when you go out than you declared when you went in.

Tell Billy [William Sessions] his old friend Mildred English was just up from West Georgia where she heard of his meanderings.

The only thing we don't have is the ticket they are supposed to give us saying we are to be met in Paris. I had to call the travel-woman up over the long distance to tell her it wasn't in with the packet. So she says she will send it by the Msgr. as she don't think it will come in time to send to me. I am sure he will have enough to do to keep up with his extra set of teeth, so I don't expect to get it.

Cheers & we hope to see you,

FATHER JAMES McCOWN TO THOMAS F. GOSSETT

Although Father McCown cannot meet Katherine Anne Porter, he had read her story, a classic anti-Communist critique of Latin American Marxism. Abandoning her midwestern bourgeois roots, "Laura" journeys to Mexico to teach school and associate with Mexican revolutionaries. The chauvinism and unwanted advances of an older revolutionary leads to Laura's disenchantment with Marxism. Father McCown's familiarity with Porter's story perhaps contributed to his anti-Communism in the late 1950s. After O'Connor's death he would, as later letters reveal, alter his political views considerably by advocating the impeachment of President Reagan because of his policies in Central America.

PASS CHRISTIAN, MISS.

MARCH 20, 1958

And it was with something like nostalgia that I read your good letter proposing among other things a trip to Flannery's . . . I am very sorry that I have to decline such an appealing invitation. At the time proposed I have to be on hand to conduct a retreat. No other arrangement was possible under the circumstances. I certainly would like to meet Katherine Anne Porter. Quite coincidentally I have just read her "Flowering Judas." She certainly is a vivid writer, with lots of compassion in her makeup. I sure would like to know something about the background of one who could write that story. And it is her earliest listed work too! Your whole program looks most appetizing.

Flannery certainly is getting excited over her trip to Lourdes. I hear from her regularly, though not frequently, and her letters are full of the trip. I'd sure love to get her recorded reactions. Even her reactions in prospect are rich enough. You know what would be fun? For you and Louise and Flannery to come down and visit me. My mother would love to have you as her houseguests in Mobile, and a trip down the coast here would be most interesting. The best part, I think, would be visiting the fishing villages and fishing docks near here. Also of interest would be the wonderful variety of seagulls that are hereabouts. No, Flannery's calumny is only partially true. There's lots else.

My work is demanding, interesting, and irregular. Right now my doctor tells me to take it easy for a week or so. So I am lounging around like a retired WPA worker. Give Louise my best. I sure miss you both, and, of course, have intended writing you since I left Macon.

God bless you,
Fr. McCown

KATHERINE ANNE PORTER TO
FLANNERY O'CONNOR

A coreligionist of O'Connor's, Porter alludes to the tragedy of Good Friday evident in the appearance of Easter lilies. The observation better illuminates the title of Porter's story "Flowering Judas." The title specifically evokes the brief triumph of betrayal on that terrible day.

ROXBURY ROAD, SOUTHBURY CONNECTICUT
6TH APRIL EASTER SUNDAY, 1958

Dear Flannery: I'll never forget you standing there in the new spring landscape watching your peacocks coming towards you in their kind of waving, floating amble,—such a smiling <u>pleased</u> look in your eyes, it did me good to see it.

It was a long trip home, stopping by way of New York to go to Martha Graham's new show, and then to a party for her afterward. There I saw Eudora Welty, and told her I had seen you on your very own territory and how delightful it had been: and then we talked about you, your writing, a subject we enjoyed agreeing upon—we think you're a marvel, as do a great many others.

I hope this reaches you before you set off for that European journey, for I want to tell you how glad I was to see you, and how I should like to see you again; I wish you <u>might</u> come to see me sometime, even if not now—later maybe!

My Easter lilies shed tears on Good Friday, just as they are supposed to. But alas, I got up early to see the sun dance, on rising, and he never showed up! It is a dull dark rainy wintry day, no Easter at all, but this is my favorite feast day, just the same, and I wish to send you my recollection and good wishes to celebrate it and to thank you and your mother again for such a pleasant time.

FLANNERY O'CONNOR TO THOMAS GOSSETT

O'Connor makes fun of the pilgrimage to Lourdes. She also mentions photographs of Katherine Anne Porter's visit, including her admiration of the peacocks.

MILLEDGEVILLE

16 APRIL 58

Can't you all come over Sunday afternoon and pay us a visit? If no calamity presents itself we are leaving Monday for our Morons Abroad Excursion. The week after the luncheon with Miss Porter and you all my mother spent in the hospital—the result of having hit herself on the edge of the kitchen sink so that she bruised her kidney. This left me unmotorized for a week and we didn't get the slides off as soon as we expected; however the man assures us he will have them by Saturday, and I can put them in your hand.

I am thinking about filling up my leather travel diary before I go and leaving it at home, as I am supposed to be a creative writer. This strikes me as strictly sensible but I haven't mentioned it to my mother as I don't think she will think it is moral.

Cheers and we'll hope to see you Sunday.

FLANNERY O'CONNOR TO
FATHER JAMES McCOWN

The pilgrimage takes on an apostolic dimension with the archbishop Gerald P. O'Hara (Diocese of Savannah), meeting O'Connor and her mother at Lourdes and facilitating a later general audience with the pope at the Vatican. O'Connor was "personally greeted and blessed by Pius XII."[14]

11 MAY 58

I am certainly much obliged to you for your prayers for my mother. The Clines must have got an exaggerated report though. She didn't have any operation. She hit her side on the kitchen sink and bruised her kidney and had to be in the hospital a week but apparently she is all right, but please continue to pray for her for a blow there could cause permanent damage, though they don't think it has. This happened three weeks before we were to go to Europe but the Doctor said she was allright to go so we went and we just got home last Friday. The upshot of my trip to Europe is that my capacity for staying at home has been greatly increased. I picked up the first germ I met on the other side and was sick almost the whole time. Lourdes is a beautiful little village completely defaced by religious junk shops. I took the bath, from a conglomeration of bad motives. I doubt if anybody prays in that water. People say the miracle is that no epidemics are caused. Everybody washes in the same trough. If the one before you has running sores, you get right in after him, wearing the sack he took off. Also they pass around the cup and everybody drinks out of it. I feel sure I left as many germs as I took away however and doubtless this experience was good for my soul, though no pious feeling went with it. All I wanted was to get out of Lourdes as soon as possible. The crowds there were enormous and mostly peasants.

The arch-Bishop (O'Hara) met us at Lourdes and again at Rome and arranged for us to be in the first seats at the general audience, after which the Pope came down and we all shook his hand and kissed his ring. The Pope seemed alive to me in a way nobody else I have ever seen has. I suppose this was holiness—a kind of super-aliveness that I have not beheld before. It was worth the trip to see this. The old man fairly springs when he walks. He runs up and down the stairs to his throne.

Billy [William Sessions] met us in Lourdes and was as per usual. No change in him.

I am very glad your brother [Robert McCown, S.J.] likes those stories. The thing in the *Commonweal* was distressing mostly because it occurred there.[15] However, this is nothing I'm not used to. Incidentally, when we were in Paris, at the airport, Regina saw a priest that she began to stare at. "Doesn't Fr. McCown have a brother?" she says. "That priest looks exactly like him." The priest looked to me about sixty years old and I tried to convince her it couldn't be your brother but she was sure it was—he was a kind of glum character in a beret but there was a certain likeness or would have been if he had looked more cheerful. She was determined this was your brother and said "Fr. McCown" in a loud voice, but he didn't bat an eye so she was finally convinced. Anyway, you have a dour aged double in a beret in Europe if you are interested.

FLANNERY O'CONNOR TO FATHER SCOTT WATSON

O'Connor links writing to prayer and beseeches intercessions as she struggles to finish The Violent Bear It Away. *While she introduces Jesuits to the literary realism of her fiction, she also beseeches intercessions from them as a believer.*

13 MAY 58

Thank you so much for your prayers for my mother. She was in the hospital a week but no operation was necessary and she is apparently fine now. We have in fact just got back from a pilgrimage to Lourdes, which was very exhausting and from which it will probably take me some time to recuperate. Pilgrimages are mighty distracting and I think my prayers are better said at home.

Please continue to pray for my mother and for me. I am at that stage in my novel when I can't do much for myself and where some outside wisdom will have to visit me to pull it through.

FLANNERY O'CONNOR TO KATHERINE ANNE PORTER

Porter led a peripatetic, bohemian life and was married several times. Realizing her friend could benefit from a pilgrimage to a shrine, O'Connor emphasizes the healing qualities of Lourdes.

MILLEDGEVILLE

GEORGIA

23 MAY 58

I had hoped to write you an I-am-here note from Lourdes but most of what I intended to do, I didn't. I hope you'll visit there sometime. While the village is hideously pockmarked with religious junk shops, the grotto is alive with something else entirely. The conjunction of faith and affliction speaks very well for faith. No one who isn't in the position of Job avoids glibness on the subject.

Actually, this is to tell you how much we enjoyed your visit.

The Gossetts were over yesterday and told us you had finished your novel. Ah Lord, what a feeling that must be! I am very glad and will be gladder to read it when it is out.

The enclosed is from the head peacock with his regards. He remembers anyone who looks at him with the proper appreciation. Not long ago there was a cow-trading man here who watched him strut for some time. When the performance was over, he said, "Don't that rascal have long ugly legs? I bet he could outrun a Greyhound bus." The bird bore it very well.

KATHERINE ANNE PORTER TO
FLANNERY O'CONNOR

The reference to the peacock parallels a similar response by the priest to the bird's sacramental presence in "The Displaced Person." Porter affirms O'Connor's description of Lourdes and the prospect of her own pilgrimage.

JUNE 5TH, 1958

Dear Flannery: Not often do I inflict my handwriting on any one, but I have a triple-copy page (and you know what that means) of *Ship of Fools* in my typewriter and almost my one working superstition is that it's <u>very</u> bad luck to take an unfinished page out of the machine. Well, of course [it] doesn't bring bad luck, it's just a misfortune in itself <u>not</u> to finish! Yes I am making final copy now and feel much better about almost everything.

Maybe the head peacock will be pleased to know I have his stately feather properly displayed between two thin sheets of glass—a really ornamental object that delights me. I send you thanks, and convey to him, please, in your mysterious language to them, my admiration.

I should love to go to Lourdes, and believe I may some day, even so soon as next year . . . I have hesitated a long time here, looking at your straight simple words about the "conjunction of faith and affliction" and there is something I want to say, but I know now I cannot—the right words are too deeply hidden; and yes, I am sure this means I should not speak, for the danger is glibness, as you say.

The heavenly summer is here at last, full of singing birds and blooming shrubbery. This time next year I'll still be in Virginia, and maybe you can come to visit me there!

FATHER SCOTT WATSON TO FLANNERY O'CONNOR

The letter written on the feast of the founder of the Jesuit order indicates, prophetically, that a story had reached a strategic audience. O'Connor's story is a cautionary tale for Jesuits in its revelation of secularizing trends in the order that O'Connor perceived in the late fifties. The narcissistic protagonist in the story is attracted to a Jesuit not because of his orthodoxy but because of his literary education and aesthetic sensibility. The source of orthodoxy in the story is an elderly diocesan priest who rebukes the protagonist for feckless literary pretensions.[16]

JULY 31, 1958

FEAST OF ST. IGNATIUS

Father McCown lent me his copy of "The Enduring Chill." I read it with the greatest interest, and these few words are simply to tell you how excellent I think the story is. I particularly liked its spiritual and psychological depth and its artistic unity. Father James Brodrick, S.J. one of our best known writers (he has restricted himself almost entirely to history and biography), happened to be here when I read your story, and so I took the liberty of lending it to him also. He liked particularly well, as l recall, your delineation of the one-eyed Jesuit; and while he found your story a bit gloomy (he was sick at the time, and looking for something in a lighter vein), he commented on its admirable style, which merely proves that he knows something good when he sees it.

Recently too I read your "A View of the Woods," in the *Partisan Review,* an extraordinarily gripping piece . . . For heaven's sake don't take the time out to answer this. Far better to devote time and energy to work on your new novel, which I trust and pray, is now progressing happily . . .

FLANNERY O'CONNOR TO FATHER SCOTT WATSON

O'Connor assigns progress on her novel to the Lourdes pilgrimage and interces-sions by the Jesuits. X-rays also showed her hip "to be unexpectedly improv-ing" and she could "walk around the house without crutches." She also passed a driving test. O'Connor acknowledges that "the Lourdes pilgrimage may be responsible."[17]

17 AUGUST 58

I must thank you for your note anyway because I appreciate it very much. I am almost too close to these stories to form any critical opinion of them so any criticism, favorable or unfavorable, is always appreciated.

My novel seems to have taken a turn for the better. We paid a visit to Lourdes this spring—my mother and I—and I prayed for my crea-tive bones rather than the other kind. The thing about Lourdes is that you are not inclined to pray there for yourself at all as you see so many people worse off. However, perhaps my prayers were answered to some extent.

Many thanks again for your interest and prayers.

FLANNERY O'CONNOR TO
FATHER JAMES H. McCOWN

O'Connor mentions William Sessions, who had been a Fulbright scholar at the University of Freiburg (1957–58), where he studied with Martin Heidegger. Sessions wrote O'Connor about consultations with him and other famous thinkers. I attended an academic conference many years later sponsored by Southern Denmark University where Sessions recounted his interactions that year.[18] *In seminar discussions, Sessions's sense of humor was evident. His first words to me were, "You mean you had to come this far to drink some Jack Dan-iel's?"*

O'Connor also departs from Caroline Gordon's praise of Dorothy Day.
Once a Marxist, Day retained a hostility to capitalism, corporations, and in-
come taxes. By contrast, O'Connor paid taxes and admired the business acu-
men of her beloved parents. O'Connor occasionally praised philanthropists such
as John D. Rockefeller, whose foundations provided financial support. On the
other hand, Day writes to C. J. Kelly, a "friendly critic," "If Mr. Rockefeller
offered us [Catholic Worker Movement] $100,000, indeed, we would not take
it. We would tell him to go and give it back to the miners in Colorado from
whom he stole it."[19]

MILLEDGEVILLE

I OCTOBER 58

Enclosed please find your French friend from Butler. Everybody
has been writing her up since she returned from her summer trip to
France.

Billy Sessions is back too and according to him he is about to lose
his mind. The descent from Freiburg [University in Germany] to
Carrollton [Georgia], from the great university to West Georgia College is such a severe shock to his nerves that he don't know if he'll
make it. But I don't reckon he will have to endure it long as it doesn't
look as if in another ten months there'll be any more school teachers
in Georgia. I shudder to think what's ahead.

I am disenchanted with the Catholic Worker myself. Some of
their pronouncements on the South are highly naieve [*sic*] and all the
pacifist stuff and income tax stuff is painful.

I certainly want to see your brother's article [Robert McCown,
S.J., "Flannery O'Connor and the Reality of Sin"] when it comes
out. These woods do not harbor any copies of *The Catholic World* but
if you will let me know when it appears, I will order off after one
through some of my city friends.

The local cleric treated us to a Pat-and-Mike last Sunday. These
fall as upon the dessert air but he is not deterred.

O'Connor mentions (November 15, 1958) that she is becoming better known in the larger academic community in Minnesota, perhaps because of the influence of Allen Tate and Caroline Gordon who taught at institutions there. O'Connor reveals continued interest in interfaith connections.

I am reading a book called THE ECLIPSE OF GOD by the Jewish theologian, Martin Buber. These boys have a lot to offer us. At your bookstore I hope you sell a book called HOLY PAGANS OF THE OLD TESTAMENT [Jean Daniélou]. Also you ought to read DOCTOR ZHIVAGO. I thought everybody was praising it just because Pasternak was a good Russian, but not so—it is a great book.[20]

FLANNERY O'CONNOR TO THOMAS GOSSETT[21]

O'Connor refers to her fellow Georgian Joel Chandler Harris, author of the Uncle Remus stories. She wishes Tom will be "as wily" as Brer Rabbit in rebuking unjust, shabby treatment from the academic community.

MILLEDGEVILLE

20 NOVEMBER 58

We have been reading about your dismissal in the paper and think you have been treated in a low-down fashion. I hope you tear up that briar patch before you are through with it.

We have missed seeing you and Louise [Gossett] his fall.

FLANNERY O'CONNOR TO
FATHER JAMES McCOWN

Dr. Gossett's academic "trial" is delayed. O'Connor is also amused about consumerist churchmanship as a sign of heterodoxy. With O'Connor's encouragement, Father McCown a few years later became friends with Walker Percy.

Father McCown may have shared O'Connor's misgivings with Percy who satirized consumerist religious practices in Lancelot *and* The Second Coming. *In the latter, Jack Curl, a trendy Episcopal priest who has jettisoned clericals for a jumpsuit, has reduced his vocation to entertainment and fund-raising. He is perplexed in a conversation with Will Barrett who asks him several times if he believes in God.*

20 DECEMBER 58

MILLEDGEVILLE

Tom Gossett was over here last night & he sure was pleased you called him up. Those jokers postponed his hearing until after Christmas so it is still hanging. He was telling me that _____, a now Methodist minister, is a lapsed Catholic. He says _____ says that when he left the Church at the age of 18, all the Catholics came after him with guns and knives. Too bad they missed, from all I hear of him.

Merry Christmas to you and your mother and brother. We wish they would send you to Atlanta to help out Fr. Jerrold. I hear they are going to have a drive-in retreat house. I reckon you honk and a Jesuit runs out and hears your confession. It's later than you think.

FLANNERY O'CONNOR TO FATHER JAMES McCOWN

O'Connor is saddened (December 23, 1958) about friends leaving the Church and encourages them. She mentions a successful academic conference.

In fact I seem to have nothing but friends who have left the Church. They have all left because they have been shocked by the intellectual dishonesty of some Catholic or other—or so they say, frequently of priests. It's only partly that but it does account for a good deal. I wish we would hear more preaching about the harm we do from the things we do not face and from all the questions that we give Instant Answers to. None of these poor children want Instant

Answers and they are right. Do you ever read that Fr. Murchland [Bernard] in the *Commonweal*? He is one of the best writers the Church has in America, besides Fr. Weigle [Gustave] . . .

I don't know what kind of conspiracy that was at Minnesota. Powers [J. F.] and I are, I suppose, the only two young writers in this country who are well thought of <u>and</u> connected with the Church. We both have the same kind of horns . . .[22]

FLANNERY O'CONNOR TO TOM GOSSETT

MILLEDGEVILLE

7 JANUARY 59

We just heard yesterday about your Reinstatement. I am trying to think of a Charlye Wigginish exclamatory remark but I am an old lady and don't have that kind of energy. We hope you'll be coming to see us and give us just the details.

Cheers,

FLANNERY O'CONNOR TO LOUISE GOSSETT

O'Connor describes the difficulties at a conference where she had substituted for the novelist Eudora Welty. She uses a vital term that reveals her perspective on conventional American history, noting she felt "unreconstructed." The term had been coined by John Crowe Ransom in perhaps the best essay, "Reconstructed but Unregenerate," in I'll Take My Stand *(1930). Ransom means that after the Civil War, refugee Georgians during Reconstruction were not "reborn" spiritually into the civil religion of American exceptionalism and the "new birth of freedom" of the Republican nationalist victory narrative. The defeated and their heirs, like O'Connor, remained "unregenerate" and dissented from the civil religion of democracy. Ransom as an editor and teacher was also instrumental in publishing O'Connor's stories.*

MILLEDGEVILLE

1 MARCH 59

Dear Louise,

We were real cheered to hear from you on 1 Feb as the bidnis letters say. And I was glad to be introduced to Bro. Juniper. I suspect him of being Anglican.

We haven't seen Tom since he brought his class over but I mean to drop him a note to come over and tell us the latest. We certainly hope you all won't be leaving next year. That would be a blow to us all and I am afraid the Rev. Pres. Martin will be at Wesleyan forever unless there is an appropriate thorn in his side at Mercer.

Out of twenty writing students at the University of Chicago there were two who had some talent and the rest were strictly from hunger. The classes went off all right because I could write and they couldn't. It gives me the needed confidence. Malamud [Bernard] is coming to do the same thing next month. At the public reading there was no public. I read "A Good Man Is Hard to Find," omitting the paragraph about the little n———— that didn't have any britches on. I felt very unreconstructed in that liberal territory.

I believe I have finished my novel. Somebody said you didn't finish one, you just said to hell with it. I am working it over and find it hard to let go. I look at it one day and think it's the worst novel ever written, the next day I manage to find possibilities in it, etc. The name of it is going to be THE VIOLENT BEAR IT AWAY. (". . . the kingdom of heaven suffereth violence, and the violent bear it away." Matthew 11:12.)

The geese are laying and the peachickens have started screaming and eating up my mother's crocus, so everything here is coming along with the season.

Give my regards to Isobel Rogers.

Cheers to yourself,

FLANNERY O'CONNOR TO
FATHER JAMES McCOWN

O'Connor cites the generosity of a philanthropic foundation and praises a favorable portrayal of a religious. She also notes difficulties in traveling.

MILLEDGEVILLE

1 MARCH 1959

A book you ought to read is THE ROOTS OF HEAVEN by Romain Gary, and you can get it in a Cardinal Editions paper back for four bits. It has a Jesuit in it that I think is modeled on Pere Teilhard de Chardin, the paleontologist. There was a piece on him not long ago in the *CommonWheel*. Anyway, this is a most inneresting book and ought to be in your bookstore.

I hear General Cline is leaving for Texas, or has done left. They will miss you.

I am going to be supported for the next number of years by the Ford Foundation. The Lord has blessed me with a Patron!

The trip to Chicago was awful. Plane grounded in Louisville and an eight-hour bus ride after that to Chicago. After I got there it was all right and the students weren't better than students anywhere else that I could see, at least not the writing students. A man named Joel Wells from *The Critic* showed up at the reading and came back and said who he was and then vanished, but at least he came.

We haven't heard the latest on the Gossett affair but I mean to get him over here shortly to give it to us

Merry Easter,

O'Connor recommends a biography of a nineteenth-century Catholic convert, Orestes Brownson—a journalist and political thinker. Brownson is little read or studied in American classrooms and appears in few textbooks. Abolitionist

writers—*Douglass, Thoreau, Emerson, and President Lincoln*—on the other hand, have been canonical figures for generations. Study of Brownson leads to a questioning of their historical assumptions that have shaped conventional American history for a century.

Up until the Civil War, Brownson was a leading apologist for the Catholic faith in the United States. Brownson's writings were vital in shaping the Vatican's understanding of sectional disputes that would lead to the Civil War. Brownson thought the war could have been avoided or its carnage mitigated considerably had the American War for Independence been used as a model of restraint. While O'Connor's reputation has grown, Brownson's has become obscure. Brownson regarded in the mid-nineteenth century many of the Abolitionists as irrational zealots (for example, John Brown) and leading Transcendentalists who justified their conduct as theologically heterodox. In later generations the radicalism of the Abolitionists and the eccentricities of Transcendentalists have been normalized in American classrooms and textbooks. By contrast, Brownson was influential in the listing of the Abolitionist novelist Harriet Beecher Stowe on the Index for heterodox theological views. He also did not support President Lincoln's reelection in 1864. Brownson decried the increase of unitary executive power in President Lincoln's exercise of "war powers" and his suppression of dissenting journalists. He also criticized Lincoln's conscription measures, in which Irish Catholic immigrants, some of whom did not speak English, ended up in the Union army. Like Nathaniel Hawthorne, Brownson was a "Peace Democrat," not a "Lincoln man." He argued that a "War for the Union" should not destroy the Southern aristocracy. The American Revolution served as a precedent that evinced compromise and restraint. Brownson believed Lincoln's presidency was a radical departure. Study of Brownson's writings challenges the central premise of conventional American history that casts Lincoln as the custodian of the essential principles of the original War for American Independence. Brownson's views were often vilified for their criticism of Republican war policies ordered by Lincoln and executed by General Sherman and others. Brownson believed Sherman's prosecution of "total war" against civilians departed from the tactics of General George Washington in the Revolutionary War and constituted a serious abrogation of a Catholic just war. Brownson's dissent from the nationalist political narrative of *the Civil War is a vital yet neglected part of the historical record.*[23] *O'Connor was knowledgeable of the narrative by way of Brownson's biography, which she recommends to Father McCown.*

MILLEDGEVILLE

GEORGIA

3 APRIL 59

I am enjoying reading about poor old Brownson [Orestes]. Converts do have a hard time in the Church and his story seems particularly sad, in as much as if they had left him alone he would probably have made more of a mark on his Protestant friends.

I sent you a Mary McCarthy, which I don't want back. The Lowells [Mr. and Mrs. Robert] took me to dinner at her house one night. I didn't open my mouth all evening. It was powerful intellecchul talk that went on. It finally got around to the Church and she said that when she was a child and went to Communion, she thought of it as the Holy Ghost because that Person of the Trinity was "the most portable." She also said that the Eucharist was a symbol, upon which I finally gained my tongue and chirped, "Well, if it's symbol, to hell with it." After that I was heard from no more. I don't know whether her attitude is like Joyce's or not. She has a book called *Memories of a Catholic Girlhood* in which she says more or less why she is above the Church. I haven't read it, but I guess your answer would be there. She has a second husband named Bowdon Broadwater who seemed to me rather nice.

Tom Gossett has accepted a job in Texas for next year. Presbyterian college and a lot more money than what he got at Wesleyan. Part of his reinstatement agreement was that he wouldn't come back. Apparently all the alumnae is trying to get rid of that _____, but he is glued there apparently. A few weeks back Tom came over one afternoon and as we had Mass at five o'clock, he went with us. After it was over, he asked why Fr. _____ didn't come out and shake hands with the people. Haw, we says. He couldn't think of anything to say if he shook their hands. Tom said well Fr. McCown did it. You should have seen the church on St. Patrick's day—green carnations.

FLANNERY O'CONNOR TO CAROLINE GORDON

MILLEDGEVILLE

IO MAY 59

Dear Caroline:

You heard the subterranean note in Cal's [Robert Lowell] voice correctly I guess. Bob Giroux spent last Monday and Tuesday with us and said Cal hospitalized himself before the party. He thought it a good sign that he did it himself and didn't have to be forced to. Giroux had just been to Gethseminie (sp?). He stopped over in Atlanta and visited the Trappist monastery in Conyers, which he said was much better looking than the one in Kentucky, or at least will be when they complete it. All the people in the outlying areas go to look at the monks—like going to the zoo.

I'm glad you have set out on The Air of the Country. With all the other things you do I don't see how you find time for it but I suppose after teaching it is a real relief to do it. It will be a big treat for me to see it.

I read at Wesleyan last week—"A Good Man Is Hard to Find." After the reading, I went to one of their classes to answer questions. There were several young teachers in there and one began by saying, "Miss O'Connor, why is the Misfit's hat black?" I said most countrymen in Georgia wore black hats. He looked quite disappointed. Then he said, "Miss O'Connor, the Misfit represents Christ, does he not?" "He does not," says I. He really looked hurt at that. Finally he said, "Well Miss O'Connor, what IS the significance of the Misfit's hat?" "To cover his head," I say. He looked crushed then and left me alone.

I am doing the whole middle section of the novel over. The beginning and the end suit me, but the middle is bad. It isn't dramatic enough. I telescoped that middle section so as to get on with the end, but now that I've got the end, I see there isn't enough middle.

I don't reckon I saw many Fugitives at Vanderbilt. The Kreigers asked for you. He read a paper which was over my head, but was very nice when he wasn't reading a paper. The Mabrys came down from Guthrie and I was glad to meet them. While I was at the Cheney's I read part of Ashley's [Brown] thesis, the chapter on *The Malefactors* [Caroline Gordon]. Ashley ought to get to work on that book and publish it. I think it's the best thing I've read on the Malefactors. If you would give him a verbal shove, he might get on with it. He is leaving Santa Barbara after this term but I don't know where he will go.

FLANNERY O'CONNOR TO
FATHER JAMES H. McCOWN

Anti-Catholic paranoia and eccentric parish activities evoke O'Connor's typical bemusement. She mentions Father McCown's professor friend at St. Charles College in Grand Coteau, Louisiana.

MILLEDGEVILLE

24 MAY 59

You said one time did I have any copies of WB [*Wise Blood*] and I have just got some so I enclose a couple.

Tom Gossett went up to the monastery a few weeks ago and he was so taken with it that he plans to go again next Friday and take me and my mamma. Did I tell you he has a job for next year at Trinity University (Presbyterian) in San Antonio. At Wesleyan the faculty has petitioned the board of trustees to ask for an investigation of _____ and a large percent of the faculty has already resigned. Carl Bennett is going to a school in North Carolina [colleague of Dr.

Gossett]. All the religion faculty has resigned—one of these is going to become an Episcopalian. He said his family thinks this is the downward path, first to liquor and then to Rome. The saying about Wesleyan now is that there is Madness in their Methodism.

The latest indignity foisted upon this congregation is a statue of Guess Who. He has everything about him but the snakes—a purple shirt, a green robe, an orange book, white gloves, gold hat—and is holding up as if for sale or edification a four-leaf clover, I mean a shamrock. This atrocity is not in the back of the church either—up smack in the front. He also has similar statues but of different sizes we hear in his bedroom, living room, kitchen, and automobile.

The Catholic ladies here have a sewing circle that meets on Thursdays—just for social purposes. On Ascension Thursday he informed them they could not sew. Sin to sew on Ascension Thursday. May I ask you if you do not think this is somewhat Extreme? Not a peep out of him this year about the sin of going to hear the bacculariat sermon. We think he was sat upon by Atlanta for that.

I had a very kind letter from a Fr. Romagosa in the wake of your passing.

FLANNERY O'CONNOR TO TOM AND LOUISE GOSSETT

O'Connor mentions that a friend and his father participated in an integrated meal at the Trappist monastery in Conyers, Georgia. The detail would have interested the Gossetts, since Tom had been suspended earlier from his academic post at a Macon college because of his support of integration.

MILLEDGEVILLE

24 JUNE 59

We are looking forward to seeing you all in August but we can't go to Pass Christian—not just the cat although I can't imagine my parent in the car with one, but just because we aren't the travelling kind. Nothing short of Europe could lure us off the place at this point . . . and as you know, we done been there already.

She sends you this picture of a cat but says when you come to leave yours in the car. Maybe this has deep psychological roots as the graduate students say; anyway they are too deep for me. I am mighty glad she doesn't have an aversion to chickens or my life might have been ruint.

We were glad to get your address so we could thank you again for taking us to the monastery. Regina sent Fr. Paul some tuberous begonias by Billy [Sessions] the last time he was here. Billy brought his daddy up and they spent the night at the monastery. The old man is from South Carolina and isn't a Catholic. It so chanced that the week end they were there, The Trappists were having a retreat for some society of Negroes. They make no distinction, so old man Sessions had to eat with them. I understand he bore up well, however.

We were at the Sanford House the other day and both Mary Jo and Miss White came over to say behind their hands that a certain lady there was none other than MRS. MARTIN. We had a good look. No comment.

Let us know when you will be here. We'd like you to spend the night but if you can't at least plan to eat with us. The cat can be served in the car.

  Cheers,

FLANNERY O'CONNOR TO
FATHER JAMES McCOWN

O'Connor recounts differences in Catholic opinion. While the Jesuits admire her, another religious order harbors suspicions about her writing. Anchored in the faith, O'Connor retains her good humor.

MILLEDGEVILLE

11 JULY 59

Reverend & Dear Father,

I hope you don't subscribe to that paper. I hope you just picked it up out of some ecclesiastical trashbasket. You and I know that somebody with a Southern accent should be teaching the Pope English. All such mistakes are a result of the fall.

The Gossetts say they are going to see you on their way to San Antonio. We wish we could come with them but we are the original Stick-in-the-Muds. I have just energy enough to pick up the eggs out of the chicken yard every morning.

There is a very funny book on death and Judgment (a novel) called MOMENTO MORI [sic] that you should read and recommend in your book store. By a lady named Muriel Spark[s]. The extra copies of your brother's article came in very handy [Robert McCown, S.J., "Flannery O'Connor and the Reality of Sin"].

The Revrundpaster here had in two sisters from Warner Robins for three weeks to teach the vacation school—straight from you know where they were. So one of them hears that I am a Catholic writer and requests to see my book immediately. So I bundled a copy of yr brother's article with it. We never heard the verdict. She took it all away with her, leaving the message that she hadn't had time to read it. I wonder.

I am typing my novel [*The Violent Bear It Away*] for the last time and it should be out in the spring with all the other crocusses.

Do you subscribe to the Davenport *Messenger* [Iowa]? If you do not let me know and I will send you a subscription. I get more out of it than out of the *Comminwheel*.

O'Connor makes an allusion to a Jesuit perhaps derived from Willa Cather's Death Comes for the Archbishop. *Riding a motorcycle instead of a horse,*

Father McCown traversed the rugged American Southwest like Cather's Father Latour did a century earlier in the novel.

MILLEDGEVILLE

GEORGIA

2 AUGUST 59

Well you are getting farther and farther away from civilization but I guess the people in Texas need to be saved worsen us Georgians and Mississippians . . .

I hope you will be allowed to wear a cowboy hat and spurs along with the Roman collar.

Maybe you can introduce your brother to a better brand of conservatives. Some of the new conservatives, such as Russell Kirk [*The Conservative Mind*], can barely be told from the better liberals.

Your subscription to the Davenport *Messenger* [Iowa] will have begun in the middle of August and sent to Texas. Mary McCarthy may be in Europe OR she may not wish to correspond with no wily Jesuit.

O'Connor requests prayer from the Jesuits. She is thankful for the few accurate interpretations of her fiction and plans for Father McCown's brother to review her forthcoming novel.

MILLEDGEVILLE

14 NOVEMBER 59

Thank you for the quick reply, which sets that out of my head so that I can go about my business. It is very good to know somebody you can ask.

Honor Tracy is a woman and so far as I know that's her name. It is hard to tell from the book [*The Straight and Narrow Path*] whether she is a believer or not. I have a friend who insists she is, but I don't know. The book is both funnier and more serious if she is.

My professor friend and I have about covered the ground on saints. I told him he was looking for the dramatic saints of the last age, whereas the Church was successfully busy teaching people how to live their daily lives in Christ and how to die. He is now taking the line that he is a member of the <u>soul</u> of the Church, which he points out Catholic doctrine says is enough for salvation. I have sent off a letter saying it is enough for those in invincible ignorance but not enough on principle. Every time I make any kind of point, he shifts ground to somewhere else.

You are right that Coffee [Thomas P.] ought to be a better writer himself if he is going to criticize other Catholic writers ["Is There an American Catholic Literature?" *Saturday Review*, September 5, 1959]. At some time or other I may try to write a more reflective piece on the same subject and send it to the *Sat. Review.* It is not a good magazine.

I want to put your brother's name [Robert McCown, S.J.] on the list for Farrer Straus to send review copies of my book to [*The Violent Bear It Away*]. Anybody who has written on me they will send a copy to if I send the address, so will you send me the address where your brother is liable to be in December or January. That is when I expect the advance copies will go out. Pray that the reception of this book will not be too bad. It is a book that most will find very hard to take. There is nothing appealing in it. I am stealing myself for the worst.

O'Connor includes a comic strip apparently from the Sunday bulletin of the local Catholic Church. A seedy character in a smoke-filled room is reading a "forbidden book." He dies, and in judgment before an irate St. Peter he is condemned to hell.

MILLEDGEVILLE

16 JUNE 59

Thanks for all the edifying literature. I enclose you our last Sunday's comic strip instruction on bad reading. We have like examples to curdle us every Sunday. Note that the people who put this out call themselves CATHOLITE PUBLICATIONS.

Whilst you were wondering where the Clines were, they were here.

My book probably won't be out until next spring. In the meantime, this is a good one.

O'Connor mentions a friendship with a Catholic convert, Russell Kirk, who was a prolific writer, historian, and essayist. He has never been as well known among the Jesuits (and in the larger Church) as Dorothy Day and Thomas Merton. While their conversion stories are familiar, Kirk's is not. His influence is arguably as significant as Day's or Merton's. His political vision is different, and in some respects more penetrating in its analysis of the American founding and the later history of the republic.

O'Connor met Kirk when both visited mutual friends, the Cheneys, in Tennessee. O'Connor reviewed one of his many books for the diocesan newspaper. His most famous nonfiction work, The Conservative Mind *(1953), emphasized that the legacy of the American founding is rooted in the Jeffersonian tradition.[24] Decentralization, limited government, and political subsidiarity were its vital features. The Jeffersonian principles formed a bipartisan American traditionalism in the aftermath of World War II upon which Ronald Reagan relied in his landslide reelection in 1984. Kirk provided vital counsel, especially in Reagan's recovery of Jeffersonian language in his 1981 inaugural address. Reagan, ironically, as a Republican suggested the alternative to Lincolnian nationalist centralization: "All of us—all of us need to be reminded that the Federal Government did not create the states; the states created the Federal Government." Reagan's successors, in particular George W. Bush, abandoned Reagan's subsidiaritist vision and supported a stolid neo-conservative imperialist foreign policy. President Bush increased massive centralist government and was dedicated to imperial global democracy fundamentally at odds with Reagan's support of limited government and avoidance of American interventionism.*

MILLEDGEVILLE

20 SEPTEMBER 59

We were real sorry to hear about that Mr. Benton that we didn't get to call up. We don't take the Macon paper so we didn't see about it. I sent the clipping to Tom that you gave us. Apparently nobody paid Martin's letter any attention. They are stuck with him. Tom and Louise [Gossett] didn't come through here but went to West Virginia and then were going on to San Antonio. The General Clines are also in San Antonio but I don't know their address.

Russell Kirk is a Presbyterian who goes to the Catholic Church. I know two or three Presbyterians who go to the Catholic Church. It seems to be the thing for intellectual Presbyterians to do. Russell, I think, is not a Catholic because the Church is not as conservative as he is. He and I were guests at the same house in Nashville one weekend. He is nice but hard to talk to.

Well, good for old Mary McCarthy answering your letter. I imagine there may be some bitterness in her feeling about the Church but I couldn't say for sure. Wm. Alexander Percy [Uncle, Walker Percy] seemed to leave in a kind of will-less way.

My friend, the professor, writes that he finds none of the Church's doctrines intolerable and that he would come into the Church tomorrow if he thought the Church was doing a good job of making saints. So what do you say to somebody like that?

I don't think there is anything I could do about your brother reviewing my book anywhere because authors just can't suggest people to review their books; but I do hope he will review it. I think if he just wrote the magazine, told them he had written on me before and where and would be interested in reviewing that that would be the best thing.

My mother indicates that she will get YOU in trouble with the Holy Office if you miss any further appointments at her table.

Cheers,

Are you getting the Davenport *Messenger* [Iowa]? You are supposed to be.

FLANNERY O'CONNOR TO
MRS. BRAINARD CHENEY

The letter from many years before the election of Ronald Reagan presents an amusing contrast between the president's later global fame and his earlier role as a television host. The prospect of Reagan playing Mr. Shiftlet in O'Connor's story is a scene typical of her humor.

MILLEDGEVILLE, 23 SEPTEMBER 56

. . . I have just sold "The Life You Save May Be Your Own" for a television play to be put on (I think) by the General Electric Playhouse.[25] People with TV sets tell me this is a program conducted by Ronald Reagan but I don't know if that means that Ronald Reagan is going to get to be Mr. Shiftlet or not. I have got my money anyway and now I am going to try and forget about it, although that is mighty hard to do, thinking all the time that R. R. may be Mr. Shiftlet and that they will probably let him and the idiot daughter live happily ever after in a Chrysler convertible. I don't know when it's going to be and I don't want to know. With the proceeds, I have bought my mother a new refrigerator, the latest model with every attachment. It spits the icecubes at you, the trays shoot out and hit you in the middle, and if you step on a button, the whole thing rolls out from the wall . . .[26]

FLANNERY O'CONNOR TO
FATHER JAMES McCOWN

MILLEDGEVILLE

10 OCTOBER 59

Thanks for the pitchers. I was glad to see myself looking so well. My mother says the trouble with you is you can't take pictures, just don't have steady nerves, etc.

I enclose the enclosed famous article lest you have not seen it. I do not think, as the Davenport *Messenger*, that he should be condemned for putting it in the *Sat. Re[view]*.[27] When Catholics realize that their linen is sometimes going to be hung on the public line, they may get it in better condition. However, I don't think Mr. Coffee distinguishes between "letters" and journalism and I don't think he knows what prose and poetry is being written. But a lot of this needs to be said.

I can't tell my friend about the numbers at the Communion rail and the filled churches because he doesn't see any practical result from this church going. All he knows is what he reads in the papers. This is somewhat like my lapsed Catholic friend who says her mother goes to Communion and comes out of the church making uncharitable remarks about this one and that one. It don't do any good to tell this girl that this is just a characteristic of ladies of that age and generation and that it doesn't mean anything. To her it means that the sacrament has no effect. Incidentally, this girl has sold three stories in the last year and they are excellent. The Church is going to sport another very good Lapsed Cath. Writer.

Excelsior,

O'Connor seeks counsel (December 18, 1959) to defend the founder of the Jesuit order, Ignatius Loyola. The Swiss psychologist Carl Jung had paralleled Jesuit monastic community with Marxist social organization.

Also [Jung is] full of such things as equating the Communist idea of community with the Church's and Communist methods with Loyola's. You ought to get hold of it just to see what you have to combat in the modern mind. I need something that covers this end-sanctifies-means business.[28]

O'Connor also criticizes Jung's "syncretist religion":

Jung has something to offer religion but is at the same time very dangerous for it. Jung would say, for instance that Christ did not rise from the dead literally but we must realize that we need this symbol, that the notion has significance for our lives symbolically, etc.[29]

FATHER JAMES McCOWN TO
FATHER SCOTT WATSON

[handwritten postscript]

Dear Youree [Scott Watson, S.J.]: Greetings from here for Christmas and New Year. This letter will prove interesting to you, I know. Could you help me on the request contained in large paragraph above, and actually send a book with answer to Flannery? She returns books faithfully, and she deserves good treatment in a matter such as at hand—many better than I or our house minus-library could supply. Since I am keeping her correspondence, you might return this letter with a little note in enclosed envelope. Her new book "not a joyous thing that people will like" will be out soon. That's what she is referring to in the last line above. Things are beginning to hum here.

God bless you,
Hooty

FLANNERY O'CONNOR TO
FATHER JAMES McCOWN

O'Connor seeks counsel about religious regulations. Father McCown observed that "as a Catholic writer Flannery O'Connor was abreast of the most advanced theological concerns in the Church, in the early days of the great Second Vatican Council . . . Yet she was inclined to strictness with herself in anything concerned with morality and having to do with Church discipline."[30]

MILLEDGEVILLE

7 JANUARY 60

I'm sending back your book with many obligements together with another one that I think you would like.

I have been in the hospital with the disintegrating bones. They have discovered that what is making them disintegrate is the medicine that I have been taking these ten years to keep the lupus under control. So they are going to try to withdraw that and see if I can make it without it. If I can't the bones will just have to go on disintegrating. A cheerful thought.

Inform me on this point, if you will. We ate out on a Friday and as I was not feeling so hot, I didn't order the fish but just got three vegetables and desert. When this came and I tasted it, I decided that one of them had been cooked in ham stock, as it tasted hamy. My mother said if you're in doubt, don't eat it, but I said if you're in doubt you can eat it. Who was right? I ate it, intent on getting my money's worth—but of such scruples are made. I know I ain't going to hell over a plate of butterbeans, but I don't know if I have to run to confession before I go to Communion. I am always afraid of sacrilege. It turned out they were cooked in ham stock. I enquired after I had eaten them. There is something about you can use drippings but you can't use stock. I hate this kind of question.

Billy Sessions spent the night with us on his way back to Mobile. My mother is his marriage counselor. He is looking for a wife, someone who is a combination cook, washwoman and fashion model. We tell him he would run any woman crazy in short order. Your mother has been nice to him and I think Tommy and Sugar introduced him to somebody.

Do you see *Jubilee*? If you do, I am going to have some genuine Catholic writing in it in February or March ["Introduction," *A Memoir of Mary Ann, Jubilee,* May 1961]. If you don't get it, I'll send you one. It is the introduction I have written to a book by the Dominican Sisters at the Cancer Home in Atlanta. The book itself is pretty bad as far as the writing goes, but it is something which deserved an introduction so I supplied it, and am highly pleased with the result.

A happy new year to you.

FATHER SCOTT WATSON TO FLANNERY O'CONNOR

A student of Father Watson wrote:

> I was a student of Fr. Watson from 1965-67, and his colleague at Loyola University, New Orleans from 1976 until his death in 1989. Fr. Watson was born Sept. 7, 1914. He was from Natchitoches, LA—I always said he was from "the country gentry." His brother, whose name was Arthur as I recall was chair of the LA Democratic Party in the 1950s and 1960s. The Watsons were related to the proto-feminist author Kate Chopin. He entered the New Orleans Province of the Society of Jesus Aug. 30, 1932. He was ordained June 21, 1944. He earned a doctorate in philosophy at the Gregorian University, Rome, in the late forties (the degree was not actually awarded until 1972 when he finally took the trouble to get a chapter from his dissertation published). The chapter from the dissertation is available from Abe Books. Its title was "Esse in the Philosophy of St. Thomas Aquinas." The dissertation challenged the then and still current orthodox interpretation of Thomas on "Esse." [31]

JANUARY 13, 1960

About two weeks ago Father McCown wrote me to ask if I could send you something by way of answer to the old accusation that the Jesuits teach that the end justifies the means. When his letter arrived I was away from Mobile and when I returned I was so extremely busy that there was no time to engage in the little research necessary to fulfill his request. Even now I won't be able to give you as satisfactory an account as I should like.

At this time I'm having the librarian here [Spring Hill College, Mobile, Alabama], Father Benedetto (from Georgia, incidentally) mail you a copy of *Readings in Ethics*, compiled and edited by J.F. Leibell (1926). It contains an article or essay: "Does the End Justify the Means?" by John Gerard, revised by Herbert Thurston (pp. 193–207) which, I think, may serve your need. I don't know about John Gerard, but Father Herbert Thurston is a Jesuit, famous, by the way, for his constant debunking of pseudo mystics, legendary accounts of the lives of the saints, etc. The book is stamped as due for Feb. 13th, but if you should need it for a longer time, the librarian will gladly overlook technicalities!

There is another good treatment of the matter in French by Georges Goyau in the DICTIONNAIRE APOLOGETIQUE DE LA FOI CATHOLIQUE, Tome II, columns 10-17 under the heading "Fin justifie les moyens?" I didn't ask if I might lend you this volume, as I know that all librarians are strongly averse to letting volumes of encyclopedias, etc. be taken out of the reference room even for a short time; but if you judge that the piece by Gerard and Thurston is not adequate to your purpose, I could copy out Goyau's article for you. It in great part overlaps the one I'm sending you; however, it adds a few things, which I'll try to summarize for you here. In regard to Count von Hoensbroech, Goyau says that he explicitly admitted that the arguments (aimed to prove that the Jesuits have taught that the end justifies the means) which had been based on citations from Jesuit moralists, and especially on citations from Busenbaum, had had no probative force, and that Busenbaum was by no means speaking of means that were in themselves morally wrong. This was in a German review called *Deutschland*, about 1903. The Count attacks other authors on other points, which Goyau treats in detail and proceeds to refute, though the whole is too complicated to summarize satisfactorily. Another book which I consulted, T.J.

Campbell, S.J. *The Jesuits* (which has only a very brief account of the question) adds that the Count was "seriously hampered" by some of his own earlier utterances. Thus, when he left the Society in 1893, he wrote in "Mein Austritt aus dem Jesuitenorden," as follows: 'The moral teachings, under which members of the Society are trained, are beyond reproach, and the charges so constantly brought against Jesuit moralists are devoid of any foundation." (p. 288). According to Goyau, the first court to which von Hoen[s]broech brought the case, namely, that of Treves, declared itself incompetent (rather than, as Gerard says, in Dasbach's favor). But the court of appeal, at Cologne, declared itself competent and did decide in Dasbach's favor and so equivalently in favor of the Jesuits! On another point too the article by Goyau corrects that of Gerard. The latter seems to have erred in thinking that Pascal had not accused the Jesuits of teaching the end justifies the means (see p. 205). Actually he did do so in his *Provincial Letters* (7th letter). To be sure, Pascal missed the point: the Jesuits to whom he refers are simply saying that a confessor may sometimes find that a penitent has used illicit means to a good end without having been aware of, or without having reflected on, the illicity of the means; in such a case the penitent is not to be judged as formally or subjectively (personally) culpable, although what he has done is certainly wrong in itself or objectively.

St. Ignatius himself is not usually the butt of the calumniators, but Goyau has something to say about him too. He refers to the book of the *Spiritual Exercises* of Ignatius. In the "Second Week" of the Exercises the saint is urging the retreatant to consider his state of life and whether or not he ought to make some change in this regard. For example, he is a priest, then should he seek some endowed position or post or should he rather choose to practice evangelical poverty? or he is an unmarried layman, then should he seek a wife or perhaps take a vow of chastity? St. Ignatius continues: "Therefore, my first aim should be to seek to serve God, which is the end, and only after that, if it is not more profitable (i.e. if it is more expedient toward this end; the Latin has "quatenus expedit"), to have a benefice ((= an endowed ecclesiastical office)) or marry, for these are means to the end. Nothing must move me to use such means, or to deprive myself of them save only the service and the praise of God our Lord, and the salvation of my soul." ((L.J. Puhl translation, Newman Press, 1953, p. 71)). Now let us look at the very first point of the "consideration" immediately following this; St. Ignatius here tells us: "It is necessary that all matters of which we wish to make a choice be either indifferent or good in themselves . . ." In other words, he is saying that our lofty aim of serving and giving praise to God will not sanctify our choice of means if these are bad in themselves. They must at least be indifferent, that is, morally neutral, as is, e.g. taking a walk. Goyau also points out that if one consults the various means actually proposed to its members in the Constitutions of the Society of Jesus, no one will find there any means which anyone—even the most rigorous moralist—would charge with being illicit.

Goyau makes a final interesting observation. Are the Jesuits to be blamed, he asks, for thinking and maintaining that in order to judge an action, we must consider its end, its motive? In this case, it is not they alone, but all Catholic moralists that are to be condemned. All consider that together with the thing done, the end for which it is done and the circumstances under which it is done, influence the morality of any action. It is odd that Catholic moralists are so often accused of being too formalistic, too "objective", of ignoring the personal equation; yet by others (perhaps even by the same at other times) they are accused of overstressing the subjective intention or end and not paying enough attention to the objective order, that is to the exterior act.

Of course, we Jesuits, for all its objective seriousness, are inclined to laugh when we hear accusations like this. To us they are so palpably ridiculous. Certainly in the long history of the Order, some individual Jesuit might have gone temporarily insane and defended the doctrine that the end justifies the means; it is even theoretically possible that he should have gotten an article containing the doctrine past a sleepy censor, but if this had ever happened (and I know of no evidence that any such thing ever has actually happened), of one thing I'm sure, that when the thing done would come to the knowledge of his superiors, that Jesuit would be in serious trouble! The principle in question is so plainly immoral and so gravely, not to say, horribly; so, that it is incredible that anyone should attribute it to a body of men whose sole purpose, as their Constitutions lay down, is to seek the salvation and perfection of their own souls while working at the same time most earnestly for the salvation and perfection of their neighbors' souls. Yet the old canard appears in the unlikeliest of places. Just a year ago the *Sat. Even. Post* (Jan. 17) had a friendly, not too far from accurate article on the Society of Jesus, but in the midst of it the old, many-times refuted accusation, with due reference to Busenbaum, crops up. No answer or explanation was given, and one was left with the impression that perhaps this was because none could be given. Yet if the accusations were true, most of the article would have made no sense at all; for an order holding such a nefarious principle, the least praise would seem to be de trop. To do the POST justice, in a later issue they did publish a short letter from Father Joseph E. O'Neill of Fordham University setting things straight on poor old Busenbaum.

Short letter! That's what this isn't. In fact, this is precisely the kind of letter I don't like to write. I wish I had time to revise the thing so you wouldn't be tempted to think that if Jesuits don't hold wicked principles, they are (much worse!) lacking in a sense of humor and utterly self-righteous.

Instead, I must bring this document to a close. Father McCown, as he perhaps told you, sent me your request because at the retreat house where he is stationed there is as yet no appreciable library for him to consult. He tells me—to pass on to something as pleasant as what has gone before has been disagreeable—that your new book will soon be out. I've been all eagerness to hear this good news since I read in AMERICA's Fall Book Issue (Oct. 17, 1959, p. 75) "The most eagerly awaited fiction titles—by AMERICA readers, that is—will be a novel by Karl Stern . . . and the first full-length novel by Flannery O'Connor, *The Violent Bear It Away* (Farrar, Straus and Cudahy). This Catholic author is well remembered for her superb short stories in *A Good Man Is Hard to Find*." (This perfectly expressed my own sentiments, especially if one omits the words about Karl Stern).

I'm about equally delighted to hear that you are going to give a talk at the college [Spring Hill] here next spring. Don't make me explain that "about equally," let me just say that the explanation would lead me to two new letters, one describing the joy of a day in Macon reading your books, the other the joy of a day in Milledgeville visiting you and your mother.

To your mother, my best regards.

Sincerely yours in Christ,

Father Watson

[handwritten postscript]
Dear Hooty, P.C. [Fr. McCown]

I'm sorry I'm so late; truly I have been, & am crushingly busy. In a ps to my letter, I recommended Fr. V[ictor] White, O.P.'s two bks on Jung. Delighted that Flannery is to come to Spring Hill. Saw your picture (with lay retreatants) in clipping from Dallas or Fr. Worth paper—very edifying!

All good wishes & prayer,

Youree [Scott Watson]

FLANNERY O'CONNOR TO FATHER SCOTT WATSON

O'Connor anticipates a hostile reception for The Violent Bear It Away, *her new novel. She praises Teilhard de Chardin, a view the presiding Bishop of the Episcopal Church in the United States also expressed in his homily at the wedding in May 2018 of Prince Harry and Meghan Markle, the Duke and Duch-*

ess of Sussex.[32] O'Connor beseeches prayer that will soon be answered by Father Watson's commentary.

17 JANUARY 60

Thank you so much for your letter and your labor and for having the book sent. I am rather embarrassed at having put you to this, but very glad nevertheless to have the information. I was surprised to find the accusation in a book of Jung's. I have Fr. White's book, *God and the Unconscious* for which Jung contributes the introduction and I also have a book by a Belgian priest on Jung. I have read Jung myself with considerable profit, but this last book given me is full of ranting. He is about 85 or so now and I suspect he could just not hold back his hankering to be a preacher any longer.

I have been reading Pere Teilhard de Chardin's *Phenomenon of Man* and I believe that he is the great Christian prophet of this century. This is a book that makes demands on the scientist and the philosopher and the theologian and the poet; of these I think the artist will accept his vision quickest.

You should receive a copy of my book shortly if you haven't already [*The Violent Bear It Away*]. I am afraid the reception of it is going to be very poor—the grotesque infuriates everybody. Please remember me and the book in your prayers and thank you again for taking the trouble to get this information for me. I'll send the book back on time. I'm enjoying it very much.

ROBERT LOWELL TO FLANNERY O'CONNOR

Lowell makes interesting comments about O'Connor's novel, linking it to Crime and Punishment. *Comments about a famous poet may have been included because of parallels to O'Connor.*

ROBERT LOWELL

239 MARLBOROUGH STREET

BOSTON 16, MASSACHUSETTS

FRIDAY, JANUARY 30, 1960

I guess the South is in the same as the rest of this perilous world, and the imperious character of my daughter would shape up there, much as here. I don't think you've ever written about three year olds, their inquisitive, voluminous bossiness. . . .

I've just read your "Prophet" enthralled, at almost at one sitting, a day long, for I read slowly [*The Violent Bear It Away*]. A queer contrast with Moll Flanders—a product of the eighteenth century Protestant mind, so the books say—which I have been studying lately for a course. Moll is all sanity and daylight, though performing her trade inches from the gallows. Your fellow is very dark, though mostly a hero, I think, a fearful warning and yet a finger of accusation against the environment. He's a little bomb, treated lovingly in a way, a true homicidal lunatic, and somehow a true prophet. The dark explodes, as it so often has since *Crime and Punishment*.

I think you are one of the very few people, who can handle such things with irony and insight. Your plot moves much more clearly and forcibly, and there's far less humor and oddity, a gain one regrets at times . . . but in the third part it all seems to come right. I don't know whether [it] is your best book or not. Certainly it adds; the [cir]cle is held with patience, and everywhere there's a heroic struggle to be clear. I have been thinking that we perhaps have something of the same problem—how to hold to one's true, though extreme vein without repetition; how to master conventional controls and con . . . normal expectations without washing out all one has to say. This [a] hurried way of saying it sounds cynical, but I think something like this happened to Shakespeare in moving from his clotted, odd, inspired Troilus and Cressida to the madder but more conventional . . .

Perhaps I overemphasize. For the last two days, I've been looking at the three volume collected . . . Emily Dickinson, and reading her

letters and accounts of her life. Chaos! She really was a raspingly better and more serious poet than anyone in the country, and also so
innocent of control that she was nine tenths of the time an amateur,
winning through in spurts, in earnest and right by accident. How
safe all the licensed and conventional daring that now prevail seem in
comparison! The really inspired and helpless hurts. Anyway, I am
awed and cheered by you.

FATHER SCOTT WATSON TO FLANNERY O'CONNOR

*Father Watson experiences a conflict between teaching and giving O'Connor's
novel proper attention. A former student observes,*

> Fr. Watson's primary apostolic mission throughout his
> life was teaching young Jesuit students studying phi-
> losophy as part of their Jesuit academic formation. He
> taught the History of Philosophy and his notes were
> published as "A Short History of Philosophy." Besides
> history of philosophy, he regularly taught aesthetics.
> From 1965 until his death, he taught a combined meta-
> physics and theodicy (philosophy of God) course . . .
> Fr. Watson had broad interests in literature and fine
> arts. He was an expert (and published) on the poetry of
> Gerard Manley Hopkins. . . . Everyone said his best
> work with students was in one-on-one conversations.
> He was unfailingly kind and generous and referred to
> regularly as 'a saint.'[33]

*Father Watson's academic, pedagogical background enables him to place
O'Connor's novel within the canonical tradition of theology and philosophy
rooted in Augustine and Dante. The interaction of faith and reason is fundamental in Father Watson's analysis of her fiction.*

I'm glad you found the book and letter of some help. Thanks for your own interesting letter. Father Benedetto, our librarian, was 'edified' at your returning the volume so promptly (this is not, I'm afraid, the usual experience of librarians), and appreciated your little note.

In the meantime an event has occurred: your new book [*The Violent Bear It Away*]!

Unfortunately, I wasn't able to read it for several days. All the while I kept it on my desk, bright and appealing in its violet jacket. Rashly! for it was a constant source of temptations to neglect the preparation of my classes and other urgent work. I had hoped eventually to have a morning or an afternoon free in which I could drink it all in one great draught, which seems to me the proper way to begin with a work of art, leaving till later a savoring of details. But in the end I couldn't bear to wait any longer for such an opportunity, and descended to reading it in installments. External factors alone could determine the end of each installment, for I nowhere found a spot where I could, I don't say willingly, but even resignedly lay the book aside for. a time. It so gripped my attention, indeed, that though I could put it out of my hands, I could never wholly put it out of my mind.

After reading it I felt as though I had lived through a storm or perhaps a bombing. I seemed to myself to be at least a year older. This latter feeling, by the way, serves as my personal criterion for a truly powerful book. St. Augustine's *Confessions* made me feel that way and Pascal's *Pensées*. Among novels I recall at the moment *The Brothers Karamazov*. Both of you—you and Dostoevski—know how to tell a story, but Dostoevski cannot resist telling several stories at the same time though they have little or no connection, with the result that his force is, as it were, dissipated, whereas *The Violent Bear It Away*, though less than half the length of *The Brothers*, makes a stronger, if less complex, an impression.

I was interested in the technique of frequent flash-backs you employ in this novel. I don't recall ever before having seen it used to the same extent. One gets the sense of living through the same momentous experiences again and again, but each time with a richer background and so with ever greater understanding. Another point of technique that intrigued me (though I'm not familiar enough with the modern novel to be certain that it is original with you) is that you, as author, get inside of two, and only two, consciousnesses: the boy's and Rayber's. This enables you to present a number of the most important events from two contrasting points of view. You wisely refrain from intruding into the consciousness of the old "prophet" and thus, as is proper leave his inmost soul still veiled and unprofaned. To return to the flash-backs, these can, of course, be somewhat confusing at times to the reader, but on the whole I should say your use of them was quite effective. By means of them you sometimes have two narratives running simultaneously, not independently, but skillfully interwoven, closely harmonized, a sort of literary counterpoint.

There are so many features of your book I should like to praise that if I were to try to speak of them all, this letter would never be finished or, at any rate, would run on to unconscionable lengths (and my classes go unprepared!). Let me just mention your wit (in the ancient sense of the word). One example comes immediately to mind: Tarwater's complaint to his grand-uncle that he never "ast" to come to the city: "I'm here before I knew this here was here." Let me mention too the poetry of many a passage, poetry rising to its most glorious in the lyrical thoughts of the child preacher. (Let me confess: I don't recall ever having been so stirred by any "real" sermon as I was by the words of Lucette.) I must mention also the masterful use of dialog, suggesting that you may someday turn with great success to the writing of plays.

But what impresses me most about your style is its organicity. This work of yours is a true whole with its many parts all contributing to the one total effect. Nothing seems casual or accidental. Everything in the beginning is the anticipation of something in the end; everything in the end is the fulfillment of something in the beginning. To give one of the most obvious and important examples of what I mean. On page 5 one reads: "The old man, who said he was a prophet, had raised the boy to expect the Lord's call himself and to be prepared for the day he would hear it . . . He had been called in his early youth and had set out for the city to proclaim the destruction awaiting a world that had abandoned its Savior." Here anticipation of what is to come, and in the last pages of the book the boy, who has so long wrestled with God, at last surrenders, lets go his proud independence ("something he had been clutching all his life"), and, being now prepared, receives the call in an atmosphere so charged with the supernatural that others (Buford) cannot stand it, and then without looking back presses forward on his mission, "his face set toward the dark city, where the children of God lay sleeping."

To be sure, this is in a sense the whole story. Everything else ties in with this starting point, this conclusion. Moreover, the direction is kept clear. We have, for instance, that amazingly fine page or two (26–27) in which Tarwater first discovers that the city is wicked and so ought to be preached to and feels indignation that his uncle walks through this evil "no more concerned with it all than a bear in the woods: 'What kind of prophet are you?'" And when the uncle retorts: "If you been called by the Lord, then be about your own mission," the boy's face pales and his glance shifts: "'I ain't been called yet,' he muttered." Just an illustration, for there is scarcely a phrase about Tarwater that doesn't help to reveal the character of the boy and the forces working on him, in such a way as obscurely to suggest the rising struggle, the climax, and the denouement. Some Catholics and perhaps some Protestants too will be upset by your story, judging that you are, if not intentionally, at least in effect, ridiculing religion. Not thus, not thus at all, do I read your heart-gripping story. First of all, I know it is a story, that is, a work of fiction, describing characters that are possible, indeed plausible (we have all known certain prototypes). As a novelist, I take it, you ask yourself what would such characters (above all what would a boy like Tarwater) with such temperaments and such backgrounds do if confronted with such and such experiences; and your artistic imagination enables you to fore-see. what it is they are most likely freely to do. (I don't for a moment believe that Rayber was right: though Tarwater was suffering from terrifyingly powerful psychological forces, I think he retained throughout at least a minimum of free will; if I thought the contrary I should find him hardly more interesting than poor little Bishop, who, nevertheless, is a source of great interest by reason of his symbolic value & of the reactions he excites in others.) If, then, your characters and the situations in which you represent them are plausible and the reactions of your characters to these latter, if at first surprising, are in the end seen to be what we too, your readers, should have expected, how can anyone say you are ridiculing religion? Can reality ridicule religion?

Actually, it seems to me, that if you yourself, as author, are wholly objective, that is, if you do not, so to speak, get outside your story in order to pass judgment on your own characters, nevertheless the events of the story itself do encourage, if indeed they do not force, the reader to pass such judgment. Here is the judgment which one reader at least felt impelled to make. For me the old man is a symbol of truth and goodness. A symbol, no more; he is not goodness itself, but goodness as we find it on earth, mixed with dross; not pure truth, but truth mingled with error. His religion has much of true religion in it, but it has also a deal of superstition and fanaticism. If he is (in a non-technical sense) an heir to the prophets of the Lord in the Old Testament, he is also the descendant in part of the pseudo prophets against whom the true prophets lifted up their voices like trumpets (even these latter, as we know, were not—all of them—without certain glaring faults). Rayber, on the contrary, I understand as a symbol of wickedness and untruth. But he is not pure wickedness and error; there is in him much, very much that is admirable. In fact, a Christian reading the story cannot but feel sympathy for Rayber. This can go so far (I speak from experience!) that he may find himself almost hoping that Rayber will finally bring the boy around to his point of view, till something is said or done that suddenly awakens him to the realization that this "hope" is abominable, that Rayber's point of view involves the total rejection of Christianity. Rayber, I should say, is "the world," not in disembodied abstraction, but incarnated in one, very vividly depicted, individual. Nor is Satan himself absent. I assume that the "voice of the stranger" which talks to Tarwater as he digs at his uncle's grave at the beginning of the story is not only the voice of his own worse self, the proud, self-sufficient side of his conflict-torn personality, but also, symbolically, the voice of the devil (who, as St. Ignatius tells us in his *Spiritual Exercises*, is wont to disguise himself as an angel of light). So it is that when Tarwater begins to listen to him, "the stranger" quickly becomes "his friend." Perhaps at no time does Satan so clearly reveal his "serpent's tail" (another phrase from St. Ignatius) as at the moment when Tarwater, after crying out the words of Baptism, "heard the sibilant oaths of his friend fading away on the darkness." And since we have the world and the devil, it is appropriate that among the forces of evil at work in the story we have also the flesh; hence the incident of the rape, which is evil in its most visible; most tangible form, evil in all its ugliness, evil unmasked. This horror coming on top of the harrowing experience on the lake evokes in the boy that reaction which prepares the way for his definitive rejection of "evil" and the acceptance of his "call" to good. And, by the way, one does not fail to note that the rapist has eyes the color of his lavender shirt, or to remember the "violet eyes" of "the friend." No, you, as the author, don't take sides in your book but let the story speak for itself. If, however, one considers that it is Rayber's (and before Rayber, the friend's) point of view which actually leads Tarwater to the murder of Bishop (Rayber himself hadn't been strong enough of purpose to live out his principles—he could say NO to God, not do No), whereas it is the old man's influence, and all that this symbolizes, which finally breaks through the hard crust of the boy's selfishness and pride and sends him off on his way to try, however misguidedly, to save mankind, one cannot, I think, doubt what the story says and, through the story, reality itself; namely, that religion is right, irreligion wrong. In a sense the truth shines out all the more clearly in that religion as embodied in the story is disfigured with human weaknesses and errors and irreligion decked out in the attractive garb of reason, arid science, and commonsense (as the misere of the human element in the Church may serve as a foil to set off the splendor of the divine in it). One argues: If even so imperfect and faulty a religion as this is far better than irreligion even when persuasively presented, how incomparably superior will be the true and perfect religion. And if hitherto he hasn't so much as conceived this, perhaps now he will at last begin to look for it. Religion, the story says, is not only ideally better, it is more humanly satisfying. Irreligion, as Rayber's sufferings go to prove, is unlivable, a burden too great for man to bear.

All this, and much more, is what I personally drew from the novel. Very probably not all will draw the same. It could well be that not everything which I found in the work was explicitly intended by the author! Nevertheless, I maintain that somehow everything, or nearly everything, of which I have spoken did get into the novel, that it's there and not just something concocted by me. Moreover, besides the great lesson spelled out by the story, that happiness comes only from God and from submission to His will, there were other things that it taught me. Thus never before, l believe, have I so clearly realized the tremendous-importance of Baptism nor the central position in the Christian life of the Eucharist (for me the "Bread of Life," which Tarwater at first despised and for which at the end he discovered he had an enormous hunger, is a most appropriate symbol of the Eucharist—which in turn is a beautiful symbol though far more than a mere symbol—of the heavenly banquet and so of the beatifying union with God, the hope which gives life its supreme meaning.)

There will be many, I suppose, who will see little in your novel but the powerful influence a strongly emotional old man can exert on a child entirely submitted to his care; yet I don't see how they can wholly miss a far more powerful influence, namely that of the imaged ideas which act in and through the "prophet," but are not properly his, being in great part, though with many corruptions, expressions of some of the great truths of Christianity. Even the most Rayber minded reader should at least perceive that for all its age Christianity still has left in it, as Chesterton puts it, enough fire to burn the world to rags. And this insight should excite that wonder and interest which is the good ground for the seed of the Sower.

Before closing let me add that if you haven't read C.S. Lewis' *Till We Have Faces,* I'm sure that you would enjoy doing so. It is a tale, remotely like your own, embodying the conflict between naturalism or rationalism and supernaturalism or faith. The former is at first made to appear extremely attractive, the latter quite repulsive; gradually, however, Lewis has his story bring out the deficiencies of rationalism and the beauty of true religion. But, though admirable in many ways, the book has too much of fantasy or myth and not enough of unity. Interesting throughout and lovely in places, it lacks the drive and the power of *The Violent Bear It Away.* Let me thank you most sincerely for your kindness in having a copy of your book sent to me; but let me thank you far more for the much greater gift—to me and to so many others—of the story itself and the soul-shaking experience it offers. My eyes are scorched. I seem to feel seeds opening in my blood.

FLANNERY O'CONNOR TO
FATHER JAMES McCOWN

The letter commemorates George Washington's birthday. O'Connor appreciated the difference between the birthday of the country's first president and commemoration of President Lincoln's birthday, later blurred in the hybrid day now celebrated as Presidents' Day. The meaning of national holidays was vital to O'Connor and reveals the precision of her historical perspective.

Father McCown offers to read O'Connor's new novel twice. He also plans to send her a novel popular among high school students at the time because of its existentialist themes of angst and rebellion. O'Connor dealt with the same themes more dramatically in The Violent Bear It Away.

MILLEDGEVILLE

GEO. WASH. BIRTHDAY

FEB. 22 [1960]

Thanks for your letter and the offer to read the book twice [*The Violent Bear It Away*]. It isn't out until the 24th but there was a long piece on it in the February *Catholic World*. Your brother [Robert Mc-Cown, S.J.] put them onto me so now they are giving me the whole hog treatment. It is a very good piece. There will be a review in the Feb 27th *Saturday Review* and I think there will be one in *Time* this week.[34] Don't know whether the *Time* one will be favorable or not. You never know what they are coming up with. A Fr. Quinn, a friend of mine at the University of Scranton, wrote me that he was to review it for *America*.[35] You may see that one and me not.

I'd love to have the copy of *The Catcher in the Rye*. I read it years ago but would like to read it again.

I haven't heard from your mother but I will look forward to meeting her in Mobile and I will invoke your memory if I see any azalea bushes.

Fr. Watson was mighty nice to send me the answer to the end-means business. I passed it on to my Loyola-hating friend, and I trust he profits by it, but it would be some loss to him if he had to stop hating Loyola.

Our best to you,

FLANNERY O'CONNOR TO FATHER SCOTT WATSON

6 APRIL 1960

Here are some I don't think you will have seen. Some of them are mighty entertaining. Observe particularly the *New York Post* and *San Francisco Chronicle*. I was so very pleased to see you at the airport and I only wish I could have sat down and talked to you while I was there. That answer to your question about the symbolism in the book was not satisfactory, but I find it hard to collect my thoughts when I am on exhibit, as it were. If you get to the Library to see that Duhamel [P. Albert, *Catholic World,* February 1960], I would like to know what you think of it.

FATHER SCOTT WATSON TO FLANNERY O'CONNOR

The commentary of Father Watson and his colleagues was vital to O'Connor's novel being properly understood. Most critics approached the novel from a secular perspective through the lens of religious science. Father Watson and his brother Jesuits read the novel as both credentialed academics and believers in a rare combination of both erudition and faith.

PALM SUNDAY
[APRIL 10, 1960]

Thank you for sending the reviews which I read with great interest. You could write another book about the reviewers of your latest, and there's no doubt the reviewers of that other book would find it utterly grotesque in this tragicomic affair the comic sometimes prevails, as in the review by the smiling Mr. Hogan of the *San Francisco Chronicle,* who finds your "comedy" so "gay" and "lighter than you think"; and sometimes the tragic, as in the review by Dawn Powell of the *N.Y. Post,* in which your story disappears in a "swamp of confusion" that is by no means picturesque. (The lady outrants your prophet, without, however, manifesting the least trace of any prophetic gift, not even enough to be aware that the story is not set in Georgia!) Yet there are consolations. If there is an Orville Prescott, there is also a Louis Dollarhide. It is doubtless no mere accident that the Mississippi man understood your novel far better than most of his Northern and Western confreres. For one thing—and it is not a little thing—the Southerner knows his bible, knows what prophets are.

At least no one is so foolish as not to admit that you write well. As a matter of fact, the reviews are, for the most part, highly laudatory, which leads one to ask: What would they have said—what would they not have said—if they had really understood your work? Please God, some day they will understand.

But perhaps the misunderstanding is not so complete in all quarters as one might be tempted to believe. Since you were here I discovered the following remarks in the *National Review* (April 19, 1960). They occur in an article on "Spring Fiction" by Joan Didion. She speaks of five novels, one of which is yours (the others by Sagan, Colin Wilson, John Braine and Terry Southern respectively). After a paragraph on Mr. Southern's book (*The Magic Christian*, the only other one Didion liked), she comes, in the last paragraph, to yours: "Miss O'Connor, whose merciless style and orthodox vision were established by *Wise Blood* and the collection of short stories called *A Good Man Is Hard to Find*, again focuses upon the problem of redemption. A difficult, perilously stylized book, *The Violent* is at every point controlled by Miss O'Connor's hard intelligence, by her coherent metaphysical view of experience, and by the fact that she is above all a writer, which is something different from a person who writes a book—and somebody ought to explain the difference to Mrs. Sagan, to Mr. Wilson, and to Mr. Braine." I took the liberty of showing the reviews you sent me to Father Murray and to Father Benedetto; their reactions were similar to my own. Father Murray, in turn, showed me your comment on the "God-intoxicating hillbillies," which we both found very witty.

It was so good seeing you again. Next time you must stay longer. My respects to your mother.

FLANNERY O'CONNOR TO THOMAS AND LOUISE GOSSETT

O'Connor cheerfully observes confusion about titles at a breakfast honoring Georgia writers.

MILLEDGEVILLE

23 MAY 60

I have just recently come back from my annual pilgrimage to the Macon Writer's Club breakfast, where I was introduced as the author of *The Valiant Bear It Away*. You go to all them pains to name a book something and then . . . Next Thursday we are expecting Norman Charles who took your place to bring his something or other class over. All Wesleyan is basking in great peace.

We'll certainly be here when you come through and will look forward to seeing you. If you are cat and dogless, stop the night with us. We have the new addition in running order. Miss White and Mary Jo came out and christened it for us by spending a Tuesday night and Wednesday.

About the questions: I did a lot of writing on *Wise Blood* in New York and Connecticut—in fact all of it except the beginning which was done at Iowa and a little of the end and a little rewriting which was done here. Three or four of the stories in the collection were written in those parts too. I'm born and brought-up Catholic, not a convert.

Fr. McCown is in Lake Dallas, Texas—Monserrat Jesuit Retreat House. I went to lecture in Mobile recently (at Spring Hill) and I had dinner with his mother and a passel of his brothers and sisters. They are all very much alive; you'd know them all for McCowns.

My mother is coping and sends you her best. We'll be hoping to see you in September.

FATHER SCOTT WATSON TO FLANNERY O'CONNOR

Better appreciation and understanding of O'Connor's novel occurs in praise from a prominent Jesuit journal.

JUNE 1, 1960

Thank you for the copy of *Critique* and the accompanying note. I can easily understand that you were pleased with Ferris's article as a whole. It is decidedly the best treatment of your novel that I've seen. May it mark the beginning of a better general appreciation!

Perhaps my long letter to Father Gardiner was not wholly without results. Did you notice that in "America Balances the Books" (*America*, May 14, 1960), he comes back to *The Violent Bear It Away* (which he lists first among the five best works of fiction of the season) and gives a much briefer, but much more understanding review? Yet, though he now sees that Tarwater at the end is led "to take up again [why again?] the prophetic mission," he thinks that he is driven to do so "by some dark compulsion." Personally, as I said in my long letter to you, I see no reason to conclude that Tarwater does not retain his essential freedom in the great decisions of his life, above all in this last, though the forces of good and evil exert on the one side and the other a fearful and most powerful pressure. This, I think, is well expressed in the last paragraph of Ferris's essay. In the paragraph just before, however, there is something with which I would disagree and which seems indeed to contradict what is said in the last paragraph. No doubt, "the passion of fanaticism and despair" have a part in Tarwater's answering the call, but certainly I would not say that there was no "passion of religion," or that the boy's answer was "a capitulation to circumstances rather than to God." I daresay this is one of the things with which, as you say in your note, you "don't go along."

But then I'm sure you wouldn't go along with much that I'm saying or have said, so let me not criticize any further our friend, Mr. Ferris. Moreover, if reviews of his or her book must often appear to the novelist as droll, if nothing worse, amateurish comments directed to the author personally could easily become ridiculous, if not indeed outrageous. If I have all along been bold in the expression of my views, it is because I have relied on your Christian charity and patience!

FLANNERY O'CONNOR TO FATHER SCOTT WATSON

It was good to hear from you and I was pleased with the item from the *Nat. Review*.

There have been other summings-up this season that were less pleasing.

I have just got out of the hospital and we are embarking on a new course of treatment which seems risky but is necessary, so I would be obliged for your prayers.

I am going to have something in the February or March issue of *Jubilee* that I want you particularly to see. If you ever get this way, we would certainly love to see you. The best kind of Christmas to you.

FATHER SCOTT WATSON TO FLANNERY O'CONNOR

Father Watson invokes Aristotle's emotional theory in discussing a story. Caroline Gordon's earlier recommendation of The Poetics *to O'Connor remains influential. William Sessions, on the faculty of Spring Hill College, has shared with Father Watson recollections of visiting O'Connor and has distinguished himself as a fine teacher. Sessions continued over the years to present his colorful, vivid recollections of O'Connor in lectures and panel discussions at colleges and universities.*[36]

FEBRUARY 14, 1961

I just read your entertaining—though much more than entertaining story in *The Critic*. It's an interesting story well told. It's also fine satire. But beyond this is your fresh, constant vision into the strange mixing of good and evil, the grotesque blending of greatness and littleness, in Man and in the "Causes" to which he devotes himself. Perhaps it is, at least in part, the same vision which Our Lord Himself expressed in the Parable of the Wheat and the Cockle so intertwining that it's hard to separate one from the other. Be this as it may, "The Partridge Festival" is a piece of powerful irony, providing a catharsis of a kind that would have surprised, but delighted old Aristotle. Sincerest congratulations!

We were all very sorry indeed to hear of the sufferings you have had to undergo, and we surely hope the new treatment is proving successful. You can be sure of a remembrance in our prayers. Lately I've been remembering you by name daily in the Memento of the Mass.

Your good friend Bill Sessions has told me a lot about his visits with you. He is doing well here. He's an excellent teacher and is much appreciated as such.

I know your energy these days is limited, so don't waste any of it trying to answer this. Just offer up one of your more difficult hours for a special intention of mine, and I shall hold myself deep in your debt.

FLANNERY O'CONNOR TO FATHER SCOTT WATSON

The letter notes a remarkable occurrence. An O'Connor story appears for the first time in a Catholic publication. O'Connor is also thankful for prayer. Publication, intercessions of the faithful, and her own suffering are all connected.

20 FEBRUARY 61

Thank you so much for writing me about the story ["The Partridge"]. That is the first story I have ever had in a Catholic magazine [*The Critic*], but I presume that is the first Catholic magazine that would have printed one of them.

The piece I told you I was going to have in *Jubilee* has been postponed until the April issue ["Introduction," *A Memoir of Mary Ann*]. I particularly want you to see it.

I am feeling better and I think that with all the prayers of my friends, I'll make it. I'll remember your intention.

FATHER SCOTT WATSON TO FLANNERY O'CONNOR

Father Watson observes that O'Connor's introduction to a memoir provides a hopeful perspective to a vital philosophic movement. Thomas Merton also would note a similar hopeful reorientation in Walker Percy's The Moviegoer, *also published in 1961. Both O'Connor and Percy provide a theistic dimension and an American context to a European philosophic movement widely understood to be atheistic.*

JUNE 2, 1961

Your article is unusual. It was not what I had expected it to be—the life of Mary Ann ["Introduction," *A Memoir of Mary Ann*]. Actually, it was something better: a quite moving, quite profound study in a vividly concrete setting of some of the great questions that men ask themselves, or should ask themselves. There's a professor at the Jesuit theologate at Louvain [University, Belgium] who likes to begin each new thesis with a few paragraphs from Mauriac, Graham Greene, or some other contemporary man of letters that will somehow present the theological problem in however rudimentary and disguised a fashion. It seems to me your article would furnish this professor with an admirable point of departure, and, more than this, with not a little of the solution. As a philosopher teacher, however, I was particularly interested in the Christian Existentialism of your approach. Only your writing has more of the tang of reality than that of most of them, try for this as they may. The best comparison would be with Dostoevski, who, as you know, is considered a forerunner of the existentialists of the 20th century. Only, you are fully Catholic, and he is not.

Father Rimes, head of the College Chemistry Dept., happened to read your article and said to me, quite spontaneously, what I like about Flannery O'Connor is her realism, or I guess a better word for it would be sincerity, or love of truth. I don't remember his exact words, but this was their tenor! I thought you might be interested in the analysis of a cold-blooded scientist!

Bill [Sessions] lent me the issue of *The Kenyon Review* [Ohio] with your delightful (strong!) satire on the sentimentally compassionate mother et al. ("The Comforts of Home"). A finely wrought piece.

I'm happy to see you're getting a better press in *America* [Jesuit journal] these days. I'm referring, of course, to the May 13th issue.

It's time for prayers, so I must stop. Tomorrow I leave for Tampa, where I shall give a retreat to some Sisters. Please remember this in your prayers.

MILLEDGEVILLE,
4 OCTOBER 61

FLANNERY O'CONNOR TO LA TRELLE

O'Connor responds to a young teacher who is writing a thesis on O'Connor's fiction. She provides commentary on her relationship to her native region and clarifies a label often applied to her.

Dear La Trelle,

The questions you ask are sort of hard to answer, mainly I think because the writer's thought doesn't run in the same categories as that of the person viewing his work from outside. I don't think of myself as having a "purpose as a Southern writer." My purpose as a writer is to write well and see as truly as possible and in as much as Southerners are the people I see, they fall under my general intention of seeing things as they are, There is nothing about this "purpose" that develops; it simply is. It was the same when I first started writing as it is now.

People write books on the subject of what is Southern literature and you can make a big thing of it, but I think probably an unsubtle definition like: Southern literature is literature in which Southerners are accurately reflected: is as good as any other. Using a definition like this, I wouldn't consider a book like *Clock Without Hands* or

Breakfast at Tiffany's Southern literature, even though they are written by Southerners. I have an ingrained suspicion of "southern" writers who sit in judgment on the South from up-state New York and such like places. The real Southern writer when he sits in judgment on the South is sitting in judgment on himself.

Books have been written also on the mind of the South [W.J. Cash, *The Mind of the South*]. The fiction writer attempts to show what it is, but he seldom cares to write essays on the subject. However I have written one which you will find in Granville Hick's symposium, the LIVING NOVEL, which should be in your library. If it isn't I'll be glad to lend you my copy.

When you come home for thanksgiving, come out and see me and we can talk about these things. They are probably easier talked about than written about. I'd love to meet Miss Strong and her mother if you'd care to bring them over.

All the best,

FLANNERY O'CONNOR TO ROBERT M. McCOWN

O'Connor thanks the brother of Father James McCown, Robert, for his essay. A native of Mobile, Alabama, he earned a B.A. and an M.A. (Honors) in 1954 at Oxford University, where one of his examiners was C. S. Lewis. He also later became a novitiate in the Society of Jesus. He was ordained in 1963 at St. Joseph Chapel, Spring Hill College. He died in 2012.

MILLEDGEVILLE

GEORGIA

1 DECEMBER 61

I am very grateful to you for writing this essay about my novel ["The Education of a Prophet: Flannery O'Connor's *The Violent Bear It Away*"]. If you have seen some of the other things written about it, you will know just how grateful. What you say about the book exactly reflects my intentions when I wrote it and I intend to write *The*

Kansas Magazine and get myself a few copies to have on hand as a defensive weapon.[37]

Most of the theories proposed about the book make my hair stand on end. Any analysis seems to be acceptable so long as it is not obvious, and when you stop to think that students are trained to read this way, the prospect of submitting your writing to continual misunderstanding becomes right cheerless. I am glad there is still someone at large who can read.

When I was in Mobile year before last, I enjoyed some of your mother's hospitality. I admire all the McCowns.

Sincerely,

Flannery O'Connor

FATHER SCOTT WATSON TO FLANNERY O'CONNOR

Thanking O'Connor for her reissued novel Wise Blood, *Father Watson parallels its themes to works by canonical and biblical writers. He also recognizes that a story could serve as an introduction to O'Connor's* The Violent Bear It Away. *This letter and others reveal how sequencing of the stories is vital in understanding O'Connor's fiction.*

SEPT. 1962

I notice that all your friends, intimate or not, call you by your first name (in part, perhaps, because it is a strange and strangely attractive first name), and as I certainly wish to be counted a friend, if only a poor friend (like a poor relation), I shall do as the others. Moreover, your own most friendly custom of signing your letters "Flannery" encourages me to think that I'm not overbold. Your book and note came while I was away making my annual retreat at our novitiate at Grand Coteau (where the good God sends rain to my spiritual roots); since then I've been unusually busy with a number of more or less urgent details; hence it is only now that I finally find myself free to acknowledge your kindness. Thank you very much for the copy of

Wise Blood. I'm "extra-grateful" for the autograph and "most grateful" of all for the friendship it so succinctly expresses.

When I get a chance I certainly wish to reread *Wise Blood,* and don't doubt that I'll find it still more gripping than the first time I read it. Your note to the second edition is truly helpful. The one short paragraph is packed with important ideas, each one of which deserves a commentary but I'll spare you this. Just a few passing words. Your characterization of *Wise Blood* as "a comic novel about a Christian malgre lui" is the sort of pithy description one would look for in a first-rate critic. Most authors—at least contemporary ones—don't seem to have so clear a notion of what they are trying to do. What you say of the exact nature of Hazel Motes' integrity is particularly illuminating and strikingly put. As to what you say of the "many wills conflicting in one man," St. Augustine, as you doubtless know, talked long ago of the divided will and before him St. Paul had dramatized the struggle between the two "wills." During my retreat I read a little book by the famous Austrian theologian Karl Rahner (called *Happiness Through Prayer*), which contains some stimulating pages on the mystery of freedom, though Father Rahner stresses rather how the present action of a man embodies his whole past or, at least, may do so. Presumably, not all our "wills" are free or not equally so at any rate. "God alone knows what is in man," writes Father Rahner. "No one knows what really to make of himself in his poor distracted heart; whether his real self lives in his longing for a greater love of God, or in his unacknowledged and unrepentant grumbling at the immeasurable demands of this love." Yet if the nature and precise location of free will are mysterious, the fact of freedom is certain. Authors who deny this fact, not only in theory, but in practical conviction play havoc with their lives and simultaneously make it impossible for themselves to write great literature. That you hold firmly to freedom while not limiting the mystery is one of your strengths as a writer.

I meant to talk about your novella [*The Lame Shall Enter First*] published in *The Sewanee Review,* but have run on at such length about other things that now no time is left. Let me just say that if we compare *The Violent Bear It Away* to a great, leaping fire we must liken *The Lame Shall Enter First* to a "hard gem like flame" by reason of its lesser scope, its admirable conciseness, its sculptured quality. It was fascinating to see the same great theme of the failure of rationalism to satisfy the heart of man undergo a new and dexterous development. Yet in its greater simplicity and clarity it will also serve as an excellent introduction to the novel.[38] Incidentally, I shall recommend both works to a young friend of mine, and former student, who, it seems, has sold his unbuyable faith for a mess of rationalistic pottage that can never quiet his soul's hunger. Please pray for him. I've not yet had an opportunity to read the articles on your work that appeared with the novella in *The Sewanee Review,* but I trust they are competent. Congratulations on the ensemble as well as on the new edition of *Wise Blood,* with its handsome format, cover, jacket.

CHAPTER 3

"HER KIND OF LITERATURE: PLACES AND FOLKS"

While O'Connor finds herself increasingly immobile, letters in this chapter show her keen interest in "folks" traveling to interesting "places." The chapter begins with her letters to a convert friend, Elizabeth "Betty" Hester. O'Connor praises her stories and a play by their mutual friend, William Sessions. A steadfast Catholic convert himself, Sessions grasped the deep bond between Hester and O'Connor. He encouraged a portion of O'Connor's letters to Hester be included in the seminal, *The Habit of Being*. Sessions notes that the correspondence comprises "the richest letters in the book" and that the collection itself "has been . . . compared to the letters of Keats."[1]

O'Connor, also in 1960, writes her fellow Georgian Roslyn Barnes, whose spiritual odyssey differs from other friends of O'Connor such as Betty Hester and Robert Lowell, who left the Church. Like O'Connor, Barnes attended college in Milledgeville and graduate school at the Iowa Writers' Workshop. O'Connor writes her about professors and experiences they have in common. Barnes dedicated her 1962 master's thesis, "Gerard Manley Hopkins and

Pierre Teilhard de Chardin: A Formulation of Mysticism for a Scientific Age," to O'Connor. Barnes would become a missionary in the Papal Auxiliary Volunteer Corps for Latin America (PAVLA), a lay movement sanctioned by Pope John XXIII. O'Connor recommended and counseled her in becoming a missionary.

Roslyn Barnes undertook rigorous spiritual formation in Mexico. She endured the severe discipline of the legendary, controversial Monseigneur Ivan Illich. Since Father McCown knew of Msgr. Illich and had himself ministered in Mexico, O'Connor enlists him to write Miss Barnes. Her thoughtful letters in reply introduce a global perspective on the writings of both O'Connor and Walker Percy that would continue in later years.

Both Barnes and Father McCown shared their love of Mexico with O'Connor. While she is often skeptical of Father McCown's literary skills, his chronicle about a pilgrimage in Mexico in 1962 wins O'Connor's praise. McCown's unpublished account delights and entertains O'Connor and her mother. Father McCown regaled both with his stories. (He would continue to send Regina O'Connor his travel narratives after O'Connor's death in 1964.)

Father McCown masters the literary genre of the Jesuit order. What he says about his later African narrative applies to the Mexican chronicle: "I fondly, rashly, hope that this could be a sort of contemporary 'Jesuit Relations,' in the tradition of the early newsletters sent back to Europe by early Jesuit missionaries to the New World."[2] Such narratives often recorded the perils faced by religious—Roslyn Barnes was no exception. She disappeared in Chile and was later presumed dead.

FLANNERY O'CONNOR TO ELIZABETH HESTER

O'Connor traces a central theme in her fiction to antiquity. She also addresses mundane matters about propriety of dress, likening descriptions from a neighbor to a character from a story by a famous author.

MILLEDGEVILLE

8 AUGUST 59

Dear Betty,

We sure have been enjoying your candy but we won't be for much longer as my mother set it out yesterday where my uncle's eye could light upon it and he went to it, she said, "like a cow to a salt lick." I thank you too for the books. I am reading the mythology one and bringing back my early days. I grew up on the Greek and Roman myths and was well up on the infidelities of the gods before I knew what infidelities were. There is much betrayal there too. You say I am concerned with that theme, but how could anybody not be? The violent bear it away. Relax, forget for an instant, and you find yourself betraying.

After you left Mrs. Armstrong said between smacks on her gum, "Is that lady a nurse?" I said no. "Well," she said, "she sher looked like a nurse. I would have said she was a nurse right off. She looked so efficient and all." They stayed about an hour. Were you there when she told about her shorts? Some Oconee [Georgia] ladies came and told her she wouldn't be liked if she wore those shorts in Oconee. She said, "Listen here, you ladies, I don't know who sent you up here to tell me that but you tell them I have a lot more shorts than I have dresses and if anybody changes their ways around here, it's not going to be me." Now she says all the women in Oconee wear shorts. Another lady stopped at her g[arden] one day when she was working in the flowers in her shorts. The lady said she had on real short shorts, didn't she? Mrs. Armstrong said, "yes and this is only June. The hotter it gets the shorter they get. You just wait until August." Mr. Armstrong never says a word himself but he listens to every word she says as if its pure music. Wednesday, we had a letter from her saying that the peahen died the next day, that she thought it got too hot. That made me kind of sick. I wrote her I'd buy the cock back if she wanted to get rid of him, so I am hoping they will come back this afternoon and bring him. My mother says its no telling if they went right home with those birds or not. Anyway, the hen was not sick when she left. Anyway,

Mrs. Armstrong is straight out of Ring Lardner and I think her words are as golden as her old man does.

The enclosed may be of same use to you. I thought I had sent it before.

I will buy what you say about a story starting with a love split in opposite directions, though desire seems a better word to me than love. It seems to me you can only love the good, but you can desire the bad.

The next time you come we are going to take you to the Sanford House, the asylum, the reformatory and the Sinclair dam. Can you wait?

Cheers

Due to the travails of Caroline Gordon, O'Connor asks her friend to give a story the kind of scrutiny Gordon had provided. O'Connor asks only a very few friends for such commentary.

WEDNESDAY

Dear Betty,

I would be much obliged if you would read the enclosed diversion and let me know what you think about it. You will have to be Caroline on this as I think she is too distraught to send it to right now.

Long distance from Eel Lopez Hines tells me that I must get aholt of the Sept 5 *Saturday Review* and see the article in it on Catholic Writing. Marvelous Sueperb and Etc. She read most of it to me over the phone, and it did sound sane. Sanity delivered in her shriek has a curious effect of intoxication.

Cheers,

F

O'Connor patiently listens to an Episcopal professor enumerate a Catholic stu-
dent's problems with priests and nuns. O'Connor is strengthened by rereading
Cardinal Newman.

MILLEDGEVILLE

5 SEPTEMBER 59

Dear Betty,

In spite of all that Billy [Sessions] says is wrong with your novel there are a good many things right with it too, but I suppose it is a good thing he put it across to you if it pulls you up from making your characters discuss religion. This always should be avoided. I spent 7 years avoiding it in this last book of mine. Some people can do it but it is always dangerous. If you were stupider you would write better fiction because you wouldn't conceptualize things so much.

We got week before this a post card from the lad saying he would be with us for dinner Tuesday (card arriving Monday) and on Tuesday instead of him we get a telegram: AM SICK. HOPE TO AP-PEAR THURSDAY. It so chanced that we were having company Thursday and going out Friday so I forthwith wired him that I couldn't see him Thursday or Friday. So we haven't heard from him again and don't know what the state of his poor health is. Maybe grandmaw was too much for him.

All good Catholics become anti-clerical sooner or later. It is a noble and honorable tradition. All the sins of the priesthood have been visited on me lately via Dr. Spivey [Ted R., professor, Georgia State University] who has a Catholic student whom he is trying, or so he says, to keep in the Catholic church. The girl came in when she was 15, is now 18, went one year to a Catholic college which she could not abide and in her three years in the Church has met nothing apparently but "lying" nuns, stupid mechanical Catholics and neu-rotic priests. I have never known a nun myself who would deliber-ately lie so what I presume the girl is talking about is "intellectual honesty" and I pointed out to Dr. Spivey that you had to have an intellect before you could be accused of intellectual dishonesty. However, it is a losing battle. I guess the little girl is looking for an excuse to get out, and she will find it, meanwhile giving Dr. Spivey many excuses for not coming in.

I have just read over Cardinal Newman's Apologia [*Pro Vita Sua*]. Have you read this at all or have you read it lately. I hadn't read it in about ten years, but it was very enlightening.

Never heard a word more from the Armstrongs. My heart is broken.

Cheers,
Flannery

O'Connor notes a story has elicited criticism from her mother. She was vigilant in reading her daughter's stories with an eye to the offense they might give locally. O'Connor recounts, by contrast, larger perspectives after having read a philosophic work by an influential priest and journal articles about Catholic literature.

MILLEDGEVILLE

19 SEPTEMBER 59

Dear Betty,

Well I have a sad tale to tell. "The Partridge Pageant" will never see the light of day, or at least not for many years. I should have known better that to start with it, but I went careening through it like a hoop. Milledgeville had one of the things in 1953—its Sesquicentennial and the Saturday before the festivities, a fellow name Stembridge shot the chairman of the pageant committee and another lawyer and himself. Of course, it was the greatest thing that had happened to Milledgeville since Sherman passed through. When my mother read it [the story] she was horrified, declared it would cause the families of those people suffering and so forth. Maybe when I am 60 years old and all the families are dead and gone, I will reach my withered paw into the trunk and pull out this, but for the present, it is just one for the pot, a nest egg. I almost sent it on before I showed it to her, but I thought she might as well see it. Then I knew by her reaction that it probably would hurt those people, so there is nothing to do but forget it. Maybe I can give somebody else the grass bag. I put your notes up with it, but I don't have the feeling to correct any of those things now.

Euthyphro was a dumb fellow whom Socrates met outside of the courts of law, and questioned on the nature of justice. Euthyphro was going to court to sue his father. This piece of erudition is not native to me. I have just finished Guardini's *The Death of Socrates*, which if you would be interested in, I will send you.

Thanks very much for sending the *Sat. Review.* It certainly is a lousy magazine. Do you want it back? What did you think of the article? I think the *Messenger* is quite wrong to criticize him for putting it in the *Sat. Re.* As I pointed out to the old soul, until Catholics realize that their linen is sometimes going to be hung on the public line, they will not get it in better condition. I think he confuses journalism and letters, and his remarks on fiction and poetry don't indicate that he knows what is being written. Even if there are not so many fiction writers, there are some very fine Catholic poets. But his other pronouncements I can accept vigorously.

Tuesday Miss Betsy Locheridge is to come down here and interview me for the Sunday supplement. You will probably find me tricked out in the personality of the Georgia Farm Girl or Good-Earth-Loving Author or something equally horrendous. Hoping to remove such possibilities, I have prepared a list of questions with answers, typewritten, which I shall hand to her to incorporate. "Here Betsy, I have done half the work myself!" Isn't <u>Betsy</u> a very unlikely name

Billy [Sessions] discussed his "entire weltsmelts" (spelling mine) with Peter, who is supposed to have plenty of bedside manner. I can visualize the scene.

Modified cheers,
Flannery

O'Connor praises a loose association of writers and implies that her correspondent is a member of the community. Betty's manuscript, perhaps The Joys of the Fittest, *has been submitted, via O'Connor, to her agent. O'Connor also reacts to liturgical innovations.*

MILLEDGEVILLE

17 OCTOBER 59

Dear Betty,

   . . . The proofs are back in New York and I have recovered some of my insensitivity to it and hope I don't lose it again. I enclose Jack Hawkes letter because it will interest you. It is a most tactful document. He has a strange and wonderful mind. I am not sure what he means by "demonic" as he uses it; frequently he leaves me behind, but I think what he says is just & good ["Flannery O'Connor's Devil," *The Sewanee Review,* Summer 1962]. Except that I am very partial to Enoch. In both cases what he thinks lowers the interest is the very thing that makes the book possible as a novel. This is inevitable I suppose when your creative energy just can't encompass but one bill of goods, metaphysically.

   We don't have a Catholic literature in the sense that we have a group of writers gathered around a central motivating proposition, or a leader, but we do have something in that there are a very respectable number of good poets who are Catholics (as our friend Hawkes would have it) who are sitting in their own places writing good poetry. And this don't have to include dear Allen [Tate] or Carol Johnson either. Raymond Roseliep, Ned O'Gorman, John Logan, John Fandel, John Frederick Nims, John Edward Hardy, a couple of interesting nuns, Leonie Adams, and Robert Fitzgerald and there may be others. This is not a movement or a school; but literature is produced by people writing. There are no literary geniuses in this bunch but those are given by the Lord now and again and can't be had by improving the culture or anything.

Can't recollect reading anything Anne Fremantle wrote on Turnell [Martin] but I have a paper back copy of his *The Novel in France*, which is enjoyable if you want to see it. Also if you want to see Elizabeth Hardwick's article on book reviewers I have it as somebody sent me that issue of *Harper's* as I am thrown a bone in it by Alfred Kazin. The donor properly marked the passage, etc. The issue is very interesting.

I am one of the laymen who RESIST the congregation yapping out the Mass in English & my reason besides neurotic fear of change, anxiety, early bed-wetting and laziness is that I do not like the raw sound of the human voice in unison unless it is under the discipline of music.

I haven't heard from Elizabeth McKee about your ms, but the last person I recommended to send her something, she sent it back to them with a note that it didn't interest her. So I am cheered that she is showing yours to some people. Her scent for money is keen enough to extend as much as ten years into the future. Yes I know her personally, which is to say I have lunch with her when I am in NY. Send her your next one. I don't think you'll regret it.

Yrs,
Flannery

A book you must investigate: *The Straight and Narrow Path* by Honor Tracy.

O'Connor provides judicious, specific comments about friends and visitors.

MILLEDGEVILLE
DECEMBER 59

Dear Betty,

My mother said did I tell you how much she appreciated your looking up that book for her and I said naw I don't think I did, at which she was not well pleased. I am a very poor hand at conveying other folks appreciation, but she appreciated it. I think, since she wants to give me a book like that, I will get Malroux's [André Malraux] *Voices of Silence*. They tell me it is very fine, but I'll wait until we come to Atlanta and look at it myself.

The enclosed will show you that Thomas is not of general appeal. I think she is right; anyway, I follow, as you do too, the negative outlook on a story before it is published and the positive after. So I will put up "The Comforts of Home" until I can decide some better way to end it. I think this bears out your feeling about the gun; only it was more than the gun. I also find the Partridge story impossible. It seems almost too slight to work on but is really better as a peanut festival but I will probably sack it, even as that. You can't turn out stories like corn from a hot popper or that is what you will have— corn.

I like Carol [Johnson] and think she is very intelligent. Ashley [Brown] thinks she is shy but I don't much think so. I think she is just wrapped up in herself and her own work. Most of us are. I am myself; but being a Southerner, I have the manners to counteract it, and she being a mid-westerner is almost devoid of these necessary manners. For instance, in writing to say she had a nice time, she did not mention my mother. Who really had the brunt of it. This is not bad manners, just a lack of manners. The touch of the convent is still on her. Occasionally I would look at her, and she would be looking straight ahead, alone in the room full of people, as if the wimple, or whatever that veil is that blinkers them, were invisibly on her. There is a kind of self-centeredness peculiar to those in religious orders, where their main business is to think of their own soul and where everything is ordered around them to that end. She did more talking when you had her by herself. But after four days of them, I was pretty well shot.

We had a note from Billy [Sessions] declaring himself to be in delicate health. I'm glad he met you regardless of his motives. When he was here, my mother gave him a lecture on thinking about himself too much, and in his note he said he had found a quotation from St. John of the Cross to help him counter that tendency: Disquietude is vanity. Billy is a peculiar combination of high intelligence and ridiculous personality. The only case like it I know.

I had a letter from my Longman's editor in London wanting to know what was the significance of Tarwater's violation in the woods. This is very depressing and a hint of things to come.

Excelsior,

Flannery

The letter concerns news and observations among mutual friends. Echoes of O'Connor's stories are present in her mother providing counsel about marriage. Such wisdom plays a significant role in "The Life You Save May Be Your Own," "Good Country People," "The Displaced Person," and other stories.

MILLEDGEVILLE

7 JANUARY 60

Dear Betty,

Well that play may not have been any worse than the others, but at least in the others there were one or two characters that Billy [Sessions] knew something about—such as the colored woman in the first one; but he don't know anything about tycoons and revolutionaries. I told him it might be good for him if he took some historical incident from around South Carolina and made a play out of it, such as Warren [Robert Penn] did in *Brother to Dragons*. It seems to me that this would furnish some discipline for his imagination; he would have something to check himself by.

By all means bring that lady with you. We'd enjoy her. You name the day.

You will be innerested to know that I am on page 245 of *Remem-*

berance of Things Past [Marcel Proust], and that I have a special bed-table to put it on, one of Miss Mary's cast off possessions, as I am too lazy to hold it up. I like it a lot better than I thought I would.

I'm not making much progress on my story as I am nauseated in the morning with this new medicine. It makes you that way until your system gets used to it, which they say takes about two months. I am less enthusiastic about all things when nauseated.

The African contingent here celebrated the holidays by staying drunk throughout them.

I think my mother is less convinced that Billy, "that prize package," as she calls him, is any less silly than always. She counseled him at length about his matrimonial desires. He averred that he would make some woman a very good husband. My mother told him he would run any woman crazy in short order. I was particularly irritated by his telling my mother about that vulgar drawing that Robie Macauley stuck on my story in the Fall *Kenyon* [*Review*]. I thought it was sickening and thought it just as well she didn't see it, but as soon as he left, she said he had shown it to her. She was insensed over the drawing. So was I but thought it best to forget it, but she reinsensed me to the extent that I wrote Robie a letter about it. To do Billy [William Sessions] justice, he probably thought she knew about it, but that does not lessen my irritation.

I'm glad you gave up the Great Books if it was going to interfere with your writing what you're writing. Otherwise, I think it would have been a good thing.

Well cheers,

Flannery

As O'Connor advises in other letters, writing by a Catholic convert does not have to be specifically religious. She hopes Hester will visit by traveling with their mutual friend. In meeting journalists and critics, O'Connor compares herself to a character in her own novel.

MILLEDGEVILLE

13 FEBRUARY 60

Dear Betty,

I would not give any thought to the fact that your novel does not express your convictions as a Catholic. The convert does not get to experience his convictions in the years that experience forms the imagination, so it is quite right that what you will reflect is your need; that is right and that is enough. In the other things you have written it may have been an attempt to express your now-convictions that marred the writing. This sounds like a highly interesting book and I await it with sympathy.

The enclosed (Penguin thing) was sent me by yclept Sessions with instructions to indicate what I want. I don't [want] anything but to be polite [so] I have marked the Hopkins poems. In his letter he indicates that he will spend the day on some Saturday in February which I am to designate. I am designating the 27th and suggesting that he bring you if he is coming from Atlanta. Your presence will take the curse off him (how awful we speak of our saintly Billy) and will also deter him from getting a weak spell toward 5 and feeling that he cannot make it to Atlanta that night. If he is not coming from Atlanta, why don't you come down on the bus or if you would rather come on a Saturday when he is not coming, come the next Saturday. Any Saturday will do but the 19th of March. Another thought is that if he is coming from the monastery [Monastery of the Holy Spirit], you could take the bus to Conyers [Georgia] and let him meet your there????

Thursday *Time* sent two men down here from Atlanta, one to take pictures and the other to ask questions sent from the NY office—so they are intending to do something with it and we shall wait patiently to see what. The man took about a million pictures, in all of which I am sure I looked like Bishop [character, *The Violent Bear It Away*]. They will select the one [that] looks most like Bishop. Apparently there is a very favorable review in the February *Catholic World* by the Medieval Studies man at Boston University. I haven't seen it.

And Granville Hicks is writing something favorable about it for the *Saturday Review*. So there will at least be a mixture.

We hear no more about the scientist who may have done in Rosie.

After the interview with the *Time* man I am very much aware of how hard you have to try to escape labels. He wanted me to characterize myself so he would have something to write down. Are you a Southern writer? What kind of Catholic are you? Etc. I asked him what kinds of Catholics there were. Liberal or conservative, says he. All I did for an hour was stammer and stutter and all night I was awake answering his questions with the necessary qualifications and reservations. Not only will look like Bishop but will sound like him if he could talk.

Cheers,

Flannery

O'Connor praises Betty's excellent fiction that deserves publication. The influence of O'Connor's writing tutor, Caroline Gordon, is evident in O'Connor's suggestion for more details to improve the novel's setting.

MILLEDGEVILLE

7 MARCH 60

Dear Betty,

This is in my opinion a HOWLING success. If this fails to get published I will lose my faith in American publishers. If it is not published for the right reasons, it will surely be published for the wrong. I am going to write E. [Elizabeth McKee] and tell her I have read it and that I think it is a sure thing.

This is certainly your medium. This one is much much better than the other, very sure in every way—well paced, dramatic, and a fine control throughout of the language. If I had known when I started marking things that it was going to be this good throughout, I wouldn't have marked it up because you could have sent it to E. like it is. The things I have marked are details only, matters of syntax or grammar or an occasional image that seemed out of tone, usually too exuberant for the occasion.

There is one thing you might think of, though if you don't I don't think it will make too much difference. That is that there is not much sense of the town that surrounds the brown-sugar house. In a story like this you want to do everything that will add to the reality of characters who are extreme. I thought it was probably a small town until the airport came in and then I began to think it might be a city. A sentence, a paragraph here and there would clear this up and add to the substantialness of things. In this college town, (Milledgeville), if a member of the faculty made a suicide attempt with the reek of Liquor on him he would soon be at some other college. You had better make it plain that this man can't be dispensed with because of his academic attainments or something. Academic reputation would keep him there, nothing else. They will put up with the worst teachers if they have published a book. All you got to do is assure us he's published a book. All this sense of what surrounds them, of the real people who surround them needs to be suggested.* (This may give you an idea of why there is a deputy in my story). It wouldn't take much to do this, and I do feel it would improve it. But it is fine, really fine.

My heartiest cheers,
Flannery

PS That mountain man riding by in the wagon at break of day is Turriffic. Every now and then I paused in sheer admiration, but nothing else could stop me from reading.

*suggested only.

O'Connor is perplexed about the rejection of her friend's novel by a publisher and suggests the agent might reveal the reason why. As in previous letters,

echoes of O'Connor's stories emerge in a literary award she received. "Brenda Star" resembles June Star of "A Good Man Is Hard to Find," and the young woman giving the award is reminiscent of "Joy/Hulga" in "Good Country People."

MILLEDGEVILLE

28 MAY 60

Dear Betty,

That is strange to me that they wouldn't handle that novel. Did they give any indication why? I don't know the Minor girl and don't know Mavis except for a few business dealings. Anyway, wait and see what Elizabeth [McKee] says, not that I think she has any literary judgment, but she might tell you WHY they won't send it around. It is well written and to me it was not offensive. I sometimes think I must be pretty callus to what is offensive to other people. However, I don't know as I would have shown it to your librarian friend; but I'd be interested to know what she thought.

Miss OBD didn't ask me what I thought of her novel; had she, I was going to tell her the beautiful truth: I haven't read it. I did read the first chapter but the part does not stand for the whole. OBD and her mother are quire unbelievable. If I had created them, I would have to scratch them all out. There is no combination quite like innocence and gall.

You are right about Billy [Sessions]. Lord, give me a little of your charity.

No, don't have Dr. S. to supper. You'd be bored to tears probably and want to heave him out the window. He is just something that, like all the letters, I would like you to be in on. You will run up on him some time or other possibly. Sent you the Jung book. I found it fairly exasperating, though I have read Jung in the past and like him better. Some journalism fraternity in Atlanta awarded me something called The Brenda, named after, I regret to say, Brenda Star, Girl Reporter, a character out of the funny paper. Anyway, I did not go up there to receive the thing but Betsy Fancher went and accepted it for me, so I had to ask the ladies of the journalism fraternity to come down for tea for to bring the object. Last Saturday ten of them came, mostly it seems fashion editors with the exception of Marjorie Rutherford and the Brigadier General Editor of the Salvation Army *War Cry*. The latter was kind of five by five and wore the skirt of her uniform and a white shirt and those stockings that the elastic ends below the knees. The object was of gilded concrete, a naked girl reporter holding up a scroll against a background of their fraternity letters. As soon as they left, I wrapped it up in a newspaper and do not intend to look at it again.

I had a letter from the Sister today wanting to know when I was coming up there. I see there'll be no escaping her. Apparently the Bishop is much interested in this too. He delivered the child's funeral oration.

Cheers or something,
Flannery

O'Connor praises her friend's writing once again and places her among the masters of American literature. Nobel Prize winner, William Faulkner, once observed he was just writing about "people." O'Connor notes Hester does the same. Drawing on her own rootedness in Dante's writing techniques, O'Connor reveals Hester's stories are similarly anchored in the Florentine.

MILLEDGEVILLE
6 JUNE 60

Dear Betty,

This is wonderful, much better than the other stories, more natural and more concerned with what stories are concerned with—people. I also have the sense that you enjoyed writing it in a way you didn't enjoy the others; and all that shows. I have no advice on it at all except you take out words here and there and you redo a sentence in it that isn't grammatical. I also suggested you leave out the sentence about the nurse in his room but that's not important. I would type this over and start sending it out. Just for the heck of it send it to *The New Yorker*. I don't think they will take it, but just send it and see what they say. I am sure you could get it published at once at some place like *The Georgia Review* in Athens, which would not be bad, but I would just try the other as you have nothing to lose. You might even try *Esquire*, which has become a literary magazine I am told by Ashley [Brown], and is read in all the best barber shops. I may try them on that Partridge deal which I have written over as an Azalea Festival and got the mater's approval of; but now I don't like it myself. I don't know what I'll do about it.

Of course, you could send this to Elizabeth [McKee] and get her to send it around but I would wait and be sure she's there. I'd like her and those other two to see it. Every communication I have had from Miss Minor has irritated me.

As soon as I finish reading it to review for the Bully Tin I will send you CHRIST AND APOLLO [William F. Lynch, S.J.] which will tell you what you have already done just discovered apparently by yourself. This story illustrates CHRIST AND APOLLO to perfection. Your other stories were written by the univocal imagination; now you have written one using the analogical imagination. Wait'll you read the book and you will see what I'm talking about.

Send this to Billy [Sessions] and see if he don't agree with me, that this story is the best.

I told him I wanted him to be picking out a Saturday to bring you and him down. If he don't, come by yourself. If you would like to meet M.[aurice-Edgar] Coindreau [French translator] come on June 18.

Cheers,

F

*This is a serial letter involving items of interest. O'Connor and Hester react to
a play written by William Sessions. O'Connor encourages Hester to come over
from Atlanta when Mr. Coindreau, the translator of Faulkner's stories into
French, plans to visit O'Connor. She perhaps senses Hester will understand
the significance of the translation of O'Connor's stories into French.*

MILLEDGEVILLE

11 JUNE 60

Dear Betty,

Why don't you just send that story to *The Atlantic* and to *Harper's*
and to *Esquire* and to the *Sat. Eve. Post* while you are at it? As soon as
you get it back from one send it to the next. A note from Miss Minor
informs me that Elizabeth will be back June 20 so maybe eventually
you'll hear from her.

Yesterday Billy's opus arrived in the mail with a dollar bill attached to it. Instructions are to send it on to you when I finish with it.
I am in medias res now with no opinion yet.

No the dog-book lady didn't come. I talked to her once about the
award over the telephone but I never know who I'm talking to on the
telephone and not until I hung up did I realize she was the dog-book
lady. She sounded like a good old girl.

My opinion of Bud has gone up I must say. Some of his columns
had struck me as efforts to be cute. Which they probably were but
anyway it is consoling to know that he has to make an effort to be
cute and isn't just naturally cute. I have hopes for the *Messenger's* future. There was a nice paragraph about TVBIA [*The Violent Bear It
Away*] in the last *Partisan Review* in the Fiction Chronicle by a man I
respect, R. W. Flint. He didn't say much but what he said was ok. The
reviews get more favorable the farther away they are from publication date. This is as it should be.

The enclosed will amuse you. It is a section that Powers [J. F.]
censored out of a book called *Conversations with Catholics* that Lippincott is going to publish soon—tape recorded sessions with McDonald. A friend of mine at Lippincott sent it to me, which she wasn't of

course supposed to do so don't mention it to anybody else. I can't understand why either of them should the mummy hard to understand. I thought it dangerously obvious.

I've sent you *Christ and Apollo* [William F. Lynch, S.J.] which has some good answers to the question of what-are-you-saying. But when people ask you this, there is no answer for them except to say you are saying what can't be said otherwise than with your whole book, that you can't substitute an abstraction and have the same thing.

This version I sent you of "The Partridge Festival" has the mater's seal of toleration. I am undecided about it though I think it is a great improvement on the other version. Lemme hear how it strikes you.

Cheers,

Flannery

I forgot. Ashley [Brown] and Carol [Johnson] were here last Thursday and Friday and Carol said, "How is Elizabeth? I would have liked to talk to her." "Elizabeth who?" says I. "The girl," she said, "who came down that Saturday." So it seems you are Elizabeth, how I don't know. A. was taking her as far as he was going, Nashville. My mother said she would just as soon have a broom in the car with her as Carol. Somebody in Virginia has had a little booklet of her poems printed for her and she is going to send you one, via me; but it hasn't come yet.

6-13-60

I meant it would be bad for you. Nothing worse than ignorant folks telling you what they think of your books. That is why I am all against writers' clubs where they read their works to each other— ignorance, malice, and flattery. I am sure that lady had no malice, but she doesn't know anything. Sometimes people associated with the outside of books get the illusion they know something about the inside—very bad.

Watch out for all those theories of your own. Miss Nancy deserves just what she got from you, no more. She won't take more weight. Send it to those places whether you like it or not.

Cecil [Dawkins] is still in Waukesha and will be there until the end of June probably. I heard from her today and she asked what had happened to you. Cecil is kind of a displaced person. I suspect she needs you.

I will try to get that bottle out of that child's mouth. I changed that around and thought I had her cleared to talk but I must have done just the opposite. I will also learn to spell nickel. Perhaps. It is dreadful to be corrupting others.

By now you will have read yclept Billy's [Sessions] manuscript. I have the feeling—and I didn't say this to him because it is just a feeling—but the feeling that this might have been written by some old man who fancied himself a Bernanos type. There are a lot of lovely passages, but it seems to me imitation Bernanos wrapped around Tennessee Williams. Billy is <u>too</u> good an impersonator for his own good. He shows exactly what he has read. I liked the angel being part of the spinning equipment, but found his entrance rather startling at that point. Billy enclosed a dollar bill in the ms. He sent it fourth class for 33¢ and wrote manuscript on the outside but the mailman told my momma it would have to be first so I owe Billy 34¢ or so. Or maybe I should forward this 34¢ to you and you should send it to him 4th class. I think we might cut a few corners ourselves in dealing with William.

I accept all your kind words about how find I address an envelope. I feel myself I am very good at it. If there is One thing I can do, I always say, it is address an envelope.

If you won't come down when M. [Maurice-Edgar] Coindreau is here, pick another Sareday. I expect no more visitors unless they be unannounced.

Cheers,
Flannery

FLANNERY O'CONNOR TO WILLIAM A. SESSIONS

O'Connor is critical of her friend's play. Staging supernatural occurrences is very difficult and requires a rare gift, like Shakespeare's presentation of a ghost in Hamlet. *Pulitzer Prize winner, August Wilson, in* The Piano Lesson, *also powerfully presents a demonic presence on stage. Sessions's attempts put him among exalted playwrights, but the results are not as successful.*

MILLEDGEVILLE

23 JULY 60

Dear Billy,

I have just finished the play and while it is fresh in my haid I will tell you a few of my reactions, since I may have forgot them by Saturday next.

While I think you have made your intellectual intentions clearer than in the other version, I think you have weakened the play dramatically. It is awful <u>talky</u>. You just can't read this psychologizing talk-talk for long. The reader gets bored with Hugh and his problems. When you had those other characters there was at least some exiting and entrancing to break the monotony.

You have moved the good bit about the angel being seen as part of the spinning equipment to the very end—where it is dramatically ineffective. You need that in an earlier place to give the vision reality. That was the good thing about it in the other version, apart from its being good in itself. We believed in the vision right away. Now I do not believe in it. I think Durwood is weaker in this version. You have prepared for the angel better, but then when you come to it, it is weak. That last speech of Elena's about the angel when Durwood has the knife at her throat is bad—just wouldn't be. All I could think of is this is not Elena with a knife at her throat, this is Billy philosophysing his play. Very frequently in this version, I don't hear the characters at all—I hear you.

I think if you could combine some of the better aspects of this version without sacrificing what you had in the other version, you would do better. Of the two version[s], I would prefer the first. But I think you can do a better one than either.

I would put Harvey and the old lady back in there if I was you and I would sure move that angel coming out of the spindle to where you had it before.

Durwood is not very real to me. Somehow I still see you commenting on things through Durwood. I think you need to get more distance on the whole thing.

We'll be looking for you and Betty at high noon on
Saturday. Cheers,
Flannery

FLANNERY O'CONNOR TO ELIZABETH HESTER

SAT AFT

Dear B,

The enclosed is what I told the lad [William Sessions] but don't tell him I sent you a copy. I think he has just tried to tighten it up and hasn't succeeded and it is much worse as you say. You hear him talking through all these people. A play with 4 characters—all Bill—the theatre will die when it sees him coming if he keeps this up.

Chrs F

MILLEDGEVILLE

27 JULY 60

Dear Betty,

I've got WALK EGYPT [Vinnie Williams] in the house but haven't set myself down to it. I did read four pages and I decided it was not for me, but since you say it's good, I'll have another go at it. I judged from my four pages that it was linsey-woolsy poor-folksy, one of those where you have to watch the grass grow. I'm really a bad reader. Something don't pay off line by line I'm gone.

I'm distressed to hear what you say about Cecilia. I wrote her a note after you said about her son and she didn't answer it. I'll try again.

Sit-downs in the Legion Auxiliary! Well! We'll all have to retreat now to the UDC.

We'll be looking for you Saturday. Cheers.

F

This letter borders on becoming a story rooted in one of O'Connor's masterful plot devices: travel. The pilgrimage to Milledgeville, possible travails of the journey, and potential scandal illustrate O'Connor's storytelling gifts.

MILLEDGEVILLE

6 AUGUST 60

Dear Betty,

Me and momma we both INSIST that you come on Wednesday instead of Friday. In the first place, if you come on Friday you won't get yourself relaxed before you have to turn around and go back. In the second place it is one thing to ride with Louis going back and another thing to ride with him coming down. Coming down, his car is full of kegs, crates, cardboards boxes, rolled wire, automotive equipment, fishing equipment and other impedimenta. At Shady Dale he stops and leads up with peaches. After a ride down with him you would be in no condition to enjoy the view. Going back, he has dumped all this stuff. In the third place, if it is scandal you are worried about, you can forget it. If I investigated the past of everybody that visits us, I would have to close down the place. In the fourth place, we figure you to be the kind of company who can eat what we ordinarily eat and for whom we don't have to put on the good silver or the linen napkins. Bring some work you want to do or something you want to read. You won't even see me in the morning. You can do your own work or go to town with Regina and set and watch the bugs. If you won't come Wednesday, then come Thursday; but I'd like you to see these people if any of them are around. I mean the ones that come on Wednesday. If you insist on coming with Louis Friday, don't say I didn't warn you. TRAVEL AT YR OWN RISK.

Yesterday in the *Constitution* [Atlanta] Doris Lockerman had her colyum on Vinnie Williams's book. She mostly quoted from it, reflections on this and that. I can't say I liked the quotes.

If you have a persistent headache you ought to go to the doctor and find out why. These headaches associated with the period are often due to water retention. I know a girl that had them practically all month. You can take a hydrodiuril tablet that will probably correct it. You can't get anything done with a headache.

If you think that section of Caroline's [Gordon] novel is nuts, you ought to hear about the rest of it. She insists it is a novel but has no precedent. Which I can well see is the case. Catherine Carver read that chapter and wrote me: "Can't she be deterred?" Ashley [Brown] thinks she may pull it off.

According to Elizabeth McKee, HOLLIDAY would pay me $500 for a piece on peacocks. I am thinking about it ["Living with a Peacock"].

I am not going to turn the Sister's ms. into anything of merit along literary lines because it would be impossible. I'll just have to see what can be done with it. We spent the day with them Tuesday. It is a most impressive place.

Cheers and kindly come on Wednesday.

Yrs,

Flannery

The letter commemorates the birthday of a president not ranked on the first or even second tier of U.S. chief executives. President Benjamin Harrison was a

grandson of President William Henry Harrison, and a great-grandson of Benjamin Harrison V, a Virginia planter and signer of the Declaration of Independence. O'Connor's recognition comports with her refreshing, unconventional perspective on American history present throughout the letters.

O'Connor also addresses Betty as a peer able to recognize well-crafted works of literary realism. She asks her to read what O'Connor considers a pious, ill-written work by a religious. Similarly, a novel that became an American classic is deficient. O'Connor, however, from the time she was a student at Iowa, admits her blunt opinions had repercussions. She writes in her Prayer Journal *about a "lack of charity" and "to make my mind vigilant about that. I say many many, too many uncharitable things about people every day."*[3] *A more tolerant voice also appears in her reviews of books for the diocesan newspaper.*

MILLEDGEVILLE

BENJAMIN HARRISON'S BIRTHDAY

[AUGUST 20, 1960]

Dear Betty,

I am glad you have seen fit to take my excellent advice and get here Wednesday. As to what those people read, they don't read nothing. I have to find a story and somebody reads it after they get here, if anything is read at all. Half of them are on vacation but there will probably be a couple here. They mostly just sit around. We will meet-cha at the gate, or anyways at the spot where there ought to be a gate but is not.

When you come you can sit down and read the Sister's manuscript [*A Memoir of Mary Ann*]. I hope you can stand it. I have permission to cut out anything I want to cut out. I am afraid that the surgery will be so drastic nothing is left but a skeleton.

Thank you for the picture. It looked very much like him. He loved all those rascals, I suppose.

We had lunch with a friend in Eatonton [Georgia] last Sunday who told me there was ONE book I ought to read, namely Harper

Lee's *To Kill A* Etc. She then recited half of it, which was enough. The lady from Florida wrote me that she had read it and it was no good.

What you say about when the extreme is justifiable in fiction is in different words about what I have said on the subject in the talk I am giving at Minnesota. I am still working on it, but I felt better on reading yours. I am working on that, working on the peafowl thing, and today the Sister sent me the last section of their thing so now I have that in my lap. I am anxious to have you read their ms. It is full of awful pious stuff, phrases like "her tender heart told her," and in part sounds like a tract for Catholicism, but anyhow, it has to be done.

I was not shocked to find that in my last review in the *Bulletin* [diocesan newspaper], some knowing soul had changed the word "gnostic" to the word "agnostic." Probably didn't know gnostic was a word. Eileen maybe. Mr. Zuber [Leo J.] has the idea I like to review fiction so he wrote and asked if I would like to review *The Leopard* [Giuseppe Tomasi di Lampedusa]. It is supposed to be very fine, but I am seeing enough spots before my eyes right now; I suggested he try you. Did he? If so you can bring it with you for you will have nothing better to do here than sit on the porch and read yourself blind or walk around and smell the sweet flowers. I have two extra typewriters; but I forget you write in long hand—a reactionary way of doing things, like cooking on a woodstove.

Chrs until Wed.

Flannery

The leopard is caged & awaits my return. Thanx.

FLANNERY O'CONNOR TO ROSLYN BARNES

The tone of the letters shifts. Barnes is younger than Betty and is an aspiring writer enrolled in the Iowa Writers' Workshop. Having had her own experience with misunderstandings of a regional accent at Iowa, O'Connor is pleased a class could understand Barnes. Learning from Mark Twain and William Faulkner, O'Connor employed regional speech to her advantage in reading to different audiences. Barnes apparently is following her lead.

MILLEDGEVILLE

12 OCTOBER 60

I hope you got over your reading in the Workshop all right and got some help from it. As I recall, the first time I set out to read to the Workshop, there were so many groans as soon as I got started that Engle took the thing away from me and said he would read it himself. Which was all right with me, except he didn't really read it any better than I would have. While I am in St. Paul, I am going to read on the U. of Minn. Campus. I am quite a ham and enjoy reading. Let me know how yours turned out.

Dr. Walston and Miss Benton were out the other day and appeared able to cope.

No, don't send me a copy of Mr. Santos' book. He sent me one himself, but with no return address. It came from Manila. I have just written him care of his publishers. Thanks anyway.

Every campus is full of the kind of students you describe. You have something they don't; so try to deepen what you've got and don't let them bother you.

FLANNERY O'CONNOR TO ELIZABETH HESTER

The letter shows the wide interests of two women of letters, but Betty still remains unknown and unpublished. Having converted to the faith with O'Connor as her sponsor, Hester encouraged her friend to reread a Church father. O'Connor is also reading the galley proofs of a friend and fellow novelist. A distinguished professor of American literature has also arranged a reading for O'Connor. She also continues to express reservations about a Catholic activist.

MILLEDGEVILLE

15 OCTOBER 60

Dear Betty

I have a Gateway edition of St. Jerome's letters so when you mentioned it, I fetched it out and read some of them again. St. Jerome was a man seldom content to stop when he had made his point. Reading a book on Christian spirituality of that era, I get the impression he was responsible for a lot of heresies brought on by people who couldn't take his extremes and reverted therefore to opposite extremes. The Lord must purify the Church in a kind of negative way with the St. Jeromes. He is so rough he drives the devils out of the whole church; a big job.

Last week the galleys of Jack Hawkes novel arrived [*The Lime Twig*]. It is very short and full of suspence, though it still seems to take place in a dream. Leslie Feidler is going to do the introduction. I am terribly impressed with the writing, but of course I don't feel I know what it's all about, and I think Jack has the feeling that if I did, I wouldn't like it. If they let me keep the galleys I'll send them to you, as I think you'd get something out of it. I may have to return them.

I got my statement from Farrer, Strauss & Cudahy the other day. *The Violent Bear* [*It Away*] sold about 3500 copies. That is about as bad as you can do short of not selling any.

Billy [Sessions], my dear girl, is not invited for any more than Thanksgiving Day. I think I made this plain to him. When he wrote that he was looking forward to seeing us Thanksgiving, I wrote back that we would expect him for Thanksgiving Day. Day is not plural. Day does not include night. He will be coming from and taking himself off to, I trust, the monastery [Conyers, Georgia].

I had a call from a priest at the Newman Club at the U. of Minnesota who said Mr. Wm. Van O'Connor had heard I would be around and they would like me to do something on the campus but had no money for it so Mr. O'C. suggested the Newman Club sponsor an appearance by me. So I am going to read there if they manage to arrange it with the sisters. I will report on any inter-resting figures I happen to meet.

Elizabeth [McKee] should try Miss Nancy at *Mademoiselle* or some of those places. My communications these days seem to be with Miss Minor, who is signing checks now. She must have both foot and knee in the door.

I am glad old John Leo got his inning in on Dorothy Day and interest. I think Dorothy is sometimes pretty silly, albeit I respect her in general. I liked the Philip Sharper piece; fits in very nicely with what I am thinking these days.

Cheers,

Flannery

FLANNERY O'CONNOR TO FATHER JAMES McCOWN

Father McCown hoped O'Connor would meet his friend, civil rights activist and Catholic convert, John Howard Griffin. Having darkened his skin chemically, he traveled in 1959 through the Deep South and recorded his experiences of racial injustice. Father McCown, Jacques Maritain, and others admired the pilgrimage, while O'Connor was critical. Griffin chronicled his adventures in Black Like Me, *a national bestseller in 1961. The narrative contains a favorable portrait of Martin Luther King, Jr., who admired Griffin for risking his life to expose racial prejudice. In 1964, Griffin received the Pacem in Terris Award from the Davenport (Iowa) Interracial Council for his efforts to advance social justice. Walker Percy presented in* The Last Gentleman *a satirical character known as the "pseudo Negro" (Forney Aiken), based on Griffin. O'Connor writes McCown (October 28, 1960):*

> You ought to be in Georgia now for the real Militant Baptist atmosphere. Religious Liberty Requires Constant Vigilance.
>
> If John Howard Griffin gets to Georgia again, we would be delighted to see him; but not in blackface. I

don't in the least blame any of the people who cringed [when] Griffin sat down beside them. He must have been a pretty horrible looking object.[4]

FLANNERY O'CONNOR TO LOUISE GOSSETT

*O'Connor sends an essay to help her friend in writing a doctoral dissertation, which was later published by Duke University Press in 1965 (*Violence in Modern Southern Fiction*). The friend was a vital early commentator on O'Connor and wrote an informative overview of her writing in* The History of Southern Literature *(Baton Rouge: LSU Press, 1985).*

NOVEMBER 13, 1960

SUNDAY

Dear Louise,

Help yourself to quoting this if you think the powers at Duke would allow such & theologically motivated job to be quoted in one of their dissertations. I wish you were nearby to talk to me about some of these points.

When you get through with this, I'd like it back as I am always losing my available copies.

Cheers to you and Tom,

FLANNERY O'CONNOR TO ROSLYN BARNES

O'Connor is part of an academic panel whose members reluctantly accept literary categorization. O'Connor recommends several works to assist in religious discernment. Such works depart from the local anti-Catholic paranoia in reaction to the 1960 presidential campaign. O'Connor also approves of her friend dropping a class because of deficient pedagogy. O'Connor, taught by Caroline Gordon, Andrew Lytle, and other traditionalist masters, did not support students critiquing the work of classmates. Such teaching of methodology elevated

untutored reactions by students, while diminishing instruction by the professor,
including study of the canonical figures such as Dickens, Faulkner, Joyce, and
others. O'Connor maintains a clear distinction between the artistry of imagina-
tive writing and the maudlin self-expression of some students.

MILLEDGEVILLE

14 NOVEMBER 60

I have been recuperating from the Minnesota trip [University of
Minnesota] and the Wesleyan [College, Macon, Georgia] business. I
beat the snows out of Minnesota which was as I intended and came
home to cope with Wesleyan. They had K. A. Porter, Caroline Gordon, Madison Jones and me on a panel and nothing much was said
and I supposed nothing was expected to be, but we were handsomely
paid and that was nice. We mostly agreed we were Southern writers
and couldn't do a thing about it.

Caroline Gordon came home with me and spent the weekend.
She is a fine stylist and has taught me a lot about writing.

I am glad you are learning something about Catholicism for
whether or not you are ever able to accept the Church, you will at
least not utter the idiocies against her, the like of which have been
prevalent around here and elsewhere during the past campaign. Some
time or other, I would advise you to read *The Unity of Philosophical
Experience*, by Etienne Gilson; *Three Reformers*, by Jacques Maritain;
The Disinherited Mind, by Erich Heller. I think they would give you
some kind of a base to cope from.

I applaud your leaving the Contemporary Fiction course if it is
nothing but student reports. You didn't go there to listen to the opinions of students as ignorant or more so than yourself.

When you leave Iowa I want to see some of the things you have
written there, but while you are under Mr. Eliott [George P.] it is better for you to get your criticism exclusively from him I should think.
I doubt if I would tell you anything contradictory to what he would
anyway. He is a fine writer and he must be on the track with you if he

is making you rewrite. Nothing better. Whether he thinks you are good or bad makes no difference. He must think you have something or he wouldn't insist on your rewriting. When you think a student is hopeless, you give him back his work and say, "I have nothing to suggest. This is unbelievable!" and he goes away thinking it is unbelievably good and is quite happy.

The weather here right now is like summer. The peacocks' new tails are about halfway out and the geese are making their domestic arrangements for next year. Keep me posted. I am always interested. I was delighted you had seen Mrs. Guzeman and that the old girl is eternal. Give her my best if she remembers me.

FLANNERY O'CONNOR TO
FATHER JAMES McCOWN

Having defended "bad Catholics" such as Hemingway and Joyce, O'Connor also endorses another novelist (December 4, 1960) criticized for sexual content in a novel. Identifying a deeper religious meaning, O'Connor upholds works criticized by pious readers.

Whoever was responsible for that editorial on John Updike's novel, *Rabbit Run*, should be confined for a while. I suspect it was the Rev. Harold C. [Gardiner]. If you get a chance you might like to look at that book. It is true that the sex in it is laid on too heavy. It is so burdensome that you want to skip those parts from sheer boredom; but the fact is, that the book is the product of a real religious consciousness. It is the best book illustrating damnation that has come along in a great while. I would send it to you but that I lent it to Billy [Sessions]. If he returns it any time soon, I will send it to you if you are interested.

Nothing doing around here. I am shortly going into Piedmont Hospital to have my bones inspected. They are melting or leaking or getting porous or something.[5]

FLANNERY O'CONNOR TO ELIZABETH HESTER

O'Connor encourages her friend's writing and is gratified that her review has been published. Among other events, she also mentions medical complications requiring hospitalization.

10 DECEMBER 60

Dear Betty,

Well I am glad you are on the track again and it seems to me to be the right one. I thought a long time ago it would be the right one, but perhaps now the time is right too. I often think how it looks like I should have done a lot more, been more prolific, in the years I have had; but on the other hand, the writer has to wait for the time when the subject ripens in him. I can't be forced.

I am going to Piedmont Hospital on Tuesday and will probably be there until Friday or Saturday. Now if it is convenient, come to see me. My last x-rays were bad and it appears the same thing that is happening to the hip is happening to the jaw. So I am going to be in there for a biopsy on the bone and for them to see if there is any way to halt this process, or any way reduce its speed. My mother may come too and stay at the hotel near the hospital. She hasn't decided, but she claims that when she isn't around, nothing is done and she finds out nothing and money is wasted. So I suspect she will superintend my future hospital visits and wring the information out of them.

After I typed up the Sister's manuscript, they decided there were a few more little things they ought to put in it. So I told them they could do the putting and the typing and then I would send it off. It's really very bad [*A Memoir of Mary Ann*].

The Critic has sent me my proofs and a copy of the magazine with the first fiction in it. Two pedestrian sorts of stories. "The Gallant" one is very well written and pleasant but no more. The other is silly. Miss Nancy is considerable better than either. But as I read over my proofs, I didn't think much of "The Partridge Pageant," so I best not criticize Miss Gallant or Mr. Sullivan. A good review in there of yours. Also a letter from some reverend who says exactly the same thing you did about *No Little Thing* [Elizabeth Ann Cooper]. I meant to tell you that in his review of it in *America,* the Rev. Harold C. [Gardiner] admits he went too far in saying it was as good as Grim Grin [Graham Greene]. I say he should have thought of that in the first place and not subjected the girl to his change of opinion.

That article on Nancy Smith's place has taken ten years off Nancy's age, as good as the fountain of youth. She went out there that Sunday and the place was full of people wanting to go through. She started taking them in. Then later in the day, she put up a sign Admission ¢50. Many folks thought this meant 50¢ a car or family. She put on the sign 50¢ Each. The first Sunday she made $30, the second 42, the third 50 something. She sold old books for a dollar a piece. The people are still out there every Sunday.

Chrs,

Flannery

FLANNERY O'CONNOR TO ROSLYN BARNES

O'Connor approves (December 12, 1960) of her friend's attending Mass. The Eucharist is the fundamental sacrament for spiritual inquiry about becoming a Catholic. From this spiritual anchor all other topics in the letter emanate. O'Connor also mentions one of the "Five Black Crows," an association of priests at the St. Thomas More Parish center in Iowa City, Iowa. In 1952, Msgr. Conway began writing answers to "The Question Box" in the diocesan newspaper, The Catholic Messenger. *Finally, as O'Connor faces hospitalization, her petition in her* Prayer Journal, *"Give me the courage to stand the pain to get the grace, Oh Lord," is relevant to her own later suffering.*[6]

I am glad you are going to Mass because along with study there should be no better way of finding out if you are really interested in the Church. You don't join the Catholic Church. You <u>become</u> a Catholic. The study can prepare your mind but prayer and the Mass can prepare your whole personality. I wish that there were a book that you could give your parents that would prepare them for your interest because it seems to me you should at least try to cushion the blow if you are going to give them one. Perhaps they wouldn't read it, but if you think they would, you ought to look around for a book that would create interest in them without offending them. I think Msgr. Conway [J. D.] has a book—Questions Catholics are asked about, or something [*What They Ask About Marriage*].[7]

1/5/61

I'll do better by you than a minite [*sic*] check but not much. I have to put up with this nausea for about two months, had to cancel my reading at GSCW [Georgia State College for Women].

Thanks too for typing out the rosary meditations. My mind is a terrible wanderer once I start saying the rosary. Meditation must be a gift.

I saw a review of your friend Mr Elliott's book of stories, very favorable [*Among the Dangs*]. I will send you a copy of *The Divine Milieu,* Teilhards [de Chardin] 2nd book, if you would like it. I got two for Christmas. Let me know.

Cheers,

FLANNERY O'CONNOR TO
FATHER JAMES McCOWN

The foundational sacrament of the Eucharist and its relation to suffering is once again emphasized. O'Connor gives thanks. Other apologists testify to its effi-

cacy, such as Father Henri Nouwen. He notes, "The Eucharist is the central Sacrament of the Church. It is the place through which God really enters into our lives."[8]

MILLEDGEVILLE

22 JANUARY 61

Thanks for all the needed information and thanks for saying that Mass for me. I think I am doing all right what with all the prayers I am getting.

That introduction I was telling you about is going to be in the April *Jubilee* now, they tell me ["Introduction," *A Memoir of Mary Ann, Jubilee,* May 1961]. It is an introduction to a book written by the Sisters at the cancer home in Atlanta and I just got word from my publisher today that they will publish the book. It was so badly written that I thought I'd never find a publisher for it, but Farrer, Straus and Cudahy took it right off. I bet the Sisters a pair of peafowl that nobody would buy it so I am out a pair of peafowl.

I would like to get my hands on a book about moral theology.

I'd like to look at the lady's book if she finishes it.

2/23/61

Thanks so much for Bernanos [Georges]. That is one of my favorite books and I am delighted to have a copy of my own. I read it years ago out of the SUI liberry.

We entertained the photographer from *Holiday* for two days last week. He took over 150 pictures of the peachickens and they think they are up for the academy award. The piece will be in the June issue ["Living With a Peacock," September 1961].

I suppose some one has sent you the editorial for the high school guests out of the Colonade. The writer ran away with herself. "The happiest day in your college career will be the day you walk down the aisle and receive your pigskin."

FLANNERY O'CONNOR TO ELIZABETH HESTER

O'Connor shares literary opinions with a fellow woman of letters who still re-
mains obscure. O'Connor dislikes critical theory applied to her fiction. William
Sessions has also written a play about Francis Marion, hero of the American
Revolution. Mel Gibson in "The Patriot" (2005) plays Benjamin Martin, a
character based on Marion. O'Connor, also in a rare observation, notes the
limitations of her beloved teacher.

MILLEDGEVILLE

4 MARCH 61

Dear Betty,

I have been this week prone upon my couch, a victim of the common cold. So I advise you to burn up this letter after you read it and
wash your hands as I am still coughing and spitting and blowing and
filling up the trash cans with kleenex.

I guess you are right about Hawkes [John] and his critical powers
and I think that probably most creative people have only sporadic
critical insights. Hawkes for instance informed me that he thought
the sheriff's view at the end of the story was the literal one; at least he
asked me if it wasn't. I suppose this comes from always looking at
everything from Freud's point of view. The poor devils think that is
ALL, at least where fiction is concerned. I sent you an essay he sent of
some criticism of his friend's poetry. He said that if there was theology in it, he supposed it was very peculiar theology. From reading it,
I should say it was modern-ordinary.

I don't think Billy was consulting Walker Percy for his health—
just as one literary Catholic-convert gentleman to another, etc. He
has honored me with two communications lately, the last announc-
ing that he is working on his Swamp Fox play and will have it ready
in a couple of weeks for me & thee to look at. It appears that I am
directly responsible for this one, having told him he might ought to

try something with a historical basis to help control his imagination. I thought that would at least keep the rich bitches out of it. Anyway we shall see.

I read one story of Walter Clemens once but I didn't think it was anything extra. Never read Humphrey. Read Cicero a while back but I suppose I ought to do it again. Peter Taylor is pleasant though I'll admit not exactly soul-shattering. I think Powers [J. F.] is the better of the two because he has something better to write about and is funny. He don't write about lonely man. They are both you might say writers of manners rather than of the demonic. The great ones like Dostoievsky combine the two. I suppose Proust is the master of the manners branch. I can see no other dimension in RTP. Manners are negligible in your friend Emily Bronte, negligible in Hawkes, negligible in me.

Everytime I think how Caroline [Gordon] would have had me change the introductory paragraph of the Introduction I see anew her limitations. She will sacrifice life to dead form, or anything to grammar. That sentence: "What is written to edify usually ends by amusing" is perfectly all right. The "us" is implied and need not be put in, as you might say, "that does not soothe, that does not please," etc. I asked Sr. Bernetta [Quinn] about it and she said I was right.

Atheneum has just sent me Louis Rubin's novel to say something about [*The Golden Weather*]. It is one of those "growing up with" Louie things and deadly dull so far. I don't know what I am going to say about it because I can't hurt his feelings. The trials of politeness.

Chrs,
Flannery

FLANNERY O'CONNOR TO ROSLYN BARNES

O'Connor inquires about the reception of her friend into the Church. O'Connor also concurs with the parallels the friend has perceived between two writers. The connection would result in the 1962 master's thesis dedicated to O'Connor: "Gerard Manley Hopkins and Pierre Teilhard de Chardin: A Formulation of Mysticism for a Scientific Age."

MILLEDGEVILLE

APRIL 6I

I'm sending you two books on Teilhard but you'll have to send them back to me when you finish them as they're all I've got. I particularly like the Tresmontain one.[9] That is a good idea about Hopkins and Teilhard. I hadn't thought of it but it figures. There is a novel called *The Roots of Heaven* by Romain Gary in which there is a portrait of a Jesuit paleontologist who I am sure is modeled on Pere Teilhard.

Have you already made your First Communion and are you going to be Confirmed next, or will you do them both at the same time? I can't keep up with you, but I am very happy for you. Has Pine Mountain been informed? What are you going to do this summer?

Give my regards to Mr. Santos [Bienvenido, Iowa Writers' Workshop].

FLANNERY O'CONNOR
TO FATHER JAMES McCOWN

Diminishing her own suffering, O'Connor also reveals her approval of the presidential election of 1960. Revealing a rare political opinion may be rooted in O'Connor's friendships with "yellow dog Democrats." Because of the excesses of "Mr. Lincoln's army," such Democrats a century after the Civil War would vote for an animal before a Republican. Brainard Cheney—a journalist, novelist, critic, and speechwriter from Tennessee—as well as other friends and teachers of O'Connor—Caroline Gordon, Allen Tate, and Andrew Lytle— were rooted in the Southern Democratic ethos.[10] The orientation has all but disappeared from the contemporary Democratic party with its vocal socialist members and devotion to identity politics. Moreover, as other letters reveal, O'Connor disliked the anti-Catholic paranoia of the 1960 presidential campaign. O'Connor and her Jesuit friend also may have admired President Kennedy's Irish Catholic ancestry.

MILLEDGEVILLE

4 APRIL 61

Dear Padre McG.,

They postponed it to the May issue so kindly tear through that. If it's not there then, I am going to sue them.

I seem to be getting on very well, no major difficulties in coming off the steroids. There was unfortunately a good bit of painkiller to it, so now that I don't have it, I feel the joints considerably and do not get about as fast. But I get about. I am probably going to St. Louis in May to Marillac College. That is one of those Sister Formation places. I believe in educating the Sisters, so I am putting in me oar there whenever requested. The more I see of them, the sharper I think they're getting to be.

Ain't it nice we've got a President after eight years?

I was glad to read that Montserrat [Jesuit Retreat House, Dallas] was good for nervous tension. Now if you could bottle it, you'd have it made. Don't ever let Powers [J. F.] get in there.

My parent is as usual coping. This place is being undermined by moonshine. Every weekend the staff is loaded.

Well cheers to you,

FLANNERY O'CONNOR TO ROSLYN BARNES

Like Ernest Hemingway, O'Connor included her own cartoons in some letters. A cartoonist in high school, O'Connor drew situations and characters that often would later reappear in her stories. This letter has an amusing drawing of a "flying nun" with a bright smile comparable to the nun described at the end of "A Temple of the Holy Ghost."

6 APRIL 61

The duck and rabbit arrived somewhat worse for the wear but still relatively chipper. A friend of mine with five children appeared and they took them over with a bang. That was the last I saw of duck and rabbit. Thanks a lot. I was glad to have something to occupy their little minds and keep them from destroying the house.

I received a book the other day from Atheneum by a girl who is apparently at Iowa—Mary Elsie Robertson. Maybe you know her. I haven't got to the stories yet.

I am probably going out to St. Louis in May to talk to the Sisters at Merrilac College—a college only for nuns. They wear a bonnet that looks like this [drawing that looks like a flying nun's head].

FLANNERY O'CONNOR TO ROSLYN BARNES

O'Connor sends a religious gift. She also concurs with the friend's criticism of a writing class at Iowa in which students assert their own views about the work of classmates while the professor provides little guidance. O'Connor is critical of such pedagogy which, however, has become fashionable in many creative writing programs. I have been amazed in my years of college teaching by the reaction of creative writing students who have stared at me in disbelief when I asked if they had read Shakespeare, Dante, or Milton in their classes. Unlike O'Connor, such students assumed creative writing classes provided a forum for them to express feelings and not study the writing skills of the masters.

MILLEDGEVILLE

MAY, 1961

I am sending you a short breviary in honor of May 18. I have one and it means a lot to me as I say Prime for my morning prayers and

Compline for my night prayers. This way you are praying with the Church and not just yourself.

I have read more of St. Teresa of Avila than John of the Cross. They were very close. Some time read St. Catherine of Genoa's Treatise on Purgatory.[11]

Bourjaily [Vance Nye] would be hard for me to take too. I have not liked what of his I have read. I think anywhere that more than three writers are gathered together the atmosphere is liable to be unhealthy. Students criticizing student's work is always a mistake.

If you do come to Georgia in August, try to get down to Milledgeville for a weekend and spend it with us.

Cheers,

The Literary Guild is coming out on the 18th for their picnic like last year. You will be better engaged.

O'Connor witnessed campaigns for racial integration but would not meet with activists such as John Howard Griffin, James Baldwin, or Martin Luther King. O'Connor was thinking, however, of other forms of integration stimulated by her reading of a seminal Jesuit thinker. She seeks advice (June 17, 1961) from Barnes, who was formally trained as a physicist.

Can you tell me if the statement: "everything that rises must converge" is a true proposition in physics? I can easily see its moral, historical and evolutionary significance, but I want to know if it is also a correct physical statement. You are the only scientist I am acquainted with.

We are all freezing here as it is 15 degrees lower than the normal temperature for this time of year.[12]

,

O'Connor agrees to recommend her friend (July 26, 1961) to the Papal Aux-
iliary Volunteers for Latin America (PAVLA). In November 1959, bishops
from North and Latin America established PAVLA to respond to transforma-
tional social changes sweeping Latin America, such as the Communist revolu-
tion in Cuba in 1959 led by Fidel Castro. The prospect of other Communist
revolutionaries toppling dictatorships, severe social inequality, Protestant mis-
sionary efforts, and the ineffective catechesis of indigenous Catholics in Latin
America were challenges facing the Church. Pope John XXIII sanctioned
PAVLA and its missionary program.

I have been wanting to write and thank you for some time for
writing me about the rising-converging business, but we have had
one thing and another going on and I haven't done much that I
wanted to. Anyway, what you said was helpful and follows my own
line of thought on the subject, uneducated as that is.

I'll be delighted to recommend you for PAVLA and I think you
are wise to do something like this before you even think about becoming a Sister. And also wise to get the debts paid up. When people
lend you money for your education, they are not very sympathetic to
your becoming a missionary to any Indians before they get their
money back. Not many people will understand your wanting to do
this anyway—around here I mean—but I think it is fine.[13]

FLANNERY O'CONNOR TO
FATHER JAMES McCOWN

O'Connor notes that a mutual friend had visited Walker Percy. Percy
was removing Catholic pietism from The Moviegoer. *Such details reflect*
O'Connor's tutoring of Father McCown. She was disabusing him of the idea
that good fiction contained "polemical writing to defend Holy Church against
her enemies."[14]

MILLEDGEVILLE

23 JUNE 61

I was cheered to get my hands on *The Ballad of Peckham Rye* [Muriel Spark] beingst I had heard so much about it. I enjoyed it although I don't think its as good as made out to be. Neither is the enclosed, though it is mighty well written. Walker Percy is a Louisiana Catholic (convert). Billy Sessions went to see him last year and he told Billy he was finishing his novel and was busy getting the Catholic parts out. A necessary operation as I well understand.

Did you know that Billy is shortly to be on his way to Greece to lead back a wife, or so he hopes? He met the young lady when he was in Greece three years ago, boarded with her family for a month, the rest has been by mail. So this summer they are going to look each other over, & decide for good.

The Gossetts had breakfast with us and were in fine fettle and full of news of you. We wish they were still in this neighborhood.

Did you ever find out what and where that was that your brother wrote [Robert McCown, S.J., "The Education of a Prophet: A Study of Flannery O'Connor's *The Violent Bear It Away*," *Kansas Magazine*]. It was more than likely a lot better than what was printed in America. That was pretty good on the stories, but bad on the novels.

Before this summer is over I think I am going to have a steel head put in my hip joint, thus eventually enabling me to get about on my own two feet. I hope. Pray that the Lord means for me to do this and that the operation will be a success.

Cheers to you,

STANLEY KAUFFMANN TO WALKER PERCY

In the previous letter O'Connor mentions Walker Percy's revisions of his novel The Moviegoer. *O'Connor's stories were vital in showing Percy how to avoid religiosity in his fiction. The esteemed film critic Stanley Kauffmann, an editor at Knopf, proposes further revisions, but stresses the novel is close to being publishable. Kauffmann was familiar with existential literature and realized the novel was revolutionary in its presentation of what Thomas Merton would call a "merry kind of nausea." Kauffmann recognizes Percy's unique existential voice with its witty observations and satire of the legendary city of New Orleans. Percy was writing theistic existential fiction—and in the process putting the maligned French existentialists such as Sartre and Camus on the side of the angels. He recasts their reputation as philosophic absurdists hanging out in Paris cafés. As a reflective physician retooling himself as a novelist, Percy recognizes their contribution: "It is not inconceivable that even Sartre's atheistic existentialism may be in the end far more productive for Christianity than many present-day Christian spokesmen who deal with religion in terms of mental hygiene, business success, and whatnot."*[15]

FEBRUARY 5, 1960

The revised manuscript of CONFESSIONS OF A MOVIE GOER has now been read by several editors here and discussed at great length. I'm sorry to report the consensus is that it is not yet—in our opinion—in publishable form, and I hasten to underscore the words "not yet" in hope that this will prevent discouragement on your part. All who have read the book here recognize a talent, a unique voice, and a viewpoint of pertinence and importance. All of us feel (as, I may say, I have felt from the start) that the writer who could do what has so far [been] done is capable of bringing the work to fulfillment.

Let me get to specifics. Some of these are matters which have disturbed me from the beginning; some are matters which struck new readers more forcibly. For clarity, let me make a list of them.

Binx's search. This thread, which winds through the book, still seems to be raised with fanfare, forgotten, referred to sporadically, and rather handily tied up at the end. It needs definition, consistency, presence and force in the book. One doesn't ask for the unanswerable to be answered; indeed one of the best things in the novel is that Binx learns to live with his questions rather than to give them neat homiletic answers. But the search, which seems to be the mainspring of his dynamics at the start, peters out and flares and dies again, and then seems to be remembered hastily at the end.

Characters and story-strands are dropped and picked up (some of them) arbitrarily. Stephanie, for instance. Binx's campaign with her is excellently done, with lots of delightful detail and insight; then she disappears in mid-book. Kate (and Binx's relation to her) is established well at the beginning; then to all intents she disappears, to be revived in the latter half. Any possible interplay between Binx's feelings for Stephanie (and his other girls) and Kate is lost.

Binx's relationship with the memory of his father is unclear as a force in the book and insufficiently resolved at the end. It seems to be in some sort of counterpoise with "the search" but too much is left to even the best-intentioned reader to supply.

Characters like Sam Yerger and Jimmy and Joel are employed beyond their utility. The[y] represent the "merde" world—at various levels and we get the idea more quickly than you think. The Mardi Gras party is needed as a catalyst to propel Kate onto the train with Binx, but it, too, goes on too long. These matters could be ameliorated simply by cutting, but if you are going to do the revision we hope for, you would want to keep in mind the use of these elements in proportion, not merely the cutting of them. One way to make scenes like dinner at grandmother's with Yerger and the Mardi Gras party more interesting and useful to the book might be to integrate Binx and Kate more firmly with them: to make sure that Kate's reactions are growing with the reader and that the characters— particularly those who are appearing for the first time—are filtering through Binx to the reader. Obviously, cutting alone will not do this.

Binx's statement, 298–300, while excellently written, doesn't really take the place of consistent growth perceivable and convincing to the reader. On the other hand, his agreement to go to medical school (305)—which has been a major matter through this book—is sloughed off in one facile reply. Why had he changed?

What all the above comes to, essentially, is that instead of a collection of brilliant and moving scenes rather arbitrarily bound together as the author seems from time to time to remember to bind them, we would like to see a more organic, better composed work in which the author has all his thematic and plot elements well in hand from the start and is moving them towards a conclusion. Our feeling still is that you discovered things about Binx and his relationships as you went along, rather than seeing him clearly in his spiritual and physical environment from the start and knowing exactly who this particular pilgrim is and what his progress is to be.

There is no blinking the fact that what we are asking for amounts to a major re-writing of the book. It means that you would have to consider this a first draft: a very extensively articulated first draft from which you would draw a great deal of material (I would hate to lose much of what is there now) to be fitted into a clear and effective design. It means, figuratively, that you would have to stand off, take a deep breath, and plunge in again—to create a book whose overall design is as effective as individual pages and scenes are now. To us it would seem a great waste of moving material if you didn't choose to do this; but it is a matter only you can decide.

In spite of what must be at least some disappointment at this letter, I hope you will give the matter careful thought (there's no need to reply at once), that you will ask questions if any of the above is unclear or if there are points bothering you which I have not raised, and that you will then decide to tackle the job.

The date of delivery of the manuscript can be advanced to accommodate your convenience. You must believe that we are still strongly attracted to your talent and want very much to publish the novel that this can be.

I'm returning the manuscript to Miss Otis [Elizabeth, Percy's agent] and will await word from you.

Every good wish.

Yours faithfully.

Stanley Kauffmann

WALKER PERCY TO STANLEY KAUFFMANN

Writing from Pompano Beach, Florida, Percy is unsure he can make the proposed changes to The Moviegoer. *Percy, however, unlike O'Connor, who resisted editorial revisions to* Wise Blood, *worked assiduously at revisions. Kauffmann was always encouraging and polite and realized the potential for Percy's novel.*

FEBRUARY 11, 1960

Dear Mr. Kauffmann:

Naturally I am disappointed you all didn't like it better. As I had written Miss Otis before I heard from you, there are changes I want to make, whether you accepted it or not, but nothing like the radical overhaul you seem to suggest. My own feeling is that I am getting pretty close to what I am aiming at. There are lapses and gaucheries here and there which need to be taken care of, some strained-for effects and some sophomore posturing, and I want to make a few additions. But it will come to no more than tinkering and polishing—I think.

It is not that I disagree with you that a complete re-write, from a higher level of consciousness so to speak would make a better book. The trouble is that the endpoint which I would approach in that case appears to be different, to judge from your letter, from the endpoint you have in mind. Your calling attention to dropped characteristics and interrupted story-strands is certainly valid novelistic criticism, but it does not seem applicable here—at least it does not strike a chord for me. *Passage to India* is a much better constructed novel than *Nausea*, but *Nausea* would be wrecked by a revision along these lines. I suppose I am trying to say that the fragmented alienated consciousness, which is Mr. Binx Bolling, cannot be done up in a novel in the usual sense of the word. At least I would not have the stomach for the job. Also, I am working on something else.

This is not to defend the book, of course since it either stands or falls with the reading, but only to explain my position.

I am asking Miss Otis to return the manuscript to me for a short-term rumination and for whatever changes come to mind. If, after that, you would like another quick look, I'll gladly send it to you. I am still obliged to you for an indispensable energy-charge at a critical point—as well as for $250.00. But truthfully I doubt if there is much use in resubmitting it to you, for even if you decided then to accept it, I hardly see how you all could take it on with the enthusiasm and unanimity without which I'd rather you didn't take it on at all.

Again my thanks to you personally and best wishes to Knopf, a fine house (you all published the greatest book of our time, Camus' *The Stranger.*) Are you and the Stanley Kauffmann, astute critic and inveterate moviegoer of *The New Republic*, one and the same?

Yours sincerely,

WALKER PERCY TO ROBERT DANIEL

Percy outlines the fortuitous events that led to The Moviegoer *winning the National Book Award, the firing of Percy's editor, who supervised the successful revisions, and the recognition of the novel by the president of the United States. The influence of Percy's novel on U.S. presidents extends to President Obama. In David Maraniss's biography* Barack Obama: The Story, *the chapter "The Moviegoer" presents the young, pre-political Obama as a rootless searcher similar to Binx Bolling in Percy's novel. The characteristic followed Obama into his presidency, where he was often seen as polished and elegant but aloof.*

MAR 19, 1962

Rob:

Your Ohio agents are a hell of a lot better than mine. I didn't learn till today what the real story was, and you are substantially correct.

Somebody sent me a clipping from Thursday's *NY Times* which out-and-out told the story which I had only inklings of during the three days in New York. If you're really curious and want to read a curious tale look up a story headlined "Critics Hear Tale of Novel's Prize" in Thursday March 15 *Times*. NY

It all sounds like a typical back-of-scenes publishing hassle—the only difference being that in this case I was the only one who didn't know what was going on.

The facts are simple. Alfred Knopf actively disliked the novel and it was shot down from the beginning—as far as promotion goes. It was bought apparently on the say so of Stanley Kauffmann who was shortly after fired (for another reason)—leaving *The Moviegoer* a sort of lame duck. I had heard many stories that such was the case, but laid it to the usual comforting of author. Well—along comes the National Awards and the three judges, Stafford, Gold and Gannett. Nobody ever heard of *The Moviegoer*. But A.J. Liebling happens to pick it up because *Time* said something about New Orleans. And what with Liebling's interest in Louisiana, he went out and bought it. Liked it and gave it to Jean. She liked it and sold Gold and Gannett. I guess.

What it comes to is that Ole Earl Long is responsible for my small success.

Hope I soon have a chance to tell you of my adventures with Alfred and Blanche in the company of Shelby and Gwynn.

The only thing tangible that has come out of it so far (besides the $1,000 and the telegram from Kennedy) is a sale to paperbacks (I don't even know which). ·

Either Oberlin or Swarthmore would be great, but I keep hearing good things about Swarthmore.

A Juhan is offering you a house. The last time I heard a Juhan talking about you . . .

Best Wak

FLANNERY O'CONNOR TO
FATHER JAMES McCOWN

Precarious health, travel, marriage, theological reading, and the prospect of
sudden death comprise the uncertainties of faith. Father McCown had also en-
couraged O'Connor to read another O'Connor, Edwin, author of The Last
Hurrah *and* The Edge of Sadness *(winner of the Pulitzer Prize in 1962).*

MILLEDGEVILLE

2 AUGUST 61

I sure was sorry to hear about Fr. Moody. He was probably over-
worked. I guess he is now in a better position to pray for the rest of
us. I will have a Mass said for him.

Thank you for the Jone [Heribert, *Moral Theology*]. This looks formidable. If I pick up any sins in it, you will hear from me.

The doctor said I couldn't have the operation, too dangerous for
my state of health. So now I can forget about it. What you know you
can't get rid of don't worry you as much as what you think you might
get rid of.

We had a card from Billy [Sessions] the other day and he declared
he is going to be married August 3 in Athens [Greece], so Spring Hill
[College, Mobile, Alabama] is going to have something new in faculty wives.

I want to see your brother's article when it comes out. The enclosed appeared in *Renascence* [Robert O. Bowen, "Hope vs. Despair
in the New Gothic Novel"]. You see why I am anxious to see something decent written about it. The worthy who wrote this does not
know what the Church teaches about predestination or free will.

I haven't read the Edwin O'Connor yet. I wait for the paper-
backs.

We are going to Boston on the 25th to visit aunt, then to New
York for two days for me to go to a Ford Foundation conference and

then home again all in less than a week. It could be shorter and I'd like it better. No kind of a traveler now.

Cheers and thanks,

FLANNERY O'CONNOR TO THOMAS GOSSETT

O'Connor, in a feat of her metaphysical imagination, links the purchase of swans and transport of birds to her literary reactions to works by her peers.

MILLEDGEVILLE

22 AUGUST 61

We wouldn't mind getting rid of a pair of peafowl but the difficulty is in shipping them. For shipping they have to be crated up by somebody who knows how to do it right. However I know where you can get some and cheap and they will crate them properly. I enclose a price list of the Miami Rare Bird Farm. These people are going out of business and so everything is half-price. I have this list because I am negotiating with them about a pair of white swans. They have one pair left and they are selling it for $65 because the hen is blind in one eye. All I need to make life complete is a one-eyed swan around here.

The man you write to is Mr. Alton V. Freeman at the address on the top of the price list. $30 a pair is very cheap for peafowl. I paid $65 for my first pair. When you get through with the price list, I'd be obliged to have it back. If I wasn't a po writer, I would buy a couple of everything he's got here in the bird line.

I also enclose that cheering letter from the professor at Rice, which I told you I'd send you. When you have been sufficiently depressed by it, send it back.

I have just read Malamud's new book, A NEW LIFE, which will be published some time soon. It is a terrible disappointment, poor and plodding. I hope he recovers. I have also read Carson McCullars,

CLOCK WITHOUT HANDS, shortly to be published. It is the worst book I have ever read in my life. Complete disintegration.

Cheers to you all and we wish you would return to Texas by way of Georgia. If there's any possibility let us know.

P.S. I have seen peafowl in Michigan so I presume they would do all right in West Virginia. However, they need a barn or outhouse or garage or something where they can retire when it is too inclement.

FLANNERY O'CONNOR TO FATHER JAMES McCOWN

O'Connor reports cheerfully about interesting happenings. A friend continues to entertain with reports about his marriage ceremonies, rituals that interested O'Connor. Several of her stories, such as "The Life You Save May Be Your Own" and "A Stroke of Good Fortune," deal with unusual marriages.

MILLEDGEVILLE

5 SEPTEMBER 61

Did you see my article about peacocks in the September *Holiday* ["Living with a Peacock"]? A very fine picture went along with it. I have just bought a pair of swans so maybe after I have had them ten years I can write another article for *Holiday*. The Gossetts bought some peafowl from the same place I bought my swans. They said they were going to call you up when they went through Dallas.

We have had several cards from Billy [Sessions] about his marriages—one in the Greek Orthodox and one in the Catholic. The Catholic one was first but the Greek Orthodox obviously impressed him the most as he got to wear a laurel wreath on his head and there was somewhere in the ceremony that they had bon bons in a silver dish. We expect them to come through here and spend the night with us and we will hear it all in detail.

The Sisters' book [*A Memoir of Mary Ann*] has been accepted by the Catholic Digest Book Club (whatever that is), has been bought by *Good Housekeeping* for their Christmas issue, and has been bought in England by Burns & Oates [*Death of a Child*]. They have kept the prayers burning underneath it and brought it to a boil.

It looks like we are going to be integrated by the atom, don't it?

Tensions between the Soviet Union and the United States escalate and threaten nuclear annihilation. O'Connor displays consistent good humor. She mentions a lecture she would soon deliver. Phrasing from a famous Jesuit has also given her an apocalyptic title for a story.

MILLEDGEVILLE

13 OCTOBER 61

Thanks generally for the religious information and advice for the magazine with the article about the fall-out ethics and your brother's [Robert McCown, S.J.] piece in it. I sure did like your brother's piece and as for the other I am prepared to shoot any scoundrel that uses air intended for the family. First of course I will have to learn to shoot and then we will have to build the shelter. We keep talking about it but we haven't started digging.

Some time I would like probably to go to a retreat. Right now, I am struggling to go to St. Louis to talk to the Sisters at Marillac College. I was supposed to go last spring, but the old lady that is president had to have her ear operated on. At least now presumably she can hear what I have to say. I have a story in the current issue of *New World Writing* #19 called "Everything That Rises Must Converge." I would send you one but I haven't got one.

Cheers and many thanks,

Did you know Bishop Hyland [Francis A., Atlanta Archdiocese] has resigned on account of poor health? I hope the Lord will send us a good one.

FLANNERY O'CONNOR TO LOUISE AND THOMAS GOSSETT

O'Connor notes that Tom Gossett's legacy endures at Wesleyan College, Macon, Georgia, in the appointment of a new professor in Southern literature. The academic field of Southern literature was becoming popular with professors from the outside. Institutions in the South increasingly hired academics with little to no regional roots to teach Southern literature and history. Their perspective often entailed "reconstructing" native Southerners by disabusing them of regional attitudes, practices, and speech.[16] O'Connor is often bemused by such efforts that appear in the deracinated attitudes of academic characters in her stories such as Joy/Hulga, Asbury Fox, and Rayber.

MILLEDGEVILLE

8 DECEMBER 61

Maybe I had better just write a book called *The Bear That Ran Away With It*. That sounds to me like a title that could go places. If you see *New World Writing*, I have one in it called "Everything That Rises Must Converge." That one will probably get called "Every Rabbit That Rises Will Engage."

The Carson McCullars is the worst book [*Clock Without Hands*] I have ever read in my life. I haven't read the Warren [Robert Penn] as I avoid the historiky [*The Legacy of the Civil War*].

Our staff has already started celebrating the season with unstamped whiskey. I don't know whether they are still celebrating Thanksgiving or started celebrating Christmas but the effect is the same.

The lady who is teaching Southern Literature at Wesleyan these days is from Connecticut.

Merry Christmas,

FLANNERY O'CONNOR TO
FATHER JAMES McCOWN

O'Connor once again cites Robert McCown's illuminating commentary about The Violent Bear It Away *and mentions a sound review by a professor.*

MILLEDGEVILLE

16 DEC 61

I hope you are back from being refreshed by the Mexicans and will have a cheery Christmas. I certainly did like your brother's piece—at least there is somebody besides Bowen [Robert O.]. Bowen incidentally is at the University of Dallas. Some body wrote me he was a big man on some right-wing indignation committee. I should think he would be good at that.

Did you see the Gossetts? I sent your mama one of the sisters' books. They're all going around in circles at being authors. They're getting stacks of letters and donations.

We are expecting Billy Sessions and his Greek wife this afternoon for to spend the weekend. Every body who has met her says Billy really did himself proud.

Cheers to you and please remember something I am trying to write in your prayers.

O'Connor is editing a narrative about Mexico that Father McCown was writing. In an earlier letter (March 4, 1962) she called the narrative a "travelogue," praises the sequence of episodes, and hopes the narrative will be published.

MILLEDGEVILLE

11 MAR 62

The second installment was enjoyed as much as the first and we await the third [*With McCown in Mexico*]. I have just read a book called *American Catholic Dilemma* by Thos. F. O'Dea in a new paper-back edition and if you read that you would probably decide you were needed more in the U.S. than in Mexico. If you haven't read it, I'll send it. Right now we are the lump that needs leavening. Our Lady of Guadaloupe will take care of Mexico. I hope the Gossetts get to read this account and I still wish you would make something out of it to publish.

O'Connor mentions commentary about her writing. She also notes the publication of Ship of Fools *by Katherine Anne Porter. As other letters reveal, Porter helped O'Connor achieve greater international recognition.*

MILLEDGEVILLE

28 APRIL 62

Maybe I have arrived in conservative circles and just don't know it. I take it you copped this issue from somebody. Do you want it back? This Robert Drake is somebody who reviewed my book once in *Modern Age*—another conservative journal ["Miss O'Connor and the Scandal of Redemption," Fall 1960, 428–30]. Well, says I, if it takes a conservative to appreciate my works, it takes one, that's all. Thanks also for the other cheerful article. I mostly agree with the lady, at least that you can't do anything about it.

I am fixing to take off Tuesday to lecture at Rosary College and Notre Dame. Last week when I was at Converse [College, South Carolina], after my talk a gentleman from Texas came up and asked me if I would come to their school. I forget the name of it but it was 60 miles from Dallas (East Texas State Teachers College???). I told him I might sometime.

I am glad your mother is learning to make the most of her wheel-chair. Dividends can be gained from such if you know how to do it.

Ship of Fools hasn't come my way yet so it doesn't look like its going to. I think I can wait on the paperback. She started out as a

Catholic and I think has more or less ended up one, though not exactly a ring-the-bell and slap-the-book one. She eloped at the age of 16 from her convent school window and has subsequently (according to Caroline Tate) enjoyed seven husbands. She's very pleasant withal, has had dinner here twice and I was on a panel [Wesleyan College, Macon, Georgia, March 27–28, 1960].[17]

FLANNERY O'CONNOR TO TOM AND LOUISE GOSSETT

St. Mary's University in Notre Dame, Indiana, is conferring an honorary degree. O'Connor had become good friends with Thomas Stritch, a Tennessee native and revered professor at Notre Dame University. The nephew of Cardinal Stritch (Chicago), Thomas Stritch helped O'Connor achieve notoriety in the Notre Dame community. Stritch and O'Connor also were mutual friends of Mr. and Mrs. Lon Cheney, and both visited them in Tennessee. In another letter to Father McCown, O'Connor notes, "St. Mary's College at Notre Dame is going to give me an honorary Doctor of Letters . . . Catholic colidge, note."[18]

MILLEDGEVILLE

16 MAY 62

Dear T & L,

We will put out the flags for June 4. Let us know the hour. If we are too tired to feed you, will go to the Sanford House, so don't hesitate to appear at any hour. Also spend the night if that would be convenient. Your cats will have to keep to their cage says my parent, so you can prepare them for a traumatic experience of one kind or another.

You mean you didn't get a cock and a hen? Write them and say you been jipped. I don't know if they are still in bidnis or not but they probably are. If you can't get a hen, you may have to pen up those cocks until after the season. I will look in the Go. Market Bulletin.

I'm getting my HaHa Degree from St. Mary's College. The question is will real doctors of Philosophy speak to me?

Let us know your plans.

FLANNERY O'CONNOR TO ROSLYN BARNES

O'Connor informs Barnes (June 29, 1962) that she has signed a movie contract for "The River." Subsequently, several more stories became films: "The Displaced Person," the American Short Story series (1979), and Wise Blood *(1979), directed by John Huston. Good Country Pictures has secured the rights to many O'Connor stories and* The Violent Bear It Away *for television and movie production (www.goodcountrypictures.com).*

Well I'm glad you're really there. I've heard a lot about Msgr. Il-lych [Ivan Illich] from two friends of mine who know him—Caroline Gordon and [Erik] Langkjaer. You must need somebody violent to run an outfit like that. I want to hear more . . .

I have just signed a contract with a young man [Robert Jiras] to make a movie of "The River." The Lord only knows what he will do with it. He has been trying for 5 years to get the money to do it and has just succeeded in getting enough to start. He's never made a movie before & I'm sure isn't aware much of the religious meaning in the story. We shall see.

We had the cub scouts yesterday and the nursery school this morning. Shot killed a 5 ft. water rattler while the nursery school was here but no one was any the wiser.[19]

FLANNERY O'CONNOR TO
FATHER JAMES McCOWN

O'Connor was impressed with Roslyn Barnes's missionary formation (August 5, 1962). Barnes was one of the few from the Papal Auxiliary Volunteers for

Latin America accepted by the Intercultural Documentation Center at Cuernavaca, Mexico. Founded in 1961 by Msgr. Ivan Illich, a native of Austria, the center offered language courses to missionaries from North America, including volunteers from the Alliance for Progress, a program supported by President Kennedy. Msgr. Illich, however, was critical of such efforts in general because he thought they failed to eliminate "apostolic tourism" in North American missionaries. He was dedicated to eradicating a superior Western perspective originally associated with Spanish colonialism that persisted in the attitudes of some North American missionaries sent to Latin America. Msgr. Illich was critical of the core progressivist perspective and the cultural values of industrialized nations. In particular, Illich believed that the faithful of Latin America should not be expected to conform to the American values of social equality, standardized public education, and material prosperity. Msgr. Illich required an extensive commitment of several years by North American missionaries. The process entailed the divesting of missionaries of "Americanism" and their embracing the indigenous cultural traditions of the faithful of Latin America.

The enclosed is a letter from a young friend of mine who is a Papal Volunteer at the school in Cuernavaca, and I am sending it to you because I know if you know about her you will pray for her. Send me the letter back but remember her. She's a convert of about two years, very bright, and with a real vocation. Her family are violently opposed to what she is doing but she goes her own way. She says Msgr. is straight out of Dostoievsky.[20]

FLANNERY O'CONNOR TO ROSLYN BARNES

O'Connor mentions (September 17, 1962) that the matriarchy of the local college is concerned about her friend's welfare. O'Connor expects a report from a faculty member dispatched to Mexico to see the situation firsthand. O'Connor writes (September 24, 1962) that Msgr. Illich won the approval of a college matriarch.

H.I. Green finally appeared and gave us a very funny account of her visit to Chula Vista [original villa at the center]. She took up the 1st 20 minutes expressing her relief that you were among nice people. All along she must have been thinking that you had fallen in with cut-throats and assassins. She seems to feel better about the religion too—that you haven't just been took. She thinks that man [Msgr. Il-lich] is the "growing tip." According to her he is antiAmerican. She was most impressed with the scantness of the meals. No foolishness. She said you had a "little service" in the morning—I presumed this was Mass—and a "little program" at night—everything was trans-lated into the language of WCG and I had to translate it back. I fig-ured the "little program" was benediction or compline. I wish she could have stayed six months.[21]

FLANNERY O'CONNOR TO FATHER JAMES McCOWN

O'Connor distances herself from a right-wing activist who had publicly criti-cized Dallas merchants for selling imported goods from Communist countries. She also praises again the article on her novel by Robert McCown.

MILLEDGEVILLE

18 AUGUST 62

Thanks for the edifying editorial. That Bowen [Robert O.] must be getting crazier and crazier. I enclose an antidote.

In the last issue of *The Critic* there is an interview with me by Joel Wells and he mentions your brother's essay in the *Kansas Magazine.*[22] I sent it to him.★ I told him I hadn't corresponded with your brother about *The Violent Bear It Away* and he wrote in the interview that I hadn't corresponded with him at all. However, I don't think it makes any difference. The point was just that he arrived at his analysis with-out discussing the book with me.

I hope you will get sent where you will do a lot of good but as I think you will do a lot of good wherever you are sent this about cancels itself out.

Roslyn's name in Roslyn Barnes, Aptdo. 479, Cuernavaca, Morelas. I am sure that if you wanted to write her and tell her that you are a friend of mine who loves Mexico and I asked you to pray for her and you are doing it, that she would be encouraged. Since she's such a recent Catholic, she doesn't have too many people to pray for her and I am very sorry at it. I forget. She might not like my sending you her letter so you had better not tell her that. Apparently when you go to do that kind of work you have to get over what they call "cultural shock." It didn't seem to bother you, but it must be pretty bad on her.

The box of old *Integrity* magazines now [illegible] has just arrived and I have put the contents on the bookshelf and will read some of them with interest and keep them all for you—so when you want them, you know where they are. I wouldn't think of throwing them away.

Cheers and best to your mamma.

★ The Kansas Magazine to Wells

FLANNERY O'CONNOR TO ROSLYN BARNES

O'Connor informs her friend that prayers by O'Connor's colleague are rooted in a shared love of Mexico.

MILLEDGEVILLE

26 AUG. 62

Well I am much cheered that you have got over the mid-term and are still there, not that I had any doubt about it. I have a Jesuit friend, Fr. McCown, whom I asked to pray for you. He is a great lover of Mexico and has done everything he could to be sent there but he is 51 so they say he's too old (which seems ridiculous). Anyway he may write you a letter and tell you he's praying for you.

ROSLYN BARNES TO FATHER JAMES McCOWN

O'Connor's prayers are answered in the new friendship between Barnes and Father McCown. He tore up Barnes's letters only to patch them together. They reveal a new perspective in Barnes's cheerful, seamless blending in with Latin American peoples peppered by discussion of the writings of O'Connor and Walker Percy. Barnes provides an unusual context for understanding their fiction. She also praises Father McCown's Mexico narrative, With McCown in Mexico.

CASILLA 1280

U. DEL NORTE

ANTOFAGASTA, CHILE

Remember me? I wouldn't be surprised if you didn't after having gone so long without hearing from me. Just returned day before yesterday from the summer's wanderings, & found your magazines waiting for me. Thank you so much, I will enjoy them, & use some of them for my students too. Peru is a strange savage sort of country. The people express themselves mostly in a wild sad music. They give you the impression of being dazed, as having received a blow at the Spanish Conquest from which they have never recovered. In the . . . , most of them do not speak Spanish. They have degenerated terribly since the days of the. . . . They do not seem to remember their past. They chew cocoa leaves and live in a kind of dream or semi-conscious state. I visited a few weeks with a friend on the shore of Lake Titicaca, 2 ½ miles high. She is an intelligent young woman, Superior of a new Franciscan convent of 4 nuns. We all studied together at Cuernavaca. They brought a stereo and popcorn when they came, so we had glorious music and midnight snacks along with our perfect view of lake civilization, so I had a real retreat. All one has to do to observe the rule of perfect silence is to step outside the door.

I was also in Santiago, & in the south of Chile, which they call, "the Switzerland of L.A." It is really beautiful, snow-capped mts.

lakes & lakes & lakes, thick forests and fields of sunflowers and roses. Active volcanoes too. An eruption destroyed in . . . a month ago.

Guess what I came across that trip down South?—a priest with a library. He is only in Chile since a few months. The mission office nabbed him to give direction & retreats to all the people that wanted it. Small world, he was spiritual director to the young priest that gave me instruction 3 yrs ago. Has much training in psychology & psychiatry & his specialty seems to be direction. So you don't have to worry about my library anymore; am quite well fixed up for the next months. Am enjoying Ign . . . immensely, have you read him? *The Psychology of Loving* is excellent. Another thing I acquired in Santiago is a Spanish guitar. Here we go-Ay! falisco!

I like the chapter you sent from your book. Before you ever wrote me when Flannery told me she had a priest friend who was writing a book on Mexico, I shuddered to think of it! It would either be sentimental, or it would condemn the indigenous culture as "pagan." Yours has done neither—congratulations! It is really good and accurate, as only a love which has nothing in it of condescension could have made it. My only suggestion would be that you might leave out the term "brain-washing" in relation to CIF [Center for Intercultural Formation, Msgr. Illich's school] . . . I . . . is too often accused of that & people might take you seriously. CIF is having its troubles right now, you know. The new training center at Po . . . , P. R, has taken the majority of the students. Nobody can play dirtier than religious, Father, when the Devil gets into them. Most of the priests & nuns from my . . . have got up a petition to have Msgr . . . fired & have sent it to Fordham Univ. My Franciscan friends were almost the only ones who refused to sign it.

Holy Thursday was my 3rd birthday in the Church. Christ remembered that it was our anniversary, and we were together . . . How is your Mexican friend who entered the convent? Write me and tell me about your summer—I mean, winter. Hope you're having the kind of Easter you want to have. Bye for now. Your friend,

FLANNERY O'CONNOR TO THOMAS AND LOUISE GOSSETT

O'Connor's friends are interested in the Second Vatican Council. She recommends books that will assist their inquiry.

OCTOBER, 1962

I guess you all are glad that you are already shut of your doctrines.

I was glad to hear that you really have a legitimate pair of pea-fowl, even if the hen doesn't mind her eggs always like she ought to. The one I gave the Cancer Home in Atlanta also didn't mind her eggs the first year she was there. The second year she produced two peachickens. This year I brought up five—all hens. But my one-eyed swan died. I think her trouble was old age and I think I didn't have a mated pair. I think her supposed mate was her last year's hatch. He doesn't seem even to be aware that she is gone. One of my litry friends wrote me that it was a shame to lose "so Oedipal a bird."

I am going to get a look at Texas next month, East Texas State College; then I am going to the University of Southwestern Louisiana, then Loyola, then Southeastern Louisiana State College, all this bang bang bang. I hope I survive. Then for a long time I am not going nowhere.

If you are interested in the Council, read a book called *The Council, Reform and Reunion*, by Hans Kung (Sheed & Ward). It's the best thing on it and you will enjoy it.

My mamma and several bull-dozers have dug a new pond. Now she is doing over the tenant house. All her ducks are in a row.

Keep us posted on your goings and comings and when we may look for a visit.

Cheers,

P.S. Fr. McC. has been moved from Texas but I don't know where yet.

FLANNERY O'CONNOR TO TOM GOSSETT

O'Connor worries about an ambitious lecture schedule all in the midst of an understated reference to the Cuban missile crisis of October 1962. O'Connor took the prospect of nuclear exchange in stride—the possible catastrophe could interrupt her speaking tour.

MILLEDGEVILLE

27 OCTOBER 62

I just don't see how I can work it in on this trip though I would love to come. Maybe we can work on it for next year. I feel as if I've already taken on more than my energy is good for on this round— four talks in six days, cold war permitting. I even have to ride on something called Trans Texas for three and a half hours from Dallas to Lafayette. My doubts about this trip get graver by the minute.

When you lay hands on Fr. McCown's address I'd really like to have it. I'm glad they've finally sent him somewhere he can function in his native capacity.

I'll send you a report on my opinion of Texas if I can generate an opinion in a day and a half.

Cheers and thanks & I wish I could come.

Yours,

*My trip is Nov 15–21—all the wrong days

FLANNERY O'CONNOR TO TOM AND LOUISE GOSSETT

On a lecture tour O'Connor mentions she saw the home of a controversial American general. The model for right-wing military characters in movies such as Seven Days in May *and* Thirteen Days, *the general was known for anti-Communist extremism. His views provoked President Kennedy's assassin, Lee*

Harvey Oswald, to try to kill him just weeks before murdering Kennedy. A CNN documentary aired on November 22, 2013, the fiftieth observance of President Kennedy's assassination, featured a segment on the general's attempted murder.

On the same lecture tour O'Connor briefly met Mr. and Mrs. Walker Percy one evening at Loyola University, New Orleans.

MILLEDGEVILLE

GEORGIA

25 NOVEMBER 62

Dear Tom & Louise,

The first thing I was shown in Dallas was General Walker's house. Do you know this landmark? It is a battleship grey two-story monstrosity with a giant picture window in front in which you see a ceramic Uncle Sam with a lamp on top of him. Texas and US flags flying on the lawn. The people that showed it to me thought it was funny too. I didn't run into any arch conservatism, but I caught it on the wind. The head of the department there is a Dr. Barrus originally from Iowa and very nice . . .

In Louisiana they were all talking about a Representative Wellborn Jack, who is apparently harassing the colleges to see they don't hire anybody with wild ideas.

When I went to Hammond, they told me that a Dr. Doyle would drive me back to New Orleans the next day. This proved to be Joan Doyle and she proved to be very fond of you all. I was impressed with her.

Thanks for F. McCown's address. I forthwith wrote him and have a letter in return. He says he's in hog heaven.

Cheers and Merry Christmas. I'm starting early.

FLANNERY O'CONNOR TO
FATHER JAMES McCOWN

O'Connor mentions in the next two letters her copyediting her colleague's "Mexican letters" which she offers to present to a publisher. A master of sequencing in her own stories, O'Connor advises him about the order of episodes.

MILLEDGEVILLE

12 FEBRUARY 63

I think this is going great and just the way it should. I had a few objections, mostly stylistic, which I marked with a green pencil. I am such a loyal child of you-know-where that I begin celebrating The Feast immediately after Ground Hog Day. I think the title is fine. I would get farther along in it before I started worrying about a publisher. When you do get more of it to show, I'll write my editor at FS&C and see if they would like to see it. You'll probably just have to try them all until you hit the one that likes it. I gather that the retreat at the end of the trip will kind of gather all this up into some kind of appreciation of Mexico and God's image in the world. Anyway, it ought to work up to a kind of quiet underplayed climax like that I should think. I want to see the rest of it.

I should speculate that a publisher would not want your pictures because it would make the book too expensive, but I don't know of course.

I hope you manage to stay out of the hospital. Maybe your ulcer didn't like Mexican food, as well as you did. If you should get around by General Walker's house, let me know if the ceramic statue of Uncle Sam in the picture window really has a lampshade on top of it. Of late it has seemed to me that perhaps my imagination supplied the lampshade. The statue I am sure of.

The cold has clobbered us three times. My mother spends all her time plumbing.

Cheers to you & don't fail to send me the rest of the book. I'll be particularly interested in the closing chapter.

FLANNERY O'CONNOR TO ELIZABETH HESTER

Changes in a movie version of "The River" elicit O'Connor's displeasure. She also is skeptical of pedagogy in local schools and critical of a future academic conference. The situation in the schools led O'Connor to write a penetrating essay, "Total Effect and the Eighth Grade." Therein she prophetically identifies "the devil of Educationism that possesses us" and which can be "cast out only by prayer and fasting."[23] O'Connor identifies the spiritual root of "educationism," whose deleterious impact she traces in many letters in this collection, as well as in The Violent Bear It Away. *Her observations raise philosophic questions about the rationale and wisdom of both public and parochial schooling rooted in "educationism." O'Connor consistently notes the widening gulf between "schooling" and wisdom.*

2 MARCH 63

Dear Betty,

How many Perrys are there for pity's sake? I thought there was just this one man. If there are two against him, he might as well fold up. What is it, man & wife? Always a bad combination. Whatever they have is not the nasty parents deal because Mr. Jiras tells me the man wants to get rid of Bevel's father altogether and have the mother be ready to get married again. While she is off getting herself a man, I gather, the child is sent off with the baby-sitter for the whole weekend. Mr. Jiras wants me to help them with a couple of new scenes ["The River"] between the child and Mr. Paradise and with the preacher, but of course I am not contributing a line to something I disapprove of—which will be a great excuse for me not to contribute my services. Actually, I don't care what they do with the thing, but I definitely prefer the Gene Kelly kind of crap to this kind.

Quote from latest communication from Dr. A. [Ashley] Brown: "You can inform Betty that Iris Murdoch's annual novel will be out soon. This one is about a unicorn [*The Unicorn*]."

Mr. Sherry after his visit here went home and thought it over and then wrote and asked me if I would contribute an article every month to his supplement. I have told him no but that I will contribute an occasional one and have agreed to do something for the first issue. I have been right disgusted with all the sentimentality wasted on those teachers who were giving Steinbeck and Hersey to the 8th grade so I am writing on that. Ralph McGill had an idiot column on it in which he implied that Hersey was much better than Hawthorne.

Miss Leone is still going strong, hanging onto her cock.

Thursday, Friday and Saturday I will be at a Symposium at Sweet Briar and will be wishing I was not. Also there is going to be a philosopher named George Boas, a theologian named Hopper, and art critic named James Johnson Sweeney (friend of Tom's), a pianist I forgit her name and old John Chiardi [Ciardi] who is everywhere anybody else is.

"Everything That Rises Must Converge" has got the O. Henry prize this year. I was much surprised as I had forgotten that that prize existed. Somebody from Harvard is now running it.

I am right worried about the state of the Wm. A. Sessions and have written Billy to render an account of himself.

Cheers,
Flannery

FLANNERY O'CONNOR TO FATHER JAMES McCOWN

Juxtaposed against Father McCown's narrative about Mexican faith is O'Connor's description of the increasing alienation of some academic communities in the United States from theological orthodoxy. The observation has be-

come prophetic in the triumph of hostility to Christianity on many American campuses today. She invents a famous phrase that summarizes well the theological essence of her lectures and apologetics. Because of fashionable theological trends in the academic world, O'Connor was unexpectedly becoming an apologist for orthodoxy.

MILLEDGEVILLE

4 APRIL 63

I can't find anything much to complain of in this, in fact nothing [*With McCown in Mexico*]. Whether you can get it published will depend pretty much on what the whole looks like when you finish it. I don't know what publishers think about travel books. I am thinking you might just try Sheed & Ward and see what they say.

I hope the debutants edified you and visa versa and all. I have just been to a symposium at Sweet Briar in Virginia on Religion and Art and did I ever get a stomachful of liberal religion. The thing began with a paper by George Boaz on Art and Magic. I don't know exactly what he meant to say but he left the impression that religion was a good thing (or at least unavoidable) because it was art and magic. They had a Methodist-Universalist there who talked about how the symbology of religion was decayed and then it ended with John Chiardi [Ciardi, *How Does a Poem Mean?*] told them about how God was a grandfather image and they had better shuck it.[24] I gave them a nasty dose of orthodoxy in my paper but I think it passed as quaint. It is later than we think.[25]

Pray for my friend Roslyn. She has been sent to a new University [Universidad Católica del Norte] at Antofagasta, Chile, where I gather things are pretty bleak. It's a Jesuit University but apparently nobody practices the religion but the Jesuits and Roslyn. I am afraid she will get impatient there and I hope to the Lord she don't undertake to reform the Jesuits.

I friend of mine who lives in Brazil is sending me an example of native religious art—a crucifix in a bottle. She says she hopes I won't be too appalled. It has not arrived yet.

A happy Easter to you and remember me to your mama and sister and brother.

FLANNERY O'CONNOR TO LA TRELLE

While several letters recount misreadings of The Violent Bear It Away, *O'Connor reveals in a pithy paragraph the scriptural inspiration of the novel and its root in ascetical theology.*

MILLEDGEVILLE,

14 FEBRUARY 63

Dear La Trelle,

I was cheered to hear from you and receive that snappy valentine. I had been a little worried after your note Christmas and wanted to write you but had lost your box number up there. Now I have it written down in my book. If I can manage not to lose the book.

About Matthew 12:11. The King James version has it ". . . the violent take it by force," but I thought "bear it away" sounded better. What they take by force or bear away is the kingdom of heaven itself. The violent in this case are the people who are willing to act upon their faith and act vigorously. St. Augustine and St. Thomas say the violent here are ascetics. Anyway it is the kind of passion for the things of God which makes asceticism possible, which puts nothing in the way and lets nothing interfere with winning heaven. Old Tarwater is this kind of Christian. All the saints are. I guess John Wesley was. Call it a single-minded assault upon the kingdom of heaven, often accomplished in part by self denial. By doing the will of God.

I am going to be at Sweet Briar College, Va March 7–9 and at Troy State April 23–4. I'm going to the University in Athens sometime this spring but the date hasn't been fixed. Don't let me miss you when you come.

There are two articles in here that I think very good. You can see if you get anything out of them and send them back to me when you get through with them.

That degree was a Doctor of Letters, St. Mary's College, Indiana, 1962.

If I can recommend you for a teaching job just put my name down. I don't know any of those schools.

FLANNERY O'CONNOR TO ELIZABETH HESTER

O'Connor speaks of sentimentality in the movies, which she labels "tenderization," and worries about distortions of a film version of her story. Her observations draw on one of her most penetrating statements:

. . . we govern by tenderness. It is a tenderness, which long since cut off from the person of Christ, is wrapped in theory. When tenderness is divorced from the source of tenderness, its logical outcome is terror. It ends in forced labor camps and the fumes of the gas chamber.[26]

MILLEDGEVILLE

16 MARCH 63

Dear Betty,

By the enclosures you will see that the young man is a dead-ringer for his paw with a touch of something foreign thrown in. A long breathless letter accompanied these, detailing how the master of the house had nearly had a collapse what with overwork and strain and so forth but how now things were looking up. Jenny [Mrs. William Sessions] is going to Greece for part of the spring and all of the summer as she has a small legacy there and Billy will go back to Oree County [Horry County, South Carolina] to his momma and poppa. And thus is it with the Sessions.

The Perrys sound fair gruesome to me. I have been reading about the picture here and there. It is always called "tender." I think they are only trying to make Mr. Jirases movie ["The River"] into something "tender." So we shall just have to wait and see how well Mr. Jiras resists its tenderization. If they are going to make it tender I hope they make it so dam tender that it will make a million bucks and I will become so filthy rich that I can quit going to symposiums in Virginia . . .

As for it, it was like all the rest of them. I wouldn't know what to tell you about Chiardi [John Ciardi]. He has a magnetic personality as far as students are concerned. If he were a crooner they would squeal. You feel he has said the same thing to students so much that if his mouth were plastered up, it would come out of his ears. This is probably true for anybody who is articulate and does much of this. Boas [George] moderated the whole thing and at the end of it when he was summing up the "conclusions" or the non-conclusions more likely, he said, "And it's been a great pleasure for me personally to be here at Bryn Mawh College" [Bryn Mawr, Pennsylvania]. It was Sweet Briar [College, Virginia], of course.

Miss Leone is failing fast, but Miss Winnifred Fowler is about to make it and Elizabeth is delighted because [she] bet that Miss Winnifred's daughter was thinking that she was going to get to spend all that money at last.

Cheers,

Flannery

ROSLYN BARNES TO FATHER JAMES McCOWN

O'Connor encouraged Father McCown to continue writing Roslyn Barnes. He sent her letters to Thomas Gossett. Formed by the severe discipline of Monseigneur Ivan Illich, Barnes seeks counsel, as had O'Connor, from Father McCown.

CASILLA 1280

U DEL NORTE

ANTOFAGASTA [CHILE]

SUNDAY [SPRING, 1963]

Dear Fr. Mc C.

I just returned from vacation and reunion in Santiago, to find your letter and the books awaiting me. Many thanks! I am very anxious to get into *Christ and Apollo* [William F. Lynch, S.J.]. I remember Flannery's recommending it very highly, but I was unable to get a copy at the time. Thank you so very much. I found a letter waiting from Flannery, too. Her handwriting was so shaky, she must still be terribly weak. But at least she seems to be out of danger, and that is a great deal!

I am afraid I have expressed my viewpoints badly to you. I do believe that consecrated virginity is <u>one</u> Christian ideal. But I do not believe that it is <u>the</u> Christian ideal, and I do not believe that the consecrated virgin is more "pure" than the partners of a genuine love relationship expressing itself through sex. There are pure virgins & impure virgins, and pure lovers and impure lovers. For me the degree of purity depends absolutely on the degree of love and loving self surrender, whether the Beloved is God Himself or God incarnated in a human person. Fidelity is an element of genuine love, and I do not approve of the treatment your little Mexican unwed mothers have received from their men. (But any real woman will give herself to the man she loves regardless of what the consequences are for her, just as you would give yourself completely to God even if you knew He was going to send you [to] Hell). Love is the important thing. Only thru love can there be any <u>real</u> purity and <u>real</u> charity, in whatever state of life. You mentioned not having run into a good book on this subject. I recently was given a very good one to read by the priest who has charge of us gringos in Chile—Fr. Charles Magram, MM—you ever meet him in the States? It's called *In Defense of Purity*, Hildebrand [Dietrich von]. It provides some good insights.[27]

Ixmiquilpan must have been a wonderful experience. The little

Sisters are certainly charming. Actually, this Order seems to me the ideal for . . . life—it perfectly celebrates the incarnation of God in the everyday world. They do not "retreat" from the world—they penetrate it. Theirs is a beautiful vocation. I have often wished it were mine, but I know it isn't. But for me it is the ideal for the woman living the life [of] consecrated virginity. When I came thru Arequipa last summer, I visited the little Sisters there, and found them just as radiant and gay.

Time to be closing now—second semester is under way, and I still have an afternoon of work ahead of me. Let me know how your work goes in the States now, and your book too [*With McCown in Mexico*]. Don't forget my "principito."

Yours,

Rosalyn

FLANNERY O'CONNOR TO LOUISE AND THOMAS GOSSETT

O'Connor expresses her skepticism of academic honors. Her professor friends who were treated poorly by academic officialdom, as other letters reveal, would probably have appreciated O'Connor's views.

11 MAY 63

We're supposed to be where we're going on the 1st so we'll be a-going there on the 31st. I call it down right revolting. I'm getting another stinking degree at one of them fancy colleges up there and I would much rather stay at home and visit with you all. Are two non-negotiable degrees more negotiable than one? No. Anyway, why don't you all come back through here? We can discuss Texas since I been there now.

Let us know how you find your West Virginia peacocks. Mine are all strutting in the middle of the road this year and are very trying to the colored folk's traffic. They come up the road at 80 mi per hr. have to stop and dislodge the bird who gives them a kind of modified course as they do so. Not at all good for race relations.

Cheers,

The letter borders on becoming a story. O'Connor identifies with her rural characters in dealing with hostile commentators and the national government. An honorary degree shows a cheerful association with Southern literature that O'Connor avoids in other letters.

MILLEDGEVILLE

4 AUGUST 63

I don't see how you all are making out up there without the consolation of a peahen and having mud in the bathtub and toting your drinking water from the spring. I think you had better get you a place in Georgia. I can then supply you with peahens and even a duck or two. I have this muscow duck that hatched nine in March, six in June, and is at it again underneath the back steps. I can look through a hole and see her setting. Each set she has hatched has been taken over by a bantam hen so that the muscovy could go back to her social life, which is very intense. There were six hens in the first set, I gave away the second. But next March, by my calculations I should have upwards of sixty infant muscovys. Muscovys are quackless ducks but adept at sign language.

I haven't read that Irving Malin book [*New American Gothic*]. Somebody wrote me about it but left me with the impression that I had been condemned, insulted, knocked down and drug out in it, so I thought well there's no use my raising my blood pressure by reading it. How I keep so calm is I just keep in mind on feeding myself and my chickens and resisting the pressures of the Federal Govermint. I write a few stories but I don't know how to interpit them.

We were awful sorry to miss you in June and that doctors degree don't do me a bit of good either. They gave away six of them—

bargain day at Smith [College, Massachusetts]. Most of them were Smith graduates and scientists, buggy or social, but when they start looking for somebody in literature they have to go South, naturally.

We wish you all would take this way back. I might even attempt to speak on the subject of angels in fiery furnaces or artificial niggers and mercy if you were here in person.

Cheers,

KATHERINE ANNE PORTER TO FLANNERY O'CONNOR

The next few letters trace the renewal of the friendship between Katherine Anne Porter and Flannery O'Connor. By 1963 Maurice-Edgar Coindreau had translated some of O'Connor's fiction, and she was becoming popular in France. Coindreau had made Faulkner's fiction accessible to his countrymen who were interested in the Mississippian's unexpected existentialist themes in regional settings in The Sound and the Fury *and other novels. Both Albert Camus and Jean-Paul Sartre found Faulkner's writing compelling, especially Camus, who was also translating Faulkner as he edited* Combat, *an underground newspaper during the Nazi occupation of Paris. Coindreau recognized that O'Connor drew on Faulkner's achievement with her own resourceful techniques. In 1958, he began translating O'Connor's stories. The fruit of his efforts appears in Porter's letter in which she informs O'Connor of her celebrity in France.*

SUNDAY AUGUST 12, 1963

PARIS, FRANCE

Dear Flannery:

Maybe you have a clipping bureau service of some kind, or your publishers for you. I have never had either, except for three months after my novel came out, which *The Atlantic Monthly* took for me: I never see anything printed about me or my work unless some friend or relative sends me it. So I am sending you this. Not long ago my translator here asked me if I could suggest any young American writers for her to translate, and I said, "Flannery O'Connor." She had never heard of you. I said, "No and the French never catch on except fifteen years later." I mentioned Faulkner, totally unknown here when Steinbeck was considered the great American writer. I said, "Malcolm Lowry is just being heard of here, and his publisher in America sent me the page proofs of *Under the Volcano* just seventeen years ago! While you people were having kittens about Henry Miller!"

Etcetera. I could run on this way for several paragraphs. Well, we were in Galignani's librairie—a huge place,—looking around, and there on a table with a show of writers translated from English, you were! or rather, two books of yours! Marcelle Sibon (the translator and my old friend) prides herself on keeping up the best writers in English as they come. She suffered chagrin, as the French say, and serves her right. And I asked Galignani himself, if he sold many of your books. And he said, "Very nicely, nothing sensational, it is just that she has her readers!"[28] And Flannery, I glowed with pleasure, for what honest artist could ask for more? And I <u>know</u>, because from my first book I had my readers, and I still have them, and my unchanging affection for them and delight in them; I never expected or wanted more, and all those quite hundreds of thousand persons who seemed to have bought the *Ship* [*of Fools*] and, so it has been said more than once, were unable to read it, have after all made no difference except that now I have a modest fixed income—I can't of course really have the use of the money because the Revenoors will take 91 percent of it, and I just don't feel that generous! Any way, not to Revenooers.— But nothing has changed in my life or my good solid relation with my readers, and that is something to treasure! You have, after all, enormously more of a reputation than I had at your age or for many years after, and I don't doubt as much or more that I have now: that is purely relative and personal and is not what I am talking about. As you well know.

Yesterday this piece came in the mails from Marcelle, and I was pleased to see it, and send it on. I have gone through here the same exhausting treadmill of reporters, camera men, translators, critics, writers, cocktail parties, teas, lunches, interviews, and have got away half-alive as usual. But coming back nicely in a little apartment over in the Lion de Belfort section, not stylish, just a good place to be, and have really disappeared, and am getting to work again.

At last I am getting out that long-delayed collection of short stories I prefer, and I chose your "A Good Man Is Hard to Find." My I hope you will let me have it; it is a marvelous and terrible story, I want to try to say something about it in the preface I am writing for the book.

I never forget you standing among your peacocks and I remember well the speech you made at that writers' conference [Wesleyan College, Macon, Georgia]—I hope you are well and merry and working just as you would like.

FLANNERY O'CONNOR TO MAURICE-EDGAR COINDREAU

O'Connor continues to endure physical suffering without complaining. As several letters reveal, Regina O'Connor's vigilant health care made possible the continued writing of O'Connor as her condition worsened.

MILLEDGEVILLE

12 MAY. 64

Dear M. Coindreau,

I am cheered to hear you've finished the translation [*The Violent Bear It Away*]. I wish my news were as good. I had to have an operation in February. It was a success but it set going my chronic trouble (disseminated lupus) and I have just got out of the hospital again and am supposed to stay in bed, no company; no work. My aunt Mary (the one in town) had herself a heart attack in April and she is now out here with us, recuperating along with me. All this being the case, I think September would be better. I had a blood transfusion yesterday which is why I have the energy to write you a letter. This is one of those diseases where you are allergic to your own protein or some such foolishness. Anyway I am doing what the doctors tell me to and writing my stories in my head. By September I hope to have thrown this off. My mother is fine so far and sends you her best. She's running a hospital though, and without much in the way of help.

If you want to write me some of the points you want to talk about, I can be thinking of them and write you as I get to feeling stronger.

Maybe by September, Equinox [donkey] will have a brother or sister. He has just started to learn to bray and he practices a[t] six o'clock in the morning and all the peacocks try to drown him out as they apparently don't think much of his voice.

I have a new story in the current *Sewanee Review* ["Revelation"] which you may like and can probably find in the Sweet Briar College library.

Again I wish we could make it June, but I guess Sept. will be better.

The following letter dates a few years back to the French translation of Wise Blood. *O'Connor asks that her tutor's explanatory introduction be removed from the French edition. O'Connor is amazed that Coindreau, having made Faulkner's characters accessible to the French, also renders the atheist preacher of* Wise Blood, *Hazel Motes, understandable to foreign readers.*

MILLEDGEVILLE

GEORGIA

4 DECEMBER 58

Dear M. Coindreau:

Caroline [Gordon] Tate has told me that you plan to come South in the spring and I write to ask if you may be coming through Milledgeville and if so if we may have the pleasure of a visit from you. We should love to have you stay overnight with us or any length of time you find convenient. Milledgeville is very much of the South and I should like to show it to you.

I also write about another matter: Mrs. Tate's introduction to WISE BLOOD for the French edition. I have felt uneasy about an introduction for some time but my thoughts on the subject have only recently crystalized into a decision. I do not believe an introduction is advisable for this French edition.

The French are too intelligent to need telling what a book is about and I am sure an introduction would only irritate them and put any discussion of the book on a factional plane. I have written Caroline and explained that I think a living author should allow his book to stand on its own and that I prefer not to use an introduction. I think she will understand.

Should I write to Gallimard and request that there be no introduction or is it enough to have taken this up with you? I am anxious to have the matter settled.

I am very pleased that you are the one translating my book. It is hard to imagine. It is hard to imagine a M. Hazel Motes. My French is feeble but I look forward to attempting to read the translation, and I hope that we shall see you this spring.

Sincerely,

O'Connor once again praises Coindreau's translating. He apparently was familiar with successful French editions of novels by Sinclair Lewis and Erskine Caldwell featuring rural preachers. Coindreau made the dialect of such characters accessible to the French.

MILLEDGEVILLE

GEORGIA

18 JANUARY 59

Dear M. Coindreau,

We are delighted that you will be able to come down in April. I expect to be here all during April except from the 22nd to the 25th. Milledgeville is not accessible by train but buses from Atlanta and

Macon come in at various convenient times during the day, and if you will let me know when you will arrive, we shall be there to meet you.

It had not occurred to me that the French wouldn't know about itinerant preachers; however I don't think Caroline's introduction would throw any light on that aspect of the matter. An article on the subject I would be very fine or perhaps a translator's note describing the itinerant preacher as a Southern institution. Being a Catholic I have never heard an itinerant preacher myself but the atmosphere in the South is permeated with their effects. One doesn't have to attend camp meetings to get the general idea.

I have never read either *Elmer Gantry* [Sinclair Lewis] or *Journeyman* [Erskine Caldwell], but I'll try to rectify this lack before you come.

Thank you again for your letter and the prospect of a visit.

Sincerely,

Flannery O'Connor

MILLEDGEVILLE

GEORGIA

19 JULY 59

Dear M. Coindreau,

I don't know whether this is address enough to reach you, but I hope so. I have been assiduously collecting clippings about evangelists for you and enclose three, one on horseback and two of the juvenile variety, one of these being female. I am wondering what the word is in French for lady-evangelist.

We were pleased to get your card from Spain. Our day in Barcelona was one of the most pleasant we had, made so I am afraid by the fact that there were geese in the courtyard of the Cathedral.

This summer I have done a good deal of rewriting on my novel

[*The Violent Bear It Away*] but yesterday I sent it to the publisher for good. I think it's a great deal improved from the time you saw it.

I haven't heard much from Caroline [Gordon] except that she in engaged in the business of getting a divorce, a very doleful affair.

All my peacocks are shedding and are walking around in a very bedraggled condition. No one wants to take pictures of them now. My mother and I are both hoping that the next spring you will come down to see us again. Spring is much the best time to be in Georgia. The heat is terrific here now and will be well into September.

I do appreciate all you are doing to make *Wise Blood* palatable to the French, and I'll hope to hear more about it later.

Our best to you,
Flannery

MILLEDGEVILLE

GEORGIA

1 NOVEMBER 59

Dear M. Coindreau,

Caroline [Gordon] finally visited us last weekend and we sent her back with an assortment of messages for you, chief of which was that we will most certainly expect you to spend Easter with us and we are already looking forward to it.

I enclose two very edifying clippings that I have been saving for your collection. They are a little weather-beaten by now.

Caroline seemed in pretty good spirits, all things considered. The divorce won't affect her Catholicism unless she decides she wants to remarry which she couldn't do and remain in the Church. After having done battle these many years, I shouldn't think she'd be tempted to marry again, unless she lost the use of reason.

I am hoping my French will be sufficient for me to read your introduction on evangelism. It is too bad this couldn't be an illustrated introduction, with photographs of the Methodist preacher on horseback, the boy carrying the ball for Christ, and Lord Joseph and Son. Perhaps you had better write a whole book on this subject.

All the best to you from my mother and me,

Yours,

Flannery

MILLEDGEVILLE

GEORGIA

5 JANUARY 60

Dear M. Coindreau,

The book [*La sagesse dans le sang*] arrived this morning and I am delighted with it. I can get the gist of the introduction on one reading but it will take me several to know what it is actually about. Do you think that if I perfect my French on LA SAGESSE DANS LE SANG I will speak French like Hazel Motes or Mrs. Watts [Leona] if I ever get to Paris? I might not then be received in the best society.

My editor at Farr[ar] Straus and Cudahy sent me the NFR bulletin. ES&C should be sending you THE VIOLENT BEAR IT AWAY in a week or two. I hope you like it as revised, and I certainly hope you will translate it. I notice, if my French does not deceive me, that in the introduction to *Wise Blood,* you mention the new book and indicate that the great-uncle in the new one bears some resemblance to Hazel Mote's grandfather. He does; though he is a less puritanical figure, more the real prophet.

We appreciated your Christmas cards, my mother the farm and me the birds. It has been very warm here. With the result that the peacocks are ahead of the season and are strutting all over the yard. Usually this does not begin until late February.

You said once that I should send a picture to Gallimard. I don't know if that is still necessary, but I enclose one which I have just gotten around to having taken, and you can send it if you like.

We are expecting to see you at the Easter vacation.

Again my very great thanks to you. I am going to read every word of LA SAGESSE DANS LE SANG!

Yours,

Flannery

GEORGIA

18 JULY 60

Dear M. Coindreau,

Well, here are the pictures that came out and as you can see they are very pale and anemic, which is the case with most pictures I take. However, I think the ones of you sitting on the porch are good if you don't mind straining your eyesight to see them.

We certainly enjoyed your visit and next year when you come we will try not to present you with so many ladies who talk so much. Mrs. Freeman paid us a second visit a week later and I see she never runs down or out of conversation.

I am much relieved that you are going to look over that gentleman's translation of my stories, as I was not very confident it would be a good translation.[29] Now I won't worry about it.

Who should call this morning from Princeton but Mrs. Gordon Tate Herself. She is going to visit an Aunt in Chattanooga and will come by here on the 26th, arriving on your bus. I hope that no stray dogs will show their faces during her visit and that we can keep down all animal incidents, etc.

The card you sent us from the station in Atlanta was edifying and we hope you'll continue to keep good company, read good literature and keep us posted on your comings and goings. We'll expect to see you next year moreover.

Our best,

Flannery

FLANNERY O'CONNOR TO KATHERINE ANNE PORTER

As O'Connor's fame grows, she complains about unflattering pictures of her. She concurs with Porter's praise of her most famous story which O'Connor enjoys reading at literary gatherings. She also finds a Bible verse applicable to journalists.

MILLEDGEVILLE

GEORGIA

17 AUGUST 63

Thanks so much for the clipping. My French is just bad enough for me to take great pleasure in it—I'm not able to disagree with him because I don't know exactly what he's saying except that I live on a vast estate among many beasts and I can agree with that. I'm glad you don't remember me with the fretful expression of this picture. The fact is I think photographers are the lowest breed of men and just being in the presence of one brings out my worst face. I have just recently had a bad experience with those people at *Jubilee*. I let their photographer come here (which I should have had more sense than to do) and you should see the result. This is a beautiful place but in his pictures it looks like Oklahoma in the duststorm. I look like one of the Oakie women after years of wrath and semi-starvation. I asked them not to use the pictures but they informed it was too late and used them anyway.

I am glad to think of you in Paris writing, escaping the cocktail parties if not the revenuers. I guess on the latter score you just cain't win. I don't make any money to speak of, but I have to keep going to college festivals etc to pay my income tax every three months. I haven't figured it out. Something must be wrong somewhere.

I'm sure Harcourt, Brace will be glad to have you use "A Good Man Is Hard to Find" in your collection. I certainly will but I don't have any say-so in the matter. I'm going to Hollins and Notre Dame of Maryland and possibly Georgetown this fall and am going to read that story. It's the only one of mine that I can read aloud without laughing and it's about the right length—but after I read it I feel as if I've been shot five times.

I hope that when you come back you'll be coming to Georgia again sometime and will come to see us on our vast estate and let me show you the many beasts. The other day I had a letter from a paper in Atlanta asking me to give them my favorite Bible verse. Wrote them I didn't have one (the idea!) but later I decided that if the occasion ever came up again, my favorite verse would be from the end of Jonas: "And shall not I spare Ninive, that great city, where there are more than a hundred and twenty thousand persons who don't know their right hand from their left, and many beasts?"

KATHERINE ANNE PORTER TO FLANNERY O'CONNOR

Porter assumes a place in an international community of writers. Following up on Caroline Gordon's predictions in chapter one, Porter places O'Connor in the canon of modern American literature. O'Connor's position leads Porter to conclude prophetically that America's national literature is largely chauvinistic and diminishes writing by women.

LAST WORD FROM VILLA ADRIENNA, PAVILLION

POUSSIN, I9 AVENUE DU GENERAL LAOLERO,

PARIS, XIV LA FRANCE

20 OCTOBER I963

Bits of common knowledge I have picked up lately. . . . My avenue used to be Orleans, and they did not re-name it for the first husband of Pauline Bonaparte, as I thought vaguely, but for the French General who, according to French history, liberated Paris single-handed on that July Day in 1944. Well, they can have it—The French are not the only nation who are busy revising history. There is a legend afoot that Ernest Hemingway did it, with a jeepload of GI'S. (American version).[30]

That's about all I've learned lately. Here is that news cutting I mentioned, and I see you are on the same page at least with Mary McCarthy, "whose place in contemporary American letters is so very particular one can compare her (reputation) to that of Madame Nathalie Sarraute [French novelist and critic] with us."[31] There is such a thing as fractured English, too. Well, anyway, it's a pretty good review of your now celebrated *Brave Men Do Not Run in the Streets*. Meaning, I am sure, that they are Hard To Find, or Do Not Grow On Bushes. This Kanters is the man who keeps writing about the "Jewish Renascence" in American literature, and seems to think the American short story began with Dorothy Parker. But just the same, he nearly knows what he is reading in your stories, he is limited but good as far as he goes: but a man who thinks of Sarraute and Parker, McCarthy and O'Connor in the same review is not to be trusted in the long run, and a nice long run you're going to have, that's certain.[32] And you will for some time find yourself teamed with any number of unlikely running mates—I was for years upon years compared with Katherine Mansfield. My own view was, and is, that we were both women, both named Katherine, and both wrote short stories, and there the resemblance ends. Then it was Willa Cather. Then it was Hemingway and even Faulkner, now and then. And now I have graduated into the society of Flaubert, Melville, Stendhal, Henry James, and even to Tolstoy. Fast company, I call it, and it does me no earthly good, and it is the device of lazy-minded third-rate reviewers who can't read them. They have heard these names or perhaps know certain persons who have read them but I daresay that is all.

There are at least half a dozen weekly literary and art newspapers, *Les Arts*, *Le Figaro Littéraire*, *Les Lettres Françaises*, *Nouvelles Littéraires*,

L'Express, etc., besides of course the serious bookshaped ones (and they really are newspapers, full of gossip and lively shop talk, with quite often a long chatty piece about American literature, which they seem to discover scrap by scrap, and they hardly know any of the younger ones) and of the older for years they knew nobody but Steinbeck and F. Scott Fitzgerald!! They were fifteen or twenty years getting around to translating Faulkner. But anyway, there was a long piece about the younger generation—some of them looking a little shopworn by now—and how they were trying to find the right man for the place left vacant by Hemingway and Faulkner—the candidates were carefully selected from their "set"—Bellow, Roth, Salinger, Styron, et al., even with Truman Capote and John Updike trailing along: and there you were named alongside Carson McCullers, not of course as Candidates for the exclusively male honor of heading up our national literature, but as its ever-blooming peripheral female adornments!

Well, on to other things . . .

For months I have been trying to decide where to go and what to do next, here in Europe or Spain or Greece: and I cannot think of any place I want to go, or anything to do: I don't even want to come back to the USA and wouldn't for anything stay in Paris a day longer than I have settled for: and this means quite simply that I want to get located somewhere reasonably permanent and dependably quiet, and work. I am quite bored and tired of everything in the world except the lovely prospect of getting my books and papers around me once more, and the uninterrupted days and weeks and months of writing . . .

I hope I shall see you again sometime soon. I hope you are doing well and also doing whatever you want! This picture of you is better than the other, but it isn't flattering, either. I like best your self-portrait, and if you have a photograph of it, I wish you would give me one! I'll swap, if you like. I haven't got a hand-painted one, but I have one that looks somewhat like me, for the present, and will be glad to send it when I am back in the country. (I remember well Marianne Moore's warning against sending unsolicited photographs.) I do it in hell's despite, of course.

Hasta luego!

With affections

Katherine Anne

There has been a Marvelous joyous carnival of mourning for Edith Piaf and Jean Cocteau, and it was <u>real</u>! They died as they had lived, with style and grace and their proper eccentricity; and Paris loves anybody who can live anarchically and be delightful entertainment at the same time. So do I. I loved them both, and I shed my few difficult tears for them, and I miss them—especially Cocteau, who was exactly of my generation. KA

FLANNERY O'CONNOR TO KATHERINE ANNE PORTER

O'Connor distances herself from other popular women writers of her generation and prefers association with a televangelist.

MILLEDGEVILLE, GEORGIA

10 NOVEMBER 63

Thanks so much for the clipping. You never know what kind of company you're going to keep next but I think I prefer Mary McCarthy to Carson McCullars. These translations give me a very uncomfortable feeling. A French review of *Wise Blood* was illustrated by a big picture of Billy Ghrame. But then I prefer Billy to both those ladies.

I have been looking around for a picture of my self-portrait. I used to have some but I haven't turned one up so far, but I have been taking pictures around here and I thought you might like to have these. The peacocks were losing their tails at the time but I think the swan and the burros are nice. I had two swans but the lady passed away and since then the cob has been in love with the bird bath. I made enough on my last trip to order me two new swans as I am determined to raise some. They are supposed to be on their way now from Miami.

I hope you are back and have your things around you. All my best and thanks again.

FLANNERY O'CONNOR TO LOUISE AND TOM GOSSETT

O'Connor expresses concern for their beloved Jesuit friend. At this time, he was engaging in an exhausting regimen of retreats and travel.

MILLEDGEVILLE

22 SEPT 63

We have about et up your mama's bread and drunk up that bottle of wine and we <u>still</u> remember your visit with relish. So I hope you can hit us again in June. I can propose a new menu. Shot killed a hoot owl last week and they ate him for supper. I thought I had better find out what he tasted like so I asked Louise how he was and what he tasted like. She said he sho was fine and he tasted about like <u>hawk</u>. So if they kill another, I'll be tempted to claim him and put him in the deep freeze for special guests.

We didn't think Fr. McC[own] looked so hot. I know he was pleased you saw his mama.

Mine sends greetings. She is against owl in the deep freeze. Contrary as usual.

Cheers,

FLANNERY O'CONNOR TO
FATHER JAMES McCOWN

O'Connor mentions facilitating a new friendship for her friend with Walker Percy. She also mentions her contributions to local ecumenical observances. This letter and several others show O'Connor's playful theology which she may have learned from reading Dante. The Florentine presents animal characters in scenes of complex theological revelation, such as the talking eagle's long speech in the Paradiso *about the salvation of virtuous pagans. The participation of O'Connor's farm animals in religious celebrations reveals the Dantean element of playful joy.*

MILLEDGEVILLE

11 DECEMBER 63

Merry Christmas to you and your mama and brothers and sisters. I'm glad you could get shut of Atlanta over the holidays and that you got a visit to Walker Percy. Hep yourself if you want to lend him my book [*The Violent Bear It Away,* probably]; however, as it is out in paperback, he might rather get a copy of his own and not have to fool with sending it back.

I'm glad you're growing Andalusia worms in the state capital. That should add something to the capital.

One of our burros is being lent to the First Methodist church for their Christmas service. I hear tell he will walk across the front of the church. The other two burros are being lent to the Christian church. That is our contribution to the current ecumenical spirit. And we'll get to see what Protestantism does for their characters in that short time.

CHAPTER 4

"REMOVING CHOICE SOULS SO SOON"

This chapter features letters of Flannery O'Connor to Ward Allison Dorrance, another writer tutored by Caroline Gordon. She wrote O'Connor from Paris in 1953 that she was showing Dorrance O'Connor's stories. Some years later Dorrance was a professor at Georgetown University when O'Connor lectured there in 1963 at the 175th anniversary of the university's founding. O'Connor encourages him to finish his novel, *The Party at Mrs. Purefoy's*. She also recounts the difficulties of living on a dairy farm and provides an admirable portrait of Regina O'Connor.

The letters to Dorrance, moreover, impart moving details about O'Connor's final months before her death—what she was reading and what she was thinking. Dorrance was also very ill (he had emphysema). Right up to the end, O'Connor plies the craft of fiction as Caroline Gordon had taught both her and Dorrance.

As O'Connor weakened, the letters chronicle how the steady diet of theological reading in neo-Thomist theologians and philosophers changed. A friend from New York, Janet McKane, had urged

O'Connor to read C. S. Lewis. Dorrance also sends books by Lewis in which O'Connor delights. Both Dorrance and O'Connor in their dire physical conditions discovered the apologetic power of Lewis, what he called "mere Christianity." Lewis's writings both comforted and inspired O'Connor as she was assembling the stories that would make up *Everything That Rises Must Converge*.

O'Connor's untimely death was a great loss to her friends. Father McCown comforts the bereaved, Tom and Louise Gossett. Father McCown's relentless pursuit of social justice also continued after O'Connor's death. His theological and political views, however, would depart from what O'Connor called in a letter a "nasty dose of orthodoxy." McCown tested his new views on Walker Percy. As much as Percy enjoyed McCown's travel writings, he would criticize his drift into anti-Americanism. Percy was rooted in the political realism of John Paul II, who survived the twin tyrannies of Nazism and Communism through theological orthodoxy.

Father McCown's friendship with Percy after O'Connor's death reveals the continued mediation of her faith-based political positions. Percy endured the senseless murders of both Martin Luther King and Robert Kennedy and the protracted Vietnam War. During this violent, dark period, Percy adroitly managed, unlike Father McCown, to embrace both anti-Communism and the civil rights movement. Percy, like O'Connor, also maintained allegiance to his Southern roots. He had little patience for the distant sanctimony of commentators, critical of segregation as a purely regional failing of Percy's native Mississippi. For Percy, Detroit, Newark, and Boston were no paragons of racial accord.

Unlike several of O'Connor's friends after her death, Father McCown never left the Church—anti-Americanism and advocacy of Latin American liberation theology, however, influenced his thinking, as the correspondence in this chapter reveals.

FLANNERY O'CONNOR TO JANET McKANE

O'Connor is grateful for her friend's correspondence. O'Connor also discusses the emotional problems of another friend, a "confessional poet."

MILLEDGEVILLE

GEORGIA

31 MARCH 1963

Dear Miss McKane,

Thank you so much for the Lourdes book and the book of Miss Tabor's [Eithne] poems [*The Cliff's Edge: Songs of a Psychotic*]. I have been sick in bed with my annual spring cold and I enjoyed them both then. I would like to show the poems to one of the chaplains at the state hospital here. I don't know if I mentioned it but we have in Milledgeville the largest mental institution in the world. They have just got onto religion out there and now they have three Protestant chaplains. One of them, a Presbyterian, called on me not long ago. He had read some of my stories. He had been an engineering student before he went into the ministry and he didn't know much about literature but he was interested in poetry. I sent him off with a couple of Robert Lowell's books. Robert Lowell is a friend of mine who was in the Catholic Church for a while and who is plagued by recurring phases of mental illness. I told this minister that I thought every mental institution ought to have a resident writer. There are a lot of them (patients) who are well enough to do more with themselves and their time than weave baskets. I think he would be much interested in this girl.

I also enjoyed the article on Vaughn. That was just the beginning of the trek away from the liturgical and the farther the world gets away from it, the harder the writer's job. Do you know a book by Wm. F. Lynch called *Christ and Apollo*? I think it is in a paper back now. You would like it.

The "passive diminishment" is probably a bad translation of something more understandable. What he means is that in the case he's talking about, the patient is passive in relation to the disease—he's done all he can to get rid of it and can't so he's passive and accepts it. (de Chardin) [Teilhard].

You are very kind to offer to look for books for me that I can't get. I may call on you some time. Right now I am pretty well supplied. I don't have many Catholic friends who are interested in reading. The ones who are have left the church, the ones who don't read, manage to stay in. An exaggeration, but this is the way it often seems. I can't think of any of them that I could present a copy of *Eve and the Gryphon* to right at the moment. I only just recently got hold of two paperback books I ordered from the Paulist Press—*Unless Some Man Show Me*, a book about the Old Testament I have been told is good and *Love or Constraint* which is about "some psychological aspects of religious education." If you haven't got them or haven't read them, I'll pass them on to you when I read them.

I hope you have the best kind of Easter. I am very grateful for your interest in me and my work.

> Yours,
> Flannery O'Connor

O'Connor shares the breadth of her reading which included the Protestant theologian, Karl Barth, and reports about the Second Vatican Council convened from 1962 to 1965.

MILLEDGEVILLE

15 JUNE 63

Dear Miss McKane,

This is certainly it. I guess that in order to keep something in mind we exaggerate it and then when we see it again we find that it is more subtle than we had thought. It's really the Child who is laughing, the Virgin is only smiling. I don't remember the hand being off. Now I'm more anxious to see it again than ever.

You must be psychic all the way around because in the *Cross Currents* you sent, you had marked the review of Karl Barth's book, the same one I received a few days ago to review [*Evangelical Theology: An Introduction*]. I am making slow headway with it. Although it is not difficult it is a little wearing to read such a good man who thinks that believing in the Catholic church is idolatry.

I'll keep the *Metropolitan Bulletin* a while before I return it as I'd like to read these articles in it. The pictures I've seen of German Medieval carving have always fascinated me. In a lot of ways I'd like to be able to write like they carved. But then I've never seen anything but pictures except for my two fading trips to the Cloisters.

Have you read the Xavier Rynne book, *Letters from Vatican City*? It is a much expanded version of some letters that were first in *The New Yorker*, and I guess it is the best report that we'll have on the Council.

I guess you are about through teaching for the year. What do you do in the summer? I look forward to the summer because I can stay at home and work and don't have to go anywhere.

Best,

Flannery OC.

MILLEDGEVILLE

3 AUGUST 63

Dear Janet,

Did you get the two books I sent some time before I thanked you for the article on Chagall? I figure you didn't. The mails are very peculiar. Anyway I sent the Raven book & a copy of the British ed. of *The Violent Bear* etc [*It Away*], also a letter enclosed thanking you for the cards and commenting on same.

Thanks a lot for the leaflet. I'm most glad to be getting them again.

I'm still struggling to get through Karl Barth. I like what I read though.

More again
Yours
Flannery

A devout parishioner of Sacred Heart Church in Milledgeville, O'Connor applies a theme of her story, "The Displaced Person." A few years after the suppression of Catholics by the Marxist government of Cuba, the local parish experiences the effects with the appearance of displaced Cubans in the local congregation. O'Connor also beseeches prayer, since traveling for lectures is becoming more difficult.

MILLEDGEVILLE

I OCTOBER 63

Dear Janet,

Thanks so much for the veils. I've always wanted one of these and somehow never got around to getting myself one so I am terribly pleased to have them. You are adding several cubits to my height against firm Biblical admonition. I am 5'4", weigh 115, so I guess the larger one should go to somebody that could grace it properly. We have a large Cuban population in our church and they wear them. They, incidentally, seem to be either exceptional Catholics or have no use for it at all. Most of the ones we have are doctors and their families. They have positions at the state mental hospital. Most of them are at church every time the door opens. I had always supposed Latin American Catholics universally indifferent, but it is not so.

The burro arrived, has been named Equinox by my mother, and his picture is enclosed. Also one of my swan drinking out of the bird bath; he is very fond of the bird bath. The burro is pictured at 1 hour old behind our house in the orchard. He looks kind of hangdog in the snapshot but he's actually very lively and gallops around bucking and kicking.

I am going to give a talk called "The Catholic Novelist" in the Protestant South at Notre Dame of Maryland and at Georgetown and at Hollins I am going to read "A Good Man Is Hard to Find" with commentary.[1] The lecture never suits me and I keep changing it, usually probably making it worse rather than better. I despise the traveling, am always afraid the plane is going to be fogged in and I won't get where I'm supposed to be and one thing and another like that. So please remember me in your prayers especially from the 14th through the 19th.

Thanks for the leaflet and the Sign and the piece on Buber [Martin], all of which I'm enjoying. I've just got through reading a book called *Atheism in Our Time* by Ignace Lepp. I recommend it highly.

Flannery

FLANNERY O'CONNOR TO WARD ALLISON DORRANCE

Having spoken at Georgetown University, O'Connor acquires a new friend. Because of their common background, she enjoys a special candor. Road signs, which play a significant role in "The Life You Save May Be Your Own" and other stories, also appear in O'Connor's own experiences.

MILLEDGEVILLE

20 OCTOBER 63

Dear Cudden Ward,

Do you know your letter of 12.X. was here waiting for me when I got back? If I had got it before I left, I would have been down sitting on that yeller sofa waiting on you. And I would have told you my lecture wasn't about what the Protestants do to him but what they do for him; in fact I rather lay that on and leave them thinking they're all going straight to hell because they weren't born in Georgia. On the way driving to Milledgeville, we passed one car that had JESUS SAVES painted in red on the back bumper and a truck that said FREE FOR ALL BAPTIST CHURCH AND NURSERY SCHOOL. If I weren't a Catholic I could only be happy in the Free for All Baptist Church. Or could I? Anyway, I loved having breakfast with you and I hope I stirred my egg the right way and left you thinking of me as a solid, sane, not altogether inscrutable addition to your universe.

May I send you a copy of the new edition of *Wise Blood* that has a note to the 2nd ed by me in the front of it to mark the occasion? Let me know.

Meanwhile cheers to Mrs. Purefoy [character, Dorrance's novel] & love,

WARD ALLISON DORRANCE TO FLANNERY O'CONNOR

Dorrance comments on the reissue of O'Connor's first novel, Wise Blood. *William Faulkner had observed in the 1949 Nobel address that his fiction created "out of the materials of the human spirit something which did not exist before."* Wise Blood *is similar in its allegorical levels of meaning, specifically the "anagogical level" that O'Connor embeds in her novel and stories. Dorrance also mentions their mutual friend, the editor of* The Sewanee Review.

2. XI. 63

Dear Cousin Honeybug:

This has been delayed because, just after your visit, the doctors told me certain things, the gut of which is that I may stop fretting about how I am going to live after my retirement; the dear fellows will be bug-eyed if I reach that age. Well, well. I have been so unhappy in this world, you'd think I'd be happy to leave it, and I expect I shall be when I've had time to look about me & tidy up and not take off like a pagan. Meanwhile I feel at least the shock I'd feel if I'd fallen down a flight of steps or been told, between bites of an apple, "Pack some things. We're off for Alaska." The shock was bad enough that I put aside writing . . .

Your letter was hilarious . . . what you said about Miss Regina, I mean . . . but hilarious for me in almost a holy way this is the way to your writing because where artists come from, as you say, is the first question, and you and she and I did most certainly come out from under the same log. God grant her a long life, free of pain & muddle-headedness, "ed puis le paradis a la fin de ses jours."

Your book, triumphantly, was of a piece with Miss R. & the holy way. I don't know if you meant I should write you my opinion of it, but I feel moved to say:

1) The Holy Ghost seems to me to have started you out with certain advantages that other writers cannot reach by mere talent, much less by study or by will.

2) Your whole pitch, for instance, is putting new wine into old bottle—a vast and a deep source of strength.

3) Your main "holt" (your biggest bottle) is what I call the fairy tale for adults. Here the field is strewn with the bodies of fallen men. Hawthorne (in all his works, if you ask me) and Henry James in such as *The Altar of the Dead* & *The Beast in the Jungle*.

4) You get away with it where they fail for at least two reasons which I see:

a) You constantly keep the abstractions on your anagogical level tied down into not only the necessary naturalistic level but into a naturalistic level that lifts the hair on the back of my neck. Take your scene in which your boy eats with his hat on with the women in the dining car . . . or the one in which the chap in the ape suit surprises the spooners. I stare at those pages, fascinated, and have to put the book down and get up and walk around a bit before I can go on.

b) Here you seem to know that the usual naturalistic level won't do. You are dealing (no matter what your ultimate "meaning") with <u>fantasy</u>.

What do you mean by a "low blood count"? How are you now? . . .

Meanwhile I'm not sure my story-that-Andrew-Lytle-won't-touch is worth any drain on your strength. Think it over again. If it would amuse you, or keep you company in a lonely spell and if you'd take it with the understanding that you could throw it away, or wait six months.

Love to you & the Lady in
the Red Coat,

FLANNERY O'CONNOR TO
WARD ALLISON DORRANCE

O'Connor has inspired Dorrance to work on a novel. Reading his writing has also influenced one of her funniest stories. She notes many writers lack roots in region, custom, or speech. To demonstrate her contention, O'Connor describes the particular situation on the dairy farm where little has changed in a century. She deeply admires her mother's authority in defusing volatile situations.

MILLEDGEVILLE

3 NOVEMBER 63

Dear Cudden Ward:

I'm glad I put a chunk under Mrs. Purefoy [*The Party at Mrs. Purefoy's*]. You put a chunk under me. I came home and read your four stories over and then I wrote me one ["Revelation"]; at least, I'm most through with it and I'm pretty sure it's good, not just good, but right like those are right. I suppose this is what a little human communion with a real writer can do for you, but I don't go along with you on liking their company as a general rule or because they're writers. They've got to come from somewhere. Too many of them don't come from anywhere, don't belong anywhere, and couldn't if they tried.

You would have to see my ma in action. I can't do justice to her.

We've got a very 19th-century operation here. Three colored people live here in what was the guest house to this house—Louise and Jack, husband and wife, and Shot, their boarder; Louise and Shot work for us, Jack up the road. The guest house was right next to ours but Regina and a negro named George Harper put it on telephone poles about twenty years ago and rolled it out of earshot (a two story house itself) but not out of sight. Now we are connected to it by an electric bell. The bell is for us, if we get scared, to call them, but more often it rings over here. It rang last week and Short came stomping over to say Louise was drunk and had thrown potash water on him. He brings her the liquor and then comes running over here when she goes wild, which she every so often [does]. We've had these negroes going on fifteen years. Regina gave her a lecture the next day, saying that one of these days she was going to put his eyes out. "Yes'm," Louise says, "I hope I gets at least one of them." She stays mad with him about a day.

Regina's big aim is to stop the flow of liquor in here, but I tell her she might as well try to stop the Mississippi from rolling on. She gives them all sorts of lectures about how nice folks do and when they are about to kill each other, she says, "Now let's not have any more of this unpleasantness. Bring that shotgun over her and leave it." What she has is no doubt whatsoever about her authority . . . I'd ask them [farm workers] to please bring the shotgun over, or some fool thing. She listens to their lies very seriously, and I mean they lie like artists. It's never a matter of finding the truth but of which lie suits you best the moment to accept in its place.

This is the right and only place for me to be but even with all of it here, as you say, you have to be chosen. And the problem is to make it believable, too, because to the rest of the world, it's not. They don't think this kind of place or life exists anymore, and if they saw it, they'd think it shouldn't.

Enclosed is the book. It's not to read but to throw at anyone who joggles you.

FLANNERY O'CONNOR TO "CHILDREN"

O'Connor's friend Janet McKane taught school in New York City. O'Connor replies to letters from her students.

MILLEDGEVILLE

GEORGIA

NOVEMBER 5, 1963

Dear Children,

Thank you for all your letters. I was glad to hear you liked the peacock feathers and the picture of Equinox and his mama. Equinox says he is sorry nobody has offered him a pair of lavender shoes or a hat. He thinks he'd look pretty good in them. He sends you all his best regards.

Sincerely yours,

Flannery O'Connor

FLANNERY O'CONNOR TO JANET McKANE

O'Connor encloses a clipping of a "lady" evangelist who will preach locally. Such gatherings may have influenced similar scenes in The Violent Bear It Away.

NOV 1963

Dear Janet,

Thought you might like to see this lady. If you had done Salvation Preaching with your accordion playing, you might still be playing it.

She's right up the road from us.

Thanks for the *Metropolitan Bulletin* & your letters. I've got an eye infection so don't want to continue using them now. Hence this scrawl.

Cheers,

Flannery

O'Connor writes as a regionalist, noting, as she does in other letters, playful theology associated with ecumenism in the local community.

MILLEDGEVILLE

GEORGIA

9 DECEMBER 63

Dear Janet,

Thanks so much for the children's letters and the veils and the copies of *Ramparts* [Catholic journal]. I will have a veil to put in all my pockets so that when I get to church I can just reach in for one. Thanks a lot. The little boy who addressed me as Miss Flannery is doing it the Southern way. Here all the children call you your first name prefixed by Miss—Miss Regina and Miss Flannery we are.

I was much surprised to see the piece in *Commonweal*. I don't know who Rupp is or if I met him there. You meet so many people at these things, talk to them a split second and they are gone, and I'm no good at names. I met mostly students there anyway. It's always odd to see the interpretations people put on things.

Regina was delighted to have Ernest for a mother's day present as that put us in the way of getting Equinox. At this writing Equinox and his ma will go to the Hardwick Christian churches pageant because Ernest has been invited to go to the First Methodist. He is supposed to walk across the front of the Methodist church, led by a deacon or deaconess I hope, and as he is a great cut-up, he'll probably let out some kind of noise in the middle of it. He has an unearthly bray which he delivers at full gallop. Maybe Methodism will do something for him.

I'll be looking out for this yellow mystery.

Cheers to you,

Flannery

FLANNERY O'CONNOR TO
WARD ALLISON DORRANCE

O'Connor courageously accepts dire illness and possible death, which both she and her friend face. Using an electric typewriter enables her to put limited energy to greater use. She recounts the reaction of family members to the reissue of Wise Blood.

MILLEDGEVILLE

10 DECEMBER 63

Dear Cudden Ward,

If you have got shut of Lawrence and tidied up your desk before death and not left a mess for your friends to clean up, you are ready to get back to work on Mrs. Purefoy [*The Party at Mrs. Purefoy's*], and with a free mind and a free soul. Every sentence ought to be like one of the dates the crow brought St. John Whatshisname in the desert. I think I envy you—the amount of notice of death anyway. I hope I get as much. My desk is a buzzard's nest. It'll take me a week or two to get it in a state I can properly leave it in. I hope you drop in your tracks though and don't have to hang around in bed. I am prepared for that for myself. In one of my affluent years I bought me a Smith Corona compact 250 electric typewriter and I'm going to get one of those hospital tables that swings across the bed and set the electric on it. It requires about 75% less energy to use an electric typewriter. I use it now for a lot of work and I can work four hours at it at a time without getting tired and I'm good for about an hour and a half on the manual.

Miss R. [Regina] would say, "Well we've all got to go but you're not dead yet." She tends to clichés delivered briskly. I notice about Southern ladies of her generation that when they've found the cliché to clap on the occasion, they take great satisfaction, as if life had been rendered its due at least as far as the language is concerned. I had considerable qualms when she read *Wise Blood*. She hadn't read anything since *Ivanhoe,* of course, and I thought Oh Lord, this will shock her to death and embarrass her and so forth and so forth. But after it was accepted she demanded to read it so I handed it over and she took the ms. off to bed with her in the afternoon—we "lie down" after dinner which we eat in the middle of the day—and I waited for the first groan or moan or explosion or whatever. After about a half hour I began to hear these gentle snores. Then I had an 82 year old cousin in Savannah who had been very good to me and I was worried about her reading it too. I thought it's going to kill her, she'll have a heart attack or a stroke or something and I'll go around with her on my conscience the rest of my life. But it didn't do anything to her either, except increase her rectitude. She sat right down and wrote me a letter beginning, "I do not like your book. There is enough trouble and misery in the world without your adding to it."

Thank you for commenting on it. That about better ventilation I will try to remember. I think the second one is better ventilated, it's also less of a fairy tale, though a disembodied devil does preside over it partially, but I'm not really much of an observer, I mean I see what knocks me down but I never have gone out of my way to look and I should. If I get it fixed up to my satisfaction I am going to send you a copy of this story I have just written because there will be a piece of your finger baked in that pie. About the nouminous and all.

Merry Christmas to you & Mrs. Purefoy.

FLANNERY O'CONNOR TO FATHER SCOTT WATSON

O'Connor confuses a title of a famous novel, perhaps because in another letter she notes her dislike of the story. She herself endured admirers at literary gatherings confusing the titles of her stories.

12 DECEMBER 63

I did appreciate your card when you were in the Atlanta airport with nothing to read but *How to Kill a Mockingbird*. The Atlanta airport is bad enough by itself and I don't know how long that particular book could be expected to deaden you to it.

We still hope that one of these days we'll see you in Milledgeville again. I plod along in my work and I guess you do too. It's something to be able to plod, and I'm thankful for it.

My mother and I hope you'll have a fine Christmas and the best of New Years.

FLANNERY O'CONNOR TO WARD ALLISON DORRANCE

12-13-63 [POSTCARD]

Heavens no! Nothing in your last offended me. I was real pleased with what you said and glad you felt like saying it. I understand the state of shock but get out of it as it will interfere with your work and you have plenty to do. I expect to hear more of Mrs. P. [Purefoy] if Lawrence doesn't. Happy Christmas.

Love, Flannery.

W. Dorrance appends a phrase of explanation: "This is an answer to a letter of mine in which I said that she (in her writing) 'got by pure outrage.'"

FLANNERY O'CONNOR TO WARD ALLISON DORRANCE

This postcard features rural character Chess McCartney leading a parade of goats. O'Connor approves of her friend's succinct comment on her storytelling strategy.

[CHAS. or CHESS McCARTNEY and His Goat Caravan]

Pure outrage for the new year.

Cheers,

Flannery

FLANNERY O'CONNOR TO
WARD ALLISON DORRANCE

O'Connor seeks expert opinion about "Revelation," written while both she and her friend are quite frail.

MILLEDGEVILLE

5 JANUARY 64

I had decided I wouldn't send you this because you being low on energy you ought to use what you've got for Mrs. P. [Purefoy], but you've asked for it so here it is—double. And I want the criticism and don't fear to offend me. My feelings are made of pig iron. I really need an eye on this. When I finished the first version I sent it to an old editor of mine in New York to look at. She wrote me it was one of my blackest stories. I had thought it was one of my lightest. She thought the main character, Mrs. Turpin, was mean and evil. I thought she was funny and innocent and big, one of those country women that are usually in touch with forces larger than themselves. So I concluded the story was a failure and I did over the end—second version. I want this woman to have this vision. I want it to be a real revelation. Maybe I've tilted the sack too fast there but I went just as slow as I dared. Anyway tell me what you can and which version is best; if either.

I'm supposed to send it to Andrew [Lytle, editor of *The Sewanee Review*] but he'll probably give me hell too. I want to get it right first. I can't criticize but I can react, if you want a third eye on yours.

Maybe you're sick of eyes on it. I'm sick of this one but I've got to keep at it.

I've been in bed all during the holidays—low blood count—but I am picking up now. This here is the electric typewriter you're being writ to on.

I can see you've got no bidnis smoking but maybe they'd let you dip snuff. There must be something [in] it, they [farm workers] love it so. Makes them sort of drunk in a nice way.

Two days ago Miss Regina was out in her red coat frisking her small magnolia. Everything was bowed over with ice. Today is a good spring day and the peafowl have begun to holler.

CAROLINE GORDON TO FLANNERY O'CONNOR

Gordon notes the reaction of students to an O'Connor story read aloud in class. Having also endured the painful dissolution of her marriage to Allen Tate, Gordon speculates about living with religious. She, like C. S. Lewis, reveals that sickness can actually become a kind of retreat. Lewis writes of spells of illness that turn into quiet times of delight in reading two or three novels in as many days.

JANUARY EIGHT, 1964

I don't think of you as a "writer." Well, that doesn't sound very nice, does it? I mean one of those writers whose works I <u>have</u> to read. Reading one of your stories is, for me, always an adventure and a delight, as you must know. I have just got back from wanderings that were pretty fatiguing and found your ms. on top of the pile of accumulated mail. I have read one quarter of it so far. Took it in hand and dashed with it to my seminar in fiction which gathers at half past seven on Monday evenings. I explained that I was taking the liberty of sharing this reading with them because Miss O'C. has the humility of the true artist and, I felt, wouldn't mind said sharing. I, myself, don't yet know what you are up to but the reading went over big. I have a notion of what I think you're up to and I suspect that you are working in this story a kind of magic (wrong word, that!)—anyhow, shall we say you are using a technique you have used before in some of your best stories: a technique which induces the reader to most willingly suspend his disbelief. You do it by making him laugh his head almost off. My students responded heartily. They laughed till some of them had tears in their eyes. Don't see how you could expect to accomplish more than that in six pages. More on this subject later.

I am awfully sorry to know that you had to take to you bed during the holidays. Do let me know how you got on. I can't help being anxious about you.

My aunt, who is eighty six years old, announced that she was being hostess at her last Christmas dinner on this earth. I realized that this was a command performance, changed my reservations, (made weeks ago), and set off on a giro that I egotistically believe, would have daunted Odysseus. However, the Lord, as so many of the theologians point out, mercifully veils what is to come from our sight . . .

I aspire to end my days with the Carmelites, so I stayed over a day in order to trek over to the Madonna Residence in Brooklyn. It is a huge building, fronting on that imitation Place de la Concorde which was set up in honour of the Grand Army of the Republic. Opposite is the Brooklyn Public Library and the Brooklyn Art Museum. The sight of the place sharpened my desire to get in there but the sister who finally consented to see me was pretty discouraging. Still, she admitted, we do have vacancies . . . Yep, I thought, thanks to the Grim Reaper . . .

I recount my adventures and misadventures at such length, partly because I want my friends to share some part of my sufferings, and, also in the hope that being forced, as it were, to participate in mine, may help a little bit, even to console you for having to be in bed during the holidays. Being in bed is tough any time, but I must say that if I have to take to my bed, I would prefer to take to it during the holidays. Two years ago I had the worst attack of flu I have had since I was sixteen. (It felt like the kind you had then. "Spanish Flu." Katherine Anne [Porter] had it and it turned her hair grey.) I was put out of circulation by losing my voice. A man I was trying to talk to long distance finally said, "I wish you'd hang up. You sound like a bat trying to talk." I thereupon got into bed and had one of the happiest Christmases I ever had. But some of my friends in Princeton refer to that Yuletide as "that time you said you had the flu."

How did the Methodists take Ernest's balking at the door of the chapel? No doubt they were polite about it but I bet my hat they had dark subterranean thoughts, such as what can you expect of a jackass raised by Papists. I am going to put him in Needle point yet! I had my Needlepoint and my *Divine Comedy*, plus Charles Williams' *Figure of Beatrice* along on my wanderings. If I hadn't had something to really occupy me I think I would have been locked up somewhere along the route . . .

I must get back to my mountain of real mail—mail that has to be answered. I'll be writing you about "Revelation" later. I'm quite excited about it.

Much love for you and Regina. Do let me have some news when you feel like writing. I know you wouldn't take to your bed without good reason but maybe you needed a rest in more ways than one. You've been working pretty hard, haven't you?

CAROLINE GORDON TO FLANNERY O'CONNOR

COPYEDITING OF "REVELATION"

The narrative is fragmented because it was written apparently at different times from New York City. Gordon is accompanied by Erik Langkjaer, the Danish textbook salesman O'Connor dated briefly. O'Connor perhaps told him about Gordon, but in the commentary Gordon seems unaware of their association.

At the end of copyediting, perhaps influenced by Mrs. Turpin experiencing a "visionary light" settling "in her eyes," Gordon is reminded of Dante, the pilgrim, looking to the stars at strategic times in his pilgrimage. She recom-

mends that a storyteller read the Florentine. *This counsel about the parallels between Dante and O'Connor opens up a rich fount of comparison. In Flannery O'Connor's fiction, we can see the potent parallels and influences of Dante's comic strategies that she uses to lead her audience to ponder sacramental theological truths through violence.*[2] *He establishes the techniques of "divine comedy," upon which later writers of similar theological interests draw. O'Connor's handwritten notes to the 1933 Modern Library edition,* The Divine Comedy of Dante Alighieri, *edited by C. H. Grandgent, show a close familiarity with the poem's allegory. At the end of the* Inferno *she writes that hell is*

> an exemplification of everlasting punishment without free-will. You could not have hell as Christian conceives it—pagan doesn't blame man as much since man is not wholly to blame for his sins. State of hell is state of rebellion against the divine order. Sinner in hell contradicts his own reason—against duty also.[3]

The girl's face is "seared," not "seered." In this masterly story it is Mrs. Turpin, who, like a blind seer in a trance, seeing all her own mischance, drifts, not down to Camelot, but up that there ladder of humility, celebrated by the A.A. Dante Alighieri, St. Bernard of Clairvaux and Franz Kafka—if in reverse. (At least, as I see it.) . . .

Again, if I were doing it, I'd break the mother's explanatory speech up a bit. Perhaps by a gesture, I'd let "Mary Grace goes to Wellesley College" stand for a second, anyhow, as the pleasant lady's explanation of her daughter's eccentric behaviour. Then, as I see it, this admirable woman who, herself, has suffered so much from Wellesley College (nice bit of projection, that,) will realize that her audience will not have any notion of what Wellesley College can do to disrupt family lives and will hasten to specify some of the results of going to Wellesley College—like reading all the time, etc . . .

. . . The man [Allen Tate, perhaps] whom I considered the finest man I knew has run off with my money and blackened my reputation and had the nerve to ask me to lunch with him last Monday.

. . . I had been told that if I wanted a quiet place in which to converse with a friend I would do well to go [to] the Café St. Germain on East Forty Seventh Street. I accordingly walked over there with Eric Langjkaer. We had some private business to discuss and I had asked him to meet me in the Scribner Book Store because I did not want to go upstairs to the editorial offices; I was afraid I might encounter So and So whom I would just as soon not see; he edited my last book. Erik did not seem to mind meeting me downstairs. But when we got to the restaurant we were both a little taken aback to see Scribner's new editor-in-chief sitting all by himself at a table over in a corner . . .

One final objection. I do not believe that she can hear either the "hoard" (or "horde") of souls. She cannot hear any one of those souls any more than she can hear a hog or a railroad train or any object or person. She hears the <u>sound</u> emitted by the object or person.

You are making for the anagogical level. One doesn't use colloquialisms or idioms there for the reason, I hazard, that there everybody understands everything anybody else says.

Allen [Tate] has expressed astonishment at my story, "One Against Thebes." It is the stars in the final paragraph that puzzle him most. He says they "work" but he can't see why they work. The answer seems simple to me. Anybody—my nine year old girl, Mrs. Turpin—can look up and behold the same stars that Dante beheld as he emerged from Hell:

The beauteous burdens of the sky,

Fletcher translates the line.

Have you been reading *The Divine Comedy*? Or were you smarter than I am and read it years ago? I have just finished reading it, for the first time, in what I begin to suspect, is a mis-spent life. Owe it to Ashley [Brown]. He kept going on about how I had learned thus or that technique from Dante and I finally told him that, like most of my contemporaries, I had read the *Inferno* all the way through but had progressed no further. He replied: "You'd better."

So I started in this Fall and, now that I have finished, I am going to pursue the plan I have followed for fifteen years with St. John of the Cross. Soon as I get through the whole works, I turn around and start in again at the beginning.

It seems to me that you—or I or any other fiction writer—can find any technique we can muster right there, used to perfection by Dante. All these things I keep trying to tell young people—he can show them to them better than I can ever hope to show them.

FLANNERY O'CONNOR TO JANET McKANE

As O'Connor's energies continue to dissipate, she is thankful for the kindnesses of her friend.

MILLEDGEVILLE

11 JANUARY 64

Dear Janet,

The two books came yesterday and I believe the Chagall [Marc] is the most beautiful I have ever seen. The other is different order of things and it is interesting to compare the two religious imaginations. I am very grateful to you and appreciate them more than I can say. It troubles me though that you should spend so much money on something that you are not here to enjoy with me. Let us own these books together and let me send them back to you after six months or so and I have absorbed them into my bones and you absorb them into yours. This kind of book ought to be shared. I feel like the proverbial bloated bondholder—only of the arts—to have them and I insist that they travel back and forth between us.

I feel better and as you see am able to be up operating the electric typewriter, a great invention. I am like the late Pope a "powerful fork" (big eater), with emphasis on proteins, do exactly like the doctor tells me always and take quantities of iron. My kind of anemia is the kind that doesn't respond to liver but does to iron. I take it in the latest form, six pills a day of something called SIMRON, which is the best form possible. I support the Merrell Laboratories single-handed with my purchases of SIMRON. I will do as you say and stretch occasionally but I am afraid that if my thoughts were too pleasant the quality of my prose (not as exhibited in correspondence) would decline.

I work a little every day but am not up to my usual three hours, and hour and a half and I am shot, and a lot of time has to be taken up with business that accumulated while I was in bed. A student in Chile wrote and asked me to correspond with him and tell him "my ideas about life" as he had to write a paper on me—that sort of thing.[4] Also such stuff as: "I am in the ninth grade and next week is Georgia Authors week and our teacher told us we had to pick a Georgia Author to write about and I picked you. Will you please send me some interesting biographical information and tell me what books you have written." And then there are the ones who are writing their Master's Thesis and send you a list of questions.

Thanks also for sending the *Metropolitan Bulletin*. My mother has been sick with the flu and she enjoyed it while she couldn't be up. Incidentally, don't you want these back? You may keep a file of them. Let me know. And my great appreciation again for the beautiful books and let me know what you think of my plan that they should travel.

Cheers,

Flannery

FLANNERY O'CONNOR TO JANET McKANE

Typically eschewing literary labels, O'Connor rejects the term "gothic," often applied to her fiction. The term has been popular over the years with academic commentators drawn to the sensational, dramatic scenes in O'Connor's stories and labeling them "gothic."[5]

22 JAN 64

MILLEDGEVILLE

Dear Janet,

Thanks for your letter and various clippings and what not. I'm feeling better but not up to any full scale letter. I'm glad you like my notion of sending the book for a summer in the Bronx. It will come. Dont send me the piece out of *Renascence* [Marquette University] on the Gothic novel. Sounds very bogus. My work is not gothic and I dislike the whole conception intensely.

Its in the 60s here today and the birds have begun to strut and I feel like we are getting somewhere toward spring. Can't get there too fast for me.

FLANNERY O'CONNOR TO WARD ALLISON DORRANCE

O'Connor with typical good humor refers to Caroline Gordon's epistle of January 8, 1964. O'Connor tolerates Gordon's grammatical instruction and also praises her mother's practical skills.

MILLEDGEVILLE

28 JANUARY 64

Thanks a lot. The reason we know some of the same things is we went to school to the same lady [Caroline Gordon]. She has beat it into my head on so many occasions that you have to show the eyes or whatever it is you've got to show that by now I've just about made it instinct. But I always need somebody to tell me if the thing is finished and that I've got a dull thud in there. I'll get rid of the dull thud. I don't know about the svelt-like. They read words like that in the papers and even the farm magazines and then they go put a like behind it and make it their own.

I had thought I wouldn't send this one to Caroline because I hadn't heard from her in a long time and I thought I might be in her black books; however I heard from her, so I sent it. She liked the story all but a couple of sentences which she proceeded to analyze grammatically insofar as it was analysable. She is a great hand at grammar. She wrote me six pages about grammar and another six about her Christmas vacation, which was all on broken-down trains and planes that didn't fly and misconnected busses—from Lafayette to Chattanooga to Princeton to Lafayette. What that woman has is Vitality. She went to see the Carmelites, for she has this idea of ending her days in one of their establishments. I think she would end the Carmelites. Anyway their instinct for self-preservation will keep them from taking her.

I'm writing another story now but its not funny and its all will and just drag drag drag. It's also not credible, which don't help any. So what I said about being dried up doesn't seem so funny to me. Its just like you said: you have to be chosen. And in between times of being chosen, you have to keep on writing.

I'm all right now but Miss Regina has had the flu. Her policy is never to admit anything but perfect health, however she was pretty obviously poorly this time and had to stay in bed a week and suffer my ministrations. She thinks I'm an incompetent when it comes to doing anything and she appeared right surprised that what had to be done got done. Now she is up again and back to her usual winter plumbing activities. We have an ancient labyrinthine mysterious system of water pipes that have to be cut off and drained and usually freeze and break anyway, but she knows it down to the last pipe-fitting. The place is also complicated electrically with two wells and two pumps and a water tower. My nightmares concern being left to cope with the pipes and wires.

You do what you feel like about sending me your story. I can't help you like you can me but I want you to know I'm around if I ever could. If I ever get this one I'm working on anyways believable, I'm going to send it to you but I promise not to send but one copy. That was inconsiderate of me.

I hope you are more involved with the typewriter & less with [illegible]

Cheers

FLANNERY O'CONNOR TO JANET McKANE

O'Connor senses her time is running out and uses her energy to work on a second collection of stories that would be published after her death.

11 FEB 64

Dear Janet,

Thanks so much for your card from New Rochelle and the *Metropolitan Bulletin* and so forth. Your generosity exceeds my free energy. My blood is back up now so I am working like mad and hope to keep it up so that <u>possibly</u> I can have a book of stories out in the fall. The ms. will have to be delivered in May if I do and there is most too much work needed to get it done but I am going to try anyway.

My two new swans arrived and look pretty good but only time will tell if they're a mated pair. They sit facing each other and converse a lot so I hope thats a good sign.

Maybe sooner or later I will get to write you a leisurely letter but I dont know when.

Cheers,

Flannery

FLANNERY O'CONNOR TO TOM AND LOUISE GOSSETT

As the result of increasing health problems, O'Connor cancels a lecture tour and a visit to her friends in San Antonio.

MILLEDGEVILLE

18 NOVEMBER 64

Dear Tom & Louise,

I sure do wish I could come but I have had to cancel all the lectures—Boston College, Brown and the University of Texas—and I have very shortly to go to the hospital and be cut upon by the doctors. I suggested they ask me again next year but I don't know. This is all fairly sudden. I WASN'T LOOKING FOR IT.

Thanks for asking me anyway. If I were coming, I would accept.

Fr. McCown seems to be in Houston. He sho do move around aplenty. Tell him not to forget to send me your lunatic book. Just right for hospital or recuperative reading no doubt.

Cheers,

FLANNERY O'CONNOR TO FATHER JAMES H. McCOWN

The next two letters concern immediate hospitalization. O'Connor also notes that Father McCown has become a nomadic retreat leader and lecturer. For almost a decade O'Connor has beseeched prayers from her Jesuit friends and Janet McKane.

MILLEDGEVILLE

20 FEB. 64

You do flit from place to place. One day I get a pamphlet from Houston + the next day a magazine from Mobile. Thanks a lot for both. We'll give the men the Knights of Columbus pamphlet. That other must have been a joke.

I am being operated on Tuesday here and will be in the hospital 10 days or 2 weeks. Rather serious so kindly commend me to the Lord, formally & informally and ask my friend Fr. Watson to do the same—if you stay in Mobile long enough to receive this.

FLANNERY O'CONNOR TO JANET McKANE

22 FEB 64

Dear Janet,

Well I didn't have much respite for work. I have to go to the hospital Monday for an operation—abdominal—and I'll be there about ten days. So I appear to be a fit subject for your prayers at all times. I'd just as soon you didn't write me for the next ten days because I won't feel like reading anything. I'll be full of tubes and jacked up to the apparatus of transfusions and what not. I'll count on your good prayers.

      Cheers,
      Flannery

FLANNERY O'CONNOR TO JANET McKANE

O'Connor is thankful for an illustrated book that imparts spiritual strength as she recuperates from surgery.

9 MARCH 64
M'VILLE

Dear Janet,

Just a note to tell you that I am back at home and the operation was a success, and thank you for your prayers and the book of Bible illus. which is wonderful. I feel like a train has run over me and am going to take your advice and let things fade for a while. I dont feel like writing letters or even much like reading them. I guess it'll take a couple of months. I'm still running a fever. I'll feel better when I can throw that off.

      Many many thanks,
      Flannery

FLANNERY O'CONNOR TO FATHER SCOTT WATSON

O'Connor replies to Father Watson who had written her a moving letter in which he invoked a Franciscan formulation about "Sister pain" in discussing the death of his brother.

15 MARCH 64

I was real sorry to hear you had lost your brother. I know the pain of a loss like that's greater than any kind of physical pain.

I came out very well from my operation. I have no strength yet but I guess that will come back in time. Then I will just pray to have something to write that will be worth the expense of energy.

I am going to have a story in the Spring *Sewanee Review* ["Revelation"] which I hope you will see. I thought it was good until I read the galleys and they always affect me adversely.

Now I just *hope* it is.

Thank you again for your prayers, I will remember you and your brother in mine.

FLANNERY O'CONNOR TO LOUISE AND THOMAS GOSSETT

O'Connor congratulates Tom for the positive review of his book, Race: The History of an Idea, *in a popular magazine. O'Connor's fiction did not fare as well in such publications. O'Connor also demurs from reading a long narrative about the Spanish Civil War. She perhaps preferred the more concise* For Whom the Bell Tolls *by Ernest Hemingway.*

20 MARCH 64

MILLEDGEVILLE

Thanks for that hog-sloppin card. It was real inspiring to me and I think I will get well at once. The operation was a success and the doctors are very pleased with themselves but I am still just creeping about and exercising my natural aptitude for doing nothing.

I was real pleased to see that *Time* took so heavy to your book ["Intellectuals as Racists," March 13, 1964]. Better to have those *people* for you than agin you even though they don't have much sense. Preacher McCown hasn't sent it yet. Incidentally I hope I can save my soul without reading *The Cypresses Believe in God* [José María Gironella Pous].

We hope you all are going to Virginia by way of Georgia this year. I've got two new swans as my old one "passed on," as genteel folks say. These new ones are very different from the old ones as to personality. They jabber constantly and the old ones were about 100% silent. Anyway, I hope I have the opportunity of innerducing you to them in June.

FLANNERY O'CONNOR TO JANET McKANE

O'Connor continues to appreciate Janet's thoughtful gifts. O'Connor continues reading C. S. Lewis, earlier recommended by her friend.

28 MARCH 64

Dear Janet,

How did you know I liked mugs? I drink my coffee out of one every morning and think they are vastly superior to cups. Thank you so much for thinking of me. I like this one a lot.

As for the state of my health that is pretty uncertain at this point. The operation was a success but it kicked up the lupus, which with me means kidney complications, and I have been put back on the steroid drugs. They (steroids) have saved my life before but at the same time they do much side damage to the bones.

The doctors don't say much but "we're walking on eggs now." I've been through all this before and it doesn't mean much to me. One thing suits me about as well as another. It may be summer before I can really get to work. Fortunately I have a natural aptitude for doing nothing.

I am reading CS Lewis' *Letters to Malcolm*. You would like it.

Cheers,

FLANNERY O'CONNOR TO LOUISE AND THOMAS GOSSETT

Having read a narrative sent by her friends about Africa, O'Connor speculates about ethnology. The subject was germane to Tom Gossett who was one of a handful of academics offering new courses at the time in African American literature and history. O'Connor comments about the connection of African Americans to Africa itself.[6]

31 MARCH 64

MILLEDGEVILLE

I'm really enjoying *Out of Africa* [Karen Blixen]. I like [Blixen's] the *Seven Gothic Tales* but they are all I had read. I think Regina may like *Out of Africa* too if she ever lights long enough to read a chapter of it. Our natives aint native, but I recognize in them some of the qualities she talks about. There is no straight answer in their book.

I am still more or less in bed and have been put back on cortesone but I hope not forever. I have taken a swipe or two at my electric typewriter but don't think I'm ready for it yet.

Everybody here is getting ready for the Garden Club Tour of Homes. My position is usually over the ink spot on the dining room sofa, but this year somebody else will occupy my post.

Cheers and thanks again for the Baroness Blixen and let us know when we can expect you in June.

,

FATHER JAMES McCOWN TO THOMAS GOSSETT

Father McCown writes from Atlanta, Georgia, hometown of Martin Luther King, Jr. Just eight years after Gossett's dismissal from a Georgia college for his support of desegregation, Father McCown reports favorable reception of Gossett's scholarly work on race, including O'Connor's praise. While O'Connor was in frail health, Father McCown notes that he had visited her novelist friend, Walker Percy, who supported the Jesuit order's social activism in behalf of racial justice.

IGNATIUS HOUSE

6700 RIVERSIDE DRIVE, N.W.

ATLANTA 5, GEORGIA

APRIL 9, 1964

Chronologically here is how my awareness of your book [*Race: The History of an Idea in America*] developed. I mean that it had been published. First your letter, telling me that a copy was being sent me. This arrived, or rather was waiting for me, Monday when I arrived back in Atlanta after my southern sojourn. Since I was very busy getting my Macon talk together (more about this later), I could not answer you just then. Then when I hit Macon I thought I was breaking some fresh news when I told them about your book, only to learn that the whole literate part of the city has been buzzing with excitement since it was written up in the March 13 *Time*, which, as luck would have it, I had missed completely on my travels ["Intellectuals as Racists," March 13, 1964]. On my way to Macon I stopped for a most satisfactory visit with Flannery. She immediately launched into an enthusiastic recital of the virtues of your book, which she was ⅔ through. I wanted to borrow her copy to take to Macon to tell them about it, but she wouldn't part with it. All I could borrow was the dust jacket. Then, when I returned to Atlanta you had found time to write me another card telling me what direction to expect my copy from—and all this before I had had a chance to so much as drop you a line! Am I embarrassed!

Congratulations a thousand times over, Tom! I am so proud of you and your work and of being a friend of yours. Naturally I have not had the chance to read RACE but will eagerly await my copy from the publisher. The writeup in *Time* which I feverishly found after half of Macon had told me about [it], was wonderful. I don't know how justified their one adverse criticism of RACE is, but certainly they are over all in deepest admiration of it. The closing line of their review is terrific. Flannery was so visibly pleased over it that it did me good.

Flannery: She looked almost as good, I thought, as when we saw her in late August. Her color is still good, though I thought I caught a hint of purplish cast that I think is one of the symptoms of the lupus or the medicine. She looks far from emaciated or weak, though, once again, she might be a little puffed from the medicine. For, there is no doubt about it, the lupus has been reactivated by her illness, though I got the impression that it was not as severe as feared. She is back on the medicine, but she brushed my anxious inquiries aside by saying that she took it for ten years in the past and survived it, so she is not fearful of going back on it. The "it" is cortisone, I think. She is not doing any work now, but is resting a great deal. Mrs. O'Connor was her bouncy self, and real agreeable. Her sister and niece were there too. Came in just after I arrived. The reason for their presence was that Mrs. O's other sister Mrs. Cline, is critically ill, not expected to live, just a matter of time. The young lady, Flannery's cousin [Louise Florencourt], was one of the most beautiful young women I ever met, a lawyer, from Washington, D.C., about 35 years old, who responded to my inevitable nosiness about her unmarried status with the quick reply, "when I find a man who can support me in the manner I am accustomed to live, I'll gladly marry him." I stopped at Flannery's during a dry two hours in the middle of a heavy rainy spell. As I went to get into my car six peacocks, probably celebrating the lull in the rain, did their stuff at the same time. It was shattering.

My reason for going to Macon was that the parish library was celebrating its tenth anniversary with a big blowout at the country club, and I, having been partly responsible for its inception, was to give the talk at the dinner. Well, I chose the ambitious subject NEW HORIZONS IN CATHOLIC LITERATURE. My idea was to talk on just some of the more popular novels that were of Catholic interest, so I wrote Flannery and asked her to name about five important such and to write just a paragraph on each. This and a letter to my brother plus my own cogitating was supposed to build up into a nice talk. Well, it did work that way pretty much. The crowd was pleased with my talk, and I had a marvelous time. There were 180 men and women at the dinner at $2 a piece, at noon on Wednesday. I thought that a wonderful response. The whole affair went off so nicely. It was at that dinner that I displayed the dust jacket of your book and told them about it, only to find out that they all knew. Remember Filomena Campbell? She made the remark to me that Wesleyan will be another ten or fifteen years getting over your departure. Incidentally, at her invitation one of the professors from Wesleyan and his wife were there, name forgotten . . .

I can't wait for your trip north this summer. And, don't forget to stop in to see my Mother in Mobile. She was so pleased over your visit, and has so often spoken of you. And now that you, Tom, are famous, she will be terribly disappointed if you don't stop by.

Did I tell you that a few weeks ago I spent the better part of a day with Walker Percy, author of THE MOVIE GOER? Flannery says he is very good. Certainly he is one of the most charming people I ever met. He is a doctor, but he (along with five others) contracted TB in his internship from working in a lab on TB specimens. So he does not practice medicine now.

If you plan to come along the gulf coast of Mississippi again, let me know so I can give you some names of friends in Pass Christian and Biloxi, Miss. Thanks for your kindness to me. God bless you. And, again, Tom, congratulations.

WALKER PERCY TO FATHER LOUIS J. TWOMEY

Percy's friendship with Father McCown was part of a network of Jesuits dedicated to social justice and works of mercy. Percy was influenced by their efforts and took an active role himself in instituting programs in the local community.

APRIL 3, 1968

REV. LOUIS J. TWOMEY, S.J.

INSTITUTE OF HUMAN RELATIONS

LOYOLA UNIVERSITY

NEW ORLEANS, LA.

Dear Father Twomey:

I am writing you on behalf of a group of interested persons in Covington who wish to initiate a Head Start Program and a Day Care Center here. It is our hope to enlist the aid of Loyola University in sponsoring our application to the Office of Economic Opportunity toward this end.

The leader and moving spirit of our group is Fr. Willis V. Reed of Covington, a Negro, and the chief beneficiaries of the program will be the Negro children of the area, though we would hope of course that deprived white children would participate as well.

The need is great, as I am sure Mr. Reed has told you. For one reason or another, St. Tammany Parish has failed to participate in any of such programs made available. A year or so ago, for example, the League of University Women tried to start a Head Start Program but were refused the use of public school facilities. The main stumbling block has been the unavailability of a building adequate enough to meet O.E.O. standards.

Our hopes have been revived by the news that certain excellent new facilities might be available at the Novitiate of the Eucharistic Sisters of St. Dominic which is close by Covington. The building, as I understand it, includes classroom space, kitchen, toilets etc. In fact, Sister Stanislaus of this order first approached us with the suggestion that they would like very much to see their extra space so used.

We would greatly appreciate the good offices of Loyola University in this matter as well as your own advice in getting such a program under way. Ours is a group of responsible persons, black and white, including a pediatrician and an attorney, who would do whatever they could to assist such a program.

I understand there is a time element involved here, that the Eucharistic Sisters have to make a decision about the use of their facilities in the near future. So I am sure that they as well as we would hope to hear from you and Loyola in the near future.

With kindest personal regards,

    Sincerely yours,

    Walker Percy

    P. O. box 510

    Covington, La. 70433

FLANNERY O'CONNOR TO WARD ALLISON DORRANCE

Sharing a common regional history with her friend, O'Connor details a gathering of the larger family, including matriarchs. Caroline Gordon also remains in contact. Another esteemed editor and teacher of O'Connor recuperates from serious surgery. O'Connor praises C. S. Lewis again.

MILLEDGEVILLE

9 APRIL 64

Dear Cudden Ward,

I am real pleased to have the picture and such a fine picture! You appear to be made out of some kind of thinking rock. I'll send you one of me but I'll have to find one at least a quarter this good. I don't like photographers in general. A magazine sent one down here last year and the first thing he said to me was, "I can't take a good picture of you. Your resistance is too great." He took a lot of pictures however and in every one I looked like one of the Oakie women and this place looked like Oklahoma in the dust storm. Whereas this is really a beautiful place. But he had never photographed anything but migrant fruitpickers and holiness preachers and the inside of flop houses. Anyway I will find you a decent picture when things quiet down here. We are in the state of waiting.

I may not have mentioned that my mother's oldest sister, Miss Mary, lives in the family home in town. She's 81 and sort of the matriarch of the family. The cook found her on the floor last Thursday week and she has been in the hospital since, no hope for her, but they all have wills of corrugated iron, and she is holding her own. But all the family has been called and is in and out and there is much confusion. My mother has these three living sisters—Miss Mary, Miss Cleo, and Miss Agnes. Miss Cleo's domain is Atlanta and Miss Agnes' Boston. Miss Cleo has a lawyer son, aged 32, who is still under her wing, and Miss Agnes has four high-powered daughters who seldom let her speak, though she continually tries. One of the daughters is here now and another on the way. They are all givers-of-orders, not takers. My aunt doesn't know how sick she is because she's full of cortesone and she's giving orders too from her hospital bed. Regina has the real responsibility and is running herself to death.

As for me you see I am at the electric typewriter, but only to write you a letter. I'm not in for business yet. I don't need any surgical instruments, just a shovel and a spoon and a pile of dirt and not to be tired. I can see pretty well when I'm tired but I can't think. I have a cold so tear up this letter when you read it and go wash your hands. You can get colds through letters. I read hit [it].

Caroline [Gordon] called me up from Purdue last week. She was in high gear, sounded like something sixteen—talking to her grandmother. And two weeks ago the Mabrys [Mr. and Mrs. Thomas] were through here and called me up. I was in bed with fever so they didn't come out, though I would have very much liked to have had them come. The Cheneys [Lon and Fannie] wrote me they had been to see Andrew [Lytle] and he was in a big old fashioned bed and in some pain.

10 APRIL 64

Cut off the bottom of that one and was going to write you some more as this is another day and I have some more energy but Miss Regina hollers in "You know what he (doctor) told you. Get away from that typewriter." All he told me was to take it easy. I was going to say something about Miracles but I guess it involves too much use of the brain at the moment. I thought you might like a book I've got called *On the Theology of Death*, by Karl Rahner—he's about the best of those German theologians. It's one of those books I didn't understand but it makes you bolder. Let me know if you'd like it. German theologians may bore you. He don't write good like Lewis [C. S.].

I hope you are feeling fitter.

FLANNERY O'CONNOR TO JANET McKANE

O'Connor sends a card with a beautiful drawing of the original executive mansion in Milledgeville where the governors of Georgia resided until 1868, when Atlanta became the state capital.

4-11-1964

Somebody sent me this paper so I thought you might like to see what our old Governor's mansion looks like—now used as the home of the President of the college [Georgia College and State University]. Our house in town is next to it and was used as the Governor's mansion while this one was being built. All this in the 1800's of course but its still in good shape.

I don't think I could stand to read the thing in *Renascence* [Marquette University]. Sounds horrible. That is a terrible combination— nun, musician and Yankee. Any of them alone would be supportable but the combination! Fathers above. Poet to the outcast! What rot. I have a suspicion that a good portion of the outcast are outcast for good reason.

My aunt continues to hold her own.

Cheers,

F

O'Connor recounts different details of religious observances. She also thanks her friend for enrolling her in the prayer ministry of the Cenacle Sisters.[7]

18 APRIL 64
M'VILLE

Dear Janet,

Thanks for the *Metro. Bulletins* & the cenocle pictures of Sisters Sumot & O'Connor. What I want to know is how they manage to endure those starched white head-cuffs cutting into their faces. I have a friend who is a Daughter of Charity. She calls her habit "the iron lung."

I feel better but the reason I write so bad is that my hands swell. The steroids make you retain water in the tissues. Right now I have about ten pounds of excess water in mine . . .

I hope you survived your British guests.

My aunt received the last rites Monday after which she took a decided turn for the better. She can't sit up yet but we believe she's going to make it.

Our pastor is a victim of clerical taste. He has just done over our church, consulting nobody but himself—PINK. It looks like a nursery.

> Cheers,
> Flannery

FLANNERY O'CONNOR TO
WARD ALLISON DORRANCE

Writing on Easter Sunday, O'Connor works assiduously on stories for the second collection. The writings of C. S. Lewis lead to a recollection of parochial school staffed by Irish religious. Lewis's presentation of "supernaturalism" may have influenced the dramatic endings of stories such as "The Enduring Chill" and "Revelation," which appear in O'Connor's second collection, Everything That Rises Must Converge.

EASTER 1964

MILLEDGEVILLE

I was in the middle of *Miracles* [C. S. Lewis] when the *Letters to Malcolm* [Lewis] arrived so I put up *Miracles* and read the other, as being probably what I need more personally. I do need it and am grateful to you for sending it. I went 6 years to a parochial school as a child and I've been unlearning those six years the rest of my life. Not that it didn't have its virtues too, but in those days most of the sisters were either just off the boat from Ireland (and says Miss Regina should have been in the kitchen and not in any class room) or they were genteel Victorian ladies. They taught you a very measuring religion . . .

To keep that [lupus] under control you have to take the steroid drugs. I took them constantly from 1951–61. They eat your bones up but it's a matter of being dead with good bones or alive with bad ones. So now I am on the steroids and if you want to do any specific requesting, as you pray for me, pray I don't have to stay on them long.

They fill you full of nervous energy but its not the kind of energy you can do much work on.

The other day Tom Mabry [*The White Hound: Stories by Dorrance & Mabry*] called me up. They were passing through . . . Anyway it's a great pleasure to be reading C.S. Lewis on the subject. And I was liking the one on miracles too. That stuff is right up my alley. I couldn't close the book and make anybody believe in miracles but what his kind of a book does is something for the imagination. I read a lot of theology because it makes my writing bolder. I'd like to read it twice if you don't want it back at once. I guess where we both want to locate our characters is right on the border of the natural and the supernatural—so that the reader don't know which is which at the moment . . .

I hope you can read this such as it is. I can really only think on the typewriter.

Cheers

FLANNERY O'CONNOR TO WARD ALLISON DORRANCE

The scenario in the letter perhaps influenced "The Enduring Chill," featuring a sickly writer confined to a rural farmhouse. Asbury Fox in his insipid whining, however, should not be confused with the cheerful, long-suffering O'Connor. She also is thankful for the unstinting care Regina O'Connor provides.

MILLEDGEVILLE

8 MAY 64

I've been thinking about you and hoping you haven't got yourself in the hospital again. Which is exactly what I did for ten days. My aunt grandly survived. She was in the hospital a month and I was on the floor above her and we both got to go home the same day. She had to come out here with us because she's not well enough to go to the house in town. So Miss R. [Regina] has all her worries under one roof and I think that is easier for her.

The lupus has got me and I am slowed down considerably. No work for the next month or two, but I think I have a story in the head and maybe if I calculate about it these two months, it'll be ready to come out when I get rolling again. Which I finally aim to get d. v.

My aunt has never been one for the country but she seems pretty content. We were afraid these 30 peafowl would disturb her but she is just deaf enough that they sound pretty good to her. She has announced that they don't holler as loud as they used to.

Cheers, and let me hear how you do.

FLANNERY O'CONNOR TO JANET McKANE

O'Connor revisits the perspective of children that occurs in a memorable story, "The River." She discusses farm animals in which her friend's young students might be interested.

12 MAY 64

MILLEDGEVILLE

Dear Janet,

I'm delighted with the mugs and as soon as my mother had opened them for me, I proceeded to have some coffee in the one with two holes for fingers—very much intrigued by those two holes for fingers. However I am pleased with all of them and will have my coffee in a different one every day. Thank you so much . . .

Thank the children for me for their letters and tell them that Equinox is learning to <u>bray</u>. He just started this about a week ago and he sounds almost like Ernest, his pa. He is separated from his parents now and is in a plot with a pony (Shetland) by the name of Tommy Traveler. Tommy Traveler is a baby pony, in spite of that name. I watch them out of my window.

Your French friend's trouble sounds grim—very European and somewhat medieval. I hope she gets over it.

Cheers to you and much appreciation.

Flannery

FLANNERY O'CONNOR TO LOUISE AND THOMAS GOSSETT

In the midst of trying circumstances O'Connor shows good humor and once again praises her mother's care. O'Connor would use her own repeated visits to the doctor in a funny story, "Revelation."

MILLEDGEVILLE

12 MAY 64

Well our state has changed considerably since you least heard from me. I have been in the hospital again and now am in bed full-time. That operation started up the old trouble (disseminated lupus) and I am back on the cortesone and doing none too well—though I feel no pain, only weakness. Yesterday I had a blood transfusion (you get up and go after it) so today I got the energy to write some letters. In addition to me here, we have my aunt Mary. She grandly survived her heart attack and is out here with us. So my parent is running the Creaking Hill Nursing Home instead of the Andalusia Cow Plantation. Or rather she is running both.

If my trouble runs its predictable course, I reckon I will be in bed all summer. I haven't had it active since 1951 and it is something renewing acquaintance with it. I am not supposed to have company or go anywhere but to the doctor, which I do once a week. Maybe you all will be coming back this way in the fall. I sure hope for better things then. It's a good thing I cancelled that trip to Texas in May. Let us hear from you anyhow.

FLANNERY O'CONNOR TO
WARD ALLISON DORRANCE

Perhaps sensing her student's days are numbered, Caroline Gordon and the abbot from the Trappist monastery in Conyers, Georgia visit O'Connor. She is determined to finish her second collection of stories. O'Connor is thankful for her mother defending her rights as a patient.

PIEDMONT HOSPITAL

ATLANTA, GA. 6/2/64

Dear Cudden Ward,

I am as cheered about that house as if I could come down the chimney of it and pay you a visit. But you see by the above where I am paying a visit at right now. I've been in this one ten days and am like to be ten more. Miss Regina is staying with her sister Cleo and stays here at the hosp. in the day time and demands my rights for me.

The other day who should blow in to the hospital to pay me a call but Caroline [Gordon], together with the Trappist Abbot and another monk friend of hers. She was in high spirits. Her next book on creative writing, she says, is going to be called *Craft Ebbing.*

Nothing fits in a hospital. The bed table is too high so you can't write on it without breaking your arm. I just wanted you to know I was thinking of you in your new house.

Cheers,

FLANNERY O'CONNOR TO CAROLINE GORDON

O'Connor is thankful for the vigilance of Regina O'Connor in facilitating continued writing. O'Connor seeks counsel from her beloved tutor for one of her last stories as she did years earlier for her first novel, Wise Blood.

MILLEDGEVILLE

11 JULY 64

I finally got out of Piedmont after one month there. An old lady here wrote me that anyone who could survive a month at Piedmont had nothing to worry about as far as health was concerned. I've been home three weeks today, confined to two rooms, am not supposed to walk around, something about they want all the blood to go to the kidneys, but my momma arranged the table so I can get out of the bed right into the electric typewriter. Enclosed* the result. Would you mind looking at it and letting me know what ails it or if you think it's fit for my collection? It'll be the usual great favor.

Did you find out how old swans have to be to lay? Mine do nothing but sit in their tub or on the grass.

Never ride with the clergy if you are not immediately ready to meet your maker. They kindly offered to bring me home from the hospital but I declined even before your description of your ride to the airport. I hope Florida is doing Fr. Charles some good.

Love,

Flannery

*Parker's Back

FLANNERY O'CONNOR TO JANET McKANE

MILLEDGEVILLE

20 JULY 64

Dear Janet,

Thank you so much for having the mass said at the cenocle and please thank your friend for her note (Sr. Sumort). My blood count has dropped again and I just don't have the energy to answer any letters. I'll appreciate the book you are sending when I am better. My mother appreciates your thought of her and that is enough. She doesn't really have time to look at anything.

These pictures were taken in April but just got developed.

Cheers,

F

Going to hosp for another transfusion etc

FLANNERY O'CONNOR TO CAROLINE GORDON

O'Connor appreciates her friend's scrutiny of her story as health problems continue to impede completion of the second collection. O'Connor deflects from her own suffering to the well-being of others.

MILLEDGEVILLE

21 JULY 64

I do thank you for the remarks. I read both versions and hope to do a little something about it all but I don't know how much as the lid has been put back on me. I go to the hospital tomorrow for another transfusion. The blood count just won't hold. Anyway maybe I'll learn something for the next set of stories. You were good to take the time.

One of the sisters at the Cancer Home wrote me that the Rev. Fr. (I presume she meant the Abbot) had had a siege of being in the hospital. She said he had some torn ligaments in his arm but didn't say what happened to him. I'm glad Fr. Charles is better. Cheers to you and pray for me.

Love,

Flannery

REGINA O'CONNOR TO JANET McKANE

Janet received notification of O'Connor's passing. O'Connor's funeral Mass at Sacred Heart Church in Milledgeville took place the next day.

WESTERN UNION TELEGRAM 1964 AUG 3 PM 4 59

FPA111 AC310

A MLA036 RX PD MILLEDGEVILLE GA 3 328P EST

MISS JANET MCKANE

2767 MARION AVE NYK

FLANNERY O'CONNOR PASSED AWAY EARLY THIS AM. THANKS FOR ALL YOUR KINDNESS

REGINA CLINE O'CONNOR

FATHER JAMES McCOWN TO LOUISE AND THOMAS GOSSETT

Father McCown and the Gossetts learned of O'Connor's death a few days after her passing. Writing from the retreat house of his own formation, Father Mc-Cown provides counsel about the loss of a dear friend. As a graduate student at the Iowa Writers' Workshop O'Connor wrote in her Prayer Journal, *"The nearness [to God] I mean comes after death perhaps. It is what we are struggling for and if I found it, either I would be dead or I would have seen it for a second and life would be intolerable."*[8] *Father McCown is assured that his friend experiences God's holy presence.*

OUR LADY OF THE OAKS (MY ASSIGNMENT FOR THE YEAR)
RETREAT HOUSE
GRAND COTEAU, LA.
AUGUST 24, 1964

Louise, you write the most graceful newsiest letter! Yes, I did receive your letter 'way down in Mexico (more later about that), and had all sorts of good intentions about answering. Then when I got home I became overwhelmed with all I had to do, so I really did nothing. Like the mountain flowers and the Heidi atmosphere, this climate and place has its own "relaxing" effects.

The first news I got at home was about Flannery. But since she had died a week before I arrived, I was sure you had heard. I was prepared for the news mainly by your letter. Like you, I had assumed that she was not mending. But then your letter and a letter from her young friend Miss Barnes, teaching in Chile, gave me much concern. Sure enough, there were two letters from Macon with clippings about her death. A letter from me in Mexico must have reached her too late, I wrote her mother, of course, but haven't heard from her. Poor woman. What has she to live for now? Well, I know how you feel about our precious Flannery, and you know how I feel. God has His own reasons for removing from our needful world such choice souls so soon. But it is an exercise in Faith to accept it. That faith tells me that the souls in Heaven can by their prayer achieve more good among us wayfarers than they ever could by their efforts on earth no matter how skillful they may be. And I <u>believe</u> this. But it is not easy to adjust my human feelings to it. I am especially sorry that my brother Bob [Robert McCown, S.J.] never met her. I know he will feel bad because I urged him to take a day out of his trip recently to visit her. But he was in such a hurry he decided to see her "on the way back." He is in England taking his last jot of training as a Jesuit. We call it "tertianship," and it is a final spiritual discipline that has in it a minimum of scholarship and a maximum of <u>affective</u> training. He will be back in May to go to work in college teaching . . .

Could you come by here on your way home? I think you would
be doing violence to your trip to bypass Grand Coteau. We are right
between the towns of Lafayette and Opelousas, La., deep in the real
Cajun country. And such damp beauty you never saw . . . And if you
come through Alexandria, Louisiana, I would like for you all to meet
my charming sister Helen and her beautiful family of seven children . . . And, of course, if you do come through Mobile my Mother
remembers you fondly and would love to see you again.

Love

Fr. McCown

ROBERT GIROUX TO ROBERT FITZGERALD

*O'Connor's editor and friend describes a memorial Mass. The ecumenical inter-
faith congregation testifies to O'Connor's wide appeal. Giroux also notes that
even in death, O'Connor is misunderstood, evident in an obituary in a national
magazine. Giroux asks Fitzgerald to write an introduction to the posthumous
collection of her stories,* Everything That Rises Must Converge.

29 EAST 66TH ST.

NEW YORK CITY 21

[AUGUST 1964]

I am most grateful for your letter. The Mass for Flannery on August 7th at St. Patrick's [Cathedral, New York City] was something
of an occasion. The celebrant was a poet, Fr Francis Sweeney of Boston College (a friend of Tom and Valerie [Eliot]) and a great admirer
of Flannery's, who had had a letter from her only two weeks before
her death. Though he had never met her, they corresponded, and she
was to have participated in a writer's conference on his campus last
April. Boston priests are much more liturgically advanced than New
York ones, and Fr. Sweeney spoke the Mass to the small group in the
Lady Chapel and expected responses in Latin and got them, to the
amazement of local monsignori who don't yet know what dialogue

is. Father wore <u>white</u> vestments because the Blessed Sacrament was exposed at the main altar, but as he explained white is a mourning color too, and it was truly appropriate for Flannery.

It was quite an ecumenical occasion, and about one third of those present were not Catholics and perhaps not Christians, though all were there out of love of Flannery—Catherine Carver, Eliz. McKee, Arabel Porter, Margaret Marshall, etc, etc. John Farrar came from my firm and Hal Vursell. Several Georgia people in town, Maryat Lee and Alexander [sic] Sessions [William], who could not get to the funeral (August 4th) in Milledgeville. Paul Horgan (who had taught F. at Iowa) turned up.

I've written Regina about the occasion, and I do believe it is one that Flannery would have been pleased with. It would not have happened as it did without Fr. Sweeney (who has good friends on the cathedral staff); if I had tried to arrange it myself, I do not believe I could have. I could not reach Caroline [Gordon] but got Percy Wood in Princeton; she was away in New England.

We have eight stories for EVERYTHING THAT RISES MUST CONVERGE, and Katy Carver tells me she saw two stories that F. wanted to add—"Judgement Day" and "Parker's Back." I hope there are no executor complications with the estate. I have not (understandably) heard from Regina.

Robert, would you be willing to do a preface for the book? Something personal and perhaps biographical about Flannery, as well as critical if you so elect? This should be a memorial to her. We want to bring it out in early Spring, if possible. So few people seem to have the facts straight. Did you see that irritating *Time* obit—"backwoods Georgia" indeed. You and Sally knew Flannery in a way that few did; she was not easy to know. Will you consider this as a formal offer from Farrar, Straus and Giroux (as we will be as of January 1st) to write the introduction? I do hope you will accept.

    With all my love to you and Sally,
    Yours ever,
    Robert

FATHER JAMES McCOWN TO THOMAS AND LOUISE GOSSETT

Father McCown notes that O'Connor's pithy statements just months after her death are becoming quotable. Her memorable phrases in later years have made her one of the most quoted American authors. Tom's book also occupies a vital place in its revelations of unknown aspects of American history, as noted by Father McCown. Gossett's tracing "race," the "history of an idea," had an impact on the Jesuit order's dedication to racial justice and diversity.[9]

> HOLY NAME OF JESUS CHURCH
> 6383 ST. CHARLES AVENUE
> NEW ORLEANS 18, LOUISIANA
> FALL, 1964

Somewhere I have your ecstatic letter written after our *viaje mexicana*, so my response to it will not be very sensible, since I cannot find it. However, I just wanted to write you about this and that. A half a dozen people sent me clippings about Flannery. They have been on top of my desk getting yellow. I don't know what to do with such things. Please take what you don't already have and throw the rest away. Also enclosed is a real nice letter of Flannery's, possibly the last of any length that I got. I found it in a Manila folder where I had a talk I gave in Macon last year. The occasion for this letter was that talk. The Catholic women of Macon asked me to speak on "Catholic Authors," so I asked Flannery to write me a "short paragraph" on some of her preferred ones, or to give me any other ideas she might have. Her line "If they are good they are dangerous," ought to be immortalized. The markings on the letter were made by me, because I read this letter to the ladies, only omitting the part about her health. The Louise, dear Louise, at the bottom of p. 2 is not yourself but a colored woman who works for the O'Connors, and Shot is her husband. We had fishing worms and a dollar tip to draw us together.

Tom, I am so proud of the recognition that RACE [*Race: The History of an Idea in America*] is getting. It deserves every single bit of it. It fills a very real need, it seems to me . . .

I am going to take a day off today and ride down to Pass Christian. I love it there. I have to prune some grapevines I planted there years ago.

Love,
Fr. McCown

ROSLYN BARNES TO FATHER JAMES H. McCOWN

Roslyn Barnes is the first American to teach the fiction of both O'Connor and Percy in a Latin American university. Discussion of a crucifix also perhaps reveals the impact of the incarnationalism of O'Connor's "The Displaced Person" and "The Artificial Nigger."

CASELLA 1280

U. DEL NORTE

ANTOFAGASTA, CHILE

WEDNESDAY SEPT 23, 64

Dear Fr,

It was a pleasure for me to find your letter waiting when I returned here from September vacation yesterday. I visited in the South, and now it rains for the first time in 15 months—Spring is coming now. In Santiago with another girl, a new volunteer. I climbed up the mountainside outside the city to the Benedictine Monastery, my favorite place there. The view is breathtaking from the top! And the chapel of the monks is my idea of what a church should be. Very very simple, lots of windows in plain glass of different shades of gold, no statues cluttering up the place. The altar is blond wood, very plain, and Mass is offered facing the congregation. The candles are big and fat and are just set flat on the altar with no holders. The monks—most of them German—chant and afterwards give you tea and bread before the long walk back to the highway. They are friendly and have simplicity and live close to the earth. It is good to be here. You're going to miss that kind of thing in the parish where you are, aren't you? I'm so sorry. For someone who loves what Mexico is, your assignment is going to be hell, I guess. So's mine. The last thing the Chileans are is simple and spontaneous.

Thank you for offering me just simple friendship. Please don't think about whether you are giving me what I need or not. To love and be loved—what else is there to need?

I would like very much to meet your friend Walker Percy. I read *The Moviegoer,* and like it so much that I'm using it in a literature course of mine. He is a medical doctor, isn't he?

I also know Mrs. O'Connor, and got a plucky note from her too . . .

I have a straw crucifix on my wall. I happened to look up and see it just now—it's from Mexico, and it's the only crucifix I've seen I really like. You know the kind you find in all the marketplaces, nothing unusual. The color is gold, and I think of Christ Glorified when I see it. I don't think one ought to go around being "resigned" to things, do you? And I remember a lovely passage from Ivon le Fort. Do you know it?

"Then I said: 'Lord, it is a crown of suffering, let me die of it.' But the voice spoke: 'Know you not that suffering is immortal. I have transfigured the Infinite: Christ is risen!' "

Well on that cheery note I had better be on my way. Oh, it was so good to hear from you! I wish I could meet you in person. Thanks for offering to send me the books, but better not to send them yet, because I don't know how much long I will be here, perhaps only 2–3 months more. If I should happen to come back to the States in February or March, could I stop by a few days to see you in La [Louisiana]? I'll be broke—but might if you know some respectable sisters who have a respectable couch? Would be so glad to have your opinion on my thesis. At the moment it is in Peru, with a Mother Superior who

I'm hoping will give me a job next year.[10] But when she returns it, I'll send it your way. Thanks for your interest.

Good-bye for now. Let me hear from you.

WALKER PERCY TO THOMAS MERTON

In the previous letter Barnes notes she is teaching Percy's The Moviegoer *in Latin America. The novel is gaining international readership. In January 1964 Thomas Merton writes Percy to ask if he could help arrange for the novel's publication in France. Percy happily assents to more international exposure.*

FEBRUARY 14

Dear Tom Merton—or Fr. Louis as the case may be—

I remember the "Fr. Louis" from another book you wrote—

Your letter meant much to me—I am a slow writer, easily discouraged, and depend on luck, grace, and a good word from others.

You make me want to read Julien Green [French-American novelist and playwright]—

Yes, please send me an abstract calligraphy!

No, *The Moviegoer* was published in Denmark, Italy, England, but not France—yes, tell the guys at Le Seuil [French publisher]!

I am reading your poetry.

ROSLYN BARNES TO FATHER JAMES McCOWN

Barnes's formation with Msgr. Illich and her study of O'Connor enables her to understand Latin American history first as a Catholic and secondarily as an American. The historical outlook is different from the conventional, predominantly "American" perspective rooted in progressivist history. The American story looks different, as Barnes reveals, when the narrative originates in the pre-colonial appearance of Our Lady of Guadalupe. Most textbooks, instead, locate American beginnings in colonial New England.

Dear Father,

How good it always is to hear from you! Would you let me read your book on Mexico? I'd love to. I liked the chapter that you sent me that time. I'm doing a—well, I wouldn't dare call it a book yet, but maybe someday—on Our Lady of Guadalupe. I think she's a "Displaced Person" and I want to put her back where she belongs: in her pre-hispanic theocultural setting. I think she came to <u>fulfill</u> the precolumbian religious concepts, which were beautiful and sound, not to replace them. So I'm studying prehispanic theology and trying to figure out as well as I can the terrific appeal which she had for people of those beliefs from the beginning. I think the idea was to sanctify the authentic, indigenous spirituality, not to make them adapt a European form of Christianity. Anyway, that's my idea. I'm glad I don't have a Supervisor to decide its fate. It is going to be very difficult. I don't know if I can do it, but it's so lovely to study the ancient ritual and beliefs. They were so beautiful, and many of them are still practiced, though usually in degenerate forms in many Indian communities. I hope Ixmiguilpan works out for you. The . . . never did get cultured, it seems. The Aztecs called them "barbarians." Actually the Aztecs were far more civilized and virtuous than their Spanish conquerors. One of Cortez' soldiers commented: We have never imagined anything like this in our wildest dreams . . . was bigger than . . . or Seville at the time and more beautiful than Venice. A good writer on pre-hispanic Mexico is Miguel (?) Leon-Portilla. Paul Westheim, too and Jacques Soustelle. All these have a certain "sympathy" that deepens their comprehension considerably. Vaillant's book—the one you mentioned—is not really good and has some serious inaccuracies. Neither is another "popular" version, the one by von Hogan. Alfonso Caso is very good . . .

You know I have doubts that the Feb. trip is going to result. Unless a job turns up in the US—and that's unlikely in the middle of the school year—I may stay on in Chile until next September. I will write my aunt about Flannery's letters. I left them in her house with other things to keep. I had not thought of writing an article on Flannery, though it had entered my mind to do someday a criticism of her stories. It will always be one of the sorrows of my life that I never did get close to her really. With me she was extremely reticent and I didn't know how to get her to reveal herself to me. We corresponded regularly and I was and am devoted to her. Why didn't any real intimacy happen? I don't know. Maybe partly the presence of Mrs. O'C. Or maybe she needed to be strong so much that she couldn't let herself become vulnerable the way you do if you let someone come very close to you. Maybe she suffered so much it was better not to look directly at how much or let anybody else look. F. invited me to see her—and then she kept her distance. Of course, we never had a chance to talk alone for any length of time. I often wondered, and do wonder now, what exactly it was that kept us strangers to one another when we should have been so close. I never had the nerve to ask her. Did I fail her someway? I don't know. And I don't know how close others got to her. I wouldn't dare do an article on her, though of the "personal type." I have an "intuition" of her—but it's no more than that . . .

Well—a biography?!—I was born and bred in Ga. along with Flannery + Brer Rabbit, a small town named Pine Mountain. I went to college in M'ville the first 4 years—that's how I got to know F.— and then went to Iowa for grad. work. And here I am in L A [Latin America]. That's a pretty lame excuse for a biography, I know. But you'll just have to know me in person, Father. This is one [of] those times when words just don't suffice! What about you? Are you from the South originally? I know you have a brother who's a Jesuit, too. Did he once publish an article on F.? I saw one awhile back by a Robert McC. [Robert McCown, "The Education of a Prophet: A Study of Flannery O'Connor's *The Violent Bear It Away*"] Is he yours?

I'm enclosing an "experiment" of mine. Please tell me what you think of it?

Thanks for the "perfume." Consider yourself, "lightly hugged and chastely kissed!"

Con mucho cariño

Roslyn

P. S. What are the "J" and the "H" for?

Barnes notes a Maryknoll priest instructed her about a sacrament through a story by O'Connor. The same religious offered a Mass for her, perhaps the only one celebrated for O'Connor in Africa. Barnes also inquires about tension between religious who write literature and their superiors.

CORREO AEREO

THURSDAY EVENING

Dear Fr.,

You are so good to me and without ever having even so much as seen me! Do you suppose your Bishop would give me a dispensation to hug you? Anyway, consider it done by Panagra—It wasn't perfume, but it was equivalent—equivalent and yellow and organdy. OK? . . .

Thank you for welcoming me to New Orleans. I hope the trip works out, but can't tell yet, until I know more or less what my future's going to be like after Christmas. . . .

A Mass was offered for Flannery in Tanganyika [now Tanzania, Africa]. By the young Maryknoller who gave me my first 3 mo. of Instruction. I knew him when we were both in Writer's [*sic*] Workshop at Iowa, and he used Flannery's "The River" to teach me about the Sacrament of Baptism. An awfully nice person. His novel was coming along well. But his Superior won't give him permission to publish it. Well, maybe someday—But it seems to me that some way ought to be provided of protecting religious from the errors and prejudices of Superiors. Look at what happened to Fr. Teilhard [de Chardin], and Sahagun [Bernardino, *General History of the Things of New Spain*] himself was threatened with the Inquisition for his invaluable research. I realize that all Superiors can't be superior. There are bound to be mediocre ones. But since this is true, why can't there be worked out some system of protection from them? Has the Pope thought of this? Of course he probably doesn't run into such things with his Superior . . .

Will close now—am out of paper, news, and time. Write me when you get a chance, & take it easy on the Cuba libre's—

affectionately,

Roslyn

Writing from Chile, Barnes notes that she is teaching O'Connor's fiction. She is grateful for the depth of O'Connor's friendship. O'Connor is instrumental in Barnes's conversion and her reading a famous Jesuit. Barnes, also through O'Connor, came to understand the meaning of love. Her description illustrates Msgr. Ivan Illich's spiritual formation had a profound impact.

CASILLA 1200

U DEL NORTE

ANTOFAGASTA, CHILE

FRIDAY AUGUST [1964]

It was very good to hear from you this morning.

Yes, Flannery means very much to me. I do share your grief. I teach her stories in my classes, but it's not the artist I miss. It's the human person. Some friends have written to me saying what a loss that so fine an artist with so much to give should die so young. I don't really agree with them. I feel that Flannery's vision and interpretation of Reality had matured and would not have changed. And her style of writing was good enough to express that vision clearly and powerfully at times. She would have written more. But would it have been different? No, the real loss is for me her herself, the human person. Of course the bonds of love, and knowledge are never broken and I can still say "She means a lot to me" and not "She meant a lot to me." But death does take away her face, hands, the sound of her voice, things we need and miss so much. And there's always apprehension, at least for me. What is she experiencing . . . What is life-after death really like? What is it like for her?

The news of her death was news I hadn't expected. When [I got] back from Santiago (winter vacation) the end of July . . . from her awaiting me. She said she was still in bed, but then went on to talk about her new swans, saying she hoped to . . . more time with them in a month or so. Her letter, as usual, [was] cheerful, although the handwriting was very faint and shaky. Then about Aug. 10 I got a letter from a friend of mine who works as a fiction editor for a NY magazine. The first thing that fell out of the envelope was a newspaper notice of F's death. Yes, I do have most of her letters to me but in the States. Of course I would be happy to loan them to your friend. Like yours they aren't profound, mostly about everyday things, peacocks, neighbors, the farm. Light, humorous, always cheerful and simple. I did often regret that she never talked with me about the things that were most serious for her, because I loved her and sensed her alone-ness. But I respected and accepted her reticence since she felt the need for it. In a sense you might say she helped me about the Church. She was the one responsible for my conversion: She made me read Teilhard de Chardin, who is certainly my "spiritual father" far beyond any other, as she knew, I think, he would be. Her fiction itself had its influence on my way of thinking. Once in a great while she would make a comment or a suggestion. But she never never tried to advise or convince me about anything. The times she directly spoke to me about religion are so few, I can tell them to you quickly. Before I knew anything about the Church, a friend of F's died, and wrote her a letter of sympathy. Somehow in the interchange of ideas [and] letters, she had the occasion to explain Purgatory to me, very simply and beautifully, in only a sentence or two. A year later when I wrote her I was taking instruction she advised me to go to Mass every day so that I would become Catholic as a "whole person" . . . would never make me become Catholic, she felt. I can't recall now the exact way she said this. It was much more beautiful than the way I have written it. And later, when I thought of entering PAVLA she warned me against ignorant priests and nuns. If only I had taken her more seriously in that! I was too idealistic and I almost paid for it with my faith. I never let F. know about my troubles with the Church, but maybe she guessed I was asking for trouble in my naivete and wanted me to know a good priest. So she asked you to write to me. Not that she told me that. She told me you were writing a book about Mexico and thought I might be able to help a little, especially in explaining Cuernavaca. So you see—of direct help, there was hardly any. Mostly, she just gave me her friendship and accepted mine. And the example of her beautiful fidelity and clear honest thinking were always there to give me confidence. I hope she really cared for me and was not just "doing her Christian duty." One of the things that has hurt, shocked, and scandalized me most is the distortion of love I have found in so many good Catholics. It makes one feel so very bad to be an object of charity, to be used as somebody's spiritual exercise or good-deed-for-the-day, etc. To be loved "for God's sake" is so often not to be loved at all. I cannot bear this. For me it is a form of prostitution, and no less disgusting than the form the Church condemns. Our director here, Fr. Magsam, has explained to me that it's bad spirituality, that Christian love is very different from this, that this is not the Church's ideal of loving, etc. Yet I run into it almost constantly in good Catholics, so that it seems to me that the Church does commonly teach what is admitted to be bad spirituality by this very human, intelligent and experienced priest. If you are writing to me to do your duty, please don't do it any more—I'll tell St. Peter I excused you from it if you have trouble at the gate.

The Mass and the Sacraments and the Mysteries of Christ's life mean very much to me. But the Church and some of its "elite" have hurt and shocked me so deeply that I know I may never recover from the damage. I have suffered so much these past 2 years that God's love seems almost like a dream to me and sometimes I can't feel that I believe in it at all. Fr. Magsam tells me this is only the effect of pain and that I do have faith. I don't know. I'm glad F. didn't know all this. It would have hurt and worried her. And who knows? Perhaps everything will still be all right and the things that have happened to me Providential after all . . . Am enjoying Christ & Apollo [William F. Lynch, S.J.] very much. Thanks for sending it. Did F. tell you that I dedicated my MA thesis to her? It was on GM Hopkins & T. de Chardin, a comparison.

I am a "me-tooer" too in what you say about love. But I think that love on earth must have elements of ugliness, as the Passion of Christ itself did. In this world both saints & lovers look grotesque and repulsive. And the world of loving is so much more chaotic than the world of hate. To commit oneself to love is to ask for destruction— Christ's experience is the proof of it. If only we were all so capable of taking destruction as He! I know that a woman loves in a very different way than a man. Her love approaches closer the way God loves. It has an element of Divinity even when it looks extreme and grotesque, ugliness you say. The face of love can be ugly as well as beautiful . . . Do you like Tagore? There is a beautiful sentence of her which says, "Amor: cuando . . ." Don't forget my principito . . . Please excuse me if my letters have seemed rude. L'AMOUR is something I can't discuss un-passionately. You will have to write CIF that you know one missioner who has certainly succeeded in acculturating "beyond the call of duty!" . . . We will miss F. so much. I like you more for knowing the Church hasn't educated you out of feeling. Here's hoping for a return home to Mexico for us both!

Your friend, Roslyn

The last specific date from Roslyn Barnes with her whereabouts in Chile documented is in a letter of November 17, 1964, to Father McCown. Sally Fitzgerald notes that "she disappeared in the course of her mission work. All efforts to trace her or learn her fate have failed."[11] *O'Connor herself ominously wrote of her friend on January 22, 1964:*

She is presently lost in the wilds of Chile, the last letter she was somewhere for Christmas that was just like Nazareth, no water no lights not nothing but holy Indians and mud houses and she was eating it up.

The theme of this collection reappears, albeit tragically. "Good Things Out of Nazareth" recur in the letters of Barnes to her mentors, Flannery O'Connor and Father McCown. Her reading and teaching of the fiction of O'Connor and Percy in Chile indicate their initial global impact.

CAROLINE GORDON TO ROBERT GIROUX

From Milledgeville, "Good Things" continue to come "out of Nazareth." Gordon reports of publishing contracts for O'Connor's fiction in Japan and Germany.

MARCH 11, 1966

I saw Walker Percy last weekend—for the first time in twenty-five years, he says. (The years have gone over my own head so fast I haven't been able to keep count.)

I have just finished reading his new novel [*The Last Gentleman*] and have written him a carping letter about a few minor technical flaws. But I told him and must now tell you that I am delighted by the book. Simply delighted!

If I read it right, this is the Odyssey of a Southern Prince Myshkin through regions as strange as Odysseus ever visited. The events which, at times, are almost incredible, take on the Dostoyevskyan stage of the modern novel. A book which could only have been written by a Southerner, packed as it is with knowledge and wisdom about that region and other strange regions.

I trust that what I am saying is not too hi-falutin for your publishing purposes. I am not skilled in writing blurbs as I never write one unless I am crazy about the book. If I do write a blurb I want it to be serviceable. And I have found that where new novels are concerned you have to tell people what to think about them. I don't mind trying again if you want me to.

I visited Regina O'Connor recently. She was busy signing contracts with Germans, Japanese and other folk. We stopped at Andalusia a little while on our way back to Atlanta. Not a human being in . . . One of my companions said he was explaining Flannery's stories to the Japanese, but I suspected that he was refuting something Allen said when *Gone with the Wind* came out: that its wide popularity would set the art of fiction back two hundred years. It seems to me that Flannery did a lot to offset that influence. And now you've got Walker! I congratulate you!

Best wishes, as ever,

WALKER PERCY TO JOHN WILLIAM CORRINGTON

Perhaps influenced by Caroline Gordon's teaching him as an aspiring novelist in the 1950s, Percy plans to offer a course at Loyola University in New Orleans some years later.

APRIL 10, 1967

Dear Bill,

If you still wish to sign me up for next year, I'll sign. Though, to tell the truth, I feel somewhat inferior to the girl in Miller's [Williams] poem.

> a girl, anonymous as beer
> telling forgotten things in a cheap bar
> how she could have taught there as well as I.
> Better.

It will, in any case, be unlike any English course ever taught anywhere. It will be a medical-pathological-psychiatric-anthropological approach to modern fiction which will probably set out with *Notes from Underground* and have nothing to do with Hemingway and Faulkner (whom I leave to you).

Slightly more seriously: I do vaguely contemplate a treatment of the modern novel from the point of view, not of stylistic considerations, but rather from what is known in Europe as a philosophical anthropology: more specifically, the consequences for fiction of such generally pervasive views of man as modern scientific positivism and existentialism.

A Wednesday-night deal like Miller's would be fine with me. I should think not less than 5 nor more than 10 students, though I shall leave that with you, as well as the actual students selected. Matters not to me.

Should like to leave myself the following escape hatch if it is practicable Would it be possible to put this on a semester-at-a-time basis, so that, in the event I see in the first semester this thing is a general bore to all concerned (but selfishly, mainly to me) I can cut out? And Loyola gets half their money back.

As yet, have not decided whether to work in some creative writing—perhaps reading one semester and writing the next. As I understand you you're willing to leave it open.

Best,

WALKER PERCY TO ROBERT DANIEL

Percy declines to attend the celebration for a mutual friend at Sewanee, Tennessee. Percy has taught the course mentioned in the previous letter and devised a syllabus.

NOV 4, 1974

Dear Rob:

Thought we were going to make it up there for Allen's [Tate] birthday. We ain't. We don't have time to drive and in airplane's too expensive—$200.

Recalling your kind invitation last summer to put us up, I thought I'd better release to (bishop's?) bed. I don't think I'll be missed much. Lewis Simpson said he heard the event was getting out of hand—too many people.

I'll be working for your pupil, Jerry, next semester—a novel workshop—a Quixote enterprise at best—I've no idea how to do such a thing—This semester's "novel of alienation" has gone pretty well—only trouble: the students talked less than I had expected, so I had to talk more. My best student: a boy named Bob Daniel—from Miss State U. I took your advice and made up a definition of alienation—even a syllabus!—beginning at the Fall, Genesis 3!

My liver is better—spirits also a degree high. Look forward to 1975 and booze—

Phin says he stands ready with all manner of advice on Province—

Love—

Wak

P.S.—Shelby's [Foote] vol iii is out in advance copies [*The Civil War: A Narrative*]. A real knock-out, I think—

W—

Percy in the previous letter mentions a syllabus. The outline is vital in understanding how his fiction is rooted in the Western theological and philosophic ethos. O'Connor's stories are vital in reinforcing Percy's syllabus, especially the stories of alienation such as "Good Country People" and "The Enduring Chill."

Optional Background Readings

I. Alienation in the Judaeo-Christian Tradition

The Fall (Genesis, chapter 3)

Alienation of the Believer-Sinner (Psalm 6)

Alienation of the heathen: Strangers with the world about you,
no covenant to hope for, and no God (Ephesians 2)

Misery of life in the fallen city of man (St. Augustine, *The City of God*, Book 19, chapter 5)

Life without Christ: All that is in the world: the lust of the flesh, the lust of the eyes and the pride of life (I John 2:16)

Man's estrangement in the world (Blaise Pascal, *Pensées*, section II)

> Man's disproportion in nature (paragraph 72)
>
> Man's concealment of his plight from himself through diversion (paragraph 139)
>
> The doctrine of the Fall is incomprehensible to man yet without it man is incomprehensible to himself (paragraph 434)

The alienated self: The despair of the self which has not become itself (Søren Kierkegaard, *The Sickness Unto Death*, p. 44 ff.)

Man's nature: Man as pilgrim and wayfarer (Gabriel Marcel, *Homo Viator*)

II. The Revolt of Naturalism: Alienation Denied, Man as Organism among Organisms

Man as organism evolved through adaptation and natural selection (Charles Darwin, *The Descent of Man,* chapter 1)

Man as responding and learning organism (I. P. Pavlov, *Conditioned Reflexes*)

The satisfaction of needs and growth through experience (John Dewey, *Intelligence in the Modern World*, p. 801ff.)

Utopia without God (*Walden II*)

III. The Mind-Body Split and the Beginning of Modern Alienation: The Ghost in the Machinery

The isolated cogite: I think, therefore I am; the absolute separation of the *res cogitans* from the *res extensa* (René Descartes, *Discourse on Method*, part IV)

IV. The New Secular Alienation

A. Alienation seen as a moment in the historical process: The alienation of the worker from himself and his work in capitalistic production (Karl Marx, *Economic and Philosophical Manuscripts of 1844*, p. 100)

B. The Revolt of the Left-Over Self against Scientific Naturalism and Humanism: The Great Literary-Artistic-Philosophical Secession

Charles Baudelaire, *The Flowers of Evil*

Fyodor Dostoevski, *Notes from Underground*

Vincent van Gogh, "Cypresses": World-things portrayed as symbols of the alienated self

Pessimism and wasteland in man's most spectacular century (T. S. Eliot, "The Love Song of J. Alfred Prufrock")

The triumph of technology and the despair of man (Jacques Ellul, *Hope in Time of Abandonment*, chapter 1)

Some alternatives to current alienation; the revolt against reason and the hatred of science: Consciousness III, Cure or Cop-out? (Charles A. Reich, *The Greening of America*; Theodore Roszak, *Making of a Counter Culture*)

V. Alienation Systemized: The Existentialists

The Three Stages of Existence (S. Kierkegaard, *Concluding Unscientific Postscript*, pp. 261–26)

Heidegger's *Dasein* and the Fall of the Self into Inauthenticity (*Being and Time*, pp. 210–19)

Self as Nothingness: The Hole in Being (Jean-Paul Sartre, *Being and Nothingness,* pp. 73–79)

VI. Peculiar Position of Southern Literature vis-a vis the Modern Literature of Alienation

The non-participation of nineteenth- and early twentieth-century Southern writers in the Great Literary Secession (L. P. Simpson, "The Southern Writer and the Great Literary Secession," in *The Man of Letters in New England and the South*)

A Southern solution to Northern alienation: *I'll Take My Stand* and the Southern Agrarians

WALKER PERCY TO THOMAS MERTON

Percy continues to write fiction in the relative obscurity of his own "Nazareth" in Covington, Louisiana. He beseeches Thomas Merton to help in his research for a novel.

JULY 13, 1967

Dear Father Louis [Thomas Merton]:

It was a pleasure to meet you. Though I must admit I felt somewhat diffident, putting myself in your shoes and imagining how much it would have put me out having that somewhat diverse crew straggling about your hillside.

It turned out later that the reason you and I were left alone Saturday morning was the expectation that somehow some great Apostolic Catholic sparks would fly and <u>Katallagete</u> would be fecundated by many noble ecumenical ideas.[12] When the truth is I haven't had an idea for months. Anyhow it was a pleasure meeting you and something I have aimed to do for some time.

Would you mind giving me the name of that book on Bantu metaphysics. It suddenly fits into a novel I am trying to conceive. It concerns, as I think I told you, the decline and fall of the USA as a consequence of its failure with the Negroes. It takes place in a pleasant all-white 100% Christian exurb named Paradise. As a consequence of internecine conflict between right-wing "patriotic" anti-Communist "Christians" and left-wing scientific-artistic euthenasic psychodelic pagans, the country falls apart, the whites more or less kill each other off, leaving a black guerilla group in control of Paradise. These latter I conceive as middle-class blacks who have turned from Christianity and adopted Bantu metaphysics. It seems proper and fitting to have the Paradise Country Club taken over by middle-class Bantus (who employ a few whites as caddies etc. and who even develop paternalistic affections for <u>my</u> whitey, cf. the Southern expression: He's <u>my</u> n_____).

Therefore, I need some Bantu lore, particularly the sacramentals of mana or its equivalent.

Sincerely,

Walker

Percy registers his skepticism about the growing dissent against the Vietnam War. He remains aloof from Merton's criticism, as well as that of other antiwar activists such as Dorothy Day and Father James McCown.

AUGUST 27, 1967

Dear Father Louis:

Most grateful indeed for the stuff on the Bantu eclectics and the reference, Sundkler's book. Am most entranced by the prospect of a society of prosperous middleclass fallen-aways from the African Castor Oil Dead Church who will have taken over the Covington Country Club Estates in 1977 following the ideological wars among the Whites.

Also much gratified by *The Long Hot Summer of Sixty Seven* with which I largely agree—although I must confess I have reservations about uniting race and Vietnam under the same rubric, since I regard one as the clearest kind of moral issue and the other as murderously complex and baffling.[13] At least it baffles me.

There've only been two sensible pronouncements following this Hot Summer that I've read. One is by John McCone [chairman, Atomic Energy Commission, 1959–1960; director, Central Intelligence Agency, 1961–1965], who said that the situation may very well be hopeless and the country may be destroyed but we must resist the temptation so to regard it. The other was said by Whitney Young: "You've either got to shoot all the Negroes or treat them with justice."[14]

Prosper in your hermitage,

Walker

WALKER PERCY TO CAROLINE GORDON

The letter reveals the different trajectories of two novelists. Percy has completed one of his most popular novels. He admires Gordon's new novel but politely implies she may have wandered from her regional roots. Gordon's novel exhibits technical skill and innovation but did not achieve the acclaim of Percy's novel.

FEBRUARY 6, 1971

Dear Miss Caroline:

I do wish you could come to New Orleans. How could you turn down the Yucatan. I must find out from Percy [Wood, Gordon's son-in-law] where to stay. I'd love to go.

So happy you got shut of *Glory of Hera*.[15] Heracles for God's <u>sake</u>. I do hope there's also some Tennessee in it.

I too just got rid of mine. *Love in the Ruins;* it ended up subtitled: *The Adventures of a Bad Catholic at a Time Near the End of the World*—the salesman at Farrar Straus said the bookstores wouldn't go for it, but I insisted on the subtitle. After all a <u>bad</u> Catholic ought to be attractive. Anyhow I'll send you mine if you send me yours.

Please give my best to Father Abbot and Fr. Charles if you get to Conyers. I'd love to join you, but I can't leave my daughter just now. I have to tutor her every night.

Fr———is crazy if he doesn't stay put right there in Conyers. He called me up, stoned in some motel in Georgia where he was traveling with a young man in a Volkswagen. I told him if he didn't sober up and go back to Conyers he'd be dead in 6 months so God bless him, I'm glad he did (God bless the Abbot too).

Love,
Walker

—Hope your brother is better

A few letters chronicle both O'Connor's and Percy's consistent anti-Communism from the 1950s. As the collective memories of the massive sufferings and cruelties of socialist/Communist ideology are forgotten, the letters of O'Connor and Percy provide a valuable record. The precision of Percy and O'Connor in the use of political words is vital given the profound ongoing confusion about "Russians" and "Communists" caused by sloppy, partisan journalism.

FLANNERY O'CONNOR TO MISS DANADIO

MILLEDGEVILLE

GEORGIA

19 APRIL 56

About the Czech and Polish publication possibility: I wouldn't want my work published in any Russian-occupied country as the danger that it might be used as anti-American propaganda is apparent. I understand some of Jack London is now being used that way.

Yours,

Flannery O'Connor

FLANNERY O'CONNOR TO MAURICE-EDGAR COINDREAU

Echoing the sentiments of the previous letter, O'Connor does not sanction the translation of her fiction in some countries. Always vigilant for possible scenes for stories, she describes a rivalry between an evangelist and a Muslim religious.

MILLEDGEVILLE

GEORGIA

27 MARCH 60

Dear M. Coindreau,

We were sorry to hear we won't see you Easter but the last of May or early June will be fine. We don't care when you come just so you get here. Let us know when and we will be at the bus to meet you.

It came up a few years ago about my having a translation in one of the iron-curtain countries. I forget which one it was. I asked Denver Lindley [editor] what he thought about it and he said he would advise against it. I wouldn't want my books used for any purpose opposite to their meaning. We would like to meet the Polish lady though [Jurast Domska]. I am going to have to be in Savannah April 30 and May 1, but before and after that we'll be here if she calls, and would be delighted to have her come down.

My friend in Paris, Ville Rolin [Gabrielle], wrote me that there was an enthusiastic piece in *L'Expresse* (?) about *La sagesse dans le sang* [Yves Berger]. I don't know if this was the one illustrated with Billy Ghrame or not. I hope Billy doesn't sue me for defamation of character. The Moslems have been giving Billy a time. I guess you read about his being challenged to a healing contest by the Moslem leader. The Moslem's message to Billy was quite insolent with brotherly love. The whole episode might have been written by Mr. Waugh [Evelyn].

I am so glad you showed my book to M. Maritain and that he liked it. I hope he will read the other one too one of those days. People seem to be finding it strange: however, there have been one or two good reviews.

WALKER PERCY TO COMMONWEAL

Percy criticizes anti–Vietnam War activism by Daniel and Philip Berrigan, both Catholic priests. A famous protest entailed Philip Berrigan and other activists breaking in to a Selective Service office in October, 1967 in Baltimore and pouring duck blood over draft records. In May, 1968 the Berrigan brothers also broke in to another office in Catonsville, Maryland, and set afire draft records with napalm.

AUGUST 3, 1970

THE EDITORS

COMMONWEAL

NEW YORK, N.Y.

Dear Sirs:

I think the Berrigans are wrong.

They have violated federal law, destroyed public property and terrorized government employees.

These actions they justify as the moral expression of their convictions about U.S. foreign policy.

It would follow, by the same logic, that a Catholic opposed to the use of public funds to promote population control could with equal propriety destroy the files of the Internal Revenue Service.

No society could long endure if many people resorted to the same violent, not to say illegal, means of translating belief into action.

But perhaps that is what the Berrigans want.

You and the Berrigans consider the United States' policy in Southeast Asia to be criminal. It is hardly necessary to point out that a great many people, perhaps as decent, as courageous, as equally distressed by the Vietnam War, do not agree with you and the Berrigans. Shall the issue be determined then by the more successful stratagem of violence?

In these parts, the Ku Klux Klan burns churches and tries to scare people in various ways. Their reasons are, to them, the best: they do it for God and country and to save us from the Communists. I would be hard pressed to explain to a Klansman why he should be put in jail and the Berrigans set free.

As it happens, I stand a good deal closer to the Berrigans than to the Klan. The point is, however: God save us all from the moral zealot who places himself above the law and who is willing to burn my house down, and yours, providing he feels he is sufficiently right and I sufficiently wrong.

The less said about Father Berrigan's comparison of his own difficulties with the persecution of the English Catholic clergy of the 16th Century, the better.

Sincerely yours,

FATHER JAMES MCCOWN, PUBLIC LETTER

Father McCown describes two pilgrimages: one to revisit Flannery O'Connor's home and the other to Nicaragua. Since his visit in 1987 to Andalusia, O'Connor's home has been listed in the National Register of Historic Places. There have been frequent celebrations there, including a twenty-four-hour marathon reading of her stories on Andalusia's front porch, commemorating the fortieth anniversary of the author's death, August 3, 2004. In August 2017, Andalusia was given to Georgia College and State University (Milledgeville). The university president stated that the donation would "help preserve, protect, and enhance the memory of one of our most influential alumni, Flannery O'Connor."[16]

NEWSLETTER
from Padre Jaime

MAY 8, 1987

FR. J.H. MCCOWN, SJ, IN RES.

SPRING HILL JESUIT COMMUNITY

4,000 DAUPHIN ST. MOBILE, ALABAMA 36608

SPIRITUAL ODYSSEY WITH "WITNESS FOR PEACE"

Dear ones

Ordinarily I get a letter to you about every three months. This time I am rushing things to reach you before I leave for Nicaragua on April 23. Dry those tears! I'll be back on May 8 full of new information on what is happening in that distressed country. I will go as a member of WITNESS FOR PEACE, a highly structured, prayerful, biblically based, ecumenical organization committed to bringing back to the people of the U.S. an awareness of what is really happening in Nicaragua, and to sharing first-hand the sufferings of the poor in that country. In two weeks we will visit many parts of the country, especially the embattled zones. We will interview people from all parts of Nicaraguan society, and actually work in the fields with the campesinos. We will return full of determination to mobilize public opinion in the U.S. to help bring justice and peace to the people of Nicaragua. I am trying to go with an open mind. I have heard of endless atrocities committed by the Contras, the counterrevolutionary army sponsored by the Reagan administration. But I have also heard serious complaints about the Sandinista government, especially its communism and its alleged persecution of religion. I hope to get some hard answers. It's hardly necessary to tell you that I hope for your prayers and best wishes. When I get home I shall tell you about my trip there, what I did, what I found out, and what I hope to do about it.

My main work now is traveling from place to place giving parish retreats, or missions, or revivals. (That last is such a beautiful word. It tells exactly what my set of talks is, a re-kindling of faith that is already in my listeners.) First I drove to Macon, Georgia, where I feel much at home, having worked there for five years early in my priesthood. Just breathing Macon air does something wonderful for me. Forty miles north of Macon I stopped in Milledgeville the home of Mrs. Regina O'Connor, Flannery's mother. First I visited the State Women's College, Flannery's alma mater, hoping to get into the O'Connor Archives. But it was Saturday & the whole college was closed. I went to Andalusia, the old farm where Flannery had lived and done most of her writing. The sign was gone, and, though the drive was open, the road was neglected, muddy, rutted. The inner gate was locked, and the weeds and woods have taken over. The circular pond where the mean swan once lived is now hardly visible because of the gums and pines and willows that crowd its edges. The house is unchanged, and I noted again what must be the highest, steepest un-bannistered brick front steps in Georgia. I had forgotten all about them. I climbed a fence and walked up to the house hoping to find a caretaker at least. No luck. Then I drove back to Milledgeville determined to find Mrs. O'Connor. I asked a native Georgian in a filling station where the Catholic church was. A long, pregnant pause, and a final, careful statement, "Never heard of it." I found the church, and remembered the fun Flannery had telling about it and its Irish-American pastor. I got no answer from my doorbell ringing. But in the church itself a genteel lady was arranging flowers. She knew all about "Mary Flannery" and Mrs. Regina O'Connor, and directed me where she lived, but with the warning that she had become something of a recluse and probably would not receive me. She said that the dear lady had been much annoyed by callers who wanted to write about Flannery, and who so often misquoted her, or tried to make something gothic about her relationship with her famous daughter. Regina now lives in the once gorgeous ante-bellum home of her girlhood. Formerly it was the governor's mansion, but was now rundown and needing a paint job. I rang the bell and pounded on the heavy front door, but had no response. I walked through a weedy yard around to the back and found clear signs of life. An elderly black man answered my knock and told me that Mrs. O'Connor was not well and did not receive visitors. We talked, and he was delighted when I told him I had known Shot, the yard man at old Andalusia. I gave him my card and he quickly returned with word of welcome. Regina was in bed, and had a nurse with her. She looked wan and wasted. She is well over ninety now. I expected her to be senile, but her sharp blue eyes and clear articulation put that fear to rest. In our conversation I thanked her for some generous contributions she had in the past made to my poor kids' camp. I said, "You have been good to me, Mrs. O'Connor." She shot back, "I sent that money for the camp not for you." I had understood that, of course, but was a little taken aback by her vehemence. Anyhow, we had a nice visit, and I was glad to see her after many years. She has been good to me . . .

The second pilgrimage concerns Father McCown's ecumenical mission to Nicaragua to assess the volatile political situation. In stark contrast to his earlier anti-Communism in With McCown in Mexico, *the narrative O'Connor hoped would be published, Father McCown's views shifted dramatically in the trip to Nicaragua. He admires the Marxist regime. The position contrasts with O'Connor's earlier letters and her unwavering theological resistance to atheistic tyranny that she shared with Father McCown. She once wrote in a classic summation: "Communism is a religion of the state and the Church opposes it as a heresy."*[17]

The subsequent Jesuit resistance to Latin American dictatorships in Nicaragua, El Salvador, and other countries and support of revolutionary governments like the one in Nicaragua led to frightful violence against members of the order. Father Henri Nouwen cites the murder of six Jesuits in El Salvador in 1989 as an example of the order's "commitment to peace and justice" and "represents the best that the Church has to give to the world."[18] *A global perspective might be invoked to assess such judgments. While some Jesuits supported revolutionary governments in Latin America, the situation in Western Europe was reversed. John Paul II, having survived Polish Communism, orchestrated a powerful witness with other leaders such as President Reagan and Prime Minister Margaret Thatcher. They helped bring about the miraculous crumbling of the Berlin Wall and the dismantling of the Soviet Union, the source of support and funding of Marxist dictatorships in Latin America.*

FATHER H. CLANCY TO FRIENDS OF FATHER JAMES McCOWN

JESUIT SEMINARY & MISSION BUREAU

MOBILE ALABAMA

NOVEMBER 27, 1991

Dear Friends of Hooty,

Fr. James McCown died of cancer at 9:18 p.m. on Tuesday 26 November 1991 at Ignatius Residence . . . the Jesuits of the community gathered around Hooty's bedside along with Hooty's sister, Rosemary.

Hooty had told me before that one of the things he liked best about Ignatius Residence was the personal and tender care he received. He did not want to die in an intensive care unit with tubes up his nose. He died as he wished surrounded by his brother Jesuits . . .

I have just returned from Ignatius Residence. Rosemary told me of his beautiful death. Hard-bitten Jesuits told me that they had never seen a holier death . . .

May he rest in peace.

H. Clancy, S.J.

FATHER ROBERT McCOWN TO SALLY FITZGERALD

Father Robert McCown, Father James's brother, never actually met O'Connor but wrote some brilliant analysis of her fiction. He outlived his beloved brother and died in 2012. Like many readers, he recognizes O'Connor's gifts as beautifully conveyed in her letters.

[NOVEMBER 20, 1981]
RESIDENCE [NEW ORLEANS]

Peace!

I just finished *The Habit of Being* and am now taking stock of the marvelous gifts it has bestowed upon my heart and mind. I am still in a kind of amazement as I try to assess the incredible depth and variety of graces that have been bestowed upon this young woman of such limited environment and experiences, of such a short and restricted life. Yet she was able to cast outward the fruit of these graces upon her family and friends, and upon the people who are fortunate enough to have read her stories. As I read I felt myself saying over and over what a marvelous gift she has been to this country, to the Church, to the human spirit! Certainly I feel gratitude and love for Flannery, but I also feel much gratitude to you for your beautiful work of bringing all this together and presenting it to us. You have been a dear servant of the Word, and I am very much in your debt.

I have heard tell of you and your husband and family many times by my brother, Fr. James (not John!—we call him Hooty) McCown. He has promised many times to introduce me to you all when the geography permits it, and that's a pleasure I am looking forward to.

Yours, with thanks and many blessings,
Robert McCown, S.J.

ACKNOWLEDGMENTS

I want to thank a dear friend, M. L. Jackson, for unfailing, generous support from the outset when I spread out copies of the letters on her kitchen table. Without her wise counsel and encouragement this collection would not have come to fruition. I also thank Kemper, Walter, and Mercer Jackson for their support. I also am grateful to Thomas Gossett and Neil Scott who entrusted several unpublished letters to me. I am also indebted to the late Beverly Jarrett. I thank the Earhart Foundation and its president, the late David Kennedy, for several grants that enabled me to lecture in Rome, Ireland, and other places. Jean Cash of James Madison University shared valuable research. I thank Ralph Wood of Baylor University who has provided helpful advice and encouragement. Likewise, Henry T. Edmondson III of Georgia College and State University. W. A. Sessions also provided personal recollections of the correspondents. I also am appreciative of Rosemary Magee's assistance at Emory University. Louise Florencourt of the Mary Flannery O'Connor Charitable Trust was also generous and hospitable on several visits to Milledgeville. I also thank Inge Kutt Lewis for her proofreading skills. I also am grateful for the specialized assistance of Michael Garanzini, S. J., of the Mary

Flannery O'Connor Trust, as well as Patrick Samway, S. J., for providing information about literary estates; likewise Robert Marx. Mark Bosco, S. J., arranged a plenary lecture at Loyola University (Chicago). Likewise, David Solomon, director of the Ethics and Culture Center, Notre Dame University. I thank Dr. Max Bonilla of Franciscan University (Ohio), former dean of the faculty, who approved several faculty grants for travel and research. Dr. Stephen Krason, chairman of the Political Science department, also provided student assistants who were helpful in research tasks. Karen Homol, faculty secretary, provided precise transcription skills, as did Toni Aeschliman. Other faculty colleagues—John and Connie Pilsner, Kaybeth Calabria, Michael Healy, Joseph Almeida, Timothy Williams, Sarah Wear, Allen Schreck, Michael Sirilla, Scott Sollom, Charles Fischer, and Robert Doyle— offered support, encouragement, and/or research assistance. The staff of John Paul II Library of Franciscan University—Katherine Donohue, Linda Franklin, and Donna Ross—were skilled in locating obscure journal articles. I also thank Marcus Grodi of *The Journey Home* who hosted an encouraging interview, as well as Steve Mirarchi of Benedictine College for his precise review. I am also grateful for Joe Goodman of Good Country Pictures who introduced me to Jay Shanker whose legal skills have been invaluable; likewise Scott Hahn, for vital contacts. I am also grateful to Fair Pines Limited Partnership, its provision of a beautiful place for editing during academic breaks, and the support of Linda Alexander. Gary Jansen, executive editor at Penguin Random House, has also provided brilliant editorial advice in the final phases. I appreciate the advice of Ashley Hong. I also have been blessed with other supportive friends—Ernest H. Stanley Jr., Mr. and Mrs. Thomas Moore, Carl Arlotta, Adam Tate, and Ralph Ancil, and his late wife, Clarissa, the late Rev. John O'Shea, the late Rev. Ray Ryland and Mrs. Ryland, Aaron Urbanczyk, James Tanaleon, Tyler Scott, John Adams, Sandy Scott, the Rev. Tony Thurston, and the Rev. Brian Cavanaugh. For others whom I have forgotten, I hope I may recall you and to offer my thanks in the future.

NOTES

CHAPTER 1: GOOD THINGS OUT OF NAZARETH

1. Penelope Laurens Fitzgerald, ed., *Robert Fitzgerald: The Third Kind of Knowledge* (New York: New Directions, 1993), 110.
2. Ibid.
3. "Correspondence," Walker Percy Papers, Southern Historical Collection, Louis Round Wilson Library (II. Other Works, D. Other Writings, Folder 219), University of North Carolina, Chapel Hill.
4. Brainard and Frances Neel Cheney Papers, Vanderbilt University Special Collections and University Archives, Nashville, Tenn.
5. Cheney Papers, Vanderbilt University, Nashville, Tenn.
6. I am grateful for Mr. Giroux's letters and telephone calls of support in which he encouraged the publication of this collection and that "he knew most of the people."
7. This letter is contained in the Sally Fitzgerald Papers, Stuart A. Rose Manuscript, Archives, and Rare Book Library, Emory University, Atlanta, Georgia. The letter was published in Sally Fitzgerald, "A Master Class," *Georgia Review* 33:4 (1979), 831–32. Fitzgerald states, "The letter of appreciation that Flannery wrote for this gift [a lengthy letter] from Caroline Gordon Tate is incomplete. Two sections of what is probably a draft remain." Paul Elie, in *The Life You Save May Be Your Own* (New

York: Farrar, Straus and Giroux, 2003), also surmises (p. 196) that the letter was never sent.

8. The dating of this letter (and others between O'Connor and Gordon), noted in brackets, is based on Sally Fitzgerald's handwritten listing of the letters by date in the Sally Fitzgerald Papers, Stuart A. Rose Manuscript, Archives, and Rare Book Library, Emory University, Atlanta, Georgia.

9. The full letter may be accessed at www.BenjaminBAlexander.com.

10. I am grateful to Jean Cash, the author of a biography of O'Connor, for informing me of these letters and their frequent praise of O'Connor and Percy.

11. *The Fugitives*, Nashville Public Television, Sept. 30, 2009. *YouTube*, https://www.youtube.com/watch?v=7O4XTjhKSSs.

12. For several years the University of the South has been undergoing an identity crisis about its historical associations with Confederate leaders and the Southern Agrarians. A student several years ago appeared in my class at a college in Ohio. He noted he had transferred from Sewanee as a "reverse carpetbagger" to study the Southern Agrarians, who were little read in classes at Sewanee. He also desired to read the tall tales of Southern humorists, the antecedents of O'Connor: David Crockett, Thomas Bangs Thorpe, A. B. Longstreet, W. G. Simms, and others. He noted the weather in the north was cold, the manners not as gracious. Importantly, though, Southern history and literature were available for study. The website of Sewanee, the University of the South, makes little mention of this vital background, while celebrating the beauty of the campus, the university's liberal arts curriculum, and its Rhodes Scholars. The omitted history of the university may be gleaned from http://www.leonidaspolk.org as well as the memoir of William Alexander Percy, *Lanterns on the Levee*.

13. See Allen Tate, "Narcissus as Narcissus," in *Collected Essays* (Denver: Allan Swallow, 1959), 248–64.

14. Poor health did not keep Henry Adams out of the Civil War. As private secretary he simply accompanied his father, Charles Francis Adams, to the Court of St. James's. Henry Adams could not fathom the pro-Confederacy views of the British and their resistance to the "Lincoln government." Sickness also did not keep Twain out of the war. He deserted the Confederate Army and later became friends with General Ulysses Grant. Twain ghostwrote Grant's *Memoirs* to help advance the Republican victory narrative of the Civil War. William Faulkner's Civil War novels and Shelby Foote's *The Civil War: A Narrative* provide the Southern counternarrative of defeat.

15. Andrew Lytle, *The Hero with the Private Parts* (Baton Rouge: Louisiana State University Press, 1966), 27.

16. In an unpublished book review of *Thomas More* by Richard Marius, Percy in his witty prose further develops views of More. The review is contained in the Walker Percy Papers, Southern Historical Collection, University of North Carolina, Chapel Hill.

17. P. Fitzgerald, *Robert Fitzgerald*, 110.

18. The Flannery O'Connor Collection, Ina Dillard Russell Library, Georgia College and State University, Milledgeville.

19. http://www.goodcountrypictures.com.

20. W.E.B. Du Bois had coined the term "Negro problem" in his seminal, vital analysis of African American spirituality, *The Souls of Black Folk* (1902). Dr. Du Bois documents the complex network of segregationist laws and practices preventing racial justice and social equality still present throughout the United States a generation after the Emancipation Proclamation. Ingrained patterns of segregation throughout American society render "the Negro" a "problem," and prevent full assimilation and social equality.

21. I was pleased to meet Mrs. Walker Percy on Valentine's Day, 2011 to discuss Caroline Gordon's letters to her husband. Mrs. Percy immediately launched into praise of Gordon dealing with the turkey.

22. Caroline Gordon was appointed professor of creative writing at the University of Dallas in 1973.

23. Nancylee Novell Jonza, *The Underground Stream: The Life and Art of Caroline Gordon* (Athens: University of Georgia Press, 1995), 305.

24. Flannery O'Connor, *A Prayer Journal,* ed., W. A. Sessions (New York: Farrar, Straus and Giroux, 2013), 5.

25. J. Bottom, "Flannery O'Connor Banned," *Crisis* 18, no. 9 (October 2000), 48.

26. *The Correspondence of Flannery O'Connor and the Brainard Cheneys,* ed. C. Ralph Stephens (Jackson: University Press of Mississippi, 1986), p. 38.

27. Cheney's political views are vital historically. Cheney embodies a political ethos that has disappeared from the contemporary Democratic party and helps account for the 2016 election debacle (probably to be repeated in 2020). Years before, Cheney in the 1950s was a "Southern Democrat," sometimes known as a "yellow dog Democrat." This variety of Democrat would vote for a "yellow dog" rather than a Republican. Democrats of this persuasion, like Cheney, had heard repeated stories of Republican war policy during the Civil War and Reconstruction from living Confederate ancestors, including dismal tales of General Sherman's "march to the sea." Brainard Cheney, Gordon, Tate, the Southern Agrarians, and Nobel Prize winner, William Faulkner, had all learned much of their history and political loyalties from the stories of Confederate veterans, not from textbooks, most written by the victors. Voting Republican for Faulkner was not an option, because of

their rootedness in an oral tradition that endures in a plethora of narratives and novels. Faulkner, the "American Virgil," rewrites American history from an oral tradition in chronicling in novel after novel the localist, defeated perspective of citizens from mythical Yoknapatawpha County. In his Nobel Prize address in 1949, Faulkner observed that he created "out of the materials of the human spirit something which did not exist before." His achievement would inspire Shelby Foote, Percy's lifelong friend, to craft America's "Iliad," *The Civil War: A Narrative.*

28. *Correspondence of Flannery O'Connor and the Brainard Cheneys,* 39.

29. "An Apology," Walker Percy Papers, Wilson Library, University of North Carolina, Chapel Hill.

30. Walker Percy, "Toynbee and the Rope Trick," Walker Percy Papers, Wilson Library, University of North Carolina, Chapel Hill.

31. I told my father about this exchange with "Mr. Tate." As a Harvard undergraduate in the 1930s my father had a course with T. S. Eliot; "Mr. Tate" reminded him of "Mr. Eliot." Like Eliot, my father was from St. Louis and told "Mr. Eliot" after class one day they both were from the same town. Eliot gave him the "stare" for twenty seconds, mopped his brow with a handkerchief, and intoned "Indeed."

32. Walker Percy, *Signposts in a Strange Land* (New York: Farrar, Straus and Giroux, 1991). In a brilliant analysis of his cultural formation, Percy argues that Roman stoicism lay at the root of the planter class. "Noblesse oblige," with an emphasis on duty, motivated planters at the top of the social hierarchy, rather than Christian charity. Inhabiting a "wintry kingdom of the soul," aristocratic Southerners, most dysfunctional Episcopalians, exercised a kind of pre-Christian stoicism. Aunt Emily in Percy's novel *The Moviegoer* personifies the code in her criticism of the mediocrity of Binx Bolling, her nephew. A skeptical lapsed Catholic, and speaking for Percy himself, Binx quips, "I had no idea what she was talking about."

33. Tate recognizes the beginnings of Percy's satirical treatment of Anglican gentility and the ceremonial grandeur of Episcopal religious celebrations in later novels such as *The Moviegoer* and *The Second Coming.* Aunt Emily in *The Moviegoer* is a dysfunctional Episcopalian who makes fatalistic pronouncements. Binx Bolling, the skeptical narrator of the novel, states that she is "an Episcopalian by emotion, a Greek by nature and a Buddhist by choice." Jack Curl, the trendy Episcopal priest in *The Second Coming,* has abandoned traditional clerical garb for a jumpsuit in order to do the "religion thing," which primarily concerns raising money. Percy's satire is exquisitely textured to the point of limiting its impact to precise readers like Tate, himself a convert to Catholicism, and having

experienced, unlike most readers, the high-toned Anglican community of Sewanee.

34. On several occasions when I enjoyed Mr. Lytle's hospitality, he was interested in kickboxing karate champion Demetrius the "Golden Greek" Havanas of Dallas, with whom I was friends in the early 1970s. Lytle was interested in "American kickboxing" but insisted the oriental roots of karate not be lost.

35. The praise made such an impression that I secured a copy of the Holbein portrait of More on a trip to England in 1983 and gave it to Lytle.

36. For a penetrating essay about Lytle, see John Jeremiah Sullivan, "Mister Lytle: An Essay," *Paris Review,* Fall 2010, https://www.theparisreview .org/letters-essays/6048/mister-lytle-an-essay-john-jeremiah-sullivan.

37. Gordon's recommendation of Jungian methodology had a profound impact on Lytle in his crafting of his most famous novel, *The Velvet Horn* (1957). In an essay about its composition, "The Working Novelist and the Mythmaking Process" (*The Hero with the Private Parts,* Louisiana State, 1966), he enthusiastically recounts "his Jungian reading" of the Garden of Eden myth in the Book of Genesis. Lytle notes that the sacred text concerns "spiritual incest." He writes in the idiom of what Percy calls "religious science," in which the novelist writes from outside the sapiential tradition of discourse. Not consulting ancient commentaries such as St. Augustine's exhaustive treatise on Genesis, Lytle uses Jungian semantics to advance the idea that *The Velvet Horn* presented an "incest of the spirit which seemed my [Lytle's] subject." Gordon advocates in several letters Lytle's Jungian approach, but O'Connor, as well as Percy, did not take her advice.

CHAPTER 2: "THE FIRST PRIEST WHO SAID TURKEY-DOG"

1. James H. McCown, "Flannery O'Connor," lecture, University of South Alabama, Mobile, April 26, 1985, n.p.

2. Sally Fitzgerald, ed., *The Habit of Being: Letters of Flannery O'Connor* (New York: Farrar, Straus and Giroux, 1979), 135.

3. James H. McCown, *With Crooked Lines* (Mobile, Ala.: Spring Hill College Press, 1990), iii.

4. The excerpts of this letter have been transcribed from the Thomas Gossett collection at Duke. A copy of the letter also appears in *The Habit of Being.* The excerpts of the letters in this collection may not coincide in some cases with the letters in *The Habit of Being,* since the volume's editor sometimes omitted passages. I have selected excerpts to maintain contextual, thematic continuity in this collection.

5. Later collected in Carter W. Martin, ed., *The Presence of Grace and Other*

Book Reviews by Flannery O'Connor (Athens: University of Georgia Press, 1983).

6.   Transcribed from Thomas F. and Louise Y. Gossett Papers, David M. Rubenstein Rare Book and Manuscript Library, Duke University, Durham, North Carolina. The letter also appears in *The Habit of Being*.

7.   McCown, "Flannery O'Connor," lecture.

8.   Transcribed from the Gossett Papers, Rubenstein Library, Duke University. The letter also appears in *The Habit of Being*.

9.   Ibid.

10. Scott Lucas, Ph.D., "Re: William Sessions," email message to Benjamin B. Alexander, February 2018.

11. Transcribed from the Gossett Papers, Duke University. The letter also appears in *The Habit of Being*.

12. Flannery O'Connor, *A Prayer Journal,* ed., W. A. Sessions (New York: Farrar, Straus and Giroux, 2013), 23.

13. O'Connor quotes from Louise Gossett's "Existence: or, Mr. Henley Never Knew He Had It So Bad." Tom Gossett appended, "This is the poem by Louise which Flannery mentions in her letter to me of Jan. 23, 1958."

14. Sally Fitzgerald, ed., *Flannery O'Connor: Collected Works* (New York: Library of America, 1988), 1251.

15. William Esty, "In America, Intellectual Bomb Shelters," *Commonweal* (March 7, 1958): 586–88.

16. I am indebted to Ralph Wood of Baylor University, who pointed out this crucial point in a lecture I was privileged to hear.

17. Fitzgerald, *Flannery O'Connor,* 1251.

18. William A. Sessions, "Then I Discovered the Germans: O'Connor's Encounter with Guardini and German Thinkers of the Interwar Period," in Jan Nordby Gretlund and Karl-Heinz Westarp, eds., *Flannery O'Connor's Radical Reality* (Columbia: University of South Carolina Press, 2004).

19. Robert Ellsberg, ed., *All the Way to Heaven: Selected Letters of Dorothy Day* (New York: Image Books, 2010), 84.

20. Transcribed from the Gossett Papers, Duke University. The letter also appears in *The Habit of Being*.

21. Dr. Gossett appends a note: "At the time I had been suspended at Wesleyan College [Macon, Georgia] mostly over the issue of racial integration (I was for it). I later was reinstated with the provision I would leave at the end of the academic year. Miss O'Connor offered me her warm sympathy at the time. If the story about me is of any possible interest, it was a big thing in the Macon newspapers. Nov.–Dec. 1958. Thomas F. Gossett, January 17, 1973."

22. Transcribed from the Gossett Papers, Duke University. The letter also appears in *The Habit of Being*.

23. Popular books and movies, such as *Killing Lincoln* (Bill O'Reilly) and *Lincoln* (Steven Spielberg), present the nationalist victory narrative with minimal references to the counternarrative of the nineteenth century present in several O'Connor letters. President Lincoln's policies and oratory have become the gold standard of interpretation as if no other views are worthy of serious consideration. "The Civil War: Legend and Lies" (Fox News), for example, retains O'Reilly's inflexible, one-sided viewpoint and reveals how O'Reilly largely forsook his Irish roots in championing Lincolnian imperialism. Occasionally, the Fox script refers to the counternarrative, but a visual device enumerating the body count concludes each episode. The numerical device dramatically registers the frightful number of lives lost in the Civil War, speculated to be six hundred thousand. The devastating number is presented as normative and necessary in a flurry of escalating figures at the end of each episode. The American Revolution, the resolution of the Cuban missile crisis of 1962, and the recent end of the Cold War and the dismantling of the Soviet Union illustrate much less horrific resolutions to protracted political conflicts. Such resolutions provide stark relief to the frightful, avoidable carnage of the American Civil War. Mikhail Gorbachev, who presided over the dissolving of the Soviet Union, stands out as a leader, for example, who pursued an alternative to frightful global war.

24. *A Political Companion to Flannery O'Connor*, ed. Henry T. Edmondson (Lexington: University Press of Kentucky, 2017), features Edmondson's essay tracing Kirk's influence on O'Connor's fiction (see "He Thinks He Is Jesus Christ!"). Jerome Foss in *Flannery O'Connor and the Perils of Governing in Tenderness* (Rowman and Littlefield) argues that Kirk was one of the seminal writers who enabled O'Connor to interact with the political thinkers of the Western tradition: Plato, Aristotle, Augustine, and Aquinas. Political theorists are writing some of the most penetrating, illuminating criticism of O'Connor's fiction.

25. The CBS-TV film adaptation, on "Playhouse of Stars," starred Gene Kelly, Agnes Moorehead, and Janice Rule, and was broadcast on March 1, 1957.

26. Stephens, ed., *The Correspondence of Flannery O'Connor and the Brainard Cheneys*, 42.

27. Thomas P. Coffey, "Is There an American Catholic Literature?" *Saturday Review* (Sept. 5, 1959): 11.

28. Transcribed from the Gossett Papers, Duke University. The letter also appears in *The Habit of Being*.

29. Ibid.

30. McCown, "Flannery O'Connor," lecture.

31. Stephen Rountree, S.J., "Re: Scott 'Youree' Watson," e-mail message to Benjamin B. Alexander, June 12, 2012.

32. While the bishop extolled Father Teilhard, the Episcopal Church in the United States has pursued for a generation heterodox theology in doctrine and discipline and has estranged the community, perhaps irreparably, from the Catholic Church. The irony of the bishop's enthusiasm for Teilhard de Chardin concerns the Jesuit's persistent quest for unity of knowledge and belief that the Episcopal Church has abandoned through its many divisive policies pursued for a generation.

33. Stephen Rountree, "Re: Scott 'Youree' Watson," e-mail message to Benjamin B. Alexander, June 12, 2012.

34. "Reviews of *The Violent Bear It Away* by P. Albert Duhamel," *Catholic World* (Feb. 1960): 280–85; Granville Hicks, *Saturday Review* (Feb. 27, 1960): 18; Anon, *Time* (Feb. 29, 1960): 118–19.

35. Father Quinn's review actually appeared in *Best Sellers* 29:4 (May 15, 1960): 76.

36. See "It Takes a Story to Make a Story: Flannery O'Connor's Life and Imagination," *YouTube*, May 3, 2013, https://youtube/pLe4ZLnhdVs, for Sessions's colorful remembrances.

37. Robert McCown's review is not included in *Flannery O'Connor: The Contemporary Reviews* (Cambridge: Cambridge University Press, 2009). For a discussion of the importance of Father McCown's article, see my essay "'These Jesuits Work Fast': O'Connor's Elusive Politics," in *A Political Companion to Flannery O'Connor,* ed. Henry T. Edmondson III (Lexington: University Press of Kentucky, 2017). Father McCown's article can be accessed at BenjaminBAlexander.com.

38. The award-winning Danish film director Jaap van Heusden adapted "The Lame Shall Enter First" for Danish television. It was broadcast in 2014 on NPO2 as "The Prodigal Son," in the *Demonic Dilemmas* series.

CHAPTER 3: "HER KIND OF LITERATURE: PLACES AND FOLKS"

1. Unpublished letter, William A. Sessions to Benjamin B. Alexander, Dec. 5, 2004.

2. James H. McCown, *Elephants Have the Right of Way* (Liguori, Mo.: Liguori Publications, 1975), 3.

3. Flannery O'Connor, *A Prayer Journal,* ed. W. A. Sessions (New York: Farrar, Straus and Giroux, 2013), 19.

4. The excerpts of this letter have been transcribed from the Thomas F. and Louise Y. Gossett Papers, David M. Rubenstein Rare Book and Manuscript Library, Duke University, Durham, North Carolina. A copy of the letter also appears in *The Habit of Being*. The excerpts of the letters in

this collection may not coincide with those in *The Habit of Being,* since the editor of the collection sometimes omitted passages. I have selected excerpts from the Gossett Papers to maintain contextual, thematic continuity in this volume.

5. Transcribed from the Gossett Papers, Duke University. The letter also appears in *The Habit of Being.*

6. O'Connor, *Prayer Journal,* 10.

7. Transcribed from the Gossett Papers, Duke University. The letter also appears in *The Habit of Being.*

8. Henri J. M. Nouwen, *Love, Henri* (New York: Convergent Books, 2017), 294.

9. The reference may be to Salvator Attanasio, trans., Claude Tresmontant, *Pierre Teilhard de Chardin: His Thought* (Baltimore: Helicon Press, 1959).

10. The last prominent Democratic politician rooted in the "yellow dog" tradition was President Bill Clinton; his wife, Hillary Clinton, lost the presidential election of 2016 largely because of a stolid imperviousness to the electoral chemistry that earlier propelled her husband to the White House. Ironically, a New York billionaire voiced the populist rhetoric of the "yellow dog" tradition, which unexpectedly helped elect him to the presidency in 2016.

11. St. Catherine of Genoa, *Treatise on Purgatory,* trans. Charlotte Balfour and Helen Douglass Irvine (London: Sheed and Ward, 1946).

12. Transcribed from the Gossett Papers, Duke University. The letter also appears in *The Habit of Being.*

13. Transcribed from the Gossett Papers, Duke University. The letter also appears in *The Habit of Being.*

14. J. H. McCown, S.J., "Flannery O'Connor," lecture, University of South Alabama, Mobile, April 25, 1985, n.p.

15. Walker Percy, "Which Way Existentialism?" Southern Historical Collection, Walker Percy Papers, Louis Round Wilson Library, University of North Carolina, Chapel Hill.

16. My experience teaching outside the South for many years has been the opposite of the pattern of institutions in the South. A college in Michigan where I taught for a few years in the 1980s had instituted a course in "Southern literature," and faculty members admired the Southern Agrarians. A few years ago, however, influenced by neo-conservative thought, college leaders normalized the radicalism of the Abolitionists in the dedication of a statue to Frederick Douglass on the campus in which he was enlisted as a "conservative." Another college in Ohio where I later taught for many years allowed the teaching of Southern literature and history as long as it was not marketed to students as "Southern literature." It could be promoted as a variety of American literature but not advertised as "literature of the American South." A

colleague seriously intoned in a meeting that "Southern" writers like Nobel Prize winner, William Faulkner, were "provincial." On the other hand, the institution's president once at a faculty convocation praised the tactical adroitness of a Confederate general who "charged both ways" in a battle. The allusion to the general elicited little response among the faculty, because apparently no one was familiar with him. Had such a favorable reference to a Confederate general been made by an official at a Southern institution where memorial statues and plaques have been removed, immediate vilification or dismissal would have probably resulted.

17. Along with O'Connor and Porter, Caroline Gordon and Louis D. Rubin participated. O'Connor also gave a lecture, "Some Thoughts on the Grotesque in Southern Fiction," which was later published in *Mystery and Manners*.

18. Perhaps because of its Indiana location and the educational formation of the Holy Cross order whose members founded Notre Dame, there seems not to have ever been much of a historical consciousness of the intersection of Catholic and Southern history. O'Connor herself is acutely aware of the alliance in her perspective on history. The moniker the "fighting Irish" and the protracted vilification and persecution by the British made the immigrant Irish Catholics in the United States natural allies with their Southern counterparts. O'Connor embodies the connection that is little known and little taught in Catholic institutions in the United States, even Notre Dame, with its conspicuous Irish identity. Most Catholic institutions are dedicated to the conventional view of American history rooted in a progressivist orientation and, as O'Connor notes, "educationism." Even though O'Connor was a popular speaker at Notre Dame and her professor friend, Thomas Stritch, sanctioned and understood her historical vision, this connection has not been systematically taught there or at most other Catholic institutions. The emphasis predictably is on O'Connor's theological orthodoxy in her letters and fiction, or, more recently, English departments are interested in how her stories reveal various kinds of literary theories such as feminism, environmentalism, and cultural studies.

19. Transcribed from the Gossett Papers, Duke University. The letter also appears in *The Habit of Being*.

20. Ibid.

21. Ibid.

22. "Off the Cuff," *The Critic* 21 (Aug.–Sept. 1962): 4–5, 71–72. The interview is reprinted in *Conversations with Flannery O'Connor*, ed. Rosemary Magee (Jackson: University Press of Mississippi, 1987).

23. Flannery O'Connor, *Mystery and Manners,* ed. Sally and Robert Fitzgerald (New York: Farrar, Straus and Giroux, 1965), 227.

24. John Ciardi (1916–86), a poet, published several collections, including *Homeward to America* (1940), *Live Another Day* (1949), *In the Stoneworks* (1961), and *For Instance* (1979). He also translated Dante's *Inferno* (1954) and *Purgatorio* (1970).

25. "Some Notes on the Combination: Novelist and Believer." A version of this address appears as "Novelist and Believer" in Sally and Robert Fitzgerald, eds. *Mystery and Manners* (New York: Farrar, Straus and Giroux, 1969).

26. O'Connor, *Mystery and Manners*, 214. A brilliant analysis of O'Connor's penetrating realism is applied to political philosophy in Jerome Foss, *Flannery O'Connor and the Perils of Governing by Tenderness*. Foss locates O'Connor in the mainstream of the imperiled discipline of political philosophy studied and taught in just a few colleges in the United States. A few critics have perceived the interdisciplinary character of O'Connor's fiction and show how it dramatically reveals the enduring issues of political philosophy. See the essays by Edmondson, Sykes, Ciuba, Roos, O'Gorman, and Alexander in *A Political Companion to Flannery O'Connor,* ed. Henry T. Edmondson III (Lexington: University Press of Kentucky, 2017).

27. Roslyn Barnes reveals wide and deep learning in modern philosophy and literature, including familiarity with Dietrich von Hildebrand. In my interactions with academic devotees of Hildebrand in the United States, however, I have not encountered a similar breadth. A Hildebrandian graduate scholar who studied at the International Academy of Philosophy (Liechtenstein) once asked me if I could tell him "something about Percy Walker." Some Hildebrandians operate within a limited network. They are conversant in conventional philosophic novelists, such as Sartre and Camus, but are unfamiliar with American existential novelists such as Percy, Ralph Ellison, Charles Johnson, and others.

28. The reference may be Coindreau's 1960 translation of *Wise Blood, La sagesse dans le sang.* Henri Morisset translated *A Good Man Is Hard to Find,* which was published in 1963.

29. *Les braves gens ne courent pas les rues* (A Good Man Is Hard to Find). Translated by Henri Morisset (Paris, Gallimard, 1963).

30. Bernhard Sinkel, in his 1988 miniseries *Stacy Keach, Hemingway* (Beverly Hills: Lance Entertainment, 2003), further popularizes the "legend" with scenes of Hemingway, a supposed "journalist," transformed into an irregular militia leader with the French Underground. After the Nazis flee, Hemingway and his band are the first to enter Paris. Hemingway, of course, finds his way to the Ritz Hotel, opens the bar, and buys drinks for everyone.

31. Nathalie Sarraute (1900–1999) was born in Russia and became a novelist and literary critic who wrote and published in France.

32. The reference may be to MacKinlay Kantor (1904–1977), novelist, journalist, and screenwriter, whose novel *Andersonville* won the Pulitzer Prize in 1956.

CHAPTER 4: "REMOVING CHOICE SOULS SO SOON"

1. The talk appears in Sally Fitzgerald, ed., *O'Connor, Collected Works* (New York: Library of America, 1988), 853–64.

2. I gave several essays I had written about the parallels entitled "Dante and Flannery O'Connor: A Study in Divine Comedy," to Sally Fitzgerald at a lecture she gave in Ohio in 1996. I was gratified and surprised in 2012 to discover she provided marginal comments to these essays and deposited them among her papers (Writings by Others 1970–1998) at the Stuart A. Rose Manuscript and Rare Book Library, Emory University, Atlanta, Georgia.

3. Flannery O'Connor Collection, Ina Dillard Russell Library, Georgia College and State University, Milledgeville.

4. This may be a student of Roslyn Barnes, a friend of O'Connor's, who was teaching at a university in Chile.

5. Irwin H. Streight of the Royal Military College of Canada gave an informative lecture at the American Literature Association meeting in Boston (2017) about the heavy metal group Wise Blood, seizing on the so-called "gothicism" of O'Connor's fiction to celebrate varieties of dehumanization and depravity in their music and shows. Such performances completely miss the point of O'Connor's stories derived from Dante's *Inferno*: violence is used as a technique to point to larger sacramental truths such as the Incarnation and the Eucharist.

6. The question has elicited different responses. The famous Abolitionist, Frederick Douglass, called himself an "American slave" instead of an "African." Dr. W. E. B. Du Bois theorized about a "twoness" of both African and American spirituality in the "souls" of American "black folk." Ralph Ellison, author of *Invisible Man* (1952), disliked the term "African American" and called himself an "American Negro." Malcolm X repeatedly criticized "so-called Negroes" and stated the term was pejorative. James Brown, one of the most "sampled" of African American musicians, in the anthem song of the civil rights movement chanted, "Say it loud, I'm black and I'm proud." President Obama has identified himself as African American as if his parents are both African American. Meghan Markle, the Duchess of Sussex, on the other hand, having similar parentage, is identified as "biracial." Issues of ethnology remain existential and varied.

7. "Prayer Enrollment," Cenacle Sisters, accessed June 27, 2018, https://www.cenaclesisters.org/Prayer-Enrollment/.

8. Flannery O'Connor, *A Prayer Journal,* ed. William A. Sessions (New York: Farrar, Straus and Giroux, 2013), 13.

9. In my experience I have not witnessed a similar emphasis on diversity in other Catholic communities outside the American South. Midwestern Catholic communities or monastic orders rooted in Irish identity have little experience with the African American ethos, revealed, for example, in not observing properly Black History Month. By contrast, both Father McCown and Dr. Gossett were native Southerners and interacted with African Americans throughout their lives and were keenly aware of their culture. Their experience was typical of most Southerners from communities with a large African American presence and history. The situation does not obtain in some Catholic communities outside the South where there are few or rare opportunities for interaction with African Americans. Other than a cursory admiration of Martin Luther King Jr.'s witness and oratory, such communities remain unaware of African Americans, their culture, and their literature. In these cases, the African American ethos remains essentially "invisible," as the novelist Ralph Ellison reveals in *Invisible Man.*

10. See Gary Ciuba, " 'School for Sanctity': O'Connor, Illich, and the Politics of Benevolence," in *A Political Companion to Flannery O'Connor,* ed. Henry T. Edmondson III (Lexington: University Press of Kentucky, 2017), 243–44. Before her death, O'Connor submitted an article from Barnes's thesis for publication in the *Review of Politics* and *The Sewanee Review.*

11. Sally Fitzgerald, ed., *The Habit of Being: Letters of Flannery O'Connor* (New York: Farrar, Straus and Giroux, 1979), 490.

12. First published in 1965, *Katallagete* served in part as a forum for Southern Christians associated with a variety of political causes. Contributors ranged from Will Campbell, the director of the Committee of Southern Churchmen (CSC) and the journal's publisher, to Leslie Dunbar, at one time head of the reformist Southern Regional Council, and the celebrated essayist, James McBride Dabbs.

13. An essay Merton was writing; see Tolson, *Pilgrim in the Ruins,* 342; also reprinted in *Social and Political Essays* by Thomas Merton.

14. Percy cites Young whose words were quoted in Merton's essay "The Long Hot Summer of 67." See Patrick Samway, *Walker Percy,* 263–64.

15. Caroline Gordon, *The Glory of Hera* (Garden City, N.Y.: Doubleday, 1972).

16. "Andalusia Foundation gifts Flannery O'Connor's home to the GCSU Foundation, Georgia College, accessed June 27, 2018, https://frontpage.gcsu.edu/announcement/andalusia-foundation-gifts-flannery-o'connor's-home-gcsu-foundation.

17. O'Connor, *Habit of Being,* 347.

18. Nouwen, *Love, Henri,* 235.

INDEX

Flannery O'Connor was born in Savannah, Georgia, in 1925. She lived most of her life on a farm in Milledgeville, Georgia, where she raised peacocks and wrote. She was the author of two novels, *Wise Blood* and *The Violent Bear It Away*; thirty-one short stories; and numerous essays and reviews. She died at the age of thirty-nine. Her complete short stories, published posthumously in 1971, received the National Book Award for fiction.

Benjamin B. Alexander, PhD, a dynamic classroom teacher with over forty years of experience, has lectured widely on American, medieval, and African-American literature, as well as political theory and public policy. Dr. Alexander currently is crafting a critical study of Pulitzer Prize–winning playwright August Wilson and Shakespeare, as well as reviewing the unpublished essays of Walker Percy and Ralph Ellison for possible publication. Visit him at BenjaminBAlexander.com.

ABOUT THE TYPE

This book was set in Bembo, a typeface based on an old-style Roman face that was used for Cardinal Pietro Bembo's tract *De Aetna* in 1495. Bembo was cut by Francesco Griffo (1450–1518) in the early sixteenth century for Italian Renaissance printer and publisher Aldus Manutius (1449–1515). The Lanston Monotype Company of Philadelphia brought the well-proportioned letterforms of Bembo to the United States in the 1930s.